African Public Theology will enrich the international discourse on public theology. Africans from different countries and theological disciplines have set out to reflect upon the threefold task of public theology. This means that they, firstly, explicate the inherent public contents of the Christian faith tradition; secondly, demonstrate the public rationality, reasonability and logic of Christian faith; and, thirdly, explore and reveal the public meaning, public significance and public impact of Christian faith.

Living on a continent with so many global concerns, the authors do their labour with pathos, ethos and logos. Driven by compassion and concern, by sound ethical values and by God's liberating logic, they bring fresh insights to various global public concerns. They challenge us to be concerned about the things that God is concerned about in all the publics of life.

This book will help us to be both faithful disciples and responsible citizens, both a faithful public church and an engaged institution of civil society, in local, global, continental and cosmic contexts.

Nico Koopman, DTh
Vice-President, Social Impact, Transformation and Personnel,
Professor of Public Theology and Ethics,
Stellenbosch University, South Africa

Every committed Christian in Africa today will agree that this continent is faced with huge problems of corruption, lies, deception, greed, murder and evil of every kind. This is the scenario which this carefully selected group of theologians seek to address as they insist that the Africa God wants is possible. Public theology is to be seen not just as the study of God but also as the study of how God interacts with his creation. Public theology looks at what faith means in "secular life" (the public arena). The writers explore a wide range of crucial areas of life today and bring encouragement and renewed vision as they consider relevant biblical teaching and Christian principles, and thus seek to discover how the church can truly be light and salt, heralding transformation and change. This is essential reading for all theological colleges and concerned Christians.

The Most Rev Benjamin A. Kwashi, DMin
Bishop of Jos, Nigeria
General Secretary, Global Anglican Future Conference (GAFCON)

D1330160

The work in this book from esteemed scholars in Africa is credible research which has addressed most of the theological issues on the ground in Africa. The various topics outlined in this book represent the challenges that affect Africans and highlight the fact that theology has to continue to engage with these topics in order to bring positive changes to African communities. I would like to commend all the contributors to this project for their deep concern for Africa. Readers will not only gain information, but will also be empowered to understand issues affecting African communities. This book will go beyond mere reading to become a resource for the academy.

Rev Gertrude Aopesyaga Kapuma, PhD
Senior Lecturer,
Practical Theology (Pastoral Care and Counselling),
Zomba Theological College, Malawi

The authors of this critical resource have demonstrated succinctly and with theological integrity, as well as in-depth research, the place of public theology in Africa. Read their in-depth account!

Thabo Makgoba, PhD
Archbishop of the Anglican Church,
Cape Town, South Africa

This book is a timely gift from the heart of Africa. It is a nuanced, easily readable collection of essays weaving together a variety of issues that belong together yet are often disjointed. Its main concern is the relationship between people's everyday lives and their faith convictions. The book profoundly challenges congregations and centres of learning in Africa and the rest of the world. Each chapter's perspective addresses theological and social issues in a critical and transformative way. A golden thread is the revisiting of African public life from different biblical perspectives. Research for the book has been done without irrelevant detail. It is highly recommended to anyone who wishes to take a fresh look at the rich and complex realities of African societies within their religious contexts.

Elna Mouton
Professor Emerita, New Testament,
Former Dean, Faculty of Theology,
Stellenbosch University, South Africa

We are thankful to God for the labour of love offered by the authors of *African Public Theology* for the people of Africa. This important work opens up a fruitful pathway towards evangelical relevance on the African continent. Indeed, for generations, evangelicals shunned the public square and escaped to the private sphere of personal morality, personal salvation, personal Bible study and personal evangelism, viewing these as the sum total of what Christians are called to be and do in the world.

The distinguished Kenyan public intellectual, Professor Ali Mazrui, described the African predicament thus: "Africans may not be the most brutalized people in the world, but they are certainly the most dehumanised." He was right, and it is this condition that challenges African theologians to theologize differently about their faith, and to explore its public relevance. Their "parish" requires it.

In their compilation of *African Public Theology*, Agang, Hendriks and Forster have made a valuable contribution for the training of pastors and theologians called to serve the African people, who in many ways are like sheep without a shepherd.

Rev Moss Ntlha, MTh
General Secretary,
The Evangelical Alliance of South Africa

This book presses right where it hurts. Once again, African theologians have demonstrated their willingness and ability to tackle issues that matter to the church in Africa. This is a praiseworthy initiative that I salute. *African Public Theology* is an invitation to get off the beaten track of doing theology. It puts forward the idea that for Africa to become the Africa we want, we must strive for the Africa God wants. It is, therefore, not surprising that the Bible is viewed as the cornerstone of this project that seeks the renewal and restoration of Africa. The time when the church only prays and proclaims change is long over. This book calls African Christians to "get their hands dirty" and become agents of Africa's transformation. It honestly focuses on key issues that need our attention, suggests new attitudes, and proposes directions for proper praxis. This book is remarkably well written and well organized, intellectually gratifying, and biblically and theologically sound.

Yacouba Sanon, PhD
Professor, Université de l'Alliance Chrétienne d'Abidjan, Cote D'Ivoire
President of the Board and General Editor, *Africa Bible Commentary*

This is an important primer for an introduction to public theology in Africa. Explaining the nature and trinitarian theological grounding of public theology, and naming a host of subjects that are concrete challenges to be addressed, the book ends by challenging the church on her task in this perspective and context. African authors are writing on African challenges from within and for the African context. However, this book is by no means relevant only to Africans; Christians in other contexts can also gain much from the insights offered here. There is honesty and self-criticism as well as a prophetic voice. Christians are called to act with competence, both theological and other as needed, to act in the public sphere, vigorously contributing as church in society without imposing itself. The public theology offered here is biblically and contextually grounded and theologically reflected, offered in very accessible language, with pertinent questions for further discussion and reflection. A most relevant and encouraging contribution for engaging the public sphere in Africa.

Rudolf von Sinner, Theol Habil
Associate Professor of Systematic Theology,
Pontifícia Universidade Católica do Paraná, Campus Curitiba, Brasil
Chairman of the Global Network for Public Theology

In our complex, postcolonial, postmodern, pluralist and global world, thinking biblically and theologically about the public witness of Christian faith has become critically important. It is urgent that we explore and bring to the fore the contribution that our faith makes to the common good and human flourishing. And this is exactly what is done in *African Public Theology*! It is a fresh and innovative book that addresses crucial issues of faith and public life for ordinary people in Africa and argues for a redeeming Christian presence in the world. The African scholars writing in this book argue boldly and convincingly that Christians have a contribution to make to the larger horizon and vision of *AFRICA 2063* and show specifically what is the unique role that African public theology can play in working towards that vision. I am sure that this remarkable collection of studies will influence public opinion, inspire public action and impact public policy. I wholeheartedly recommend it.

Corneliu Constantineanu, Theol Habil
Professor of Public Theology,
Director of Intercultural and Interconfessional Research Centre,
Aurel Vlaicu University of Arad, Romania

African Public Theology

African Public Theology

General Editor

Sunday B. Agang

Associate Editors

H. Jurgens Hendriks
Dion A. Forster

HIPPOBOOKS

© 2020 Sunday B. Agang, H. Jurgens Hendriks and Dion A. Forster

Published 2020 by HippoBooks, an imprint of ACTS and Langham Publishing.
Africa Christian Textbooks (ACTS), TCNN, PMB 2020, Bukuru 930008, Plateau State, Nigeria.
www.actsnigeria.org

Langham Publishing, PO Box 296, Carlisle, Cumbria, CA3 9WZ, UK
www.langhampublishing.org

ISBNs:
978-1-78368-766-4 Print
978-1-78368-813-5 ePub
978-1-78368-814-2 Mobi
978-1-78368-815-9 PDF

British Library Cataloguing-in-Publication Data
A catalogue record for this book is available from the British Library

ISBN: 978-1-78368-766-4

Cover & Book Design: projectluz.com

We dedicate this book to Ronald Hartgerink (1942–2019)
who listened, shared and generously supported NetACT
until we were on our feet and walking.

And let us consider how we may spur one another on toward love and good deeds.
Hebrews 10:24

Contents

Foreword

Traditional Christian theologies from the West have often concerned themselves with issues that are irrelevant to African concerns. The genius of *African Public Theology* is that it adopts an innovative approach rooted in the belief that the definition of theology as the study of God needs to be rethought. Theology is not only the study of God; it also involves the study of how God interacts with his creation. This expanded definition allows the thirty African scholars who have contributed to this book to offer fresh, pertinent and practical truths. Africa is served "real meat" rather than just crumbs from Western tables. Or to use an even more basic metaphor, this book scratches where Africa itches!

Of course, traditional theology still has its place and underlies much of the content of the book, as is clear in the chapters in Part 1 that discuss not only the nature and need for public theology but also the role of the Bible and of the doctrine of the Trinity in the formulation of public theology.

Part 2, Public Theology and Public Life, is the heart of the book. A mere glance at the table of contents will show you that the topics covered are important and relevant, and reading the chapters will convince you that the authors share a deep concern for Africa, the issues confronting Africa, and what God desires for the people of Africa. It is a passion that runs through the entire book.

Part 3, Public Theology and the Church, discusses the primary responsibility of the church in Africa as witnessing to God in Jesus Christ through the power of the Holy Spirit. It reminds us that the Africa God wants and that we dream of can only become a reality through a movement of its many peoples.

African Public Theology not only asks questions believers, theologians and the church ask but even deals with the aspirations and passions of the African continent, as reflected in the African Union's *Agenda 2063*. That agenda advocates far-reaching public policies to tackle the continent's darkest demons – bad governance, corruption, socioeconomic injustice, religious competition, tribal and ethnic conflicts and political domination. *African Public Theology* offers intentional and robust interaction and recommendations on the issues on the ground.

Many theologies ask and answer questions that people are not asking, and use language and concepts that are completely foreign and technical. In *African Public Theology*, the content is presented in a way that is understandable and interesting. Readers do not need advanced theological training in order to understand what the book is about. The editors' firm belief that public theology is not only for an elite few but involves everyone is demonstrated in the practical thrust of each chapter and the entire book. The questions at the end of each chapter encourage readers to interact with the contents of the book and apply what they have read in their own contexts.

African Public Theology is a bold statement by African theologians who are willing to take the bull by the horns and show what they can do in a new field. Though there are thirty authors from different backgrounds and disciplines, there is unity of purpose, clarity and continuity in this highly readable book. Their ambitious goal was vigorously pursued and in my mind accomplished. The authors of the book have crafted a new and fresh way of doing theology that will speak to theologians, pastors, believers, and even unbelievers. All will find the book engaging and practical.

African Public Theology is one of the most important theological books to come out of Africa in 2020 and should be a pacesetter for future African theologies. This being the case, it is a necessary resource for all African scholars and believers and for all who are concerned for the Africa God wants. I enthusiastically recommend it as required reading for all our theology courses in all our theological institutions.

Samuel Waje Kunhiyop, PhD
Former General Secretary, Evangelical Church Winning All (ECWA)
Author, African Christian Ethics *and* African Christian Theology
January 2020

Preface

In the beginning God created the heavens and the earth. Now the earth was formless and empty, darkness was over the surface of the deep, and the Spirit of God was hovering over the waters

—Genesis 1:1–2

Africa is a continent in transition with shaky foundations. However, reading the account of creation in Genesis 1–2 gives us tremendous hope. The God of all beginnings is still at work! He uses humans, whom he has created to be his image-bearers, to change the earth. His creative energy is not exhausted, but still leads us through a repeated process of creation, moving us from formlessness, emptiness, and darkness to the stage of light and abundance. As writers, we experience this as a book grows from the stage of no idea (or barrenness) to the stage where ideas are birthed that can change the world in which we live. For a book to achieve this, it must birth ideas that are capable of infusing a new consciousness, a new spirit that is able to renew, transform and repurpose human societies for the glory of God and the blessing of both present and future generations. It must birth ideas that are capable of bringing to humanity and the environment the hope of love, fidelity, honesty, justice, integrity, dignity and peace, while also celebrating difference and diversity. That is what we want this book, the fruit of a collaborative effort of men and women of Africa, to achieve.

This book too began in darkness. I had finished an earlier book, and had no idea what to do next. Then God in his creative wisdom engineered a meeting that produced a spark of light. It was at the 2016 conference of the Global Network for Public Theology, hosted by the Beyers Naudé Centre for Public Theology at Stellenbosch University, that I sat down to chat with Isobel Stevenson, the senior editor for Langham Literature. We had worked together before and were glad to meet face to face. Our talk turned to the conference we were both attending, and she said, "I need someone to give me a book on African public theology."

My heart caught fire. That night, God gave me a rough idea of what such a book might look like. The next day, Isobel and I sat down and hammered these ideas into the form that I would use to make a formal book proposal to Langham. The book was beginning to take shape, but I was aware that there was still something lacking.

In 2017, I shared my vision for this book with the Network for African Congregational Theology (NetACT), who were meeting at Scott University in Kenya. I had come to see that I should not be the sole author; the book should be a collaborative project by authors from across Africa so that it could speak to all Africa. NetACT embraced the idea and scheduled a planning meeting in Wellington, South Africa, in 2018.

With the help of a sponsorship from Langham, and encouraged by Jurgens Hendriks and Dion Forster, I took a sabbatical in Stellenbosch to work on the book. It was while I was there that I stumbled across the African Union (AU) document *Agenda 2063: The Africa We Want* (see appendix). I was moved as I watched a video about what our young people in Africa are saying and read what African leaders have done to address their concerns. It came to me that this book should not just be my book, nor just a NetACT book, but should be part of a collaborative effort feeding into the AU *Agenda 2063*, and that it should stand shoulder to shoulder with other efforts such as the Africa Leadership Study (ALS) conducted and published by the Tyndale House Foundation, and the development work of Tearfund.

At the NetACT general meeting in Wellington in 2018, two days were devoted to brainstorming, during which we drew up two lists: "The Africa we do not want" and "The Africa God wants." Our vision was to empower African Christian leaders to make the prayer "your kingdom come" a reality by starting a Spirit-led movement on our continent. Thus, we have written a handbook that theological schools and Christians in general can use to empower them theologically and spiritually to address Africa's problems.

This book is divided into three parts. Part 1 introduces the need for an African public theology and the fundamental principles underlying our approach to public theology. Part 2 discusses the application of practical theology in various fields, and Part 3 deals with the role of the church in relation to practical theology. Each chapter is followed by questions that can be used alone or in a group to stimulate thinking about how the principles in the chapter relate to each reader's particular context. Each chapter is also followed by a list of further reading for those who wish to pursue a topic in more detail.

The final chapter of the book talks about the need for a network of theologians to build on the ideas presented in these chapters. One step in the construction of this network will be regional meetings across Africa to introduce the book. But meetings cannot do the work. That is up to you, the readers, and our prayer is that you will prayerfully take up the task and join together with your peers to work towards the Africa God wants.

Sunday B. Agang
January 2020

Acknowledgements

I am deeply grateful to the many partners and collaborators that God allowed to cross my path in the journey towards the production of this book. I thank the Board of Governors of Evangelical Church Winning All (ECWA) Theological Seminary Kagoro for granting me an opportunity to take a one-year sabbatical. I am grateful to Langham Partnership for giving me a Writer's Grant in 2018, enabling me to have the time and the space I needed to read, research and write. Langham also assigned its senior editor, Isobel Stevenson, to work with me. I am deeply grateful for her ardent commitment to the project and her expertise honed over many years of editing. I am grateful to the Beyers Naudé Centre for Public Theology in the Faculty of Theology at Stellenbosch University in South Africa where I spent my sabbatical. I especially wish to thank Prof Hans Jurgens Hendriks who encouraged me to spend my sabbatical in South Africa and whose suggestions and support have greatly contributed to bringing this book to fruition. His hard work as the administrator of the project is much appreciated, as also are his fund-raising skills. I am thankful to the director of the Beyers Naudé Centre, Prof Dion Forster, who warmly welcomed me and added to his heavy load by agreeing to be one of the editors of this book. I would also like to thank Prof Reggie Nel, Dean of the Faculty of Theology, for the moral support and warm reception he accorded me when I was there. I am deeply grateful to Network for African Congregational Theology (NetACT) for organizing the brainstorming session in 2018 and for handling the grant application to the Tyndale House Foundation, and to the Tyndale House Foundation for the grant to do the regional workshops in 2019. And finally, I owe a debt of gratitude to all the authors who put their time and energy into their contributions to this book, and into serving Africa.

Sunday B. Agang

Contributors

Tersur Aben (PhD, Calvin Theological Seminary, USA) is a professor of systematic and philosophical theology at the Theological College of Northern Nigeria, where he once served as college president. He is an ordained pastor in the Universal Reformed Christian Church (NKST) in Nigeria.

Babatunde Adedibu (PhD, North West University, South Africa) is provost of the Redeemed Christian Bible College, Nigeria (affiliated with the Redeemers University, Ede, Nigeria).

Sunday Bobai Agang (PhD, Fuller Theological Seminary, USA) is provost of ECWA Theological Seminary, Jos (JETS), Nigeria. He was formerly professor of Christian ethics, Christian theology and public theology at ECWA Theological Seminary, Kagoro, Nigeria. He is also a research fellow in systematic theology and ecclesiology at Stellenbosch University, South Africa, and director of the African Research Consultancy Centre (ARCC) of the Oversea Council International (OCI) based in Kagoro. Dr Agang is the founder and chair of the International Foundation for Entrepreneurial Education (IFEE) and co-founder and vice president of Gantys Aid to Widows, Orphans and Needy (GAWON). He has published a number of books and both academic and popular articles.

Samuel Peni Ango (PhD, Nigerian Baptist Theological Seminary, Ogbomoso) is a professor of Christian education at UMCA Theological College, Ilorin, and currently the provost of the Theological College of Northern Nigeria (TCNN), Bukuru.

Kajit J. Bagu (John Paul) (PhD, University of Edinburgh, UK) manages a foundation for cognitive justice, while combining research, advocacy and writing with legal practice in Nigeria. He is the author of *Peacebuilding, Constitutionalism and the Global South*.

Collium Banda (PhD, Stellenbosch University, South Africa) is a post-doctoral research fellow in the faculty of theology at North-West University, South Africa, and adjunct lecturer in systematic theology and theological ethics at the Theological College of Zimbabwe.

Jane Adhiambo Chiroma (PhD, Stellenbosch University, South Africa) serves as adjunct faculty in the Department of Leadership at Pan Africa Christian University, Nairobi, Kenya, and runs a consultancy in research and leadership development. Previously she was the head of education at ECWA Theological Seminary, Jos (JETS), Nigeria. Dr Chiroma engages in interdisciplinary research in environmental education, politics and theology.

Nathan Hussaini Chiroma (PhD, Stellenbosch University, South Africa) teaches practical theology and serves as the dean of the School of Theology at the Pan Africa Christian University, Nairobi, Kenya, and is a research fellow at the Department of Practical Theology and Missiology at Stellenbosch University, South Africa.

Ernst M. Conradie (PhD, Stellenbosch University, South Africa) is senior professor in the Department of Religion and Theology at the University of the Western Cape in South Africa where he teaches systematic theology and ethics.

Bimbo Fafowora (PhD candidate, Stellenbosch University, South Africa) holds a master's degree in communication and language arts from the University of Ibadan, Nigeria. Her research interests are media, fake news, gender and politics.

Dion A. Forster (PhD, Radboud University, Netherlands; DTh, University of South Africa) is professor of public theology and ethics, chair of the Department of Systematic Theology and Ecclesiology, and director of the Beyers Naudé Centre for Public Theology at Stellenbosch University. His research focuses on African public theologies, the politics of forgiveness in South Africa, and Wesleyan and Methodist theological ethics. Dr Forster is an ordained minister in the Methodist Church of Southern Africa.

H. Jurgens Hendriks (DLitt, Stellenbosch University, South Africa) is professor emeritus of practical theology and missiology at Stellenbosch University. He is a founding member and programme coordinator of the Network for African Congregational Theology (NetACT).

Idaresit Inyang (PhD candidate, Stellenbosch University, South Africa) is affiliated with the Department of Theatre Arts, University of Uyo, Akwa Ibom State, Nigeria. She develops creative arts programmes for children and youth.

Ofonime Inyang (PhD, Tshwane University of Technology, South Africa) teaches courses in media drama, directing, oral literature, contemporary theatre and advanced research in the creative industries at the University of Uyo, Akwa Ibom State, Nigeria. He studies the intersection of cultural policy in sustainable development in sub-Saharan Africa with emphasis on the Nigerian and South African contexts.

Daniel Rikichi Kajang (PhD, St Clement University, British West Indies) is currently a senior governance specialist in procurement with the World Bank. He has previously served as a public health officer with the Kaduna State public service and as head of the Procurement and Asset Management Division at the National Agency for Control of AIDS (NACA), Abuja, Nigeria. Dr Kajang is an ordained minister of the Evangelical Church Winning All (ECWA).

Maggie Madimbo (PhD, Eastern University, USA) is vice chancellor of the African Bible College, Lilongwe, Malawi. She specializes in leadership studies and is the author of *Transformative and Engaging Leadership: Lessons from Indigenous African Women.*

Sipho Mahokoto (PhD, Stellenbosch University, South Africa) lectures in ethics and public theology at Stellenbosch University. He also serves as part-time minister of the Uniting Reformed Church in Southern Africa, Kayamandi, Stellenbosch.

Johnson A. Mbillah (PhD, University of Birmingham, UK) teaches world religions/comparative study of religions, Islam and Christian-Muslim relations at Trinity Theological Seminary, Legon, Accra. He was formerly general advisor to the Programme for Christian-Muslim Relations in Africa (PROCMURA), Nairobi, Kenya.

Matthew Michael (PhD, ECWA Theological Seminary, Jos [JETS], Nigeria) directs the Masters and PhD programmes of the Department of Philosophy and Religious Studies at Nasarawa State University, Nigeria. He has a research fellowship with the faculty of theology, Stellenbosch University. He also works under the auspices of the Nagel Institute/John Templeton Foundation, United States, as the senior researcher on the project Triangulated Health & Integrative Wellness.

Esther Mombo (PhD, University of Edinburgh, UK) is director of international partnerships and alumni relations at St. Paul's University, Limuru, Kenya, where she teaches courses in history, gender and theology, and ecumenical relations in Africa. She is a member of the Circle of Concerned African Women Theologians and mentors women in theological education and ministry.

Hassan Musa (PhD, Stellenbosch University, South Africa) teaches at ECWA Theological Seminary, Kagoro, Nigeria, and is a research fellow at Stellenbosch University.

Dwight S. M. Mutonono (DMin, Bakke Graduate University, USA) is currently at Asbury Theological Seminary in the USA studying for a PhD in intercultural studies. He previously worked at Africa Leadership and Management Academy in Zimbabwe as the executive director. He is associated with the International Council for Faith Ministries churches which originated in Zimbabwe. He has authored two books and contributed chapters to others.

Piet Naudé (PhD, Stellenbosch University, South Africa) is professor of ethics and director of the University of Stellenbosch Business School.

Olo Ndukwe (PhD, Stellenbosch University, South Africa) is the rector of Hugh Goldie Lay/Theological Training Institution, Arochukwu, Abia State, Nigeria, and an associate research fellow at Stellenbosch University. He teaches systematic theology, public theology and theology and development and has published books and articles in reputable journals.

Benaya Niyukuri (PhD candidate, Stellenbosch University, South Africa) is a research fellow in the Department of Practical Theology and Missiology at Stellenbosch University. He is the founding director of Paraclete Counselling Mission, a faith-based organization at Havana Informal Settlement in Windhoek, Namibia, that offers counselling and Christian education services to orphans and vulnerable children, people living with HIV and AIDS, and people dependent on alcohol and drugs.

Rahab Njeri Nyaga (PhD, Kenyatta University, Kenya) is a senior lecturer in communication in the Department of Communication, Languages and Linguistics at Pan Africa Christian University, Nairobi, Kenya. She is a member of the Public Relations Society of Kenya (PRSK) and chaired the 2019 Taskforce on Public Relations and Communication Management Law in Kenya. She is a lead author of the book *An Introduction to Communication* and has also published several peer-reviewed articles on communication and public relations. Dr Nyaga has headed departments of communication in two different universities and has served as PAC University's academic dean and as dean of the School of Humanities and Social Sciences.

Ester Rutoro (PhD, Zimbabwe Open University) coordinates the Research Based Curriculum Development Unit at the Reformed Church University (RCU) in Zimbabwe, where she is also in charge of quality assurance. She teaches research methods and statistics. Ester was deeply involved in teacher education from 2007 to April 2019 when she joined RCU. She has served as dean of students and gender advisor at Morgenster Teachers' College (MTC), Masvingo, Zimbabwe.

Alfred uw'Imana Sebahene (PhD, Stellenbosch University, South Africa) is a canon in the Anglican Church of Tanzania, Diocese of Kagera. He teaches systematic theology and ethics at St John's University of Tanzania in Dodoma and is founder and leader of the Department of Corruption Studies. He assists governments, NGOs, churches and other organizations in understanding, formulating and responding to public ethics and policy, and is also a columnist writing on ethics and human flourishing.

Theodros Assefa Teklu (PhD, University of Manchester, UK) teaches theology and ethics at the Ethiopian Graduate School of Theology, and is a research fellow in systematic theology and ecclesiology at Stellenbosch University.

Danie P. Veldsman (PhD, University of Pretoria, South Africa) is the head of the Department of Systematic and Historical Theology, Faculty of Theology and Religion, at the University of Pretoria, where he teaches systematic theology.

Part 1

Introduction to Public Theology

The opening two chapters of this book set out to explain the need for an African public theology and the nature of an African public theology. Given that such a theology must be biblical, we have a chapter dealing with issues relating to the interpretation of Scripture in the context of public theology. Then there are two chapters showing how key theological concepts affect not only our understanding of God but also our understanding of the world God has created. These concepts lay the foundations for the chapters that follow. Like all foundations, they are not always visible above the soil, but will be found as soon as one begins to dig into the ideas presented. The superstructure of public theology must rest firmly on these foundations or it will collapse.

1

The Need for Public Theology In Africa

Sunday Bobai Agang

Almost everyone in Africa acknowledges that we are currently living in an Africa we do not want. It is not that we do not love Africa – we do, passionately and deeply. There is much that is good and beautiful in Africa and much that we can be proud of in our past. But when we look around us, we see abundant evidence that all is not well in Africa.

The African Union has also acknowledged this reality and has drafted an ambitious *Agenda 2063* which advocates far-reaching public policies to tackle the continent's darkest demons – bad governance, corruption, socio-economic injustice, religious competition, tribal and ethnic conflicts and political domination. The popular version of that document concludes with the ringing words, "Our journey towards the Africa of 2063 has started. . . . Be part of the transformation!"[1]

How are African Christians going to respond to that call?

Africa's Christians

As Christians, we should be deeply concerned that Africa is tormented by so many evils and is so far from being what God desires. After all, each time we say the Lord's Prayer we pray "Your kingdom come." Are we merely praying that Christ will return and set up his kingdom one day? But that is going to

---

1. African Union, *Agenda 2063: The Africa We Want* (2015). See appendix.

3

happen regardless of our prayers. When Christ spoke about the kingdom of God, he referred to it also as a present reality – the reign of God made real in the present, even as we await its fullness.

We are the representatives of that kingdom here and now, and that is why we pray for God's help to see God's will done "on earth as it is in heaven." As the representatives of that kingdom, we should be working not just for a better society for ourselves but for a society that shows real evidence of God's love. We should want to see all human endeavours done in God's way, for God's glory.

Unfortunately, many of those who read the previous paragraph will simply nod in agreement, or utter a deep "Amen." And that will be that. They will fully agree that Christians should be concerned about these things, and will be waiting for their church or pastor to speak out against immorality and corruption. And for the rest it will be business as usual.

That in a nutshell is the problem that public theology seeks to address. For too many people, there is a disconnect between their Christian life and the rest of their life, between the sacred and the secular world. They tend to think of the church as "self-contained and institutional. Only that which is on the files in the central office is recognized as part of the Church; only those activities which are initiated and supported from that office are regarded as the Church's work."[2] It is assumed that only the clergy are really doing God's work, while what the laity are doing has nothing to do with their being God's stewards and bearers of his image. Christians in secular jobs seldom see themselves as fellow workers in a single Christian enterprise. They do not see themselves as constituting the church, or as responsible for carrying out its mission. The kingdom of God has a place in their hearts but not in their minds and lives.

Public theology speaks not only to pastors and church leaders but to every person who claims to follow Christ. It calls on each of us to take responsibility for carrying out the three tasks that the church everywhere is called to do: 1) proclaim the word which God has spoken, 2) demonstrate the way of Christ, and 3) work hard for the healing of our nations. These tasks require all the wisdom, understanding and discernment that God has given us. The challenges appear daunting, but we can draw courage from the fact that God's incomparably great power is at work in us (Eph 1:19). His Spirit will help us as we seek true moral vision, ethical wisdom and real knowledge – or in other words, as we seek to be transformed by the renewing of our minds (Rom 12:2). For it is not only our souls that need to be saved, but also our minds.

---

2. John Taylor, *Christianity and Politics in Africa* (Westport, CT: Greenwood, 1979), 7.

But before we take our first steps into public theology, let us survey where Africa is now and what Christian public theology can contribute to the transformation required to give us the Africa we want, and, even more importantly, the Africa that God endorses.

Africa's Heritage

Africa is widely acknowledged as the birthplace of the human race and has contributed much to the shaping of the Christian mind.[3] The thinking of Augustine of Hippo (354–430), an African, has shaped Christian doctrine and theology for centuries and is still influential today. In the centuries before Augustine, hundreds of African martyrs died for their faith, with their shed blood as the seed for the spread of Christianity in Europe. It was African desert monks who pioneered the monastic system that preserved the Holy Scriptures in turbulent times and laid the foundations for Western civilization.

The Indian writer Vishal Mangalwadi argues that it was the medieval monks' careful study of the Bible that led them to recognize that all human beings have dignity because they are created in the image of God and because Christ's becoming human in the incarnation conferred enormous dignity on the human race.[4] As the monks thought through the implications of this insight, they came to recognize that they were called to oppose all that undermines human dignity, and to work to protect human dignity. Thinking still further about the implications of this call, they realized that they needed to use reason, logic, science and technology to improve human life. It was their application of their minds to the implications of biblical truth that led to the growth of Western civilization.

It will be our equally diligent application of our minds to the implications of biblical truth today that will give birth to a spiritual, moral and material Renaissance and Reformation in Africa, making the African continent a place that offers hope to all. It is time to end the continent's groaning!

---

3. For more on this topic, see Thomas C. Oden, *How Africa Shaped the Christian Mind: Rediscovering the African Seedbed of Western Christianity* (Downers Grove, IL: InterVarsity Press, 2007).

4. Vishal Mangalwadi, *The Book that Made Your World: How the Bible Created the Soul of Western Civilization* (Nashville: Thomas Nelson, 2011).

Africa's Groaning

Too many Africans are suffering. Some are refugees, fleeing for their lives to escape evil governments. Others flee from their own families, who are accusing them of witchcraft and the like. Still others have been left stateless and homeless by poverty and terrorism, whose effects are compounded by the corruption that leads to further unemployment. Those who are employed are often denied just wages by their African brothers and sisters as well as by foreigners. Abandoned children suffer. Orphans of HIV/AIDS face stigmatization and poverty. Dehumanizing traditional beliefs and practices double the sorrows of widows and widowers. Herders and farmers are locked in violent conflict as environmental degradation turns arable land into deserts. Caught between these forces, many Africans have nowhere to turn. There is no one to whom they can cry for help. All they can do is groan as they struggle to survive.

As we contemplate this vista of suffering and dehumanization, we find ourselves asking the same question as Paulo Freire, who wondered whether humanization is a viable possibility.[5] Can such great problems ever be solved? Certainly, politicians have shown little ability to do so. And appeals to ancestral spirits and to African Traditional Religion do not provide a permanent solution. It is time for Christians to step up.

To be able to do so, Christians need to have a solid theology that goes beyond promising future deliverance and the salvation of our souls, and does not merely promise prosperity provided we follow the right rituals and show enough faith. The people in our churches need to be exposed to a public theology that proclaims that God cares about people and hears their groaning. He created human beings and himself became human, and he opposes all that is dehumanizing. He is a refuge for the oppressed and calls on his people to be his representatives in our world. As such, we are not called merely to give handouts to the suffering but to groan alongside them as we seek to understand and remedy the causes of their suffering. When we groan like this, the Holy Spirit hears and interprets our groans, and God answers our prayers in Jesus's name.

Africa's Theology

Public theology needs to direct Africans back to the one who is the source of power. It reminds us to go to the Lord for deliverance, strength, power and wisdom and to seek the Holy Spirit's direction in difficult moments.

---

5. Paulo Freire, *Pedagogy of the Oppressed* (New York: Seabury, 1973), 27.

But, some will say, we have been crying out to God for many years. And we have been pointing people to God. The church in Africa has shown phenomenal growth in numbers. Why then is Africa still in such dire straits? Maybe in our search for an answer we should listen to John Stott, who while not writing about Africa made an observation that applies to Africa:

> Our Christian habit is to bewail the world's deteriorating standards with an air of rather self-righteous dismay. We criticize its violence, dishonesty, immorality, disregard for human life, and materialistic greed. "The world is going down the drain," we say with a shrug. But whose fault is it? Who is to blame? Let me put it like this. If the house is dark when nightfall comes, there is no sense in blaming the house, for that is what happens when the sun goes down. The question to ask is "Where is the light?" If the meat goes bad and becomes inedible, there is no sense in blaming the meat, for that is what happens when bacteria are left alone to breed. The question to ask is "Where is the salt?" Just so, if society deteriorates and it standards decline, till it becomes like a dark night or stinking fish, there is no sense in blaming society, for that is what happens when fallen men and women are left to themselves, and human selfishness is unchecked. The question is to ask is "Where is the church? Why are the salt and light of Jesus Christ not permeating and changing our society?" It is sheer hypocrisy on our part to raise our eyebrows, shrug our shoulders or wring our hands. The Lord Jesus told us to be the world's salt and light. If therefore darkness and rottenness abound, it is our fault and we must accept the blame.[6]

If Africa is rotten today, we should not lay all the blame on African society. Rather, we need to ask the church, "Where is the salt and the light?" Is something wrong with Africa's Christian theology? Have we become so focused on saving souls that we have forgotten that we also have to save people's minds? Both our lives and our thinking need to be transformed.

The failure of African Christian theology is partly rooted in our inadequate understanding of what theology actually is. It has traditionally been defined as the art and science of the study of God, but this definition needs to be rethought. Theology is not only the study of God; it also involves the study

---

6. John Stott, *Issues Facing Christians Today: New Perspective on Social and Moral Dilemmas* (London: Marshal Pickering, 1990), 63.

of how God interacts with his creation. We need to seek to understand God's purpose in creating human beings in his image and likeness and what it means that he put them in charge of the created order. As we come to understand more about this, we can start to move away from our focus on our own interests and status and start to work to apply all our intellectual and economic abilities to bring about his intent for everything in the whole of creation to bring him glory (Rom 11:36).

A better understanding of theology will also undermine African Christians' perception that public life, or what we call secular life, is a neutral area about which the church has nothing to say. This may be part of the explanation for why a continent where so many claim to be Christian is filled with all forms of corruption and impunity, lies, deception, pride, fear and greed. Public theology looks at what faith means in the secular arena, and this definition of theology is one of the fresh truths that public theology can bring to a continent that has been living on crumbs instead of real meat.

What Africa needs is not just a Christian theology but a Christian theology that is concerned with how all aspects of human knowledge, understanding and faith in God can translate into a deep moral commitment to building a better society, one which is strong in faith, love, justice and wisdom. Such a theology can be called a public theology.

Is Africa open to such a theology? Yes it is. I say this as one who believes that God has called us to this task. But I also have secular endorsement for this stance. Aspiration 5 of *Agenda 2063* calls for "An Africa with a strong cultural identity, common heritage, values, and ethics." Under this point, it adds, in paragraph 46: "Africa is a continent of people with religious and spiritual beliefs, which play a profound role in the construction of the African identity and social interaction." While the Agenda opposes "all forms of politicization of religion and religious extremism," it does not deny that in Africa our ethics and values are shaped by our religious beliefs, or in other words, by our theologies.[7] Now is an opportune time for African Christians to reflect on theology, ethics and moral education.

Africa's Fear

But, someone will say, Christians in Africa are already talking about corruption. For years, we have been taught to believe that the continent's troubles are rooted in corruption and impunity. To some extent that is true. However, that

---

7. African Union, *Agenda 2063*, 2, 8.

cannot be the whole truth, for there is no continent in the whole world that is corruption free. Transparency International's list of corrupt countries makes this very clear. The Asian economic tigers and other developed and developing economies have continued to thrive despite the corruption and impunity that exist within them. So there must be something else that is fundamentally wrong with Africa.

We can find a clue to what this may be in the Tanzanian proverb, "Make some money, but don't let money make you." In Africa both the leaders and the led are letting money make them instead of them making money. And the reason they succumb to the lure of money is fear, which is devastating to social, economic, intellectual, moral, and ethical standards. People define themselves by their possessions and their status, and fear anything that threatens these. So they lack compassion for the suffering because they see them as a threat to their own security. Leaders fear anyone and anything that may reduce their power, and so they cannot share power with anyone but must instead maintain power over people, by whatever means necessary. Africans have become slaves to fear.

Politicians know how to play on African people's fears. They use religion, ethnicity and regionality to deceive their fellow men and women and pit them against each other. While the people are enmeshed in the conflicts these fears generate, the elite siphon off public funds to private accounts within and outside the continent. They fear the possibility of losing their status and having their goods plundered, and to allay this fear they plunder the continent themselves, often in partnership with outside groups who seek to exploit Africa's resources for their own benefit. The unpatriotic activities of African leaders leave their subjects in dire unemployment, poverty and conflicts. Yet the people are reluctant to change the situation because it is at least one that they are familiar with. They fear change.

In such circumstances, public theology equips Christians to come alongside experts in various fields and help them develop better options for work and for society. It can help Christians persuade people to let go of their fears and trust the one who calls his people to live in love and righteousness. This is a far better option than being trapped in the cycle of fear that begets corruption and impunity, which then beget fanaticism, extremism and terrorism. To dislodge these deadly evils, we need an African public theology that brings in a dimension of public discourse rooted in a biblical narrative of the origin of and solution to human fear.

Since the fall of Adam and Eve, fear has dogged the human race. When God called out to Adam saying, "Where are you?" Adam replied, "I heard you walking in the garden, so I hid. I was afraid because I was naked" (Gen

3:8–10). He and Eve resorted to using leaves to clothe their nakedness and hid themselves from God's presence because they were spiritually and physically naked. They did not understand that there was nowhere they could hide from God and nothing that would cover their fundamental nakedness before him.

Just as Adam and Eve assumed that leaves could clothe their nakedness, so Africans and their leaders assume that wealth and political power can clothe their spiritual and physical nakedness. But they find that their material success leaves them socially, morally and ethically empty and lonely – and afraid. This is why many African leaders refuse to relinquish power for decades; they are afraid that their sins will find them out. They refuse to step down because they are afraid of losing power; they are afraid of what will happen if their corruption and ill-gotten wealth are uncovered; they are afraid of their subjects whom they have not treated with respect and kindness. They are afraid of having to face a future without hope. They are also afraid of witches and wizards and witchcraft. These diverse forms of fear persist because like Adam and Eve, humans – both Christians and others – have failed to realize that wealth or power cannot repair a broken relationship with God. Africans need a public theology that will infuse a new consciousness that will transform this mindset.

The greatest weapon against fear is truth. *Agenda 2063* can only be achieved when Africans know, understand and believe the truth. Therefore, one of the reasons why public theology is necessary in Africa is that it will help Africa discover the truth that can unlock the continent's potential and release it for the greater good of the poor and rich of Africa. African Christians today need a theology that will help them and their neighbours say,

> I lie down and sleep;
>> I wake again, because the LORD sustains me.
> I will not fear though tens of thousands
>> assail me on every side. (Ps 3:5–6)

Africa's Governance

Although Africa is a religious continent, African leaders lack the moral and ethical standards that can change the continent and make it a place for all. We do not lack policies that meet global best practices. Almost all of our nations are signatories to the major declarations of the United Nations. Yet our leaders lack the political will to implement them for the greater good of their people. Consequently, Africans no longer trust their leaders.[8]

---

8. This is a global phenomenon, but is especially true in Africa – see Manuel Castells, *Rupture: The Crisis of Liberal Democracy* (Cambridge: Polity, 2019).

When the colonized nations of Africa regained their independence from the British, French, Portuguese, Spanish or apartheid regimes, the people entrusted their lives and countries to African leaders who were their kinsmen and relatives. Every year there are joyous celebrations of Independence Day across the continent as nations remember that they have escaped colonialism with its dehumanization, oppression, and exploitation of Africa's natural and human resources. But as they listen to rousing speeches on Independence Day, the people cannot be unaware that the speakers are doing the same things (or even worse) that the colonialists did to the continent. The people have discovered, to their utter dismay, that their own leaders have abused the confidence reposed in them and have taken advantage of their political positions to misuse the God-given economic resources of the continent. Africa is still full of dehumanization, exploitation, oppression and the destruction of human lives and property.

As a result, the African people have been left to wallow in huge unemployment and dire poverty. That is why Africans, both young and old, are yearning for a new Africa, an Africa that is free from a leadership that does not have its people's interests and well-being at heart. Until that comes, we are enslaved by those whom we elected to represent our interests but who have instead ruined our continent.

Public theology is needed to set Africa free by holding leaders to biblical standards. But this means more than merely criticizing our leaders when they fall short. Christians should not merely stand on the sidelines and shout advice to the players; we need to get involved in doing the hard work of achieving a goal. We need to join governments and social institutions and do the hard work of thinking through ideologies, policies and administrative issues, helping politicians draft good laws, and seeing that they are observed. It is time to end mere lip service to justice for the oppressed, the marginalized, the refugees and the stateless. It is time to come together to pursue the common good – but to do this as informed Christians whose thinking about the issues of life is shaped by Christ.

Africa's Education

For *Agenda 2063* to succeed, Africa needs transformation, innovation and initiative in education of all kinds, not least in the realm of theological education. Like our school systems, much of our theological education has used what Paulo Freire calls the banking method: the lecturer deposits information in the minds of the students, which the students then deliver back to the lecturer when their knowledge is tested. But this model is woefully inadequate for addressing Africa's problems and realizing its potential. All it does is uphold the status quo. It does not encourage students to think creatively or to consider how what they are learning applies to the context in which they are learning it.

It is past time for the banking system of education to be replaced by the problem-posing and problem-solving method of education. As Freire points out, "education is communication and dialogue. It is not the transference of knowledge, but the encounter of Subjects in dialogue in search of the significance of the object of knowing and thinking."[9] We will be looking at this more in later chapters of this book.

One of the problems with introducing such education is that we now live in an age of fast food, fast Internet, fast worship and so on. We are living in a century of impatience. So we tend to "want knowledge, but only if it comes quickly and easily. Even more dangerous than a faulty system of learning, this virtually universal something-for-nothing mentality fundamentally undermines the growth of quality thinking skills and processes."[10]

Christians too accept this mentality. We assume that all we need to do is recognize that something is wrong and pray about it, and then our work is done and we leave the rest to God. But this is not how God worked in the Bible, and it is not in line with the task he assigned Adam and Eve at creation. He endowed them with the abilities they would need to solve problems, but did not immediately reveal the solutions to the issues they would face as they set out to be his stewards over creation. They had to apply their minds to that task. In the same way, public theology calls us to apply our minds to the problems that face Africa. We are called to look closely at the problems, going beyond the surface issues to the underlying causes rooted in social structures and prevailing worldviews. That is part of what education should train us to do.

Public theology also calls on us to use our God-given creativity when looking for solutions to problems. It is not enough merely to denounce corrupt structures without offering a positive, realistic alternative. And if our alternative is adopted, it too must be critiqued; for in a fallen world, good intentions are not enough to guarantee good outcomes. God's kingdom grows from a seed – we cannot expect a fruit-bearing tree to grow overnight.

Public theology needs to provide a model of the type of moral, ethical and intellectual education needed to bring hope to Africa. Forming the Africa

---

9. Paulo Freire, *Education for Critical Consciousness* (1967; New York: Bloomsbury Academic, 2013), 126.

10. Philip E. Dow, *Virtuous Minds: Intellectual Character Development for Students, Educators and Parents* (Downers Grove, IL: InterVarsity Press, 2013), 86.

we want is not going to be a simple task. It will require a kind of education infused with a new and radical consciousness that inspires a passion for a future with hope. For as Freire says, "Without a minimum of hope, we cannot so much as start the struggle. But without the struggle, hope . . . dissipates, loses its bearings, and turns into hopelessness. And hopelessness can become tragic despair . . . [which is] both the consequence and the cause of inaction or immobilism."[11]

Africa's Hopes

As human beings, we are capable of both tremendous good and tremendous evil. In this chapter, we have highlighted some of the tremendous evils being done in Africa. These have eclipsed Africa's positive potential to such an extent that it looks as if Africa has no hope. Yet African public theology is intended to help the African people recognize that God is not done with Africa. Given that all human beings are capable of doing tremendous good, Africa can surely rise again. With us on God's side and God on our side, Africa can transcend her dilemmas and become the Africa we want, the Africa God endorses.

Public theology reminds us that the Bible teaches that everything which exists comes from God, everything which exists is kept in existence by God's power, and everything which exists is intended for God's glory. So all of life – work, leadership, wisdom, politics, the economy, enterprise, intellect, technology, science, art and the humanities, entrepreneurship, media and so on – is intended for God's glory. Grasping the reality of this fact will help us transform Africa. It will make us aware that all human endeavours in all spheres are part and parcel of interacting with God's creation, and that we must all live and work as God's stewards.

Theological education is critical in this matter.[12] And the audience for this education in public theology is not just pastors and theologians but the whole church. Every member must be encouraged to fully participate in living, thinking, and working daily with a clear grasp of the fact that all their work, education, research and life in all spheres is to be lived to the praise of God's glory. This mindset is required of clergy as well as laity, so that all see and do their work as God's work, done in God's way, for his glory. Thus we will build up what Dow calls an intellectual moral bank comprised of men and women

---

11. Paulo Freire, *Pedagogy of Hope* (New York: Bloomsbury, 1992), 3.

12. NetACT, the network of African theological schools that initiated this book, was founded on this belief, as also was the Langham Partnership.

with intellectual courage, carefulness, fair-mindedness, curiosity, tenacity, honesty and humility.[13] The lack of these intellectual virtues is causing Africans to groan. Their presence will cause Africa to flourish and fulfil the high hopes of those who drafted Agenda 63.

This book does not contain the solutions to all the problems we have identified. Nor is its theology comprehensive. But our prayer is that as you read and study it, your feet will be set on the path that will lead you to become someone who lives for God's glory and brings hope to Africa in your sphere of influence. More than that, we pray that you will find yourself part of a large movement dedicated to healing and transforming our beloved continent.

Questions

1. What does theology mean to you?
2. Read and pray through *Agenda 2063: The Africa We Want*, noting its seven aspirations (see appendix). Should Christians be concerned about these things? If so, why?
3. Can you identify examples of the split between sacred and secular in your own life and in the life of your church? How can you work in your situation to end this false dichotomy?
4. Can we apply the principles of public theology in all areas of our lives or only in areas where we have special expertise?
5. How can Christians become pillars of hope for our continent?

Further Reading

African Union. *Agenda 2063: The African We Want*. Addis Ababa: African Union, 2015. https://au.int/en/Agenda2063/popular_version

---

13. Dow, *Virtuous Minds*.

2

The Nature of Public Theology

Dion A. Forster

There is a problem with the title of this chapter, and in fact with the title of this book. Both speak of "public theology," but in reality it might be better to speak of "public theologies" in the plural, rather than public theology in the singular. Different theologians, and theologians in different regions of the world, have very different approaches to the subject. They also focus on different issues. This is not surprising given the diversity of those who contribute to public theology and the unique issues faced in each region. Even within Africa, different regions may take different approaches to public theology. However, in the midst of this diversity, it is possible to identify some common characteristics of contemporary public theology. So that is what we will do in this chapter, along with specifying the approach to public theology that we have adopted in this particular book.

Isn't All Theology Public?

Let me begin with two questions I am often asked when I talk about public theology. The first is, "Isn't all theology public?" After all, theologians do not work in secret or hide what they know – they like to publish it in books and to talk and preach about their ideas. The second question is, "Are you saying that we should be distinguishing between our 'public' theology and our 'private' theology?" The idea of a private theology appeals to those in the increasingly secular global context who relegate religion to the private sphere. They argue that religion may be practised in the home but that it has little to no place in public life, except for a ritual role at certain public ceremonies. But that is not

15

how the majority of Africans view the relationship between faith and life. In Africa, religion is not private; it is present in both positive and negative forms in all spheres of life.

This African understanding captures an important point about theology. In fact, we can identify three different ways in which those who say that all theology is public are quite correct.

- *All theological engagement and reflection inevitably has a public presence, public influence, and public consequences.* Across all the theological disciplines – from systematic theology to practical theology – theologians seek to understand a God who is lovingly at work with all God creates in all spheres of life. Because God is active in all areas of life, theology is interested in all spheres of life, and in this sense those who say that all theology is public are quite correct. Nico Koopman puts it like this: "Public theology reflects on the love of the triune God for the world. . . . At its heart, therefore, Christian theology is public theology."[1]

The German Reformed theologian Jürgen Moltmann puts it this way:

> From the perspective of its origins and its goal, Christian theology is public theology, for it is the theology of the kingdom of God. . . .
> As such it must engage with the political, cultural, educational, economic and ecological spheres of life, not just with the private and ecclesial spheres.[2]

- *Our theology influences our lives, and our lives influence, and are influenced by, the contexts in which we live.* There are no purely "private" convictions. If, for example, a Christian or a church community has religious beliefs about the structuring of gender relations in society, those beliefs will affect both their relationships with their spouse and their children and the way they treat people at work and in society in general. The influence of their beliefs will extend past their front door and will have an impact on the wider society. Their beliefs will be shown in public. But the influence goes both ways. We influence our community, and our community influences us. So we must cultivate an awareness that our worldview

---

1. Nico Koopman, "Some Contours for Public Theology in South Africa," *International Journal of Practical Theology* 14, no. 1 (2010): 123.

2. Jürgen Moltmann, Nicholas Wolterstorff, and Ellen T. Charry, *A Passion for God's Reign: Theology, Christian Learning and the Christian Self* (Grand Rapids: Eerdmans, 1998), 24.

is not shaped just by the Bible (as we like to claim) but also by the surrounding "public," that is, the society we live in. The beliefs and behaviours of the people around us affect what we as Christians believe and how we behave. This influence is sometimes neutral and sometimes negative. It is neutral when the practices we share with our neighbours are morally neutral – for example, we may share preferences for certain foods, certain sports and certain greetings. But the influence of the society around us can also be very bad for our theology – as when some parts of the church in South Africa accepted the prevailing cultural racism and used Scripture to defend apartheid, and when preachers in Rwanda accepted local ethnic divisions and urged on the genocide in 1994. Those are extreme examples; other harms may appear more minor. But the fact that our theological thinking is influenced by a range of factors, and that it can issue in actions that are harmful to others, means that we must think carefully about what we believe and how it should affect our actions. The chapters in the second part of this book are meant to help you to start thinking carefully about how your theology affects the way you and your church respond to Africa's needs.

- *The task of theology is to facilitate meaningful engagement with all aspects of life, and not just with the religious aspects of life.* We claim to believe that God is active in all of life, in all spheres of society, and that God's activity is not restricted to the church and faith-based organizations. If this is the case, we need to talk about theological truths with people in non-church contexts. The church in its many forms (individual believers, congregations, denominations, ecumenical bodies, etc.) is present in public life as the body of Christ. Hence, it participates in public discourse and public reasoning "in the many, diverse and complex, aspects and spheres, structures and institutions of public life and speaks many different languages at the same time."[3] We need to learn how to do this. In other words, we need to find ways of "translating" God's presence and putting it into public language, that is into the language used by economists, nurses, teachers, politicians, businesspeople and farmers. This "public" language will differ from group to group, and we will need

---

3. Dirk J. Smit, "Does It Matter?: On Whether There Is Method in the Madness," in *A Companion to Public Theology*, ed. Sebastian C. H. Kim and Katie Day, 1st ed. (Leiden: Brill, 2017), 75.

to use different methods and approaches when we want to discuss theology in their contexts.

In the three senses outlined above, all theology is public theology. This means that public theology is not a separate theological discipline, or a department in a seminary or university, or even a method of doing things. It is the work of "public reasoning" with, alongside and sometimes in spite of, the diverse publics in which we live.[4]

Why Does Public Theology Even Exist?

Given what has just been said, why are so many people now talking about public theology? If theology has always been in some sense "public theology," why do we now talk about "public theologies" and refer to some scholars as "public theologians"? Dirk Smit has a valid point when he asks, "Does it matter?"[5]

Smit's answer as a public theologian is that public theology as a field of study does matter because it operates differently from other theological disciplines. Given that its mandate is to reflect on the meaning, significance and implications of faith in and for public life, it cannot be constrained to a single theological discipline such as systematic theology, practical theology or biblical studies. Public theology draws on these disciplines, but it also interacts with other disciplines as it seeks to apply theology in areas that are usually covered by disciplines like economics, sociology, ecology and educational and political theory. Public theology studies the "shifting political, cultural and economic realities of the time . . . following different images, pursuing different metaphors, making different proposals, holding conflicting viewpoints, and raising new questions."[6]

In his studies of the emergence of public theology as a separate paradigm, Dirk Smit has identified six areas that have been of theological interest in recent decades:[7]

- The role of religion in public life.

---

4. Smit, "Does It Matter?," 76–77.

5. Smit, 67.

6. Smit, "Does It Matter?," 67.

7. Dirk J. Smit, "The Paradigm of Public Theology: Origins and Development," in *Contextuality and Intercontextuality in Public Theology*, eds. Heinrich Bedford-Strohm, Florian Höhne, and Tobias Reitmeier (Münster: LIT Verlag, 2013), 11–23.

- How religion and theology affect and are affected by public reasoning in society, academy and the church.
- The contextualization of theologies in vastly different social, religious and political contexts such as Africa, Europe, Asia, Australia and the Americas.
- The relationship between theologies and public struggles in contexts of injustice and conflict.
- The role that theology and the church have played in development discourses on service delivery, gender debates and issues of environmental concern.
- Theology and the public return of the religious, including religious fundamentalisms and religious violence and extremism, as well as the resurgence of interest in religion and spirituality as making a positive contribution to the lives of persons and communities across the world.

These interests have all emerged within, or in response to, changing political, social and religious contexts. They reveal the importance of linking faith and life, of having meaningful exchanges between theology and other academic disciplines, and of being aware of the need for critical reflection on the historical and contextual factors that affect our thinking.

Smit's analysis makes it clear that for public theologians the work of theological reflection is done in relation to broad social, political, economic and historical concerns. But at the same time, it is important to remember that public theology is not identical to sociology or political studies or literary studies: it has to remain theological in nature and facilitate the presence of a theological voice in public life. As Koopman stresses, the work of the public theologian is to "reflect on the meaning, significance and implications of Trinitarian faith for public life."[8]

What Does It Mean to Have an African Public Theology?

Africa is a diverse continent and public theology is a diverse field, and so there is no single definition or method that characterizes public theology. After all, public theology is "a visionary and normative project, seeking to take a position, to make a difference, to serve what matters . . . it is the urge

---

8. Nico Koopman, "The Beyers Naudé Centre for Public Theology: Five Years On," in *Christian in Public: Aims, Methodologies and Issues in Public Theology*, ed. Len Hanson (Stellenbosch: Beyers Naudé Series on Public Theology, 2007), 281.

to show the world what theology looks like. It is concerned with issues of common interest and of the common good, whatever that might mean. It is about discipleship as transformation."[9] If we were to put this definition into an African frame, we might say that African public theology can be compared to the values of *ubuntu*. As Africans, we know that we have been shaped and given our identity by our communities, and so we seek to bring together our identity as Africans in community and our identity in Christ, and offer back to our communities the fruit of our thoughts and labour so that we and our communities may see a harvest that will nourish all of us as we work together towards the Africa God wants and we long for.

The engagement and dialogue between theology and the rest of life in Africa both contributes to society (and public life) and allows society to challenge and renew theological thinking. Let us think about what this means by looking at six important characteristics of public theology and their implications in our African context:

- *Public theology must be biblical theology.* As Smit puts it, "public theology should be recognizable as theology."[10] We are not just people who happen to be Christian talking about, say, economic matters. Rather, we are people who are applying our minds to understand what has been revealed about God's purposes for all areas of life. Public theology must remain theological in its nature, content and contribution.[11] Because Christian theology is rooted in Scripture, the Bible must play a key role, as is recognized in the next chapter of this book. But we must read the Bible not only through Western eyes but also as Africans seeking its relevance to Africa today.

- *Public theology must be multilingual.* All of us speak a variety of languages. In Africa, many people know their mother tongue, other languages spoken in their region, and a colonial language. This multilingualism makes it possible for us to listen to people who come from a variety of cultures and have a variety of experiences, and to communicate what we have learned from public theology to them, whether they come from our own ethnic group, other ethnic groups in the region, or from elsewhere in Africa or the world. However, we are also all "multilingual" in a different sense, in that we use language differently in different contexts. We may use one form of a language when talking informally and another when

---

9. Smit, "Does It Matter?," 89.

10. Smit, 71.

11. Koopman, "Some Contours," 127–129.

addressing a conference. We know that different spheres of society have their own jargon and systems of argumentation and ethics. A taxi driver sees the world very differently from the lawyer who rides in the taxi. Public theologians who want to relate to taxi drivers have to use a different style of language than they would use when addressing a gathering of lawyers. So if we want to start thinking about how theology applies in a particular field, we need to know the jargon of that field and what types of argument will be understood and seen as relevant by our peers in that field.

- *Public theology must be interdisciplinary.* Anyone seeking to be a public theologian needs to know more than just theology.[12] This is because the task of theology often extends beyond a two-way conversation and involves careful and rigorous reflection across many disciplines, drawing on the expertise of scholars in various academic fields and from varied faith traditions. For example, if you are going to express a theological conviction on justice in relation to some economic issue, it is crucial that you be knowledgeable and competent to engage with that topic and are not speaking from ignorance. In some parts of Africa, you may also need to know something about Islamic concepts of justice and ethics if your arguments are to be persuasive. It is our prayer that many of you who are reading this book already have or are acquiring expertise in other fields and will use it to benefit theology and society. Then you will be able to speak with clarity, conviction and competence in a variety of settings and on a variety of matters of public concern.

- *Public theology must be competent to provide political direction.* In other words, public theologians need to be able to "provide orientation, direction, and even guidance for policy-making and decisions about public life."[13] This orienting role applies not only in relation to government policies but also in regard to situations within churches, organizations, schools and communities, in fact, in any situation where religious leaders may be asked to help provide direction. To give one example of this orienting role, Alfred Sebahene from Tanzania (author of chapter 28 in this book) has made an in-depth study of corruption in Uganda and has launched a department

---

12. At the Beyers Naudé Centre for Public Theology, for example, contributing theologians are expected to have expertise in fields such as social and economic justice, reconciliation, ecology, religion and law, religion and science, gender and health.

13. Smit, "Does It Matter?," 82.

for the study of corruption that can advise leaders from across Africa on how to deal with issues of corruption.[14]

- *Public theology must be prophetic.* As is repeatedly emphasized in chapters 28 and 29 of this book, we must not allow our theology to be co-opted by the state or by other powerful persons or structures in our society, so that we simply agree with what those in authority do. "Theology should somehow be critical, in opposition, resisting, warning, critiquing, opposing what is already happening in public life, and for most this is an aspect that belongs inherently to the gospel and therefore to the role of the church and the task of theology."[15] The church and theologians have a responsibility to critically evaluate the structures, decisions, values and formulations of contemporary life in Africa in the light of the gospel of Christ and the values of the kingdom of God. One of the challenges of this characteristic of public theology is that various branches of the church may not agree about the implications of the truth of the gospel and the values of God's kingdom. So when exercising a prophetic role, we must be sure that our position is backed up by rigorous biblical theology. We may also, sadly, often find it necessary to critique not only society but also the church.[16]

- *Public theology must be inter-contextual.* We have already noted that public theology takes place in a wide variety of contexts (different spheres of society, different geographic locations and different disciplines). While the issues, concerns and patterns of the contexts may differ, there is a great deal to be learned from the variety of these contexts. Inter-contextual engagement can enrich public theologies with deeper and more nuanced insights. That is why we hope that you will read more than just the chapters in this book that relate to your own special area of interest. It is also why we encourage you to consider joining up with others who share your concerns to form a network of public theologians that reaches across Africa, supporting each other and learning from each other. This is doubly important in this age of globalization, in which the concerns of a local community are often connected with the global concerns of other

---

14. For more information on this department, see https://www.sjut.ac.tz/index.php/directorates-departments/department-of-corruption.

15. Smit, "Does It Matter?," 84.

16. Nico Koopman, "Racism in the Post-Apartheid South Africa," in *Questions About Life and Morality: Christian Ethics in South Africa Today*, ed. Louise Kretzschmar and L. D. Hulley (Pretoria: Van Schaik, 1998), 165.

communities[17] (giving rise to the term "glocal," embracing both global and local).[18] This presents a major challenge to those who choose to work in the field of public theology as they need to recognize the importance of understanding the local (micro) context without losing sight of broader national or regional concerns (the mezzo context), while also being aware of global concerns (the macro context).

What Challenges Do We Face as African Public Theologians?

When we attempt to do public theology, we will face criticism, particularly if we seek to exercise a prophetic function. Some of this criticism will come from those whose power and actions we are challenging. Their response may be hurtful – both physically and emotionally – but it is not unexpected.

What may be more difficult to handle is criticism from within the Christian community. Some of these critics may be people who have been co-opted by those in power, but other criticism will come from people whose theology is different from ours. We need to listen to them, for sometimes we may actually need either correcting or input and guidance from people with broader theological knowledge, specific expertise, or greater wisdom than we have. So we need to weigh what our critics say against Scripture and the realities of the situation. We also need to humbly examine ourselves and see whether we are letting our community influence us when we should be speaking God's truth to the community. Study, dialogue and networks of concerned theologians and "ordinary" church members are vital to helping us determine whether we should stand by our positions or modify them in some way.

African contextual and liberation theologians have been very critical of "global" public theology, asking whether it is radical and contextual enough to engage with the ongoing struggles and realities of Black and African Christians. They are concerned that some public theologians have tried to apply Westernized views and approaches to Christianity in African contexts without fully understanding those contexts. Tinyiko Maluleke questions whether those who do this really understand the pain of African Christians who love Jesus but resent the damage wrought by colonialism and imperialism (and by well-

---

17. Frederike Van Oorschot, "Public Theology Facing Globalization," in *Contextuality and Intercontextuality*, 225–232.

18. For more information on the glocal focus of the Global Network for Public Theology, see Dion A. Forster, "Democracy and Social Justice in Glocal Contexts," *International Journal of Public Theology* 12, no. 1 (2018): 1–4; Smit, "Does It Matter?," 87.

meaning, but misguided, missionaries).[19] Rothney Tshaka makes this point even more strongly. He asserts that Africans need approaches to theology that emphasize the perspectives and contributions of Black African theologians.[20]

While their arguments have some validity, there is a risk that this approach may limit the scope of their theology to a particular geographical context (Africa), or a particular historical experience (liberation from colonialism, or apartheid), or a particular ethnicity or culture. Such limitations may hinder the ability of African Christians to share their theologies, experiences and discoveries with other Christians around the world. The result might be that Africa develops its own form of "private" theology (private to Africa, or to Black Christians) rather than making its own contribution to global public theology.

Our goal in this book is to help Africans develop a contextual public theology that takes our African history and experience seriously and that is able to operate with rigour and integrity in African public life, and beyond Africa. It is up to you, the readers and students who use this book, to become the Black African theologians whose voices need to be heard. It is up to you to interact with the other theologians who are already raising their voices.

That having been said, it would be a mistake to think that public theology does away with the need for liberation theologies and contextual theologies such as African, Black or feminist theologies, or other specific approaches to theology. We are not in competition with these theological traditions and their approaches to specific experiences or concerns. On the contrary, our aim should be to include the best of what we can learn from them, and from the theologians and Christians who use them, in order to better serve Christ and work for the Africa God wants, and we want. We need continued prophetic engagement with historical social structures and oppressive systems such as racism, colonialism, sexism and entrenched social injustice. What our approach to public theology advocates is that we should draw on the best of what comes from other theologies and from the contributions of experts from

---

19. Tinyiko Sam Maluleke, "Reflections and Resources: The Elusive Public of Public Theology: A Response to William Storrar," *International Journal of Public Theology* 5, no. 1 (2011): 79–89.

20. See Rothney S. Tshaka, "African, You Are on Your Own!: The Need for African Reformed Christians to Seriously Engage Their Africanity in Their Reformed Theological Reflections," *Scriptura* 96 (2007): 533–548; Rothney S. Tshaka, "On Being African and Reformed? Towards an African Reformed Theology Enthused by an Interlocution of Those on the Margins of Society," *HTS Theological Studies* 70, no. 1 (2014): 1–7; and R. S. Tshaka and A. P. Phillips, "The Continued Relevance of African/Black Christologies in Reformed Theological Discourses in South Africa Today," *Dutch Reformed Theological Journal/Nederduitse Gereformeerde. Teologiese Tydskrif* 53, no 3 & 4 (2012): 353–362.

other fields (such as economics, political science, sociology and history) and should engage them in a conversation that is deeply theological, very contextual and critically informed.[21]

A final significant critique comes from feminist public theologians who argue that this field is often dominated by male theologians and approaches to theology that function in ways that exclude women and women's perspectives.[22] This point applies equally to all areas of theology. We have taken note of it, and you will see that several chapters in this book were written by women. It is important to engage with the work of these theologians and with others like them and to listen to the voices of our sisters, mothers and daughters as we seek to understand and solve some of the complex problems that we face on the African continent.

Conclusion

As African Christians whose lives are shaped by Christian theology, we must recognize that we are required to focus our attention on understanding who God is and how he is at work in our contexts in Africa, not just in the church, but in all of society. Our goal is to move from belief to action, from doctrine to ethics, and from worship to mission.[23]

Our prayer is that the chapters that follow will encourage you to identify areas into which you need to delve more deeply and will help us all to work to transform our continent from the Africa we do not want to the Africa we long for – and the Africa that God desires to see.

---

21. See, for example, Nico Koopman's article, "In Search of a Transforming Public Theology: Drinking from the Wells of Black Theology," in *Contesting Post-Racialism: Conflicted Churches in the United States and South Africa*, ed. R. D. Smith et al. (Jackson: University of Mississippi Press, 2015), 211–225.

22. Esther McIntosh, "Hearing the Other: Feminist Theology and Ethics," *International Journal of Public Theology* 4, no. 1 (2009): 1–4; Esther McIntosh, "Issues in Feminist Public Theology," in *Public Theology and the Challenge of Feminism*, ed. Stephen Burns and Anita Monro (London: Routledge, Taylor & Francis Group, 2015), 63–74; Esther McIntosh, "Public Theology, Populism and Sexism: The Hidden Crisis in Public Theology," in *Resisting Exclusion: Global Theological Responses to Populism* (Geneva, Switzerland: Lutheran World Federation, 2019), 221–228.

23. Koopman, "Some Contours," 124.

Questions

1. Which of the points made in the chapter would you like to discuss?
2. In what area can you as an individual contribute to public theology? Which of the six characteristics of public theology do you see yourself as having, and which do you need to cultivate?
3. After identifying your area of expertise, start working to identify a person whose expertise is not in theology with whom you will be able to dialogue and discuss issues that arise as you work through this book.

Further Reading

Hansen, L., ed. *Christian in Public: Aims, Methodologies and Issues in Public Theology*. Stellenbosch: Sun Media, 2008.

Kim, Sebastian C. H., and Katie Day, eds. *A Companion to Public Theology*. Leiden: Brill, 2017.

Koopman, Nico. "Some Contours for Public Theology." *International Journal of Public Theology* 14, no. 1 (2010): 123–138.

Mugambi, Jesse N. K. *Christian Theology and Social Reconstruction*. Nairobi: Acton, 2003.

3

The Bible and Public Theology

Hassan Musa

Having considered why Africa needs public theology and the nature of public theology, it is time to consider the source from which we derive our theology. That source is the Bible, the written word of God which has been preserved through many generations. It contains the history of God's revelation of who he is and of his plans and purposes for all that he has created, and particularly for human beings, whom he created to bear his image. The Bible deals with the origin of life, of humanity and of creation in general and records the various ways in which God's salvation has been introduced and how humanity has responded to it. But the Bible is not merely a historical record. It still speaks to modern church contexts and plays a key role in spiritual formation and ethical direction. It is important that we continually engage with it in order to see its value and significance for our lives and communities.

Yet we live in a world of distorted vision. That is why the Bible addresses our worldviews and corrects them to fit the original vision of God for his creation. But how are we to understand and use the Bible? It has been received in different ways by different readers and interpreters at different times and in different places and circumstances. Some believe that the way to be safe from demon manipulation and oppression when sleeping is to use the Bible as a pillow. Others wave a Bible over a sick person they are praying for, or hurl a Bible against someone they regard as evil in order to drive out a demon. Some use the Bible as a tool for clairvoyance. If something is missing and cannot be found by conventional methods, they recommend using a stick or thread to open the Bible and reveal where the missing item is. In traditional evangelical circles, the Bible is used as a tool of authority especially as regards church government and the rule of life.

Given all these different ways in which the Bible is used in African contexts, it is important that we think carefully about how the Bible should be used in doing public theology in Africa. We need discernment, and discernment in turn requires that we have a good theological foundation to draw on. It is important that we understand the broad sweep of biblical theology if we are not to be unduly swayed by individual verses and incidents. So let us begin by considering the great themes of the Bible that must shape our thinking.

The Bible and Origin, Identity and Ethics

Our understandings of our origin and identity determine our ethics. This point is readily understood in African contexts, where who you are is determined by where you come from, which explains what you do and don't do. But today many in Africa find the question of origins complex, for socio-political violence has forced them to move to other locations in Africa or overseas in search of peace and food. The result of this migration, whether for social, political, religious or economic reasons, is that people's identity has been jeopardized if not totally changed.

Migration was also the experience of the ancient Israelites, and so the Bible addresses issues of origin and migration. Issues of origin are dealt with in Genesis 1–11, where it is asserted that God created everything and everyone and declared that all he had created was "very good" (Gen 1:31). There are two key points here for our understanding of public theology. The first is that because everything comes from the creative hands of God, God's creation is truly beautiful and should not only be admired but also actively protected. The second point is the dignity of humanity. Every human being is made in the image of God (Gen 1:27) and should contribute whenever possible to the care of God's good creation. Later chapters in this book outline some of the implications of these truths in particular contexts.

Even though Genesis also records human failure and the brokenness of the world, these human failings do not destroy the work of God. God does not give up because people are now deeply flawed. God's patience and grace should encourage us to be patient with the weak among us and should help us to live better with great joy and hope.

The rest of Genesis (Gen 12–50) shows how God continued to work by choosing and calling the patriarchs and matriarchs of ancient Israel and promising them blessings for themselves, their descendants and the whole world (Gen 12:3). When their descendants found themselves enslaved in Egypt, God offered dignity to slaves by seeing their suffering and graciously sending Moses and Aaron to rescue them. The respected South African theologian Dirk Smit argues that the act of "seeing" is basic to ethics.[1] God saw the plight of the Israelites in the Egyptian context and made provision for their rescue. This has provided us with the kind of ethos we need in responding to the needs of others, namely the ethos of compassion.[2]

The rest of the story of the Israelites' journey in the wilderness tells of God's continuing grace and compassion for his people despite their rebellion against his messengers, Moses and Aaron. The wilderness was a place of drought and vulnerability, but God made his companionship available to the people and supplied their needs. He also gave them the law, which was intended to teach them how to love the Lord, worship only the Lord God of Israel, and love and care for their neighbours. If they obeyed the law, they would enjoy the blessings of the land God was going to give them. Moses's three speeches in the book of Deuteronomy are intended to provide courage and direction on the ethos and ethics of the people of God if they are to live responsibly in a new land.

The law as laid out in the Pentateuch is not meant to be interpreted and applied literally today. Rather, we should see it as the source of the principles that shaped the ethics of the Israelites and should shape our thinking today.[3] Jesus provided an example of how this should be done in his Sermon on the Mount, in which he penetrated to the heart of the law and taught Christians how to focus on what God desires and to be perfect as God is perfect (Matt 5:48).

The rest of the historical account of the origins of the Israelites (Joshua to 2 Kings), the prophetic and wisdom books, and the New Testament show us how the Israelites conducted their lives in and out of the promised land. We learn how they received the land and how they lost it because of their disobedience. Their history is replete with stories of human arrogance, ignorance and rebellion, and so prepares us for the theme of salvation that is a leading paradigm throughout biblical literature and in public theology.

---

1. Dirk Smit, "Liturgy and Life? On the Importance of Worship for Christian Ethics," *Scriptura* 62 (1997): 261–262.

2. See also M. Nussbaum, *Upheavals of Thoughts: The Intelligence of Emotions* (Cambridge: Cambridge University Press, 2001).

3. Christopher J. H. Wright, *Old Testament Ethics for the People of God* (Downers Grove, IL: IVP Academic, 2011); John Walton, "Deuteronomy: An Exposition of the Spirit of the Law," *Grace Theological Journal* 8, no. 2 (1987): 213–225.

The Bible and Salvation

The theme of salvation runs in various forms right through the Bible. God's very first act of salvation occurred shortly after Adam and Eve had sinned and plunged all humanity for all generations into the brokenness of life and relationship with God (Gen 3). God rescued them from their new vulnerability by making clothing for them out of animal skin. In the rest of Genesis, we see God saving or rescuing the patriarchs of Israel from physical, social and even spiritual dangers.

The historical act of salvation to which the biblical writers most often refer is God's spectacular salvation of the Israelites from bondage in Egypt.[4] It was through the exodus experience that they became an independent people and received a religious and social identity that set them apart from the other peoples of the ancient Near East. God's salvation restored their sense of being and gave them a sense of relationship with God, with one another and even with other nations. So it is not surprising that the exodus experience has been at the heart of liberation theology.

Even the book of Leviticus, which may seem to us to focus primarily on arcane rules of sacrifice, can be read in terms of salvation theology.[5] Leviticus answers the question of what it means to be saved by saying that to be saved is to be holy. Holiness is seen as the distinctive mark of the people of God. It means that they are set apart for God so that they can be a blessing for the whole world (Gen 12:1–3) and that they accordingly live in a way that shows their love for him and for other people (Lev 19). That was why God made so many provisions for the Israelites' restoration after any kind of sinful rebellion or shortcoming. Whenever the people as individuals or as a nation were defiled for any reason, God supplied a means of restoration, with the highest point being the rituals and sacrifices on the Day of Atonement (Lev 16). The instructions of Leviticus show both God's demand for holiness and God's enabling of holiness.

Human rebellion and turning away from the love and worship of God remained key problems in the books of Joshua and Judges, but the compassionate solidarity of God always provided salvation (rescue) from their physical enemies. We see the same protection extended to the young David when he was threatened by Saul. It is not surprising that so many of the psalms

---

4. Walter Brueggemann, *Journey to the Common Good* (Louisville, KY: Westminster John Knox, 2010).

5. See A. A. Cody, *History of Old Testament Priesthood* (Rome: Pontifical Biblical Institute, 1969); M. Douglas, *Purity and Danger* (London: Routledge and Keegan Paul, 1966).

celebrate the salvation of the Lord. David and the other psalmists did not live easy lives, but God's presence made them safe and secure.

At the very start of the New Testament, we are introduced to "Jesus the Messiah" (Matt 1:1), whose name and title shows that the theme of salvation continues. The name "Jesus," like the names Joshua and Hosea in the Old Testament, means one who saves, rescues and even restores. The title "the Messiah" means that Jesus fulfils the Old Testament prophecies of a coming deliverer.

While the general understanding of salvation in the Old Testament had to do with physical rescue from potential or actual danger, the New Testament takes the theme of deliverance further into the spiritual dimension with the announcement that Jesus saves "his people from their sins" (Matt 1:21). Some may say that whereas God was at work in the public sphere in the Old Testament, the salvation that Jesus offers is private and personal. But I would disagree. The sins from which "sinners" are saved may be either public or private, seen or concealed, yet the "sinner" as a human being always lives in public. The salvation of a sinner results in a changed life, which is as visible in public spaces as a light shining in darkness. When people see the good works of a person who has been saved, they will have reason to glorify God who is in heaven (Matt 5:13–16).

Paul dwells on this theme of salvation as the renewal of life, or regeneration, in Ephesians 2. He argues that salvation reorients the people of God to live in ways that please God. Their spiritual deadness is destroyed, and they are reawakened into the real life of faith and spiritual faithfulness and fruitfulness that God desires. The new people of faith live differently: they live sacrificially and in harmony with one another because of their unity in Christ (Eph 3–4). The old ethnic walls that separated them have been broken down, and every member is now part of the glorious household of God. This sense of renewal of life brings us together and makes us worship God in spirit and in truth (see also John 4:24; Rom 12:2).

The Bible and Worship

One of the most extraordinary things that people of faith do in Christ is to come together in worship. The Bible is full of God's restorative justice and love. It constantly calls us back to God in worship. The alienation of humanity due to human rebellion has ushered us into vulnerability; nevertheless, the alien love of God has dignified us by providing new clothing for rebellious humanity. In Leviticus, the instructions on the way to holiness enable unholy or sinful people to be purified so that they can worship anew. The Psalms are full of calls to the people of God to come and ascribe all glory and honour to God in public places of worship. Worship is thus not a purely private matter, and so our theology of worship is a serious part of public theology. It is in our act of worship that we live as the true people of God. In our liturgical acts of worship we look in the right direction.[6] It is in the liturgy of prayer and worship that we participate in the reality of the kingdom of God.[7] From our worship tradition we learn to receive one another as brothers and sisters, and in it we continually cultivate a God-centred and God-honouring ethos that leads to life-transforming and even world-transforming ethics. It is in this ethical engagement with God and with one another that we see anew that we are in the world but do not belong to the world. We reject all kinds of worldliness, but we accept the world. Our public worship should thus always invite us into the holy presence of God in true confession and gratitude.

Sometimes, however, our flesh and its desires can take over our thoughts and acts so that our worship does not allow the life of God to flow in us.[8] We should not pretend that all is well and live in false piety, but should continue to seek to be renewed into the image of the One who has saved us. The renewal of our minds in the presence of God in order to serve God and one another becomes our true act of worship to God (Rom 12:1–2).

Note that our godliness is seen not in our separation from the world but in our living in the world differently (John 15–17). The eschatological theology of Revelation turns out to be a theology of hope for life and godliness rather than merely a succession of frightening images. In the end, the idea of worship will remain and reign when all evil is destroyed (Rev 18–19). As transformed human beings we will join the company of angels in singing praises to the Lord.

It is in our acts of worship that we confront the worldliness of the world and show that there is another sense of being that is better than what it has to offer. In our public theology of worship, we engage with the kingdom of God here on earth as it is in heaven. This is when heaven comes to us here and now. This is when we see the beauty of God in our salvation and in our togetherness. It is in our worship that we learn new speech that will constructively transform the world and continually keep our witness to the presence of God open. It

---

6. Smit, *Liturgy and Life?*, 261; see also Stanley Hauerwas and W. H. Willimon, *Resident Aliens* (Nashville: Abingdon Press, 1989); Stanley Hauerwas, *In Good Company: The Church as Polis* (Notre Dame: University of Notre Dame Press, 1995).

7. D. E. Saliers, *Worship as Theology: Foretaste of Divine Glory* (Nashville: Abingdon, 1994).

8. J. W. de Gruchy, *Cry Justice! Prayer, Meditations and Readings from South Africa* (London: Collins Liturgical Publications, 1986).

is in our public theology of worship that we learn new ways of living in the world as living with responsibility.

The Bible and Social Responsibility

Although we are in the world, we do not belong to the world, as Jesus told his disciples in the upper room before he was executed (John 13–17). We should thus be prepared to learn to live differently in the world, that is, to live responsibly.

This biblical theology of responsibility is seen at creation and at the exodus. When the Israelites came out of Egypt, God, speaking through Moses, called them to be a different people. God asked them to learn to hear and obey the voice of the Lord in order to be the new people that God desires. In Exodus 19 and other similar chapters, the people were consecrated in order to prepare them practically to see and know that the holiness of God must be reflected in their daily lives. God made a covenant with them in order to make them new and responsible people. The idea of responsibility in the here and now means to live with awareness of the otherness of others and to contribute meaningfully for others. This is what we do when we live together as the new people of God, both different and interconnected.[9]

In Deuteronomy the Israelites were called to show the world what it means to be the people of God by loving God and caring for their neighbour and for foreigners. Our neighbour may be someone we know well, or someone who is very different from us, sometimes even someone who seems really strange to us. That is why we need to be challenged to receive and love our neighbour. We may have to learn how to do so.

This idea of neighbourliness comes to us anew in the coming of God in Jesus Christ. Jesus speaks of himself as present in the neighbour we receive and care for (Matt 25:31–46). The person of Jesus can be seen in the faces of others, whether our friends, neighbours or complete strangers. Regardless of who they are, the way we receive and treat them reveals a lot about how we receive and treat Jesus Christ. The children we see and the unknown person who passes by, all wear the face of Jesus in front of us. The poor person in need of love and care is left for us as a test of our faith and spirituality.

The story of the good Samaritan leaves us either cold or warm. We feel cold and perhaps challenged that we too have failed a person in need. We have

---

9. Dirk Smit, "Notions of the Public and Doing Theology," *International Journal of Public Theology* 1 (2007): 431–454.

too often shown the same face of godliness as the priest and the Levite who simply passed by. But the stranger in need is now the one who is familiar to us. This is a public theology of care, which flows from a compassionate sense of what it means to be human. Whenever the truth of our humanity seems to evade us, we need to be reminded that we have an intrinsic need for love as care and that we must respond to the needs of others.

Wolterstorff applies this perspective on responsibility in his various writings on the role of "justice" in the world as a foundational paradigm of life.[10] We manifest this justice in our solidarity with all those in need amidst us, and by caring for them we practise a public theology that is useful in transforming the world into a better place for all. Writers like Heinrich Bedford-Strohm have critically engaged the socio-political and economic problems of the world from a global context in search of the meaning of life together for inclusive justice and care, and we need to heed their voices and recognize the need for renewal of our civilization.[11]

Our modern civilization was born from the West, but its origins are not solely Western. As Vishal Mangalwadi has shown, the Bible, a book from the Middle East, has played a vital role in shaping the world in which we live.[12] The biblical concept of human dignity has shaped the world's ethics, and a biblical understanding of nature has shaped the world's thinking on science. The key ideas that have made Western civil society vital and efficient are thus rooted in the Bible.

Today many in the West have little regard for the Bible; not so in Africa. Here it is still part of a vital tradition, and we thus should be encouraging people to read the Bible for all its worth in both their personal and social contexts. We need to allow it to continually transform our lives and our cultures. The Bible has always been a means of cultural preservation and enhancement, especially in contexts where it is read with care and deep reverence. This kind of reading is all we need for a more useful public theology for the future.

---

10. Nicholas Wolterstorff, *Until Justice and Peace Embrace* (Grand Rapids: Eerdmans, 1983); Wolterstorff, "Liturgy, Justice and Holiness," *Reformed Journal* 16 (1989):12–20; Wolterstorff, "Justice as Condition for Authentic Liturgy," *Theology Today* 48 (1991): 6–21.

11. Heinrich Bedford-Strohm, "Prophetic Witness and Public Discourse in European Societies: A German Perspective," *HTS Teologiese Studies/Theological Studies* 66, no. 1 (2010): 1–6.

12. Vishal Mangalwadi, *The Book that Made Your World: How the Bible Created the Soul of Western Civilization* (Nashville: Thomas Nelson, 2011).

The Bible and the Public Theology of the Future

It may be useful to ask if the Bible has any potential for doing what we call public theology of the future. This concern is very legitimate because many do not see the Bible as speaking to us here and now. They think of the Bible as a document of the past, with little or no relevance for the present or the future. But from a public theological perspective, the Bible should continually be our daily companion as we journey from the past into the future.

In saying this, I am not referring only to eschatological concerns, even though they are so much a part of what it means to look into the future through the Bible. We have been reminded of this by the theology of hope propounded by one of the renowned public theologians of the twentieth and twenty-first centuries, Jürgen Moltmann. Moltmann argues that the idea of the coming of God presents us with a realistic focus for Christian eschatological hope that should stimulate us to living well and living fully in the present even as we move into the future.[13]

Returning to Mangalwadi's thesis that the Bible shaped Western civilization, we can affirm that the Bible has been useful in creating the civilization that has served all of humanity in the recent past, and that it still holds the same potential today. If we return to the study of the Bible in our contexts with good interest and intent, it will continually engage with us in life-giving ways.

Recent research includes multidimensional approaches to biblical hermeneutics that address our myriad concerns in modern and even postmodern cultures. Gerald West, for example, has led the way in doing a hermeneutic of liberation from a biblical perspective.[14] There are so many things that we need to be liberated from in order to have the vital life of true humanity that God has called us to. These concerns are mainly ideological and include colonization, violence, discrimination, abuse, ecological abuse, religious abuse and the like. All these things are always throwing our humanity and world into jeopardy. Some of them are addressed in later chapters of this book.

Scholars like Juliana M. Claassens have suggested a restorative reading of the Bible that continuously leads us into seeing the Bible in new ways that are

---

13. Jürgen Moltmann, *Theology of Hope* (London: SCM, 1967); Moltmann, *The Experiment of Hope* (London: SCM, 1975); Moltmann, *Ethics of Hope* (Cambridge: Cambridge University Press, 2012).

14. Gerald West, *Biblical Hermeneutics of Liberation: Modes of Reading the Bible in the South African Context*, 2nd ed. (Pietermaritzburg: Cluster, 1995).

life giving.[15] Musa Dube has offered postcolonial readings of the Bible that give voice to the voiceless and bring liberation to the African continent.[16] Mercy Amba Oduyoye founded the Circle of Concerned African Women Theologians in 1989, which brings women (and men) from all over Africa together to read the Bible today and attend to its truth in their togetherness. This cooperative Bible study is very useful for contextual analysis and for finding relevant ways of doing public theology that attend to the concern of the "ordinary reader."

Gerald West has also given his time and energy to doing theology "from below" and to reading the Bible from the perspective of the "ordinary reader" who lacks formal theologian training.[17] The perspectives of these readers need to be heard. They show us where God's word is needed in the lives of people and reminds us of how God in Jesus lived with people in their contexts. They reveal how the Bible can be used as an authoritative document to orient and reorient our lives in different contexts toward a more vital public theology in Africa.

This is the way for the future of public theology in Africa. The knowledge of the past must be discussed in the present with great hope for the future in terms of responsible hermeneutics. The significance of biblical material must be open to the daily concerns of people, and we should seek to find important ways of contextualizing the truth of God's word in ways that make theology not only easy to do but very transformative in Africa and beyond.

Questions

1. Is the Bible about salvation? If so, what does salvation mean? Does it relate only to receiving eternal life?
2. How can reading the Bible help your community to engage in sociocultural, spiritual, economic and political development and transformation?
3. How would you as a public theologian respond to someone who argues that Christians today should obey the law of Moses as set out in the Pentateuch?

---

15. Juliana M. Claassens and B. C. Birch, *Restorative Readings: The Old Testament, Ethics and Human Dignity* (Eugene, OR: Pickwick, 2015).

16. Musa W. Dube and G. West, eds., *The Bible in Africa: Transactions, Trajectories, and Trends* (Leiden: Brill, 2000). See also, Dube, *Other Ways of Reading: African Women and the Bible* (Atlanta: SBL, 2001), and Dube, "Exegeting the Darkness: Reading the Botswana Colonial Bible" (presented in Atlanta at the SBL Annual Meeting, 2010).

17. See G. I. Akper, "The Role of the 'Ordinary Reader' in Gerald O. West's Hermeneutics," *Scriptura* 88 (2005): 1–13.

4. Identify a particular situation that concerns you in your community and indicate how the Bible's teaching on origins, salvation, worship and responsibility affect your approach to that problem.
5. How can you set about encouraging people to read the Bible for all its worth, not only for their personal lives but also as regards their communities?

Further Reading

Akper, G. I. "The Role of the 'Ordinary Reader' in Gerald O. West's Hermeneutics," *Scriptura* 88 (2005): 1–13.

Dube, M. W., ed. *Other Ways of Reading: African Women and the Bible*. Atlanta: SBL, 2001.

Dube, M. W., and G. West, eds. *The Bible in Africa: Transactions, Trajectories, and Trends*. Leiden: Brill, 2000.

Fee, G. D., and D. Stuart. *How to Read the Bible for All Its Worth*, 4th ed. Grand Rapids: Zondervan, 2014.

Mbiti, J. S. "The Biblical Basis for Present Trends in African Theology." In *African Theology en Route*, edited by K. Appiah-Kubi and S. Torres, 83–94. Maryknoll, NY: Orbis, 1979.

Sanneh, L. *Translating the Message: The Missionary Impact on Culture*. New York: Orbis, 1989.

4

The Trinity and Public Theology

Tersur Aben

The title of this chapter may puzzle many, for we tend to think of the Trinity as a doctrine formulated at the Council of Nicaea and agreed to by all Christian churches, but one that has little relevance to our public life and ethics. How can the knowledge that God exists as Father, Son and Holy Spirit even begin to affect public life?

The place to start answering this question is right at the start of the Bible, in the account of creation where we are told that human beings are made in the image of God.

The Image of God

Genesis begins, "In the beginning God created the heavens and the earth" (Gen 1:1). It sounds as if God is one divine individual, but closer examination of the rest of the chapter, in light of our knowledge of the rest of Scripture, suggests that all three divine persons were present. We are told that the "Spirit of God was hovering over the waters" at the start of creation (Gen 1:2). And it was by God's word (the repeated "and God said") that all things on earth were set in order and harmonized. In John 1:1–3, we are told that this Word is Christ. Therefore we can say that in the biblical account of creation, God exists as three distinct divine persons who work together to create and order all things on earth.

Genesis also gives a detailed account of the creation of human beings. It begins with God saying, "Let us make mankind in our image, in our likeness, so that they may rule over the fish in the sea and the birds in the sky, over the livestock and all the wild animals, and over all the creatures that move along the ground" (Gen 1:26). The word the NIV translates as "mankind" literally means "man" (that is, one individual man), but clearly in context it refers to both men and women, for in the next verse we read: "So God created mankind in his own image, in the image of God he created them; male and female, he created them" (Gen 1:27). What this means is that the word "man" in the creation account refers to both an individual and a plurality of persons, in the same way as "God" refers to the one God who is nonetheless three distinct divine persons. We speak in much the same way when we refer to "Africa" as a unit, despite the vast plurality of nations and people within Africa. Grasping this idea of unity in plurality helps us to understand what it means to say that God is a plurality of persons.

If we agree that God is a plurality of persons working together to accomplish creation, and that "mankind" is a plurality of persons made in God's image, then it follows that human beings were created to work together to accomplish the task that God has given them, which is to care for God's creation. And given that God's creation includes their fellow human beings, their task is also to care for each other, as will be mentioned repeatedly in the second part of this book.

That is a first application of the idea of the Trinity. But there is another point that we can deduce from the account of the creation of humanity. It is that the God who exists in plurality has one single essence or nature, and the same is true of human beings – we all share the essential attribute of having been created in the image of God. For Africa, this means that all human beings on this continent, regardless of their vast diversity, share the essential attribute of being made in the image of God. As such, all share in the divine dignity. Ethnic, political and economic differences sometimes overshadow this in our thinking and in our actions. But we should never forget that everyone, even our enemies, even the most impoverished among us, has the dignity of bearing the divine image, and so sharing something of the divine essence.

The task of public theology is to find ways to uphold that dignity in all the spheres of life and make Christians aware that truly recognizing this dignity will transform their own lives, and those of others.

The Unity of the Trinity

Trinitarian theology states that God is one with respect not only to his substance (his essence) but also as regards his will (decrees) and his actions (deeds). The Father, the Son and the Holy Spirit always act in agreement, with no possibility of conflict. As Neal Plantinga puts it, "the Father, Son, and Holy

Spirit are both freely and essentially joined to each other in a superlative unity of harmony and fellowship."[1] Jesus Christ used the preposition "in" to explain their relationship of perfect union and fellowship, saying, "I am in the Father" and "the Father is in me" (John 14:10–11).

As human beings, we find it difficult to imagine that three persons can rule in absolute unity. In African politics, leaders are surrounded by people with their own agendas, all seeking to advance their own interests. But within the Trinity, there is no rivalry. They are in full agreement on their goals and on how they are to achieve them, and none seeks to advance himself in relation to the others.

Is this not a model for how we should conduct ourselves in working to improve civil society in Africa (and globally)? If we agree on our goals for our community, can we try to be like the Trinity as we work towards those goals? In other words, can we set aside our individual egos and focus on our task rather than on our standing in relation to someone else who is pursuing the same goal?

This understanding of unity in plurality is less foreign to Africans than it is to Westerners. Whereas the West tends to promote individualism, all Africans are familiar with the concept of *ubuntu* expressed in the words "I am because we are." All Africans are aware that we live in community and that our own identity is intricately interwoven with that of others. We see evidence of this in the fact that many African languages have no words for "nephew," "cousin," "niece," or "uncle." Such words are not needed because everyone in your community is your brother or sister. Individual differences do not matter so long as one can eat and talk with one's neighbour.[2]

In living out this concept of community, Africans are also living out an aspect of what it means to be made in the image of a Trinitarian God.

The Diversity of the Trinity

One way in which theologians have attempted to underscore the distinction between the three divine persons of the Trinity is to assign names to them. The Council of Nicaea agreed that the first person of the Trinity is to be called the Father, the second person is to be called the Son, and the third person is to be called the Holy Spirit. The Council added that the Father is not the Son

---

1. Cornelius Plantinga, Jr., "Hodgson-Welch Debate and the Analogy of the Trinity," (PhD dissertation, Princeton Theological Seminary, 1982), 339.

2. Byang H. Kato, *Theological Pitfalls in Africa* (Kumasi: Evangel, 1975), 130.

or the Holy Spirit, the Son is not the Father or the Holy Spirit, and the Holy Spirit is not the Son or the Father. Still, the Council insisted that the three distinct divine persons are exactly one God, and the numerical designations first, second and third do not represent degrees of status. Rather, they are convenient terms related to the order in which the persons of the Trinity have been revealed to us in Scripture.

Although the Trinity act in perfect unity, they have different roles when it comes to human salvation. In the New Testament, God the Father is spoken of as sending his only begotten Son, Jesus Christ, the second person of the Trinity, to earth to die on the cross of Calvary to save human beings from sin and restore them to a right relationship with God. Then together the Father and the Son sent the Holy Spirit, the third person of the Trinity, into the world to apply the benefits of salvation and empower all who believe in Christ to be holistically transformed into his image. These blessings of salvation and sanctification are available to all who believe, regardless of their race or ethnicity or social class. This distinction in action is why we speak of God the Father as the creator, Jesus Christ as the redeemer and restorer, and the Holy Spirit as the empowerer.

Although the Trinity have different roles, none is inherently superior to the other. Christ repeatedly insisted, "I and the Father are one" (John 10:30). Similarly, the book of Revelation begins with a vision of the ascended Christ, who describes himself as follows, "I am the Living One; I was dead, and now look, I am alive for ever and ever!" (Rev 1:18). The risen Christ then gives John messages to seven churches, and each time he ends with the statement, "Whoever has ears, let them hear what the Spirit says to the churches" (Rev 2:7, 11, 17, 29; 3:6, 13, 22). Here the words of the Spirit and the words of the risen Christ are treated as coming from the same source with the same authority. Yet Christ also says that "the Son can do nothing by himself; he can do only what he sees his Father doing, because whatever the Father does the Son also does" (John 5:19) and that the Spirit "will not speak on his own; he will speak only what he hears, and he will tell you what is yet to come. He will glorify me because it is from me that he will receive what he will make known to you" (John 16:13–14). These passages illustrate both the harmony and the different roles of the three persons of the Trinity.

What is worth noting about these statements is that even though the Father, Jesus and the Spirit have different roles in salvation, they all have equal dignity. It follows that for us to live like beings made in the image of God, we must accord equal dignity to one another. We all have differing parts to play in God's creation, and no part should be seen as lacking in dignity merely because it is different from another part or serves another function. God "sends" his Son, and the Son asks his Father to "send" the Spirit, but in all cases the one sent is equally God. Similarly, when we are in a position to "send" others and assign tasks, we must never assume that the fact that we are in leadership implies that we have more human worth than the one we have sent. On the contrary, if we seek to live out the implications of the Trinity, we must seek to restore human dignity in all the relationships within African families, our education system, our commercial structures and all our social and political structures.

To put this another way, the Trinity teaches Africans to embrace their diversity and to regard their diversity as a source of enrichment. The harmonious coexistence of the Trinitarian persons teaches Africans to firmly embrace their plurality and to celebrate the dynamics of African identity. Just as the Trinitarian persons participate equally with one another in building the kingdom of God, so Africans have to learn to be engaged in constructive discourses with one another aimed at building a godly civil society and a strong missional church.

The Consequences of Failure to Acknowledge the Trinity

God created human beings to enjoy the same perfect fellowship of love that God enjoys within the Trinity. They were to enjoy this love with God and with each other. Initially, this was how human beings lived. But when Satan brought sin into the world, it disrupted that perfect fellowship of love. It tore apart our perfect fellowship of love with God, for we were expelled from the garden of Eden where Adam and Eve had lived in regular communion with God. It also damaged our relationships with each other, as can be seen from the way Adam and Eve blame others for their own sin (Gen 3).

At the fall human beings turned away from God and gave precedence to their own selfish desires, interests and objectives. They ceased to reflect the image of God. Like all others, Africans became self-absorbed. They did not want to please God, nor did they love one another.

But, thank God, the Father sent his one and only Son, Jesus Christ, the second person of the Trinity, to come to earth and die on the cross of Calvary to save human beings from sin. Through his death, the Son removed the negative consequences of sin, making it possible for us to again become like God in nature and character. Through the empowering work of the Holy Spirit, we will one day again fully represent the image of God as God created us to do.

But in the present, we are still scarred by sin, and those scars can warp our understanding of what it means to live in the image of the Trinity. In particular we are prone to two heresies: overstressing unity and overstressing diversity.

Overstressing unity

The first heresy we fall into as regards the Trinity is to blur the distinction between the three divine persons, treating God as if he were only one person. But the Scriptures clearly reveal that there are three distinct divine persons in the Godhead.

This heresy must be rejected because it negates the truth of biblical revelation about the identity of God. What may be less obvious to us is that it also affects how we treat others. If we deny that diversity exists within God, we may feel entitled to oppose diversity in those around us.

For instance, in a family, a husband may refuse to accept that his wife is a different person from himself and may try to force her to do only what he wants. Similarly, parents may refuse to accept that their children have their own identities and may insist that their children fulfil their parents' desires, without regard for the children's interests or abilities. On the broader social scale, we see a similar dynamic when a dominant class or group or race tries to force minor classes or groups or races to assimilate with them and assume the same identity. All these attempts to impose our wills, decisions and desires on others are oppressive and deny the fact that as beings made in the image of God, we are diverse. Dictatorship is the stamping out of the liberties of individuals by suppressing their unique individuality.

We are all familiar with the evil consequences of such oppression and of the crises it causes in families, communities and nations. Oppression does not make for the harmony and peace God wants us to have in our relationships. Instead, it makes for hatred and an absence of the love that exists within the Trinity and should exist among us as beings made in God's image.

Overstressing diversity

Some of those who resist the temptation to see God as one, rather than as a Trinity, fall into the opposite error and treat the three persons of the Trinity as if they are three separate deities. They speak as if the Father is separate from the Son and the Holy Spirit. This separation of the divine substance is heretical because it gives rise to three deities or gods. But the Scriptures reveal to us that there is only one God – not three gods.

When we see God as three deities and ignore the loving unity that exists within the Trinity, we are paving the way for individualistic thinking, which is what happens when individuals choose to live their lives separate or apart from the other individuals in society and are not willing to work together to achieve common goals. God does not live in isolation, and neither should we.

To reflect the image of God as Trinity, we need to work hard to live together in harmony across ethnic and generational boundaries. We need to redefine leadership so that it does not only benefit members of the leaders' group but seeks to address the physical and spiritual needs of all Africans.

Excessive individualism is not only a problem at the national level; it also affects families. If parents and children refuse to communicate with each other or visit each other, we are not acting like the Trinity. The same is true if they do not actively refuse to meet but simply ignore each other and see no need to relate with other members of the family.

It sometimes happens that a group separates itself from others and ceases to see itself as part of the larger community. This type of division may be based on class, race, gender or sexuality. Members of the group live in a ghetto and want nothing to do with anyone outside the group. They do not have any fellowship with others – not at church, not in the market, and not in the political arena. Instead they simply oppose any position put forward by anyone else. When such problems arise in a church or a community, we should point people to the perfect Trinitarian fellowship of love that is a model for us to act together to accomplish mutual goals.

What I call the perfect Trinitarian fellowship of love manifests itself as the kind of love that warmly and respectfully affirms the otherness of the beloved. It affirms, celebrates and communicates their otherness without reservation or fear of oppression. When this happens, God is present as a full member of the community. Indeed, God is part of any vibrant Christian community who live in harmony with one another. This is the essence of the scriptural assertions in Genesis 1:26–27 and 2:18 that God created us in his image – that image accounts for our communal existence.

Our creation in the image of God accounts for African's social nature and character. God has placed us in families, communities and nations in Africa. Each member of those groups is a distinct individual, with a distinct existence. But a perfect fellowship of love should join us to one another in will and action. African families, churches, tribes and nations should reflect this fellowship of love as they live together in unity with one another.

The Trinity and the Church

Another analogy that Paul uses to speak about the Trinitarian fellowship that should characterize African life is the fellowship of the church. Just as the one God is three Persons, so the church is one body but has many members who work together to serve the whole body. The different organs – eyes, ears, feet and hands – are all part of one unified body (1 Cor 12:12–27). Similarly, the church in Africa is drawn from many African societies and includes individuals with very different personalities, backgrounds and gifts, but together they all make up the church of God in Africa. If the church in one part of Africa suffers, the whole church suffers. And if the church in one part of Africa is honoured, then the whole church in Africa is honoured.

African's strong sense of community, which springs from the Trinity, also explains why Africans are by nature ecumenical and encourage the cooperation and unification of different Christian groups so that they can work together in harmony to bring about the kingdom of God on earth. Our prayer is that the chapters in the second half of this book will suggest new ways in which we can cooperate to achieve this goal.

Conclusion

Together, the Father and the Son sent the Holy Spirit into the world to live in those who follow Christ and to apply the benefits of salvation to them. Those who are saved from sin are now called to work towards learning to live in perfect fellowship of love with God and with one another. As they model their relationships on the relationships that exist within the Trinity, Africans will come to experience God's shalom or peace, which will make for holistic transformation of African families and educational, commercial and socio-political structures.

If we live in harmony and accord human dignity to one another, we will be both truly human and truly Africans. I thus issue a "prophetic" call on Africans to image God by transforming their communities by infusing moral integrity into their governments and civil societies so that they too live at peace with one another. In so doing, Africans will uphold human dignity, seek justice in all human affairs of life and obey the laws of God.

Questions

1. How can we better reflect the relationship of the Trinity within our own family, in our relationship as husbands and wives and in our relationship with our children?
2. What does it mean to respect the dignity of others in Trinitarian terms? What are the implications of this for our involvement in all forms of politics?

3. What are the implications of the Trinity as regards ethnic differences and the importance we attach to ethnic loyalties?
4. What implications does the fact that the Trinity is a community and that we are made in its image and likeness have for our thinking on economic matters?
5. What is the relationship between the Trinity, humanity and creation?

Further Reading

Bitrus, Ibrahim. *Community and Trinity in Africa*. London: Routledge, 2017.
Kombo, J. O. *The Doctrine of God in African Christian Thought: The Holy Trinity Theological Hermeneutics and the African Intellectual Culture*. Leiden: Brill, 2007.
Peterson, Eugene. *Christ Plays in a Thousand Places*. Grand Rapids: Eerdmans, 2005.
Rohr, R., and M. Morrell. *The Divine Dance: The Trinity and Your Transformation*. New Kensington, PA: Whitaker House, 2016.

5

Public Theology and Identity

H. Jurgens Hendriks

An Africa we do not want. . . . Africans we do not want to be . . .
"Almost everyone in Africa acknowledges that we are currently living in an Africa we do not want. It is not that we do not love Africa – we do, passionately and deeply."[1]

An American president's reference to African countries as "shithole countries"[2] is only one in a long history of racially tainted, derogatory remarks and characterizations aimed at our continent and its people, remarks that hurt and humiliate.

What makes these remarks even more mortifying is that, in some cases at least, if we are honest with ourselves, we have to admit that we are responsible for making such terms quite accurate characterizations. Historically, the African slave trade was not a financial enterprise initiated and maintained solely by Western powers. Local merchants were always complicit in the lucrative trade in fellow Africans. Local tribes were often too willing to assist colonial masters to divide and rule. Currently, South Africans are reeling as they learn that our former president and many members of his government have been corrupt and nepotistic to a degree that exceeds our wildest imagination. Foreign nationals and South African business tycoons have influenced cabinet decisions and appointments. They have had access to minerals and contracts that enriched themselves and those they bribed. The president and his key operators lived

---

1. Sunday Bobai Agang, Chapter 1, opening lines.
2. www.news24.com/Africa/News/africa-is-no-shithole-outrage-over-trumps-remark-20180112.

in extreme luxury while unemployment rose, poverty increased and basic services spiralled into decline. Because of corruption and mismanagement, some municipalities are unable to provide even potable water or electricity to their residents. Untreated sewerage flows into and pollutes river systems.

What happened to the dream-come-true rainbow nation that, to the amazement and admiration of the world, made a peaceful transition from apartheid to democracy? How does a country whose presidents have won the Nobel Prize descend to this state of affairs?

There is not a single country on the African continent that does not have a similar story to tell. Our continent groans in pain (Rom 8:19–21).

A shithole country? A shithole continent? Shithole leaders? Is it not the embarrassing and terrible truth that our own people are selling our resources to the highest foreign bidders? They are pocketing the proceeds, keeping the people they are supposed to serve in poverty and dependency. The 2006 movie *Blood Diamond* serves as a parable illuminating this phenomenon.[3] Statistically, most Africans are poor when compared to the rest of the world's people. Many are slaves to socio-political and economic systems that are dehumanizing in the extreme. Testimony to this is found in the millions fleeing the continent to foreign shores, often at great personal risk.

Nigeria's Chinua Achebe in 1958 prophetically lamented Africa's condition in his great novel *Things Fall Apart*.[4] In that novel, a man called Onkonkwo struggles to protect his village and people against inevitable change. The story ends in tragedy with Onkonkwo's suicide.

Are all Africa's stories sad stories, stories of failure? Are the odds Africans face insurmountable? Are all Africans necessarily either selfish perpetrators of corruption and oppression or the victims of it? Should those who can migrate leaving our shores, or should they allow themselves to be drawn into the vultures' banquet of nepotism and self-enrichment? How does all of this make sense given the widely accepted statements that Africa is incurably religious and is the continent with the highest percentage of Christians?[5] Isn't it time that we began asking questions about what it means to have a Christian identity?

---

3. "Blood Diamond," Wikipedia, https://en.wikipedia.org/wiki/Blood_Diamond. Proceeds from the sale of diamonds have funded wars and other conflicts in a number of African nations.

4. Chinua Achebe, *Things Fall Apart* (London: Heinemann, 1958).

5. P. Jenkins, *The Next Christendom: The Coming of Global Christianity* (Oxford: Oxford University Press, 2002).

The God Who Calls and a People Called . . .

The Bible is full of stories that give us glimpses of God's identity and ours, of who God is and who he calls.

When humankind chose to be in charge of their own little gardens (Gen 3), when they chose to construct cities with high walls and impressive towers to make a name for themselves (Gen 11), paradise was lost. God then called Abraham and took him on a journey (Gen 12). In the same way that God had created the world and blessed it, he now called this man and blessed him so that he could be a blessing to the nations of the world. God offered a way out of the disillusionment of wrong choices. Abraham's journey was the first "long walk to freedom!"[6]

Abraham's journey took time, and time is like a river – it meanders. Many years later, the descendants of Abraham were slaves in Egypt with no sign of hope on the horizon. However, a little Hebrew boy who survived among the reeds of the Nile became a prince in Egypt. He fought and killed for his kin and had to flee to the desert. There he met God, who told him,

> I have indeed seen the misery of my people in Egypt. I have heard them crying out because of their slave drivers, and I am concerned about their suffering. So I have come down to rescue them from the hand of the Egyptians and to bring them up out of that land into a good and spacious land, a land flowing with milk and honey. (Exod 3:7–8)

The God Moses met is a God who is concerned about suffering. The most powerful nation in the world could not keep God's people in bondage. Moses was filled with disbelief and terror when he was told that it was his job to rescue his people! Neither a burning bush nor a stick that changed into a snake subdued his fear. But when God revealed his *name*, something amazing happened. Although Moses could say that name, he realized that not all the words of human tongues or all the sounds that fill the world could express the full extent of that name. God is the beginning and the end of everything that exists. In the barren desert, Moses took off his shoes and covered his face because he realized that he was in the presence of the Almighty.

He went and told the Pharaoh what God commanded: "Let my people go."

The story of Israel's journey through the desert is the stuff of legends. It was a road less travelled! Exodus 32 and 33 illustrate leadership. Moses could

---

6. The reference is to Nelson Mandela's autobiography, *Long Walk to Freedom* (Boston: Little, Brown, 1994).

have had God's favour for himself and his family. He declined. He pleaded with God for the people. He was a mediator for them, and never gave up on them. He pulled them through!

Andrew Walls has said that Christianity's mission history "is not a steady, triumphant progression. It is a story of advance and recession."[7] The same is true of the story of the Israelites. A promised land can easily be lost, and life within its borders can be a nightmare . . . then and now. God called Abraham and his descendants to be a blessing to the world, to sow the seed of the kingdom of God. However, not long into their stay in the land, the people wanted to have a king, "like the nations around them." Saul became the first king but did not grasp his calling. There was war with the Philistines, and the Israelites were humiliated. A giant with the name of Goliath put fear into the Israelite army. In the stand-off between the armies, a shepherd boy named David brought food to his brothers. He volunteered to fight Goliath. It is worth listening to the conversation between a desperate king and the shepherd boy:

> Saul replied, "You are not able to go out against this Philistine and fight him; you are only a young man, and he has been a warrior from his youth."
>
> But David said to Saul, "Your servant has been keeping his father's sheep. When a lion or a bear came and carried off a sheep from the flock, I went after it, struck it and rescued the sheep from its mouth. When it turned on me, I seized it by its hair, struck it and killed it. Your servant has killed both the lion and the bear; this uncircumcised Philistine will be like one of them, because he has defied the armies of the living God. The LORD who rescued me from the paw of the lion and the paw of the bear will rescue me from the hand of this Philistine."
>
> Saul said to David, "Go, and the LORD be with you." (1 Sam 17:33–37)

David illustrates how trust in the Lord can conquer fear and help one to face seemingly impossible challenges.

The New Testament is also full of stories. One of the most beautiful of them is the story of Mary, the mother of Jesus. She was a young girl from a despised area (John 7:52) whom God called to be the mother of his Son. By every *human* standard, Mary was not fit for the job. She was a poor teenager from a rural

---

7. Andrew Walls, *The Cross-Cultural Process in Christian History* (Maryknoll, NY: Orbis, 2002), 12.

area, with no standing in society. But God called her and explained to her the significance of the coming birth of her son, his son, the Messiah. It would have been a mind-blowing experience for anyone, let alone a girl of Mary's age and circumstances. Her response leaves one amazed: "I am the Lord's servant. . . . May your word to me be fulfilled" (Luke 1:38).

There is a golden thread that runs through all these stories: If God calls and the Holy Spirit empowers, there is no ethnic, class, gender, age or any other human or natural barrier that prevents a person from becoming a vehicle for the coming kingdom of God. That, rather than their human circumstances, is what shaped their identity.

What these stories also all have in common is that in the presence of God, those called become acutely aware and are inspired by God's holiness and power. They believe God's words, and they obediently answer God's call. They grasp something, not only of who this God is but also of who they are and what they were called or destined to do. The Holy Spirit empowered their feeble faith and gave them the power to be obedient.

A few glimpses into the life of Jesus underline the same principle. He had no doubt about his identity and his call. Luke strikingly describes how "the Holy Spirit descended on him in bodily form like a dove. And a voice came from heaven: 'You are my Son, whom I love; with you I am well pleased'" (Luke 3:22–23).

It is clear that Jesus knew his identity, that is, what his Father had called him to do and what the Spirit was guiding him to do. As with Abraham, Jesus's call and ministry was also a journey, and one needs guidance on a journey. One way of receiving guidance is through prayer, as we see illustrated in Matthew 14:23. Jesus sent the apostles by boat to the other side of the lake and then "he went up on a mountainside by himself to pray." Similarly, Jesus prayed before his arrest in Gethsemane and his subsequent crucifixion. Matthew reports that "he fell with his face to the ground and prayed, 'My Father, if it is possible, may this cup be taken from me. Yet not as I will, but as you will'" (Matt 26:39).

This prayer also illustrates that it is not always easy to fulfil one's calling. Jesus petitioned his Father three times to let it pass. His Father then sent the Spirit to strengthen him. Without this community of the Father, Son and Holy Spirit, it is impossible to remain true to our calling.[8] Jesus himself explains this in his metaphor of the vine: "Remain in me, as I also remain in you. No branch

---

8. Chapter 4, "The Trinity and Public Theology," should be read in conjunction with this chapter.

can bear fruit by itself; it must remain in the vine. Neither can you bear fruit unless you remain in me" (John 15:4).

For Africa to become the Africa we want, for us to become the Africans God wants, we need to remain in Christ, be part of the vine, be in communion with the Trinity, and in that communion, bear fruit. As the passage in John goes on to explain, the first fruit of being in the vine is love for one another. Jesus explained the metaphor by saying, "As the Father has loved me, so have I loved you. Now remain in my love. If you keep my commands, you will remain in my love, just as I have kept my Father's commands and remain in his love. I have told you this so that my joy may be in you and that your joy may be complete" (John 15:9–11).

To recap: The purpose of telling the stories of Abraham, Moses, David, Mary and Jesus has been to make clear that God uses people to make a difference. Most were ordinary people with their own weaknesses, but they made a difference even when doing so seemed humanly impossible. The odds we face on our continent are many and complex. Humanly speaking, overcoming them seems impossible. However, we confess that what is humanly impossible is not impossible for God. People who make a difference do so because they know their identity and calling. They have experienced the presence of the Holy One, and they are, often hesitantly, tremblingly, obedient.

An Issue of Identity

One's *identity* is who one is, the way one thinks about oneself, and also the way in which one is viewed by the world. It refers to the characteristics that *define* one. Every person has his or her own identity and unique character traits as well as identity traits that are shared with others such as gender, age, ethnicity, language, belief, occupation and so on.

As Christians, we need to look to the Bible, to theology, to define human identity. Understanding human identity, what God had in mind when he created us, is important for our quest as Africans to find answers and to open windows of hope towards the future of our continent.

Created in God's Image and Likeness

The very first chapter of the Bible describes how God created the heavens and the earth and explains the identity and purpose of humankind.

Then God said, "Let us make mankind in our image, in our likeness, so that they may rule over the fish in the sea and the birds in the sky, over the livestock and all the wild animals, and over all the creatures that move along the ground."

> So God created mankind in his own image,
>   in the image of God he created them;
>   male and female he created them.

God blessed them and said to them, "Be fruitful and increase in number; fill the earth and subdue it. Rule over the fish in the sea and the birds in the sky and over every living creature that moves on the ground." (Gen 1:26–28)

The passage we have just read describes the identity and purpose of human beings.

- *God created us in his image and likeness*, on the sixth day, as the crowning achievement of creation. Many contemporary theologians remind us that our being created in the image of God forms the basis of human dignity. It applies to all human beings, regardless of any other traits we may share or not share.[9]

- *The Trinitarian God created humans as people in relationship.*[10] Scripture documents the continuous flow of being, communication and action between the Father, Son and Spirit. Earlier, we looked at the metaphor of the vine and the commandment to love one another as an example of the kind of bond that should bind people together. The first manifestation of the image of the Trinity is the companionship, community and relationship of marriage and family life.[11] We should grow towards that likeness. It circles out to all human relationships and the different forms of being connected to living in communities.

- *It is important to see that the diversity within this unity is creational in design.* The Father is not the Son and not the Spirit, but they are one. Husband and wife differ physically, but in more than one way they become

---

9. Bernd Oberdorfer, "Human Dignity and 'Image of God,'" *Scriptura* 104 (2010): 231–239; Nico Koopman, "Some Theological and Anthropological Perspectives on Human Dignity and Human Rights," *Scriptura* 95 (2007): 177–185.

10. Nico Koopman, "Public Theology in (South) Africa: A Trinitarian Approach," *International Journal of Public Theology* 1 (2007): 188–209.

11. *Africa Study Bible* (Carol Stream, IL: Oasis, 2016), 8–9.

"one" as the relational flow of love and action binds them together and brings them joy. Deep relational unity is built on love and understanding. It does not contradict the diversity that also exists.

- *One of the strongest traits of the Creator is that he creates and cares.* God takes responsibility for what he created. Being created in God's image is therefore linked to taking care of creation and all its creatures. The biblical terminology of "rule" and "subdue" may sound harsh, but in light of the bigger picture it concerns responsible love and care. Stewardship is an apt word to describe such care.[12]

- *The incarnation is the ultimate illustration of taking responsibility for creation.* John 3:16–17 is one of the best-known passages describing God's love. Love is the core of God's identity (1 John 4:8, 16). It is a sacrificial love to which we should respond in faith, accepting it and living in the joy of resurrection life: "For God so loved the world that he gave his one and only Son, that whoever believes in him shall not perish but have eternal life. For God did not send his Son into the world to condemn the world, but to save the world through him" (John 3:16–17).

Is there hope for our continent? The argument here is that if our identity is based on our likeness to the image of God, then God's care, healing and restoring should also be reflected in and by us as essential elements of our identity. Our purpose is to be stewards, to love this world so much that we give ourselves, our lives, to serve and heal it. Ultimately, God illustrated this identity by sending his Son to us. Even when things went terribly wrong, the caring God reached out to heal and save. Paul explains this in Philippians:

> Think of yourselves the way Christ Jesus thought of himself. He had equal status with God but didn't think so much of himself that he had to cling to the advantages of that status no matter what. Not at all. When the time came, he set aside the privileges of deity and took on the status of a slave, became *human*! Having become human, he stayed human. It was an incredibly humbling process. He didn't claim special privileges. Instead, he lived a selfless, obedient life and then died a selfless, obedient death – and the worst kind of death at that – a crucifixion. (Phil 2:5–8 MSG)

We should be growing towards this: it is, in fact, our inherent identity! The key Greek word in this passage is *kenosis*. It means emptying – loving those in

---

12. Exodus 32–33 illustrates this trait of Christian identity and leadership in Moses.

bondage to such an extent that one sacrifices one's life to help and save them. *Kenosis* means, and Jesus illustrates, that life is about selfless giving to the point of crucifixion. To follow Christ is to imitate him. Such a love is, paradoxically, the only way to hope and peace. Here power and powerlessness paradoxically coexist. Salvation implies being saved from the self and the temptations to which it so easily succumbs. If one really wants to love oneself, one should use all the power at one's disposal to serve one's neighbour!

Let us take a few steps back to gain perspective. God put Adam and Eve in charge of creation, but they wanted to be independent, to do their own selfish thing. The people of Babel wanted to build a city with walls and a tower to make a name for themselves. These stories illustrate what it means to miss the point! It is called sin. It simply means going the wrong way, not becoming what one is intended to be. Avoiding becoming what one was created to be is self-destructive. Illustrations of this sad reality abound on our continent.[13]

In Philippians 2:1–4, it is as if Paul is answering our groaning and pain about the reality of this world, of our continent and communities:

> If you've gotten anything at all out of following Christ,
> > if his love has made any difference in your life,
> > if being in a community of the Spirit means anything to you,
> > if you have a heart,
> > if you *care* — then do me a favour:
> > > Agree with each other,
> > > love each other,
> > > be deep-spirited friends.
> > > Don't push your way to the front;
> > > don't sweet-talk your way to the top.
> > > Put yourself aside, and help others get ahead.
> > > Don't be obsessed with getting your own advantage.
> > > Forget yourselves long enough to lend a helping hand.
> > > (Phil 2:1–4 MSG)

Surely these words concern Christian identity! In other words, what power we have should be used to serve and uplift, to love our neighbours and to reach out to them. Such power should not be used to grow our own garden or construct our own city.

---

13. Chinua Achebe offers a profound demonstration of this truth in the context of corruption and self-destruction in African politics in his book *A Man of the People* (London: Heinemann, 1966).

Christ himself had access to power so great that we cannot even begin to imagine it! Look at creation, the stars, the universe . . . But in becoming human, Jesus illustrated what it means to serve, to give one's life as a sacrifice. Jesus did not use his power to escape the cross. He knew that the only way towards a better world was to never use power to one's own advantage.

Abraham, Moses, David and Mary all have in common that they were obedient to God, even when that meant not having their own way, not living their own lives the way they wanted to, in order to make a difference in a world that has gone wrong. They discovered true Christian identity. They were people of the way . . . followers of Christ.

Public Theology

According to Valdir Steuernagel, theology "comes at the second hour."[14] God appears first and speaks, as illustrated by the stories referred to in this chapter. Theology is about our words and deeds *after* God has called us. Steuernagel uses Mary as an illustration of theology as "a womb thing." It grows deep inside you. It takes time to understand what the word of God means in one's context. It's a continuous journey of discernment with its share of ups and downs and often a cross along the way.

African theologian Jesse Mugambi emphasizes that Christian identity can only take shape in a specific culture.[15] If theology is a womb thing, it means it is always both intensely personal and culture bound. However, culture as such is not Christian. People created in the image of God can grow spiritually and mature to the likeness of Christ in any culture. As Christians, they can influence their culture positively. Paul in 1 Corinthians 9:19–23 explains how he approaches specific cultural groups in sharing the gospel.

Christians should be the salt of the earth and the light of the world in the public life of a specific culture. Mary, mother of Jesus, exemplified public theology in the way she always tried to discern how Jesus Christ could make a difference where he was. An excellent example is the events at the wedding feast at Cana, where Jesus turned water into wine (John 2:1–11).

Africa's fortunes will change when Christians from all occupations live and act like Mary in creating opportunities for Christ to address the need and

---

14. Valdir R. Steuernagel, "Doing Theology with an Eye on Mary," *Evangelical Review of Theology* 27 (2003): 100–112.

15. Jesse N. K. Mugambi, "Christianity and the African Cultural Heritage," in *African Christianity: An African Story*, ed. Ogbu U. Kalu (Pretoria: University of Pretoria, 2005), 516–542.

humiliation of our people. In all our cultures, Christians can be instrumental in demonstrating that Christ can make a difference.

The Times, They Are A-Changin'[16]

It is easy to list African scenarios we do not want and to dream about the continent we do want. The African Union's *Agenda 2063: The Africa We Want* is a good example of such a dream.[17] It makes sense to look at the realities confronting us from the vantage point of other disciplines.

Sociologist Manuel Castells has reflected deeply on the macroeconomic, social and political changes of our time.[18] He argues that the world is changing through the combined impact of globalization, informatization, technology and crime. Power has been redefined. There was a time when the physical power of men and guns held sway, but today the power of information has much greater effect. The results of this epochal shift are difficult to grasp, but some of it can be seen in the demise of nation-states and the way in which democracies are now influenced by the financial power of the superrich. Multinational companies and the financial elite have the best possible information available and can buy the power they need to influence people and governments.[19] Parallel to, and often in conflict with, the power of these companies and tycoons is an emerging networked society where social movements are having a growing impact.[20] Paternalism, the dominant power of men, is in decline, while families are in distress and gender turmoil is prevalent. Women are coming into their own and are increasingly represented in the labour market and in all spheres of life. In response, we have seen the rise of reactionary movements, fundamentalist religious movements and regional nationalism that opposes globalization, all motivated by fear and challenges to particularistic identities and security.[21]

---

16. Bob Dylan's song "The Times They Are A-Changin'" was written as an anthem for change.

17. See appendix.

18. Manuel Castells, *The Power of Identity: The Information Age – Economy, Society and Culture*, vol. 2, 2nd ed. (Oxford: Blackwell, 2004).

19. The phenomenon of state capture applies to this scenario. See "State Capture," Wikipedia, https://en.wikipedia.org/wiki/State_capture.

20. Manuel Castells, *Networks of Outrage and Hope: Social Movements in the Internet Age*, 2nd ed. (Cambridge: Polity, 2015).

21. Castells, *Power of Identity*, 360. See also his later work, *Rupture: The Crisis of Liberal Democracy* (Cambridge: Polity, 2019).

What is important for our deliberations is the phenomenon that Castells calls "legitimizing identity formation methods." Over millennia the church, monarchies and governments have had the power to control and manipulate information and thus to dictate identity and control the masses. The inability to read and write kept people ignorant and superstitious. However, the discovery of the printing press and the subsequent Reformation changed the world. Governments soon realized that they needed to control the press and information in order to stay in power when they no longer served their people. The dawn of the Internet, however, made such control more difficult because it spawned social media communication tools such as Facebook.

Times are indeed changing.[22] The king is dead; long live the king! These epochal shifts challenge Christian identity. New prophets use the power tools of a new era. Fake news is an old strategy in a new design aimed to protect the concerns of the powerful and downplay the efforts of social movements. There is a new ballgame in town, and truth is warped.[23] This societal transformation has grave implications for human life, and indeed for the planet.

Lessons from History and Pointers to the Africa God Wants

Rodney Stark's *The Rise of Christianity* (1997) was a multidisciplinary sociological study that analysed how, in the Roman Empire over a period of three hundred and fifty years, Christianity grew from a few adherents to thirty-four million followers within a population of roughly fifty-four million.[24] Despite persecution, 60 percent of people in the then known world were Christian! The per decade growth rate of the Christian movement was 43 percent. This led Stark to ask: "How exactly was this done?" His hypothesis was that "the basis for successful conversionist movements is growth through social networks, through a structure of direct and intimate interpersonal attachments."[25]

In my notes on Stark's book, I summarized his answer to the "How was it done?" question in five points:

22. See Manuel Castells, *The Rise of the Network Society: The Information Age – Economy, Society and Culture*, vol. 1 (Oxford: Blackwell, 1996); and Castells, *End of Millennium: The Information Age – Economy, Society and Culture*, vol. 3, 2nd ed. (Oxford: Blackwell, 2000).

23. A good example is the myriad new and superrich prophets in our continent who preach a prosperity gospel and promise health and wealth. They are vultures.

24. Rodney Stark, *The Rise of Christianity* (New York: Harper Collins, 1997).

25. Stark, *Rise of Christianity*, 20.

- *The lives of Christians were different from those of the world.* I noted Ephesians 4:1–2 and Colossians 4:1–2 as two passages that confirm the statement.

- *Between AD 165–180, a horrific plague killed a third of the population of the known world.*[26] Sources from that period mentioned how the sect called "Christians" cared for the sick and dying. The result was that more Christians survived and more people joined Christian communities simply because of how Christians cared, despite the fear of infection.

- *Christian communities had sound moral values in marriage and family life* in an empire were sexual morals were appallingly lax.[27] In Roman society, dogs and women had more or less the same status! This was decidedly not the case in Christian communities. Women, therefore, played a major role in the growth of the church. Need one say more? "There is neither Jew nor Gentile, neither slave nor free, nor is there male and female, for you are all one in Christ Jesus" (Gal 3:28).

- *The church fought racism and classism every inch of the way* (see 1 Cor 3, to mention but one passage). The unity of the Christian community was found in Christ, and their diversity was seen as a benefit and a thing of beauty.[28]

- *Christians were hardworking and dependable* – sought after employees and officials in all walks of life (see Eph 5–6; Col 3:22–4:1; 2 Thess 3:6–13; 1 Pet 2:18–25).

Two quotes towards the end of Stark's book illustrate key aspects of Christian identity:

> Finally, because Christianity was a mass movement, rooted in a highly committed rank and file, it had the advantage of the best of all marketing techniques: person to person influence. . . . what Christianity gave to its converts was nothing less than their humanity. In this sense *virtue* was its own reward.[29]

One of my former students wrote the following at the end of his assignment discussing Stark's book:

---

26. Stark, 73–94.
27. Stark, 95–128.
28. Stark, 29–47.
29. Stark, 208, 215.

What was central to the identity of the early Christians was not the developing doctrines so much as it was the continued influence of the risen Lord. It was the Lord who prompted, the Lord who sustained, the Lord who liberated and the Lord who formed the central "doctrine" of their identity.

Conclusion

For us Africans, as for people anywhere, our biggest embarrassment can also be our biggest opportunity. Seventy years after the birth of Christ, the Romans razed Jerusalem, and with it the temple, to the ground. Christians were scattered all over the Roman Empire. It was called the "diaspora." The gospel went "global." Africa's diaspora can be an opportunity.

God said to Sarah, Abraham's barren wife, that nothing is impossible for God (Gen 18:14). Jeremiah received the same assurance when he doubted whether his people and their fate could change (Jer 32:26–27). When Mary hesitated for a moment upon hearing that she should give birth to the Son of God, the angel said, "nothing will be impossible with God" (Luke 1:37 NRSV).

The stories that we referred to illustrated that with God, nothing is impossible.

However, there is a "but." One way of explaining the "but" is to say that we must live up to the image and likeness of our creator. We have to follow in his steps. Things will not fall apart, in the words of Achebe, if we remain in the vine. At the core of Christian identity is *kenosis*, emptying of the self and all things selfish.

To be is to be willing to sacrifice and serve, to cross all human divides and to help restore the dignity of others, especially the dignity of those who are different to oneself. Jesus did that, and since we are created to be his image, we are to attain that likeness.

It starts with prayer, the Gethsemane way, and the empowering presence of the Spirit.

It may be a tough hill to climb, but it was done by Jesus who commissioned us to do the same

All authority in heaven and on earth has been given to me. Therefore go and make disciples of all nations, baptizing them in the name of the Father and of the Son and of the Holy Spirit, and teaching them to obey everything I have commanded you.

And surely I am with you always, to the very end of the age. (Matt 28:18–20)[30]

Questions

1. Take a critical look at your country and community. Describe the influence of corruption and nepotism. Discuss this with others. What stands out?
2. Take one of the Old Testament prophets and describe his criticism of society and leadership.
3. Discuss the identity traits of two tribes/ethnic groups with which you are familiar. How would you explain unity and diversity to them from a Christian point of view?
4. Mission history points out that it is only in crossing boundaries that the church stays true to its core identity. Jesus did that by becoming human, and he did it with his disciples. He took them to places and people who were culturally different or who were not acceptable according to their religious beliefs. Apply this principle to your context, cross familiar boundaries and see where God leads you and what happens.

Further Reading

Katongole, Emmanuel. *Born from Lament: The Theology and Politics of Hope in Africa.* Grand Rapids: Eerdmans, 2017.

Priest, R. J., and K. Barine, eds. *African Christian Leadership: Realities, Opportunities, and Impact.* Carlisle: Langham Global Library, 2019.

Sanneh, L. *Whose Religion Is Christianity? The Gospel beyond the West.* Grand Rapids: Eerdmans, 2003.

Tickle, P. *Emergence Christianity: What It Is, Where It Is Going and Why It Matters.* Grand Rapids: Baker, 2012.

Tutu, Desmond M. *No Future without Forgiveness.* New York: Doubleday, 1999.

---

30. David Bosch argues that Christian identity was embedded in doing "public theology," in orthopraxis, and in Matthew's missionary paradigm of discipleship, as shown in the parable of the sower in Matthew 13. See *Transforming Mission* (Maryknoll, NY: Orbis, 1991), 79–83.

Part 2

Public Theology
and Public Life

The chapters in part 2 of this book set out to apply the principles discussed in part 1 to various aspects of life. We begin with a chapter on democracy, citizenship and civil society in order to stress that these are issues that concern all in Africa, not just a few theologians. This chapter is followed by one on work, for all of us work in some way or another. Work leads naturally into the questions of economics, and economics leads naturally into issues of poverty and development. Development in turn is closely related to issues of education and environmental concerns, which are also related to science, an area where Christians are often unrepresented, except in the health care sector. Given that access to health care is a human right, it is logical to place the chapter on human rights next, and then to address human rights issues in relation to gender, migrants and refugees. Migrants and refugees are often defined as "the other," and so we move on to look at others who are classified in this way because they follow other religions, with which we have to engage in interreligious dialogue.

Issues relating to the state are left until late in the section to avoid giving the impression that public theology is equivalent to political theology. But it does deal with some of the same issues including the state and the use of state power. Land issues are prominent political concerns in some parts of Africa, so the section includes a separate chapter on land.

It is often the media who hold governments accountable for their actions and expose corruption, and so a chapter on public theology and the media, which also deals with the issue of "fake news," follows. The close ties between the media and the arts are the reason these two chapters are placed in close proximity.

Finally, we deal with issues of leadership and with the training of the next generation of leaders. Some might have expected these chapters to start this section of the book, but they are left till last to discourage readers from relying on existing leaders rather than assuming personal responsibility for how they live as Christians in their own communities and places of work.

Each chapter is followed by a list of further academic reading for those who wish to dig deeper into a specific area. Readers may also want to refer to the articles related to the themes in this book in popular sources like the *Africa Study Bible*[1] and the *Africa Bible Commentary*.[2]

Note that in all chapters with joint authorship, the authors' names are listed in alphabetical order; nothing is implied about the contribution each has made to the chapter.

---

1. *Africa Study Bible* (Carol Stream, IL: Oasis, 2016).

2. *Africa Bible Commentary*, ed. Tokunboh Adeyemo (Nairobi: Word Alive; Grand Rapids: Zondervan, 2006). A second edition is forthcoming.

6

Democracy, Citizenship and Civil Society

Jane Adhiambo Chiroma

Christians who want to contribute to civil society and combat corruption need to know more than just biblical theology and biblical ethics. They also need to understand what civil society is and to have a good grasp of the meaning of democracy and of their rights and responsibilities as citizens. Public theology exists to help Christians understand these issues and become informed participants in democratic processes.

It is easy to be sceptical about democracy in Africa given the inequalities, violence, corruption, nepotism, poverty, xenophobia and ethnic politics that have characterized the postcolonial era. The constitutions of African nations may speak of democracy, but in many respects Africa seems to have turned its back on the possibility of a democracy that protects human rights, equality and participation. Yet we should not forget that it was a growing understanding of democratic values that led to the end of the exploitative colonial era and the re-emergence of independent nations in Africa. So we should not dismiss what democracy has to offer. Instead, we should apply ourselves to thinking about the potential of democracy to address Africa's societal ills. This may also involve us in rethinking our own understanding of what democracy means.

Democracy

Democracy is not simply a Western import to Africa. At its root, the word simply means "people power" and refers to the way members of a community interact to reach agreement on how to handle a particular issue. In this sense, democracy is as old as humankind itself.[1] Forms of democracy have been present in African communities over the centuries, as can be seen in, for example, the *kgotla* system in Botswana, where all members of the community are allowed to speak and decisions are made by consensus.

The concept of *ubuntu*, which was also widespread across Africa, presaged democracy in that it recognized that "I am because we are."[2] In other words, an individual's source of humanity came from synergy with the community of others. The individual had dignity, and so did the community. Each individual realized that there was a common humanity for which they existed, and that this humanity was defined by the community. This recognition made for a sense of belonging, collective participation, cooperative living and solidarity that captures the true heart of African democracy. It means that a diverse group acknowledges that they need each other to survive.

Today, however, democracy has become a more complicated political concept, open to different interpretations. Some understand democracy as meaning people power in the sense of the dictatorship of the people. In other words, they think that once a majority group has obtained power, it is free to exercise autocratic authority, including limiting the freedom of speech and religion of those not in power. The parliamentary system of government that was left to Africa as a colonial legacy has been seen as encouraging this model. Once a party wins an election, it feels free to govern without regard to the concerns of those who voted for other parties.

Others, however, interpret democracy more broadly and argue that democracy is not just about winning power in an election but is an approach to living in community that prioritizes reason, open-mindedness and fairness, and encourages moderation, cooperation, bargaining, compromise and accommodation. This more egalitarian understanding of democracy, rooted in respect for all, fits well with Christian theology, which holds that because all are created in the image of God, all are entitled to respect, regardless of their race, gender or ethnic origin.

Finally, democracy can be seen as a model in which power is exercised publicly in a cooperative way within the institutions of society or among

---

1. A. Mafeje, "Theory of Democracy and the African Discourse: Breaking Bread with Fellow Travellers," in *Democratisation Processes in Africa: Problems and Prospects*, eds. E. Chole and J. Ibrahim (Dakar: CODESRIA, 1995), 5–28.

2. John Mbiti, *African Religions and Philosophy* (New York: Doubleday, 1970), 141.

particular groups of people.[3] This style of democracy is deliberative in the sense that power is distributed equally among all the individuals within a particular institution, so that all stakeholders are also participants who can take part in the deliberation. All participants thus have an equal chance to speak, ask questions and probe during public debates. In this way, they can all work together for the common good and seek to promote economic welfare, cultural stability and institutional effectiveness.

Citizenship

Speaking about democracy as a way of living in community and involving all members of a society inevitably leads to the question of who counts as a member of a community with rights within that community. In other words, who is regarded as belonging to the community and so is entitled to take part in democratic processes. What are the boundaries of the community, and who is included and who is excluded? Who count as citizens?

In general terms, we tend to associate citizenship with location and identify someone as a citizen of a village, a town or a country. However, location is not the sole ground of citizenship, for citizenship also involves identification and emotional attachments. There are many examples of political exiles living in the West who insist that they are still citizens of their African homelands.

A sense of citizenship is also related to ethical and political value systems. Some identify strongly with the values of a particular region, whereas others see themselves as having a more national or even international vision. Some of those in the latter group define themselves as "citizens of the world" and focus on global issues rather than on regional issues.

One question that needs to be addressed here is whether people with different value systems to the majority in a community can still be regarded as citizens of the community. For example, can Muslims be regarded as citizens in a community where the majority are Christian? Our answer needs to be "yes," if they meet the requirements of location and identification with the community. We should not use definitions of citizenship as a way to exclude people who live in our community from participating in decision making in our community.

---

3. S. Benhabib, "Towards a Deliberative Model of Democratic Legitimacy," in *Democracy and Difference: Contesting the Boundaries of the Political*, ed. S. Benhabib (Princeton: Princeton University Press, 1996), 69.

Some scholars speak of citizenship as involving a type of abstract contract between an individual and the state. On this understanding, citizenship is basically a legal relationship of the kind expressed in the issuing of passports and identity documents. In other words, it involves entitlements and rights. Others, however, regard citizenship as participatory, involving the relationship of ruling and being ruled. This understanding of citizenship involves both rights and responsibilities. The responsibilities include working to uphold civil society and to hold the government accountable for what it does or does not do for the citizens of a village, town or country. On this understanding, citizenship may be seen as the association between our status and identities as individuals and the lives and concerns of others with whom we share a sense of community. It connotes identity, belonging and how each individual plays his or her part in building a democratic society. Citizenship, therefore, is the way in which we live together and organize our lives together despite our differences.

When it comes to public theology, we should be concerned both with issues of local and regional citizenship and with the wider global political and social realities that face society today. Such engagement is in accordance with the nature of the church, which is both local – "the church at Antioch," for example – and universal as the physical manifestation of the global kingdom of God. As citizens of local communities, church members should be involved in local initiatives, and as members of the kingdom of God, they should also be involved with global ecological concerns.

Civil Society and the Common Good

When we talk of democracy and society, we often tend to think solely in terms of the government and those governed. But there is another element that we need to consider, and that is the entire network of non-government organizations and community initiatives that constitute civil society. In areas where government is weak, civil society may actually have more power to change situations than any external authority. Examples of the types of organizations involved in civil society are schools, hospitals and public libraries, which are all intended to benefit all members of society, rather than just particular groups within the society. Anti-corruption organizations also have a place in civil society, for they too benefit a whole community.

For a church to be involved in civil society, its members must be prepared to work alongside members of the community who are not church members, and may even represent different religious affiliations such as African Traditional Religion or Islam. In coming together in civil society, the goal is not to debate religious differences but to work together to combat an evil like corruption, or to accomplish something that will promote the common good, that is, the welfare of the entire community. For example in parts of Nigeria, Christian and Muslim leaders have worked together to calm the hostility spawned by interreligious violence and to create opportunities for Christian and Muslim youth to meet regularly on friendly terms in, say, a sports club. Christian churches have set up refugee camps that offer shelter to Muslim families displaced by religious violence. In South Africa, groups with very different values joined together as co-belligerents to fight apartheid.

Such acts are examples of the church working in civil society in times of crisis. However, it is important that the church also be involved in such activities on a day-to-day basis if we are to demonstrate to our fellow citizens that we are truly concerned for their welfare. Given that public welfare is undermined by corruption, the church has strong reasons to be involved in anti-corruption and social justice initiatives.

Theological Grounds for Involvement in Civil Society

Earlier it was pointed out that democracy is not alien to Africa. It is important to mention that it is also not alien to Scripture and Christian theology, for a number of basic theological themes point to the importance of democratic citizenship.

The first theme is the basic Christian understanding that God is personal and relational. God exists in community, as evidenced by the relationships within the Trinity,[4] and he reaches out beyond himself to care for all creation. This same attitude should inform Christians' sense of citizenship. We should not be like Cain who denied his responsibility for his brother, but should obey Christ and love our neighbours as ourselves. In doing this, we will build human community (relationships) and see them not as an optional extra but as part of what it means to be like God.

The second theme is that all human beings bear God's image and are endowed with rights and responsibilities at creation. This implies that the human dignity of all should be respected. Democracy is in harmony with this theme, for it values the input of all members of society. As Christians, we should acknowledge that God created our fellow citizens and should object strongly when anyone speaks insultingly of a fellow human being or refers to them as a "cockroach" or an "animal."

Third, Scripture explicitly addresses the question of how we treat those who are different from us, which is a key issue when it comes to democracy and

---

4. See chapter 4, "The Trinity and Public Theology."

citizenship. In contrast to the acceptance of ethnic violence and xenophobia in many parts of Africa, the Old Testament commands God's people not to "mistreat or oppress a foreigner" (Exod 22:21) but to show love to strangers. This point is further emphasized in the New Testament concept of the truly global community of the church, where people of diverse nations and cultures can live together in peace and find their unity in Christ, who transcends all. Recognition that we are to care for those who are different from us implies that even where Christians are in a majority, they must show consideration for the minorities among them. Following Christ's example, Christians should demonstrate care for the poor, the marginalized and the stranger. If a society is judged by how it cares for its weakest citizens, then Christians should be in the forefront of those caring for them.

Fourth, the Old Testament concept of *shalom*, the Hebrew word for "peace," embraces notions of healing, wholeness and unity of relationships. *Shalom* is threatened by sin and evil. In Africa this threat often comes in the form of corruption that works against the common good of the whole society. As Christians, we proclaim the life, death and resurrection of Christ, which makes redemption and restored harmony possible, and we should be working to accomplish it.

Fifth, Christians are called to be salt and light in every human society that they are part of (Matt 5:13–14). As such, they must be good citizens, coming together with those who are not Christians to work for justice, peace and the common good of all. As good citizens, Christians will live out their values, expressing their future hope of the kingdom of God, and in so doing they will also be working in ways that will help them to accomplish the Great Commission.

Contemporary notions of democracy and citizenship are thus clearly reconcilable with Christianity, and Christians living in Africa can benefit from living as democratic citizens.

Living as Democratic Citizens

Living as a democratic citizen involves listening. This too is biblical virtue (Jas 1:19). Democratic citizens engage with others on the basis of listening before making judgments about particular issues.[5] They recognize the need to

---

5. Y. Waghid, "On the Relevance of a Theory of Democratic Citizenship Education for Africa," in *African Democratic Citizenship Education Revisited*, eds. Y. Waghid and N. David (London: Palgrave Macmillan, 2018), 1–12.

hear what other people have to say and are prepared to do the work required to develop persuasive arguments in favour of or against some action. They seek to apply wisdom gained from experience and to be able to justify their opinions and beliefs to themselves as well as to others. Careful, responsible, loving thought precedes their calls to action. They would agree with Walzer that democracy involves argumentation by citizens to persuade the largest number of their fellow citizens when making decisions.[6]

Democratic citizens do not infringe on other's rights to freedom of expression and being. In other words, they do not coerce others into agreeing with them. They are willing to work alongside others without having to be forced to do so. And they communicate their beliefs in language that is readily understood by other members of the community.

The Church and Democracy

The church in Africa has a mixed record as regards its democratic responsibilities. It has made major contributions to civil society through its provision of education and health care. However, there are also many examples of its failure to uphold democratic values. For example, in apartheid South Africa, some parts of the church failed in their responsibility to listen to all. Instead, they listened to only one voice, the voice of the state, and offered theological justifications for apartheid. Thankfully, this was not true of all South African churches. But even those that joined the South African Council of Churches (SACC) that opposed apartheid seem to have lost their way after apartheid was overthrown.

> Prior to 1994, the SACC was an incredibly strong organisation which boasted clarity of vision and theological grounding in its work. It had a strong sense of purpose and direction embedded in an authentic prophetic voice of the oppressed and voiceless. It provided a space for worship and home for the oppressed. It was seen as an instrument and beacon of hope. It enjoyed the support of the grassroots and many ordinary people wanted to be involved in the work of the SACC in different ways. It had a high international profile and was extremely well supported by foreign donors. It had a unifying force for the communities

---

6. M. Walzer, *Spheres of Justice: A Defense of Pluralism and Equality* (New York: Basic Books, 1983), 304.

and the churches. After the advent of democracy in South Africa in 1994, the SACC seemed to lack a clear vision and corporate identity. Its strong and clear theological rationale and ecumenical vision dwindled. It lacked a pastoral plan to deal with new and emerging moral, social, political and economic challenges.[7]

This example is a reminder that we cannot rest on our laurels when it comes to our role as democratic citizens. There is a constant need to adapt to new challenges in our societies and communities.

For a long time, many churches in Africa stood apart from politics, treating it as "worldly" and alien to the church. However, more church leaders now see politics as a space to exercise their citizenship rights and influence society, thus serving as salt and light. This group includes Ugandans like Bishop David Zac Niringiye and Kenyans like Bishop Okullu, who was an outspoken critic of the Kenyan government of his day. In his sermons and publications, Bishop Okullu called for justice and human rights and a multiparty system of governance.[8] He served on many national and international committees, started a financial company to provide loans for the poor and initiated development projects including educational institutions and agricultural and health programmes. Nor is the role of Christian leaders limited to criticism from outside the government. In 2007, a prominent leader in National Council of Churches of Kenya (NCCK) resigned his church position and won election to a parliamentary seat.

Other examples of Kenyan Christians exercising their democratic rights include the Pentecostal churches calling on their members to exercise their civic right to reject practices that undermine human dignity and exclusion by rejecting the draft Bomas Constitution that provided for abortion and Islamic Kadhi courts. In 2009, a committee of experts again drafted a new constitution for Kenya, and the NCCK and the Catholic Church again called for the removal of clauses allowing abortion and Kadhi courts and insisted that all religions be treated equally. Christian denominations formed the Kenyan Christian Leaders Constitutional Forum (KCLFC) to hold rallies to oppose the draft constitution.

But not all Christian involvement in politics is praiseworthy. In the 2007 general elections in Kenya, many churches were openly biased along ethnic

---

7. J. Pillay, "Faith and Reality: The Role and Contributions of the Ecumenical Church to the Realities and Development of South Africa since the Advent of Democracy in 1994," *HTS Teologiese Studies/Theological Studies* 73, no. 4 (2017): 2.

8. K. Omollo, "Bishop Okullu: A Man of God with a Heart for Justice," *Standard Media Digital* (13 Feb. 2014).

lines determined by their leaders' ethnic backgrounds. Prominent church leaders gave conflicting prophesies on who would emerge victorious in the elections and even publically anointed candidates to signify that God had chosen them for the presidency. This type of involvement by the church did not make for listening to the voices of others. Nor did it make for peace: instead it contributed to post-election violence, as also did socio-economic grievances and unaddressed historical injustices.[9] Consequently, several church buildings were burned down, and the church's efforts to step in to mediate the conflict were largely ineffective as the public no longer regarded them as unbiased intermediaries.

The next Kenyan government attempted to regulate religious practices with the aim of monitoring the activities of "preachers who abuse the freedom of worship provided for in the constitution." Currently, all religious organizations in Kenya must be registered and declare their sources of income.[10]

It is important that the church does not forfeit its prophetic voice when it becomes involved with issues of democracy and citizenship, as has also happened in Kenya where mainstream churches have been reluctant to criticize corruption in governance. It appeared that things were improving when "the secretary general for National Council of Churches in Kenya (NCCK) was appointed the head of the steering Committee on Anti-Corruption," but in reality his position made it difficult for him to "point out massive corruption in government independently."[11] It could be said that in this case, the voice of the church was co-opted by the state.

These developments point to the fact that churches in Kenya and elsewhere in Africa have gained public recognition and have seen the need to contend against injustice and corrupt practices in the public sphere. However, they also indicate that the church needs to seek a clear understanding of its role when it comes to involvement in national democratic governance. It needs a solid grasp of the principles of democracy and citizenship if it is to function as salt and light in the world and not be seen merely as another political group promoting the interests of its own members rather than of the whole society.

---

9. C. Kenga, "The Role of Religion in Politics and Governance in Kenya" (Thesis submitted to the University of Nairobi for an MA in International Studies, 2014), 6.

10. Kenga, "Role of Religion in Politics," 7.

11. Kenga, 6.

Promoting an Understanding of Democracy

It seems that our concern at present should not be whether democratic citizenship is needed in Africa (it undoubtedly is) but whether it is possible to expedite its development on the African continent so that the distracting language used by supposedly democratic Christian leaders does not undermine it.

It is simplistic to assume that speaking about democracy is enough to reform the authoritarian and repressive culture that has established itself in Africa. To make this assumption is to discount the fact that the only political reality many African Christians have known is one where there is no such thing as multiparty democracy, but instead rule by autocrats and rigged elections. For many in Africa, the main interest of an election is the bribes and free food handed out by those who are courting their votes. The only way to actually change leaders or end corruption seems to be yet another coup – even though the new leaders may prove to be as corrupt as the old.

The emergence of democratic citizenship in Africa must thus be linked to learning to think differently about authoritarian politics and oppressive practices. Church leaders across Africa need to speak out against political elites who manipulate religion and Africans' sense of community (*ubuntu*) by seeking to imply that people of other religions or of other ethnic groups have no voice in local or national politics. We need to be actively refuting wrong understandings of belonging and instead proclaim that civil society requires that everyone in the community be accepted as a member of the community, and that everyone is entitled to the same democratic rights as every other member. In other words, we need to teach what democratic citizenship entails.

Where can this much needed citizenship education be provided? I would argue that it can be provided in our schools, in our churches and in our communities.

In our schools

One step towards promoting a greater understanding of democracy as defined in this chapter is to look at its applications outside the political sphere. One key place where the young can learn about democratic values is in the education system. There democratic values should be taught by example. Teachers imbued with such values would not seek to exercise dictatorial authority but would treat children and their parents with respect. Rather than expecting students to do no more than memorize and repeat what they are told, they would seek to inculcate critical thinking skills so as to enable future citizens to weigh public policies and the arguments put forward by various groups in society.

A democratic approach to schooling would teach students to work together for common goals while also showing respect for those whose ways of life are different from their own, thus preparing them to work together in civil society. Such participation of all members of a community on equal terms is an essential element of democracy. Students should be encouraged to have a commitment to meaningful communication with others and develop an interest in learning from all those they meet. Democracy can neither operate nor develop if people from different groups live in separate worlds and never interact. Where this is the case, people hear only the views of those who agree with them and remain ignorant of the wisdom, and the needs, of those in other groups.

Given that students may live in communities where they are not exposed to great diversity, it can be helpful to promote a curriculum that exposes students to the histories and cultures of various groups of people, including major religious and cultural groups as well as marginalized ethnic, racial, gendered and social minorities. Such teaching can contribute to a sense of respect for others who are different from them and yet occupy the same citizenship space as they do. Students can be encouraged to use their imagination to understand others' feelings, experiences, despair, suffering and oppression, and so to develop compassion that can lead to civic reconciliation.

A democratic approach to schooling would also take pains to ensure that students learn about their rights and responsibilities as citizens. Education should prepare the young to participate in public debate about issues like corruption and ways to counter it. They should also learn about the key political institutions and systems within their country and develop a respect for law and justice and what it means to seek the common good of all citizens.

This education in democracy should continue at all levels, from the primary school through high school and on to university. It should ensure that all students in the education system have a sense of belonging as regards how they learn, why they learn and what they learn. As they learn how they as citizens can work together to address societal ills in their own communities, they will also develop an awareness of their potential influence in the region, the nation and the world.

In our churches

It should not be forgotten that education does not only take place in schools and universities. It also takes place in the home and in our churches. Thus parents and churches too should teach the democratic and Christian values of respect for others and of cooperation for the common good. Those who speak out against corruption should be supported, for to stay mute is to become part of the society that encourages corruption.

At the same time, churches should not be run like dictatorships, as is sadly often the case. A church cannot teach democracy if the leader is unwilling to listen to others. So churches need to work to encourage communication and cooperation between their leaders and their members, between their members in the church, and between church members and other members of society in pursuit of the common good. Churches are places where people can learn that the democratic value of respect means we can work with people with whom we do not agree about everything.

While it is true that the purpose of the church is personal and societal transformation, we need to note that God does not coerce people into living the way he wants them to live. Instead, he reaches out to them in love, hears their cries and seeks to persuade them to follow him. If we are to be like God, we must do the same. We must respect the right of others to disagree with us and not dehumanize those who disagree with us. This position fits with that of Dewey, who says that democracy requires "a type of education which gives individuals a personal interest in social relationships and control, and the habits of mind which secure social changes without introducing disorder."[12]

One other function that churches may fulfil in a democratic system is seeking to provide true information to counteract the propaganda put out by governments and the fake news distributed by both governments and their opponents. Church leaders have networks of information outside the traditional media that are controlled by politicians, and they can use church networks and media to share details about the actual state of affairs. However, in doing this church leaders must exercise great care. On the one hand they must maintain independence of the government, and on the other they must not simply become voices for the opposition. Christian leaders need to exercise great discernment and caution when distinguishing true facts from the fake news that is so widely spread.[13]

---

12. J. Dewey, *Democracy and Education* (New York: Macmillan, 1916).

13. For more on fake news, see chapter 23, "The Media."

In our communities

Friendship is an important element in promoting democratic citizenship. When people are bound by ties of friendship, they will interact more freely and be more willing to communicate their own opinions and to hear the views of others, even if they disagree with them. Friendship is thus an important basis for dialogue.

In civil society, we should thus endeavour to create civic spaces where similarities rather than differences are emphasized. For example, in Nigeria some Christians established sports clubs for youth. Young peoples shared love of sport drew them together, and ethnic and religious differences were no longer the focus. By creating this type of civic space, the differences of others who might be considered threatening are relativized, and opportunities for dialogue are created. The participants learn how to coexist in civic spaces, which is a basic prerequisite for democracy.

Note that this is not the same thing as trying to force everyone to assimilate and adopt the same identity. The participants in these interactions retain their own identities and their own cultures and religions. But they learn to work together for the common good.

Conclusion

In this chapter, democratic citizenship has been discussed in terms of relationships and associations, and not simply as a method of counting votes and determining whose vote matters. The type of democracy that will transform Africa values relationships, communication, listening, partnership and support and does not dismiss those who are different from us.

Democracy and citizenship are closely related to active citizenship in plural African culture and involve respect for human dignity and the rule of law. These should be of concern not only to political theorists but also to theologians, churches, educational professionals and ordinary Christians, for all have a role to play in management and decision making in their communities and in the wider society.

Public theology with democratic lenses can help the church to engage in deliberation about social inequalities such as poverty and corruption. Such engagement will become a culture that encourages equality among all people regardless of their colour, gender, sex and ethnic background.

Questions

1. How does understanding democracy and citizenship guide Christian involvement in public concerns like corruption?
2. How are democracy and citizenship embedded in the Bible?
3. Identify ways in which democratic citizenship can counter societal ills you are aware of.
4. Explain, giving examples, what your church can do to promote democracy.

Further Reading

de Gruchy, J. W. "Christianity and Democracy: Understanding Their Relationship." *Scriptura* 62 (1997): 323–333.

Kukah, Matthew Hassan. *Democracy and Civil Society in Nigeria*. Ibadan, Nigeria: Spectrum, 1999, 2003.

Magezi, V. "A Public Practical-Theological Response and Proposal to Decolonisation Discourse in South Africa: From #YourStatueMustFall and #MyStatueShouldBeErected to #BothOurStatuesShouldBeErected." *HTS Teologiese Studies/Theological Studies* 74, no. 1 (2018). https://hts.org.za/index.php/hts/article/view/5030.

Waghid, Y. "On the Relevance of a Theory of Democratic Citizenship Education for Africa." In *African Democratic Citizenship Education Revisited*, edited by Y. Waghid and N. Davids, 1–12. Switzerland: Palgrave Macmillan, 2018.

7

Work

Sunday Bobai Agang

This chapter is written for two groups of people: those who have work and those who have not. Its goal is to encourage us to think as Christians about what work is, why we work and what we can do to help people find work.

Work can take many forms. For some people it is working in the fields and doing hard manual labour; for others it is working in an office or a shop, or caring for a home, or running a company or preparing a sermon. Some work is physical, other work is mental, but all forms of work involve effort and are tiring. We do this work in order to achieve a purpose or meet some need, such as the need to eat or to provide for our families. But is this all there is to work? If you were to suddenly find yourself rich, would you stop working? And if so, what would you do with your time? In other words, is work something we are *forced* to do to stay alive, or is something that we do *because* we are alive? Is work a curse or a blessing? How should we as Christians think about work, value work and do our work?

These questions may be new ones for you to consider, because for many African Christians there is a disconnect between faith and work. The one is spiritual and the other is very much about material matters. We will happily skimp on our daily work in order to get to the prayer meetings, church gatherings and choir practices that are our "real" spiritual work.

But there should in fact be a close relationship between our faith and our daily work. In the book of Romans, Paul explains how God's salvation should affect our wisdom, our honesty, our relationships, our judgment, our ability to endure hardship, our character, our attitudes and our mindset – that is, our logical and ethical reasoning. All of these are essential to our work, and if salvation affects them, it will also affect how we go about our work. We need to start seeing work as an activity that humans engage in to the praise of God's glory and to fulfil the purpose for which God created us.

The Bible and Work

As Christians, the primary source and final guiding authority for our theology of work is the Bible and the theology we derive from the Bible, which tells us both what God does and how God does it. We can thus explore the meaning of human work in the light of four major biblical themes: creation, the fall, redemption and the new creation.

Creation

Work is not only done by human beings. God works. We see this in the account of creation, which concludes with these words:

> Thus the heavens and the earth were completed in all their vast array. By the seventh day God had finished the work he had been doing; so on the seventh day he rested from all his work. Then God blessed the seventh day and made it holy, because on it he rested from all the work of creating that he had done. (Gen 2:1–3)

God's work is different from ours. God created everything that is, including us, out of nothing. Any creating we do depends on using what God has already given us. Nevertheless, as human beings part of what it means to be made in the image of God (Gen 1:27) is that we are like God in doing work. God explicitly assigned work to Adam and Eve, telling them to "be fruitful and increase in number; fill the earth and subdue it. Rule over the fish in the sea and the birds in the sky and over every living creature that moves on the ground" (Gen 1:28). We are also told that God put Adam "in the Garden of Eden to work it and take care of it" (Gen 2:15). The garden was not a place where Adam and Eve could relax and do nothing all day. There was work to be done!

Recognizing that work is part of God's original creation, which he declared "good," changes the way we see work. It is not merely a burden. It is the way in which we exercise our God-given mandate of stewardship of the environment and the ecosystem. One of the reasons God gives us brains and hands is so that we can use them to work.

Nor is work done entirely on our own initiative. God is still at work, and Christ is still engaged in "sustaining all things by his powerful word" (Heb 1:3).

We are called to partner with God in carrying out his mission on this planet and so to fulfil God's purposes for creation. That is why work can give us a deep sense of satisfaction and an enormous sense of happiness.

Given the frenzied pace of modern life, we should also note that work should not be all-consuming. God rested on the seventh day, and he enshrined this rest day as a principle in the Ten Commandments:

> Remember the Sabbath day by keeping it holy. Six days you shall labour and do all your work, but the seventh day is a sabbath to the LORD your God. On it you shall not do any work, neither you, nor your son or daughter, nor your male or female servant, nor your animals, nor any foreigner residing in your towns. For in six days the LORD made the heavens and the earth, the sea, and all that is in them, but he rested on the seventh day. Therefore the LORD blessed the Sabbath day and made it holy. (Exod 20:9–11)

God gave humans six days in which to do nothing but work. The seventh day is meant for them to rest and enjoy the presence of God through worship and also to refresh, rejuvenate and revitalize themselves in preparation for the next six days of work.

The fall

Adam and Eve's rebellion disrupted our relationships with God, other people and the rest of creation, as well as our relationship to work. Adam was told, "Cursed is the ground because of you; through painful toil you will eat food from it all the days of your life" (Gen 3:17). The fall did not destroy the intrinsic value of work, but it distorted the world so that work may seem hard and meaningless. We no longer find fulfilment in our work, and we struggle to associate it with service to God. Even those who are doing good struggle to produce good results. Many toil at difficult jobs while longing for good, creative work that would enable them to thrive and not merely survive. Some reject work and try to do as little of it as possible, while others idolize work and seek their personal meaning in work rather than in God.

Redemption

Jesus became incarnate and entered the world, including the world of work, in order to redeem and transform it. He told his followers to love God and their neighbours. He also commanded them to bear witness to him and to teach others the things he had taught them (Matt 28:19–20).

Through our work and the way we do it, Christians are witnesses to Jesus Christ as the way, the truth and the life. Doing our work opens doors so that our words about Christ have credibility. People will not listen to those for whom they have no respect, and so Paul urged the Thessalonian Christians to "mind your own business and work with your hands, just as we told you, so that your daily life may win the respect of outsiders and so that you will not be dependent on anybody" (1 Thess 4:11–12). He exhorted Christians to live in a way that brings glory to God, or in other words, that prompts others to praise God and turn to him in faith. This explains Paul's advice to slaves, whose work would often have been frustrating and unrewarding: "Whatever you do, work at it with all your heart, as working for the Lord, not for human masters" (Col 3:23).

Work is not only done to win respect; it is also how we show our love for others. Paul reminded Timothy that "Anyone who does not provide for their relatives, and especially for their own household, has denied the faith and is worse than an unbeliever" (1 Tim 5:8). He implies that we work to be able to provide the goods and services that we want and other people need.

God holds us accountable for our work and will reward work that is done well. Paul's advice to slaves concluded with the words, "you will receive an inheritance from the Lord as a reward. It is the Lord Christ you are serving" (Col 3:24). The writer of the letter to the Hebrews comments, "God is not unjust; he will not forget your work and the love you have shown him as you have helped his people and continue to help them" (Heb 6:10).

The new creation

Christ's gospel transforms us and can transform all areas of life. As those who follow him and are empowered by the Holy Spirit, we are called to be partners or co-workers with God in putting things right in all spheres of life. We are called to engage in creative, redemptive and healing work, as well as work that seeks to restrain and challenge evil aspects of the prevailing culture. We are to live as signs and agents of the dawning kingdom of God. This will include working to transform our workplaces and those we work with. Of course, we cannot expect to accomplish this solely by our own efforts. Only the God who says, "Not by might nor by power, but by my Spirit" (Zech 4:6) can effect transformation.

God is initiating his coming new creation in the midst of the present world order, and he is doing this in part through the work we do for him day by day. Our present work gains significance and hope when we catch a glimpse of God's future and know that our "labour in the Lord is not in vain" (1 Cor 15:58). In accordance with God's promise, we are not looking forward to a disembodied existence but to resurrection in a "new heaven and a new earth, where righteousness dwells" (2 Pet 3:13) and where all frustrating and futile work will be replaced by fulfilling and God-glorifying work (Isa 65:17–23). There our present struggles with work will be vanquished by Jesus's reign so that we can experience the productive fruits of our work. We will no longer have to endure the frustration and injustice that accompanies so much of our labour in the present world.

Traditional Attitudes to Work

In traditional Africa, work was celebrated because it was seen as crucial to a community's dignity and their social, political and economic identity. In a communal society, to work was to participate in the life of the community and gave each person a sense of belonging and a route to meaning and status. Harvest celebrations gave families an opportunity to show how hard working they had been. So did the amount of grain drying on each person's roof. In my community in Nigeria, farming in the rainy season and hunting in the dry season were ways in which men acquired and showcased their political, social and economic prowess. Unfortunately, however, the quest to have the biggest harvest also contributed to polygamy, for the more wives and children one had, the more land one could cultivate. So while the traditional African attitude to work is good, it is not flawless.

Work in Contemporary Africa

In Africa today, we need to move beyond the idea that we work to be successful and that success is the key to happiness – regardless of how that success is achieved. We cannot expect to have the new Africa envisaged in *Agenda 2063* unless we change popular ideas about work and recognize it as a way of propagating cultural, economic, political, social and spiritual development and transforming society.

It is also important to note that work and peace are intrinsically related. To understand this point, we need to remember that in Africa "the median age is 19 years and is only expected to reach about 25 years in 2046. As such, young people will continue to constitute about half of the population of most countries on the continent in the next three to five decades." Consequently, Africa has many young people who are "(a) desperate for opportunities that promise a better life and so are (b) vulnerable to recruitment by individuals and groups who promise such deliverables. Together with other social realities, vulnerable youth populations have become easy recruits for crime, rebel militias, political gangs and extremist networks."[1]

Unless these young people find some meaningful way to use their energy, they will lose hope for the future and resort to drugs, gangs and violence. The result will be mayhem in our communities and nations. Foreign companies and local entrepreneurs will hesitate to invest in the continent, so exacerbating the situation. We as Christians will not be able to worship God in a peaceful atmosphere. This reality underscores the need for us to be thinking seriously about issues relating to work.

Redefining Work

Why does Africa have such a high rate of unemployment? Is it simply because of a high birth rate, or the exploitation of the continent and the greed of the rich, or has this situation also got something to do with our attitudes to work? We cannot deal with all of these options here, but will focus on the concern of this chapter and argue that one reason for Africa's high rates of unemployment is the way we define work. We see work as something that the government is supposed to provide. And we assume that to be worthwhile, the work that is provided must be a white collar job and provide a regular salary. Everyone wants to be a professional; no one wants to do manual labour. To correct this view requires three changes.

Redefining what constitutes work

What counts as work? Do we define work only as a job for which we are paid a regular salary? If that is the case, we are leaving many categories of work out of our thinking. For example, what about women's work in the sense of domestic tasks? Women are not normally paid to do this work, and so their work is looked down on as unimportant. But is this fair? Is their work not part

---

1. Andrews Atta-Asamoah, "Youth of Africa: Unemployment, Social Cohesion and Political Instability," UNICEF, Office of Research-Innocenti.

of the work God ordained at creation, and so worthy of respect? Or what about those who are caring for a person with a disability or an elderly parent? And does one have a job if one is an entrepreneur, or a freelancer or simply sells peanuts at the roadside? Is "work" defined by being formally employed? Again, our answer must be "no." Work is the task of caring for the world God has put us in – and that world includes people who need care. Work is not defined by a pay cheque. Work is any activity involving mental or physical effort done in order to achieve a purpose or result. Work is what humans do in order to produce a result that benefits us, our families, our fellow humans, our society or our environment and also brings the Creator, God, praise, honour and glory. All legitimate work is God's work.

Acknowledging the dignity of all work

All forms of work should be respected, not just the work of the professions. All types of jobs should be equally respected, and no occupation should be considered superior to another. This applies even as regards the work of pastors and Christian workers. No one should have to endure discrimination because of their work. In today's Africa, people worship professional jobs and despise jobs that get your hands dirty. However, the biblical concept of work is that no type of work is inferior to any other. We should not look only for secure government or private sector jobs but should do whatever our hands find to do that is morally acceptable, can help us put food on the table, and leaves us with enough left over to help others. All jobs are equally honourable in God's eyes.

Adopting an entrepreneurial mindset

It has been said that "the biblical doctrine of work is the gracious expression of the creative energy of the Lord in the service of others to create shalom."[2] Note the reference to the "creative energy of the Lord." One of the ways in which we are like God is that we are creative, and we should apply that creativity to the question of work. We should not wait for work to come to us but should apply our entrepreneurial creativity and ingenuity to creating jobs for ourselves. We should look for ways that we can work with God in creating a new earth and come alongside our fellow human beings to make this happen. Our goal should be to become productive and to look for ways for self-improvement rather than expecting someone else to give us a job. There should be far more

---

2. Attributed to Dorothy Sayers, but with no clear provenance.

freelance workers and entrepreneurs in Africa. It is when we work hard and take responsibility for making our own work opportunities that we will find ourselves in a position to have the resources to provide goods and services to our own families and others.

Work and Corruption

The widespread corruption and impunity on our continent may well be linked to a mindset that sees work as a punishment rather than a blessing. We tend to assume that the only way to cover our social, political and economic nakedness is to amass material wealth, and so we tell ourselves, "I need more power, more possessions, more respect, more admiration." But we want these things without having to work hard to earn them, and so we take shortcuts to get them by accepting bribes, underpaying our workers and stealing goods and time from our employers. We want more but will not work more to get it.

Even some Christian preachers condone this attitude by preaching a prosperity gospel that encourages "seed-sowing" and a "name it and claim it" Christianity. People are being taught that their material success depends on divine intervention rather than hard work. There are many people who prefer praying for wealth to working for it. They too may take shortcuts to wealth if given the opportunity.

But the Bible speaks unequivocally about our need to work. Paul reminded the Thessalonians, "we gave you this rule: 'The one who is unwilling to work shall not eat.' We hear that some among you are idle and disruptive. They are not busy; they are busybodies. Such people we command and urge in the Lord Jesus Christ to settle down and earn the food they eat" (2 Thess 3:10–12). Even when God miraculously provided manna for the Israelites during the exodus from Egypt, he required them to go out and collect the manna each day, and the supply of manna dried up when they reached the promised land and were able to work to meet their own needs (Exod 16). God did not provide food for people who were unwilling to work.

The Africa of our dream will remain a mirage if our ideology of work is built on shaky ethical and moral foundations. We need to develop an awareness of the sacredness of work because it is divinely mandated. It is what God ordained for the human race when he created us to bear his image and to work for God's glory, for our own benefit, for the benefit of other human beings and for the entire ecosystem. It is only when that happens that humans can enjoy happiness, satisfaction and peace – and what better definition of success could there be?

But work brings happiness only when it brings glory to God and benefits others as well as ourselves. It does not bring joy when our motives are corrupt and when we set out to exploit others and amass wealth that is not rightly ours. Work brings joy; corruption leaves a sour taste in the mouths of all affected by it.

Work and Work Relationships

While relationships between workers are important, here we will focus only on the relationships between employers and employees, and the role of trade unions.

Employers' relationship to employees

God takes the relationship between employers and employees seriously. Thus Moses exhorted the Israelites:

> Do not take advantage of a hired worker who is poor and needy, whether that worker is a fellow Israelite or a foreigner residing in one of your towns. Pay them their wages each day before sunset, because they are poor and are counting on it. Otherwise they may cry to the LORD against you, and you will be guilty of sin. (Deut 24:14–15)

In the New Testament, James reminds his Christian readers of those verses when he writes, "Look! The wages you failed to pay the workers who mowed your fields are crying out against you. The cries of the harvesters have reached the ears of the Lord Almighty" (Jas 5:4).

Paul too emphasized the need for fair dealings between employers and employees when he wrote these words to the Christians in Ephesus:

> Slaves, obey your earthly masters with respect and fear, and with sincerity of heart, just as you would obey Christ. Obey them not only to win their favour when their eye is on you, but as slaves of Christ, doing the will of God from your heart. Serve wholeheartedly, as if you were serving the Lord, not people, because you know that the Lord will reward each one for whatever good they do, whether they are slave or free.
>
> And masters, treat your slaves in the same way. Do not threaten them, since you know that he who is both their Master and yours is in heaven, and there is no favouritism with him. (Eph 6:5–9)

If we value every human being as having been created in the image and likeness of God, we will not in any away maltreat our fellow human beings who work for us. More than that, if we are Christians, we are called to be like God, who is loving and compassionate. Compassion should thus characterize all our relationships, including our work relationships. While getting work done is important, it should never become more important than acknowledging human value and worth.

God expects justice and fairness from all kinds of employers – families who hire nannies or housegirls and houseboys, the private sector, small business owners, security organizations, NGOs, entrepreneurs, firms, companies (local, regional, national or multinational) and government parastatals, the civil service, etc. God is deeply concerned about the relationships between employers and their employees.

We have all heard stories, or have ourselves experienced, situations where someone is treated unfairly, or paid very poorly, or expected to work completely unreasonable hours. How should we as Christians respond in such circumstances? Is it enough merely to say that we disapprove, or should we seek to find legal ways to protect employees from exploitation and from retaliation if they make a formal complaint about the way they are being treated?

Of course, it is also possible that some employees treat their employers unfairly, stealing from them and not carrying out work that has been assigned to them. This too is unacceptable, and employers may be justified in firing workers who do these things.

But while the extreme points on the spectrum of employer–employee relations are clearly marked, there are also grey areas in the middle. What exactly constitutes fair pay for work? How is this determined? What about those who have disabilities and find it difficult to find work – what should employers be expected to do to help such employees? What about taxes and environmental regulations and safety regulations, as well as other government regulations about labour relations or tariff laws? We need Christian lawyers and labour experts to help us approach these matters from a Christian perspective.

Work and trade unions

If the world were fully just, there would be no need for trade unions. But in a world where some have great power to exploit others, there is a need for trade unions to protect the rights of the workers. Nevertheless, Christians are divided about the merits of trade unions. Some oppose them; others support them. What does the Bible have to say that is relevant?

First, the Scripture is clear that we live, walk and work in a fallen world. In such a world, every human system will have both strengths and weaknesses, and that includes trade unions. It also includes their leaders, who like all human beings are capable of both tremendous good and tremendous evil.

By and large, the primary reasons for which trade unions were formed were good. They came into being to create safety nets for workers through checking employers' self-interest and greed, which led them to pay poor wages and not offer workers increases. The trade unions thus served as checks and balances on employers. They were powerful enough to confront the monopoly power of employers and seek higher wages, better working conditions and a fairer share of the company's and nation's profits for those who did the work.

A further benefit of trade unions is that they can help to establish a stable and well-trained workforce.[3] Some of them have programmes to train apprentices and other employees, thus relieving employers of the cost of training inexperienced workers. Well-trained employees create better and safer work conditions and result in fewer days lost because of work-related injuries or illnesses. Labour contracts also enable an employer to predict future operating costs, which helps the employer to know what to charge for a product and to plan for the future.

On the other hand, trade unions have their drawbacks and may discourage investment and improved working practices. They can even exacerbate unemployment when their demands result in employers avoiding hiring people and cutting back on or automating production. Unions may also resist any reductions in the workforce, which sometimes has the effect of forcing large semi-state organizations to be so grossly overstaffed that they cannot make a profit and have to be subsidized at enormous expense to taxpayers.[4] Furthermore, very powerful unions can lead to macroeconomic problems such as wage inflation and lost productivity due to strike action. While union members may benefit by getting higher wages, these gains may come at the cost of higher unemployment for others. These issues become a particular concern when the activities of trade unions discourage firms from investing in a region and creating more opportunities for employment. If firms fear

---

3. Material in this section is derived from Jim Woodruff, "Advantages and Disadvantages of Unions for Employers," bzifluent (20 October 2018).

4. See for example Bloomberg, Business Tech, "Eskom's Massive Workforce Problem: Over-Staffed and Over-Paid" (3 April 2018), https://businesstech.co.za/news/business/235299/eskoms-massive-workforce-problem-over-staffed-and-over-paid/.

frequent strikes and a non-cooperative trade union, they may prefer to invest in another country where they have a prospect of better labour relations.

Work and the Prophetic Role of the Church

The widespread economic and social injustices in our continent despite the high proportion of Africans who claim to be Christian makes it clear that the church in Africa has derailed from its prophetic role. We need to speak out loudly to say that we cannot have the Africa we want and that God wants while we act unjustly towards the unemployed, the underemployed and the disabled. We have sometimes closed our eyes even to such relatively simple matters as the abuse of domestic servants by church members. Nor have we spoken out when foreign companies prefer to bring employees from their home countries instead of employing nationals. Nor have we challenged our compatriots who accrue wealth for themselves while underpaying their employees. For example, in Nigeria private security companies do not pay their workers a minimum wage and offer them no job security and no health or pension benefits. And surely we as Christians should have something to say when Africa's resources are exported for processing elsewhere, when they should be processed on this continent and African people should reap the benefits. For example, there is no reason why Nigerian oil should flow to the rest of the world while Nigerians suffer fuel shortages.

We in the African church need to become deeply involved in prophetic engagements that advocate for young people and exploited workers. We should be motivated to do this not only by the repeated calls for justice and fair wages in the Scriptures, but also by the desire to see the compassion of God manifested in work relationships. Jesus offers a good illustration of what this means in his parable of the labourers in the vineyard (Matt 20:1–16). We find this parable puzzling because those who have worked all day get paid the same wage as those who were hired late in the afternoon. This seems unfair by our standards. It felt unfair to the labourers in the parable too, and they complained about it to their employer. The employer replied, "I am not being unfair to you, friend. Didn't you agree to work for a denarius? Take your pay and go. I want to give the one who was hired last the same as I gave you. Don't I have the right to do what I want with my own money? Or are you envious because I am generous?" (Matt 20:13–15).

On the one hand, this parable illustrates God's great generosity, which is something we need to remember when deciding what wages we should pay those who work for us. But the parable might also be helpful for thinking about why there were workers still hanging around hoping for employment at three and five o'clock in the afternoon. These people clearly wanted to work.

> Nothing suggests that those characters in the parable are irresponsible or lazy. More likely, they are unwanted.
>
> Who spends the whole day waiting to be hired but doesn't find success until the end of the day? In Jesus' time, these would be the weak, infirm, and disabled. Maybe the elderly, too. And other targets of discrimination, such as criminals or anyone with a bad reputation.
>
> A God who is "just," then, is inclined to show special generosity to the poor and outcast. No wonder the respectable people get anxious.[5]

In much of Africa, the people who are ready to work but have not had an opportunity until late in the day include university graduates, skilled artisans, manufacturers, refugees, stateless citizens, orphans, widows and so on. We need to care about offering all of these groups opportunities for employment and to be looking for ways to do so. Skinner states, "By dealing generously with a group of people that no other manager in town considered worth the trouble of hiring, the landowner has made a clear declaration about their value, their worth."[6]

People need personal dignity, which is associated with being able to fulfil their responsibilities and provide for their own needs and those of their families. Those who are excluded from work feel it as an assault on their dignity and self-worth. This holds true regardless of whether they are unemployed because of a general shortage of jobs or because they are disabled or because of their gender. Each of us needs an opportunity to make some meaningful contribution to the flourishing of our community, and to do so alongside other members of our society. Sometimes the obstacles to participation in work are economic or physical, and sometimes, unfortunately, they are rooted in religion, which is often used to sideline women.

The church should be at the forefront of those acknowledging the dignity and worth of every human being. We should not leave it to trade unions to speak for workers, and we should also speak for those workers who are not and will never be represented by trade unions.

---

5. Matthew L. Skinner, "Matthew 20:1–16: Justice Comes in the Evening," blog posted on 2 November 2011.

6. Skinner, "Matthew 20:1–16."

One other point emerges from Jesus's parable: the owner gives everyone the same wage for their work. It may be that it is time for the church to question the enormous disparities between the salaries of company executives and the salaries paid to ordinary workers. In some cases, the wages paid to those at the top are so high that it is impossible to spend that much money, while those at the bottom are paid so little that it is impossible to survive on so little money. More thought needs to be given to the spread of income as well as the source of income.

Conclusion

Many Africans work very hard. Many others spend long hours looking for work. All of them hope that their work will ultimately be a source of satisfaction, joy and hope, but many of them are disappointed and find little fulfilment in their work. All it seems to accomplish is to bring in money that is desperately needed to stay alive and provide for their families.

The desire to find satisfaction in our work is a valid one, born of the fact that we are made in God's image with a desire to be creative and do work that makes a difference in the world. But sometimes our dissatisfaction is less because the work is not satisfying and more because we fail to see how our work aligns with God's creational and creative purposes. We need to recognize that "our work" is not only our work; it is part and parcel of God's grand plan to enable human beings and creation to flourish. Working is one concrete way of fulfilling God's intent in creating us to be like him in loving, caring for, and protecting all of creation. Working is a way in which we can concretely demonstrate our love for God, our fellow humans and the rest of creation.

The church needs to acknowledge that not all work is paid work, but that all work should be honoured, and that everyone should have the opportunity to do something for others. Creating such opportunities will call on those who have work to acknowledge that "the money we get from our work should not be used in just any manner. God created us and gave us a means to earn a living; therefore, what we earn from work belongs to God" and should be used not only to put food on our tables but also on the tables of others.[7]

Finally, the greatest need in Africa in terms of work is a change of attitude not only as regards work, but also as regards who we are as human beings. Our attitude to work cannot change until our attitude to our fellow humans changes by rediscovering and recognizing the humanity of all. We need to

---

7. *Africa Study Bible* (Carol Stream, IL: Oasis, 2016), 144.

recognize the inherent value and dignity of each human being. Human dignity emanates from the fact that we are all created in the image of God and are all honoured in the fact that Christ became incarnate as a human being. These revolutionary ideas on human dignity have helped many generations to create a different and better future for themselves and for others.

Questions

1. What different kinds of work are done in your community? Which jobs are admired and which are despised, and on what grounds? Should a Christian understanding of work change your perspective at all?
2. How can we see all jobs as a means of demonstrating God's creativity and an opportunity to serve others and to help society and the environment flourish?
3. How can you use the Bible to infuse a new consciousness about work in Africa?
4. What can you as a church or an individual Christian do to help people find work and to create just working conditions for all?

Further Reading

Botha, Johan, ed. *Work as Calling and Worship: Challenging Thoughts for Our Day.* Arochukwu, Nigeria: Hugh Goldie Publishing; Cape Town: Lux Verbi, 2001.

Johnson, Brett. *Transforming Society: A Framework for Fixing a Broken World.* San Francisco: Indaba Publishing, 2017.

Keller, Timothy, with Katherine Leary Alsdorf. *Every Good Endeavour: Connecting Your Work to God's Work.* New York: Penguin Random House, 2012.

Volf, Miroslav. *Work in the Spirit: Toward a Theology of Work.* Eugene, OR: Wipf & Stock, 2001.

8

Economics

Piet Naudé

Theology, understood as *theos* (God) + *logos* (word, knowledge), refers to "knowledge of God." A theology that is public thinks about how the knowledge of God, primarily revealed in the Scriptures, impacts on matters of public concern at a specific time and in a specific context. This theological reflection is done and communicated in a way that is publicly understood and has the potential to affect public life.

Economics, understood as *oikos* (home) + *nomos* (law) or *oikonomia*, refers to "study of the law or rules of a household." This "household" may be a family, a country or the world; so economics studies may be the budget of a family, the economics of a country or the global financial system. Economics in its modern sense is a social science that studies the production, consumption and distribution of goods and services.

National economic systems can be classified on a continuum. At the one end are those that are centrally controlled by the state (socialism) and those where all the means of production are owned by the state (communism). At the other end are systems that largely rely on the free market to steer the economy and where the means of production and capital are held in private hands (capitalism).

After experimenting with African socialism just after the end of the colonial era, most countries in Africa now have a "mixed" economy with a leaning towards central control. This means that some sectors of the economy (education, electricity generation, water provision) are controlled by the state while others (mining, banking, trading in consumer goods) are open to free market competition or are held jointly by the state (public) and entrepreneurs (private) (e.g. telecommunications, transport).

For theology, matters of public concern certainly include questions about economics issues, for example (un)employment, national debt, wealth creation, technological innovation, poverty and inequality. These matters can be housed under the umbrella of "the economy" and make the link between public theology and economics a natural and very important one.

Why Theology Should Interact with Economics

A key reason why theologians need to know something about economics is that economics provides them with technical knowledge of and empirical data about "household affairs." For example, theologians are rightly concerned about "the poor," but without economics, theologians would not know how many people in a country live on less than, say, $2 a day and so can be classified as "poor," and how this proportion changes over time to show either progress or regression. To give another example, theologians are right to make prophetic calls against inequality. Economics helps us to distinguish between income and capital inequality and is able to measure the inequality in a given society, expressed in the Gini coefficient. This measurement runs from zero (complete equality) to one (complete inequality). The higher the figure as a proportion of 1, the higher the inequality in a given country. Examples of African countries that are very unequal are South Africa, Botswana and Namibia, while Algeria, Egypt and Ethiopia are more equal.

Some Christians argue that paying workers a high minimum wage is a good thing. Economists can provide data to help determine the optimum level of a minimum wage by taking into account the amounts paid by state social grants and the ability of a specific business sector to absorb a rise in the minimum wage without an overtly negative effect on their liquidity or ability to expand employment to others.

On the other hand, economists also need theologians who can expose and question the moral assumptions of economic systems. For example, is the idea that human beings are rational agents striving to maximize their self-interest an acceptable understanding of the human person? Or does a free market really move "freely" when the evidence demonstrates that the collective decisions and emotions of investors actually drive prices? Or is communism the best system to allow individuals the freedom to improve their welfare via entrepreneurship?

Theology with its normative (ethical) view of society can also critically examine economic policies and their outcomes. For example, is it good and fair that companies use natural resources but do not pay for them and leave it to society to pick up the costs? Mining companies may pollute groundwater, affecting boreholes and rivers, but often by the time the damage emerges, the companies no longer operate in that area or have ceased to exist. Or oil companies may pollute water resources and destroy the agricultural potential of land that local communities rely on for food. Taxpayers then have to pay to clean up their pollution. Or is it fair that all goods are subject to value added tax or sales tax, or should there be exemptions for food and other products that poorer people normally buy?

Finally, theology reminds economics that its promises of happiness and purpose through increasing personal or collective wealth exclude the important spiritual dimension of human nature. Neither the capitalist dream of becoming a wealthy self-made person nor the communist dream of an equal society ruled by the proletariat reflects ultimate realities. The purpose of human life is not to accumulate wealth for its own sake (always shifting the boundaries to "more" consumption) but to love others as God loves us and to use wealth to bless others.

Africa's Economic Challenges and Opportunities

Africa is a huge and diverse continent with fifty-four countries in which 1.2 billion people live. Each of these countries has its own challenges and opportunities. So what is said below is inevitably something of a generalization.

Economic challenges

- *Many African countries rely for their income on one commodity only.* If for example the sale of oil makes up 90 percent of state income, and the price of oil drops from $120 per barrel to $40 (as recently happened), the country will soon find that it cannot balance its books because its expenditures far exceed its income. It will have to borrow to make up the shortfall. This is how countries fall into a debt-trap, which reduces their ability to diversify their economies and create other forms of income.

- *Africa has weak infrastructure.* Economic growth cannot happen without infrastructure that allows the easy transport of goods and people. Countries need a proper road network, a good spread of railway lines and strategically positioned airports and harbours. Other important forms of infrastructure include relatively affordable and reliable electricity supplies – but only 24 percent of sub-Saharan Africans have access to electricity. Infrastructure also includes a well-functioning communication system including mobile and Internet services; a legal system that protects contracts and is transparent and fair; and a financial system that can process payments and move money easily in and out of the country, subject to exchange controls.

- *Too many African countries are politically unstable.* There are regions in Africa with perpetual conflicts and wars. There are autocratic rulers who enrich themselves and stay in power for life or until they are challenged or toppled through a violent overthrow of government (see the thirty-five military coups between 1991 and 1996). These unstable countries or parts of countries are the source of political and economic migrants who flee to safer spaces, with the result that Africa's economic development lags far behind its actual potential. The UN Refugee Agency states that sub-Saharan Africa hosts about 26 percent of the world's refugee population, adding up to more than 18 million people in regions like Sudan, the Central African Republic and parts of Nigeria.[1] What we need to work for on this continent is "an Africa of good governance, democracy, respect for human rights, justice and the rule of law."[2]

- *Rampant corruption results in the loss of billions of dollars that could have been spent on basic services like education, housing or health.* The annual Corruption Perception Index, compiled by Transparency International, defines corruption as the misuse of public power for private gain. By 2017, a total of twelve African countries were on the list of the twenty-five most corrupt countries in the world.[3] Corruption pushes up the cost of goods and services and leads to a system in which companies that operate honestly do not get business. A few connected individuals walk away with unethical and inflated profits, and ordinary people suffer. Furthermore, all of Africa's economies need foreign investment if they are to grow. But investors will only commit to projects if they are sure there will be a safe and stable business environment with trustworthy business partners, and that they will be able to repatriate profits after paying their taxes. The tenth principle of the UN Global Compact, a broad agreement for global

---

1. "Africa," The UN Refuge Agency (n.d.), https://www.unhcr.org/africa.html.

2. *Agenda 2063: The Africa We Want,* aspiration 3, African Union (2015), https://www.un.org/en/africa/osaa/pdf/au/agenda2063.pdf.

3. "Most Corrupt Countries 2019," World Population Review (4 October 2019), http://worldpopulationreview.com/countries/most-corrupt-countries/.

business, reads: "Business should work against corruption in all its forms, including extortion and bribery."[4]

- *Africa's main trading partners lie outside the continent in China, the EU and the USA.* Trade agreements that are fair and may even allow African countries preferential treatment are good for the economy. But there is very little trade within Africa because of poor cross-Africa infrastructure (see above). In other words, African countries do not trade enough with other African countries that are in close proximity and so they miss out on the benefits of economies of scale. There are not enough economic unions or strong trading blocs across Africa to allow the continent to speak with one voice in international trade. This means that Africa is easily marginalized and does not optimize its economic potential.

- *Africa is very vulnerable to the effects of climate change.* Although the continent uses less than 5 percent of the world's fossil fuel (a major cause of global warming), changing rainfall and weather patterns greatly affect the continent because of carbon emissions from already developed countries like the USA, the UK and Germany and now also from China and India. The reason for this impact is twofold: 1) Millions of people rely for their food on subsistence agriculture, and drier seasons or floods have a direct impact on food production. 2) Africa is poorly prepared to deal with natural disasters because of inadequate transport links and rapid urbanization that leads to overcrowding in townships and informal settlements which lack the infrastructure of streets, storm water drainage and sewage systems. Floods as a result of cyclones affecting Mozambique, Zimbabwe and Malawi have become much stronger and more frequent due to the Indian Ocean's warmer surface water. And droughts in West Africa and Southern Africa have become longer with higher temperatures and lower access to groundwater.

Economic opportunities

We should not only consider the negatives when looking at Africa, for it is also a continent with huge economic opportunities. Economists look at the following positive potential contributors to socio-economic development.

---

4. "The Ten Principles of the UN Global Compact," United Nations Global Compact (n.d.), https://www.unglobalcompact.org/what-is-gc/mission/principles.

- *Africa does not have to follow the long road to technology development.* It has the ability to benefit from technological advances without the pre-development phase. For example, mobile phones are now widely used for communication in Africa, which has eliminated the need to set up a fixed line telephone infrastructure. Mobile phones are also now widely used in the taxi industry and for banking, health care, farming and education. There is no reason why Africa cannot benefit greatly from the so-called Fourth Industrial Revolution and contribute to it with innovations in the virtual economy.

- *Africa has the youngest population of all continents.* Africa's median age was just below 20 years in 2010, and it is projected to be around 22.7 years by 2030, compared to the 2010 figures for Japan (45), Germany (44) and the UK (40). This means that half of Africa's population will be below 23 years of age by 2030. Economists speak about the "demographic dividend" which lies in the future, when the proportion of people in the age group 15–60 (working age) will be the highest and those younger than 15 will make up less than 30 percent and those above 60 less than 15 percent of the total population. Africa has youth on its side, which creates the potential for innovation, a locally available workforce (on the condition that education functions well) and a relatively low burden of an ageing population to carry in the economy.

- *Africa has the potential to contribute significantly towards a lower carbon economy.* The continent has abundant sun, wind and rivers to generate green energy in the form of solar, wind and hydroelectricity. Technology has already brought the price for "green" production within the range of fossil-based energy. Africa will be able to mitigate the current low proportion of people with electricity while at the same time reducing the unit price and increasing the stability of supply to households and businesses.

- *Africa has high growth potential to create and expand a new middle class.* Unlike mature economies with a stagnant middle class, the youth dividend means that more people will be entering the middle class, which is defined as people with the ability to spend between $10 and $100 per day. These are the people who buy consumer goods (appliances, televisions, cars) and invest more in the education of their children. They grow businesses, increase employment and generally contribute to a vibrant economy.

- *Africa's wealth of commodities (e.g. minerals) that the world needs creates huge potential for beneficiation (enrichment).* For example, instead of

Botswana simply mining diamonds and sending the rough stones to be sorted, cut and polished in Brussels, this finishing work could be done in Gaborone. The economic value of rough diamonds is far below that of polished diamonds, and the country can earn much needed foreign currency for itself by increasing the value of the raw product. The same thing is starting to happen in agriculture, for example in coffee and tea production and packaging, and for other mining products like iron ore, aluminium and gold.

- *There are few continents with such high and unique tourism potential.* Countries from the North (Egypt, Morocco) to the East (Kenya, Tanzania, Uganda) to the West (Ghana), Central Africa (Rwanda) and the South (Namibia, Botswana, South Africa) as well as islands like Mauritius have become choice tourist destinations. Economists tell us that tourism is the most effective job creator, with up to seven locals jobs created for each arriving foreign tourist.

With wise leaders, hard work and good policy execution, Africa is a continent that can flourish in the twenty-first century.

Christian Confessions and Economics

Although the Nicene and Apostles' creeds do not refer to economic matters directly, they can be interpreted in a way that helps us to understand God's will for the economy. If, for example, we confess that God is the "maker of heaven and earth, of all that is, seen and unseen" (Nicaea) and take up our task to rule over the earth (Gen 1:28), we have a responsibility to care for the integrity of creation. If we confess that we believe in Jesus Christ, then we are called to imitate him in not advancing only our own interests but also the interests of others (Phil 2:1–4). If we, with both the Nicene and the Apostles' creeds, confess that the church is "catholic" (meaning universal), we accept global solidarity with one another. If we confess that the church is "holy," we acknowledge that we must strive through sanctification to be like God (Lev 11:44; 1 Pet 1:15). And because God is love, we must live an economic life that embodies love for our neighbour and our enemies (1 John 4:7–21).[5] The

---

5. Nicene Creed, https://www.sacred-texts.com/chr/nicene.htm; Apostles' Creed, https://www.crcna.org/welcome/beliefs/creeds/apostles-creed.

seemingly "old" words of the confessions are in fact revolutionary if translated in terms of economic life.[6]

More recent confessional documents stemming from the Reformed tradition are much more explicit about economic matters because we have come to understand the huge impact economic systems, policies and practices have on individual people, broader society and the environment. The most prominent of these newer documents are the Belhar Confession (1986) and the Accra Confession (2004).

In the Belhar Confession, the church is called to unity and reconciliation with a view to establishing justice. In a world full of injustice and enmity, "we believe that God is in a special way the God of the destitute, the poor and the wronged." The church as the possession of God "must stand where the Lord stands, namely against injustice and with the wronged."[7]

The Accra Confession draws attention to the devastating effects of the global economic system (both socialist and capitalist) on the environment and to the increasing inequality within and between countries. According to the confession, a new empire has been created that stands against the will of God and should be resisted. "We believe the economy exists to serve the dignity and well-being of people in community, within the bounds of the sustainability of creation." It goes on to reject "the unregulated accumulation of wealth and limitless growth that has already cost the lives of millions and destroyed much of God's creation."[8]

Evolving Catholic social doctrine played and still plays a huge role in bringing economic and labour matters into the fold of Christian theological thinking. The key text in this regard is the *Compendium of the Social Doctrine of the Church*,[9] which includes references to ground-breaking statements like *Rerum Novarum*, *Gaudium et Spes* and many other Catholic encyclicals.[10] In chapter 4, the *Compendium* sets out the seven principles on which the social

---

6. For more, see World Council of Churches, *Confessing the One Faith: An Ecumenical Explication of the Apostolic Faith as It Is Confessed in the Nicene-Constantinopolitan Creed* (Geneva: WCC, 1991).

7. The Belhar Confession (September 1986), https://www.pcusa.org/site_media/media/uploads/theologyandworship/pdfs/belhar.pdf.

8. The Accra Confession, *World Communion of Reformed Churches*, http://wcrc.ch/accra/the-accra-confession.

9. *Compendium of the Social Doctrine of the Church*, Pontifical Council for Justice and Peace, http://www.vatican.va/roman_curia/pontifical_councils/justpeace/documents/rc_pc_justpeace_doc_20060526_compendio-dott-soc_en.html.

10. See Pope Leo XII, "Rerum Novarum – Encyclical Letter of Pope Leo XIII on the Conditions of Labor," (1891), Providence College Digital Commons.

doctrine stands. The *Compendium* contains subdivisions on human work (chapter 6) and economic life (chapter 7) from a Christian perspective.

Christian Criteria for Economic Life

The sources of our criteria for a good economy are first the Bible and second our confessional tradition. Let us look at five of these criteria and how they – taken together – promote human flourishing globally and in Africa.

Integrity of creation – stewardship

In the beginning, God created the heavens and the earth. (Gen 1:1)

The earth is the LORD's, and everything in it;
the world, and all who live in it. (Ps 24:1)

In the beginning was the Word. . . . Through him all things were made; without him nothing was made that was made. (John 1:1, 3)

The LORD God took the man and put him in the Garden of Eden to work it and take care of it. (Gen 2:15)

Humans were assigned the task of working in and on the created order. For too long, however, economists understood this "work" as subjugation and exploitation of the earth to satisfy our insatiable human needs. Instead of being good stewards, we were too greedy and have now reached a point where human beings have become a danger to all the earth. Geologists confirm that we live in the *Anthropocene* age, a name which implies that our impact on the environment has become so pervasive that it is recorded as part of the earth's geological record, which was previously restricted to major natural events like earthquakes or volcanos.

Public theology must be a green (ecological) theology, supporting international agreements on climate change and reminding the human species of its holy responsibility to rule over the earth as good stewards who know that we do not own the earth but work it on behalf of its real owner, God Almighty.

Business corporations should not only comply with minimum environmental legislation but should take all possible measures to mitigate their carbon footprint. There are many different practical strategies for achieving this, including switching to alternative energy sources (solar, wind), recycling waste, limiting water consumption and using technology to conduct meetings instead of travelling long distances.

Principles 7–9 of the UN Global Compact urge businesses to "support a precautionary approach to environmental challenges; undertake initiatives to promote greater environmental responsibility" and to "encourage the development and diffusion of environmentally friendly technologies."[11]

Human dignity – imago Dei

The idea that human beings are created in the image of God (Gen 1:26) and deserve to be treated with dignity is deeply embedded in the Scriptures and Christian tradition. A powerful secular expression of human dignity is contained in the Universal Declaration of Human Rights, originally adopted in 1948 and now acting as a global benchmark for politics and for business.

Here are some suggestions for how we can honour and advance human dignity in a working environment: Provide safe working conditions for employees and access to basic health care; avoid child labour; pay workers a fair wage in line with industry and country standards; set fair working hours, not exceeding eight hours per day and six days per week; create a welcoming workplace with no discrimination on the basis of race, culture, religion or gender; provide training and up-skilling of employees to optimize their human potential.

The UN Global Compact starts with two principles related to human rights, one positive and the other negative: "Principle 1: Businesses should support and respect the protection of internationally proclaimed human rights, and Principle 2: should make sure that they are not complicit in human rights abuses."[12]

Striving for an egalitarian (equal) society

Many passages in the Old Testament point towards structuring an economy for greater equality. For example, the idea of the Jubilee year points in this direction: After seven sabbatical year cycles (7 x 7 = 49), the fiftieth year is the Jubilee year (Lev 25:10–11). This year was a Sabbath year in which even the fields were to rest. The economic implication of this "year of release" was the setting free of slaves, the writing off of debts and the return of land to the original owners who had lost it in the past fifty years.

The Wisdom books of the Old Testament understand that some will grow rich because of hard work and others who are foolish and lazy will become

---

11. "The Ten Principles."
12. "The Ten Principles."

poor. Those who bury their talents – according to the New Testament parable – will lose even that which was given to them, while those who use their talents are rewarded even more. The labourer is worth his or her wages. Thus, reward for what we can call entrepreneurial activities is accepted as a reality in the Bible. A society of perfect equality where all have the same income and capital is simply impossible (Deut 15:11), and riches are seen as gifts that should be used as a blessing to others and to relieve their plight (Deut 15:4–8).

Nevertheless, a highly unequal society where landowners (owners of capital) increase their wealth at the expense of others is not ethically acceptable. Therefore the Scriptures sketch the ideal that the balance between rich and poor should be restored with periodic interventions in the economic system like the actions required in the Jubilee year.

In our modern economy, measures to keep inequalities within morally acceptable limits are two pronged: 1) empowering those outside or at the bottom of the social system by helping them acquire the skills to participate meaningfully in the economy (education is a key way out of poverty), and 2) setting up an efficient and progressive tax system that redistributes income from more well-off people to the national treasury, thus enabling the state to assist poor people with a social safety net and basic services like housing, health care, water and electricity. The latter remedy assumes the existence of a credible and transparent tax regime coupled with a non-corrupt and competent state. No wonder inequalities in Africa are sometimes so stark!

Where no formal or functioning public social system is in place, Africans have a long and proud *ubuntu* tradition that places the interests of the community before private gain. If one is able to produce more food than required in the family, the surplus is shared. If I gain business success, *ubuntu* imposes a moral obligation to share my wealth because my success is based on my being-in-community. Long before formal state structures in the modern sense of the word were instituted, Africans understood the obligation to share goods and spaces. Modernity has unfortunately led to a distortion of *ubuntu* that has resulted in a higher degree of individualism, with retention of what is gained for private use only, and a definition of *ubuntu* in ethnic terms, excluding those who are not from my extended family or ethnic group.

Special care for the weak and marginalized

The Old Testament makes clear provision for the special treatment of foreigners, widows and the poor in the books of the Law (Deut 24), the Wisdom literature (Ps 146; Prov 22), and the Prophets (Isa 1:17; 61:1; Jer 5:28). The idea also receives strong support in the teaching of Jesus (Luke 4:18) and the apostles (Jas 1:27; 1 John 3:17–18).

Given the millions of migrants and displaced peoples in Africa, we in Africa have a special responsibility to treat such people in line with the philosophy of *ubuntu*: If we are persons through other persons, their suffering is, as 1 Corinthians 12:12–26 says so clearly, also our suffering, and we are called not only to protect our own interests but also to advance theirs (Phil 2:1–4).

It is sometimes said that the civility of a society can be measured by the way it treats the "insane" people living among us. This is a way to say a society is measured not by economic growth figures but by how it treats those who are shunted to the side of society. The Scriptures support this concern. Economic policies should include a social system that provides for orphans, for the ill and for the old. The way we treat foreigners should also reflect our Christian faith. Xenophobia and tribalism send the opposite message to that proclaimed in God's word.

Assistance in a crisis

We all know that it is wise to save for a rainy day. What this means is that on a personal level, we should spend less than we earn and should save a set proportion of our income so that money is available for an unexpected event or crisis. The same holds true for a country. If a country has to borrow money to pay off its debt, then it is in a very vulnerable position when crises come.

But we should not have to rely only on our own resources; we should also be able to look to our neighbours for help. Jesus told the parable of the good Samaritan in response to the question, who is my neighbour? In other words, whom should I care for and assist? The parable involves a man in a crisis. He is overpowered by robbers and left for dead along the road. The people who come across him while he is in this crisis react in very different ways. Those who might be expected to help (the religious people who go to the temple every week) walk past with "good" excuses. The only one who offers help is a Samaritan, a man who is not Jewish, who provides emergency assistance and pays for the injured man to stay at an inn and be assisted further.

A crisis on a regional and national scale can emerge from a natural disaster like a drought or flood, wars and uprisings and highly contagious and often fatal diseases like Ebola, HIV/AIDS and cholera. No matter who is affected, the Bible requires us to assist in a crisis and do what we can to alleviate that nation's or region's burden.

In summary, a good economy from a biblical perspective is one in which –

- natural resources are used sustainably in line with our calling as stewards of God's creation.
- the dignity and rights of individuals and groups of people (labourers, employees) are advanced in the workplace and beyond.
- inequalities are within fair limits with structural interventions where necessary to ensure that the gap between rich and poor does not increasingly widen.
- special measures are taken to protect the weakest in society.
- emergency assistance is available to anyone who is in need.

The Church and Economic Issues

Let us now turn to the role of the church in economic life. When we talk about "the church," we refer to three levels of the institutional church: the local congregation and its members; the regional church in different denominational structures; and the ecumenical church as the global people of God. Let us look at the role of each in turn.

The local congregation

The local congregation is closest to the economic realities of its members and the surrounding communities. Its first task is to live out the law of love and care among its own members. The first church in Jerusalem was not admired by outsiders for its smart buildings or academically qualified pastors! They were an amazing example of a sharing community – showing love among a huge diversity of languages and cultures, looking after one another with a special care for foreign widows, breaking bread at one another's homes and praising God all the way (Acts 2:42–47)!

In modern terms, the local church must run its own finances in a responsible and transparent manner. The practice of pastors getting rich on contributions from poor congregants must be stopped, and corruption should never be associated with the local body of Christ.

The local church should also be a blessing to the surrounding communities: it should reach out with the gospel of Jesus Christ and provide pastoral and physical care as far as possible. The church must become known as a place of love with a special heart for the weakest in society, and not, as in recent times, as a place where children and women are sexually abused. Where possible, churches should link up with local non-government and aid organizations – no matter whether they are faith-based or not – as this strengthens their collective ability to serve the communities.[13] And where there are local tribal or state/ municipal authorities, the church should use every opportunity to cooperate and support such authority in matters that are fair and just so as to benefit the people of the area.

The regional church

The regional church within the rich diversity of Christian denominations should have a focus on assisting one another as the needs arise. The book of Acts tells us that when the Jerusalem church was in trouble due to hunger and drought, the regional churches were called upon to send assistance according to their ability. The power of a regional church lies in its ability to structure socio-economic care on a firmer institutional basis than is possible by a local congregation. When individual churches contribute financial and human resources to the regional church, the means available are much greater. Examples of regional church actions are church schools, clinics, hospitals, orphanages, social workers and emergency assistance abilities.

The power of joint action is one reason why even local churches without a specific denominational affiliation should open their doors and resources to cooperate with other Christian churches. The body of Christ acting in unity is a powerful witness to the love of God and a practical demonstration of that love. The idea of a church "going it alone" is not in line with the image of the church as the one body of Christ.

The global church

The global church in the widest ecumenical sense of the word has at least two callings with regards to the economy. The first is to participate in shaping economic policies by providing expert advice from a Christian perspective to international bodies like the United Nations, the World Trade Organization, the World Bank and the International Monetary Fund. Churches are the widest

---

13. Examples of small but effective local interventions to fight poverty and underdevelopment in areas like education and health care emerge from the work of the 2019 Nobel Prize winners for economics, Drs Kremer, Duflo and Banerjee. Churches could imitate their small-scale experiments and make a noticeable difference at a local level.

spread of all institutions and understand regional and local conditions. They can therefore provide input on how best to assist African and other developing economies as well as provide an alternative to allowing the advancement of global financial interests to be the sole criterion for interventions.

The second calling is to be an informed and responsible prophetic voice about global economic matters. As was said above, economics needs the constant ethical reminders provided by theology, which draws its guidelines for a good economy from Scripture. Recent examples of this happening are the Protestant churches in Germany's stance on refugees and on the 2008 banking crisis, as well as the Catholic voice on climate change in *Laudato si* by Pope Francis.[14]

Conclusion

The horizon of the church's work and its inspiration is the coming of God's kingdom. The church's resilience in its determination to care and, despite all odds, take a stand against exploitative economic powers stems not from our own commitment but from our reliance on God's promise that his kingdom is coming and that the new earth will be a gift to us. There will be a time when all tears are wiped away and the lion and the lamb will lie together in the peaceable kingdom of God. This future vision is not a way to escape economic realities but encourages us to confront those realities in the power of God's transformative Spirit.

Questions

1. Why is the relation between theology and economics important for the public witness of the church?
2. What does economics contribute to the task of public theology?
3. What do you consider to be the most urgent economic challenges in your area, and what potential for economic growth is there in your area?
4. What are the basic biblical requirements for a fair and good economic life, and what can you do to encourage these in your community?
5. What is your local church doing to bear witness to the love of God in economic terms? What more could it be doing?

---

14. Pope Francis, *Laudato si* (2015), http://w2.vatican.va/content/francesco/en/encyclicals/documents/papa-francesco_20150524_enciclica-laudato-si.html.

Further Reading

Banerjee, A., and E. Duflo. *Poor Economics: A Radical Rethinking of the Way to Fight Global Poverty.* New York: PublicAffairs, 2001.

Boesak, Allan, and Len Hansen, eds. *Globalisation: The Politics of Empire, Justice and the Life of Faith.* Stellenbosch: SUN, 2009.

———. *Globalisation II: Global Crisis, Global Challenge, Global Faith. An Ongoing Response to the Accra Confession.* Stellenbosch: SUN, 2010.

Koopman, Nico. "Theology and the Fulfilment of Social and Economic Rights: Some Theoretical Considerations." In *Theories of Social and Economic Justice*, edited by A. J. van der Walt, 128–140. Stellenbosch: SUN, 2005.

Naudé, Piet J. *Neither Calendar nor Clock: Perspectives on the Belhar Confession.* Grand Rapids: Eerdmans, 2010.

Toryough, Godwin. "The Biblical Ethics of Work: A Model for African Nations." *Verbum et Ecclesia* 30, no. 1 (2010): 1–8.

World Alliance of Reformed Churches. *Choose Life, Act in Hope: African Churches Living Out the Accra Confession.* Geneva: WARC, 2009.

9

Poverty

Collium Banda

Public theology has a deep concern about the state of affairs in socio-economic and political life. Thus it must be concerned about poverty and seek viable ways to address it. This is especially true in Africa, where poverty is so endemic that Africa and poverty are sometimes regarded as synonyms. We may sometimes assume that this is just the way things are, but poverty is not a random thing. It is caused by specific socio-economic and political factors, and we can only address it if we understand those factors and how to counter them. But first we need to have a good grasp of what exactly poverty is. In other words, how do we define poverty?

Defining Poverty

There is a sense in which poverty is in the eye of the beholder, for our definitions of poverty are influenced by our world view, economic experiences and knowledge of socio-economic and political issues. Thus one person may consider themselves poor while living in circumstances that others would envy. So it is important to avoid simplistic definitions of poverty. In fact, "there is no single, precise, standardised or usable definition of poverty."[1]

Traditionally poverty has been defined in terms of deprivation of basic goods, or a low income that limits people's access to basic goods. This definition of poverty is reflected in the statistics compiled by international bodies such as the World Bank, which speak of how many people in a region live on less

---

1. A. E. Orobator, *From Crisis to Kairos: The Mission of the Church in the Time of HIV/AIDS, Refugees, and Poverty* (Nairobi: Paulines Publications Africa, 2005), 181.

than, say, US $2.00 per person per day. By this standard, there is mass poverty across sub-Saharan Africa. But the problem with this way of measuring poverty is that it ignores regional differences and the differences between households. For example, some people who have very low incomes may cultivate their own farms and gardens. The crops they harvest supply the food they need and may be worth more than $2.00 a day; yet because this harvest does not involve a monetary transaction, it does not show up in the World Bank's records. So while the $2.00 per day scale is not irrelevant, it should be employed with caution when trying to identify who is really poor.[2]

The awareness that poverty involves many factors led the United Nations to define poverty not so much as a lack of necessities for material well-being or a lack of income, but rather as a multidimensional reality that precludes the ability to flourish. By this definition, poverty includes denial of the opportunities and choices most basic to human development, including denial of the opportunity to lead a long, healthy, creative life; to have a decent standard of living; and to enjoy dignity and self-esteem, the respect of others and the things that people value in life. This definition of human poverty acknowledges that "income is not the sum total of human lives, [therefore] the lack of it cannot be the sum total of human deprivation."[3]

These definitions remind us that in addressing poverty, it is not enough to focus on the issue of deprivation; poverty also affects the way people experience life itself. It determines the quality of their socio-economic and political life and involves all the social, political and spiritual structures that help or hinder human flourishing.[4]

If we apply the above definitions of poverty to life in Africa, we are forced to recognize how deplorably poor the quality of life is across much of Africa. Far too many Africans have limited access to food, poor nutrition, poor housing, poor sanitation, poor access to health care and education, and poor access to viable economic participation. It can even be said that a "majority of Africa's people are not simply poor; they are destitute – with hardly any means for adequate livelihood."[5] Kunhiyop cites a Nigerian Human Development

2. R. C. Tangonyire and L. K. Achal, *Economic Behaviour as If Others Too Had Interests* (Bamenda: Langaa RPCIG, 2012), 173.

3. United Nations Development Programme, *Human Development Report 1998* (New York: Oxford University Press, 1998), 25.

4. B. L. Myers, *Walking with the Poor: Principles and Practices of Transformational Development* (Maryknoll, NY: Orbis, 1999), 81.

5. M. Theuri, "Poverty in Africa," in *Theology of Reconstruction: Exploratory Essays*, eds. M. N. Getui and E. A. Obeng (Nairobi: Acton/EATWOT, 1999), 233.

Report that in many African countries, poverty manifests itself in "prostitution, exposure to risks, corruption, robbery, street life, increased unemployment, living in squalor, shanties, shacks, high infant mortality, acute malnutrition, short life expectancy, human degradation, living in overcrowded and often poorly ventilated homes."[6] Poverty is an existential reality.

Poverty and Theology

Poverty features prominently in God's mission in the Bible. We see this clearly in the account of the exodus, where God acted to liberate the Israelites from spiritual oppression, political oppression (Exod 6:8), economic oppression (Exod 1:11) and social oppression (Exod 1:15–16). We can thus say that "in the exodus God responded to all the dimensions of Israel's need."[7] God did not only save Israel spiritually; he acted holistically. The same is true of Christ who saves people comprehensively and not just spiritually (Luke 4:18–21). The church is thus called to take poverty seriously because within God's eschatological framework of salvation, God saves the whole person, including the material component that will be transformed into a glorious imperishable component at Christ's return. To ignore poverty is to fail to live up to Christ's mission to lead people into abundant life (John 10:10).

Another reason why poverty poses a theological challenge is that it is often a result of social injustice and inequality. Myers puts it this way: "Poverty is a result of relationships that do not work; that are not just, that are not for life, that are not harmonious or enjoyable."[8] In essence, poverty "is the absence of shalom in all its meanings."[9] Examples of what happens when shalom is absent are evident throughout the Bible, including in the oppression of Israel by the Egyptians, the state of lawlessness and social chaos in the book of Judges, and the abuse of the poor, the widows and the orphans condemned in the various prophetic books. In the absence of shalom, the poor are vulnerable to commodification by the rich, who trample on their human dignity and treat them as expendables for their self-gratification. This is often how the ruling elites in Africa treat the poor. Public theology needs to assert that no one is a

---

6. S. W. Kunhiyop, "Poverty: Good News for Africa," *Africa Journal of Evangelical Theology* 20, no. 1 (2001): 4.

7. C. J. H. Wright, *The Mission of God: Unlocking the Bible's Grand Narrative* (Nottingham: Inter-Varsity Press, 2006), 271.

8. Myers, *Walking with the Poor*, 86.

9. Myers, 86.

mere object to satisfy someone else's desires. We need to stand with the poor and defend their human dignity.

Finally, poverty is a challenge to theology because it destroys people's self-esteem. This is vividly captured in one woman's lament, "Poverty is pain. It feels like a disease. It attacks a person not only materially, but also morally. It eats away one's dignity and drives one into total despair."[10] The loss of self-esteem induced by poverty results in a distorted view of the self: "When people believe they are less than human, without the brains, strength, and personhood to contribute to their own well-being or that of others, their understanding of who they are is marred."[11] This marred self-understanding induces the hopelessness that leads many poor people to adopt survival methods that lead to further self-destruction. For instance, in Africa poverty is a leading driver of violent crimes, commercial sex work, and early sexual activity among adolescents and youth and is a leading cause of the high prevalence of HIV and AIDS. Poverty leads to the attitude illustrated by commercial sex workers who retorted, "Is there anything that does not kill?" when challenged about the dangers of HIV and AIDS.[12]

For the above three reasons, responding to poverty must be a priority for the church at all times, particularly in Africa where poverty is rampant and increasing.

The Causes of Poverty in Africa

Poverty is a complex reality with many underlying causes that we need to understand if we are to address it.

The colonial legacy

In light of Africa's history, one cannot speak about poverty without making reference to slavery and colonialism. Much of Africa's modern socio-economic and political terrain is a direct result of its history of colonial subjugation, exploitation and marginalization by powerful nations who enslaved the indigenous people and expropriated their fertile lands and minerals. Any strategy aimed at dislodging poverty in Africa must equip Africans to engage

---

10. S. Hunter, *Black Death: AIDS in Africa* (New York: St. Martin's Press, 2015).

11. Myers, *Walking with the Poor*, 87–88.

12. V. Magezi, *HIV/AIDS, Poverty and Pastoral Care and Counselling* (Stellenbosch: African Sun Media, 2007), 51.

with this colonial history that continues to shape Africa's economic capacity and the economy of the world in general.

Some argue that the days of colonialism and foreign occupation have long passed, but "Africans seem to be bent on transmitting a victim mentality from one generation to another instead of walking tall."[13] But what may justifiably be seen as a victim mentality is also a sign of the depth of the crippling wounds inflicted by colonialism.

There is no doubt that colonialism had some positive aspects in that it brought technology, improved agriculture, durable housing and efficient mechanized transportation networks to Africa. However, many of these developments benefitted colonial settlers more than local Africans. Furthermore, in Southern Africa the policy of separate development (apartheid) objectivized and dehumanized black people.[14] Consequently, African development always lagged behind white development. Using the example of Zimbabwe, Maundeni says that the colonial system made Africans useable but not independently accountable. It did not incorporate them into the structures of the colonial state, nor did it allow them to qualify as cadres skilled in the management of a modern capitalist economy.[15] In other words, the colonial economy reduced Africans to mere children without accountability.

While Africans have broken the political power of their former colonial oppressors, they have yet to assume full control and responsibility for their economies. In some African countries, economic power still remains in the hands of foreigners who continue to directly and indirectly control African economies. Crippling sanctions are imposed on African governments that do not toe the line. The vast mining and oil companies that operate on the continent have their headquarters elsewhere. Given that so much of Africa's economy is reliant on direct foreign investment, the ripple effects of any fall-out with overseas governments are serious. Furthermore, many African economies are heavily indebted to the International Monetary Fund (IMF) and the World Bank (WB). The evidence of the unequal partnerships between these institutions and African economies is best seen in the disastrous economic structural adjustment programmes that took a heavy toll on African countries. Africa's economic and political leadership has failed to meaningfully address

---

13. M. T. Speckman, *A Biblical Vision for Africa's Development?* (Pietermaritzburg, South Africa: Cluster, 2007), xx.

14. M. O. West, *The Rise of an African Middle Class: Colonial Zimbabwe, 1898–1965* (Bloomington: Indiana University Press, 2002), 28.

15. Z. Maundeni, "Why the African Renaissance Is Likely to Fail: The Case of Zimbabwe," *Journal of Contemporary African Studies* 22, no. 2 (2004): 199–202.

the effects of colonialism and to critically engage the neo-colonial tendencies of the world's superpowers that want to control and exploit the mineral resources of smaller nations.

Geography, weather and epidemics

Poverty in Africa is also related to geography, weather and diseases. Some of these factors are within human control; others are not.

Geographical location and the weather play a significant role in the wealth and poverty of rural communities, which often depend on agriculture for survival. Poor rains and flooding have a serious effect on food production and availability.

Africa continues to struggle with epidemic diseases that are financially and humanly costly. A poor response to these epidemics means that they affect the economy of a country. HIV and AIDS, cholera, Ebola, tuberculosis and other diseases drain national budgets, deplete the much needed skilled labour force, kill parents and leave child-headed homes, in which the older children may drop out of school to care for the younger ones. Such children are easily forced into child marriages, so perpetuating the vicious cycle of poverty. The poor are more vulnerable to these diseases because of their living conditions and generally poorer health and education. Epidemics thrive on poverty.

Incompetent and corrupt leadership

It has been said that the "main reason why Africa's people are poor is because the leaders have made this choice."[16] This statement may seem harsh and unfair given Africa's history of colonialism and the fact that weather patterns are beyond human control. However, it remains true that African leaders have made bad economic choices and have failed to deal with economic challenges. Speckman calls on African countries to realize their potential and assert themselves economically. He says, "Africans . . . are among the most disadvantaged nations of the world apparently because they constantly and wilfully undermine their own potential. They tend to define themselves in terms of 'others,' and without the 'others' they see little value in themselves."[17]

---

16. Greg Mills, quoted in P. Verster, *New Hope for the Poor: A Perspective on the Church in Informal Settlements in Africa* (Bloemfontein: Sun Media, 2012), 16.

17. Speckman, *A Biblical Vision*, xvii.

Plainly stated, African leaders have failed to lead their nations. Weak, unimaginative and visionless leadership has failed to spearhead economic recovery in many African states. It can even be said that at a fundamental level, poverty in many African countries correlates with the level of democracy. Furthermore, while some geographical and weather causes of poverty are beyond human control, the severity of their effects on people's lives can be attributed to poor and unimaginative leaders who have not sought innovative agricultural solutions in drought-prone areas.

Chitando bemoans the African paradox of a mineral-rich continent devastated by poverty and concludes that this paradox points to a "spectacular failure of imagination by postcolonial African leaders and citizens."[18] In some African countries, national leadership tends to be tribally or regionally biased instead of being nationally inclusive, resulting in civil wars and civil unrest. Such leaders distribute national resources only to the groups with which they are aligned, consigning other tribes and regions to poverty. Affirming the poor capacity of African governments to move the continent forward, Speckman says,

> Africans should be asking themselves what, if anything, have African countries done about their natural resources since the Europeans began to relinquish political power in African countries in the 1960s? How much mining and agricultural activity have Africans engaged in? What other developmental initiatives have they undertaken with success? What is the strategy for the future?[19]

A serious challenge faced by public theology in Africa is addressing the vacuum of visionary socio-economic and political leadership. Africa needs leaders who can formulate viable and sustainable economic policies. It may be that we should discourage some of the best and brightest minds from taking church positions, and instead encourage them to study business and economics. If we cannot find such leaders, then mining and processing, natural conservation and technological investments will continue to be initiated, led, owned and controlled by people from outside the continent instead of being locally led, controlled and financed. Unless the issue of leadership is addressed

---

18. E. Chitando, "Equipped and Ready to Serve? Transforming Theology and Religious Studies in Africa," *Missionalia* 38, no. 2 (2010): 198.

19. Speckman, *A Biblical Vision*, xxi.

effectively, Africa's rich soils will continue to grow poverty instead of wealth for its people.[20]

However, in Africa the problem is not only weak leadership but also corrupt and greedy national leaders who have commodified national economic resources. Many African leaders have stolen and continue to steal vast amounts of money from their nations, hiding it in foreign banks and depriving their countries of the money needed for national development. They further impoverish their nations by incurring huge financial debts to overseas lenders, using the borrowed money for their self-gratification and failing to repay the loans. The result is that Africa's coming generations are burdened with huge debts before they are even born.

Kunhiyop points out that although the external exploitation of Africa by richer nations cannot be ignored,

> we must note that there is also the internal exploitation by the rich. . . . Government officials are more interested in enriching their families and their own tribal communities. Similarly, their own townsmen expect special privileges from their own sons and daughters. In most African countries what creates an immense barrier in successfully combating poverty is the fact that the ethnic and tribal factor takes precedence over national commitment.[21]

Corruption signals the moral rottenness of leaders, and it often coexists with dictators who undemocratically hold onto power. But corruption is also a sign of the inability of governments to enforce justice and uphold the law. There are also greedy, warmongering elements who disturb the peace in many African regions, causing a serious lack of development even in mineral-rich countries such as the Democratic Republic of Congo. National leaders have demonstrated poor leadership by failing to effectively contain and deal with these groups.

Poor and corrupt national leadership triggers mass migration as people seek refuge in stable countries. Migration breaks families apart and can promote intergenerational poverty as children grow and develop without parental nurturing and supervision, which can negatively affect their social and academic progress and ultimately kill their economic power. In addition to promoting poverty by promoting cheap labour, migration creates serious tensions in host countries between migrants and locals, as evidenced by the xenophobic outbreaks in South Africa. Poor and corrupt national leadership has far-reaching economic consequences.

---

20. Chitando, "Equipped and Ready to Serve?," 199.
21. Kunhiyop, *Poverty*, 18.

Poverty and gender imbalance

Poverty is a gendered issue in that those most affected are women and children. This is a result of the unequal power relations between men and women in contemporary African society. Furthermore, "poor and marginalized women are severely discriminated against in macro-social and economic policies resulting in this group continuing to bear the brunt of poverty."[22] Social institutions such as the family, religion, culture and education are patriarchal in nature and discriminate against women. Even though many African countries have enacted laws that promote gender equality, the enforcement of these laws is often weak, and many women are either ignorant of the laws or lack the financial capacity and social support to legally enforce their rights.

The traditional tendency is that when resources are limited, girls are side-lined while boys are sent to school. Thus girls are more likely to drop out of school and enter into early marriages with older men. The default mode of patriarchal societies is also to favour men, which means that men have a higher chance of being employed than women. Public theology therefore needs to challenge gender imbalances in order to dislodge poverty.

Religious world views on economic issues

Theological ideas have a powerful influence on people's approach to economic life, for these ideas determine "people's relationships and attitudes to material things and how they should be used."[23] Religion plays an important role in economic sense-making. This role can be positive when religion creates economic opportunities, but it can also be negative, for religion can be a cause of poverty, or at least it can cripple people's meaningful engagement with economic issues. For instance, in African Traditional Religions, wealth is sometimes viewed as a product of religiosity, good luck and powerful magic rather than of hard work. Therefore, poverty or a lack of economic success is blamed on witchcraft, bad luck or angry ancestors and not on the quality of one's work, one's diligence or the nature of the investment undertaken. Consequently, some people are less diligent and careful with their economic activities but are extra diligent with religious rituals and activities that are believed to enhance their fortunes. Furthermore, some people give up pursuing their economic

---

22. B. Haddad, "Theologising Development: A Gendered Analysis of Poverty, Survival and Faith," *Journal of Theology for Southern Africa* 10 (2001): 6.

23. A. Moyo, "Material Things in African Society: Implication for Christian Ethics," in *Moral and Ethical Issues in African Christianity: A Challenge for African Christianity*, eds. Jesse N. K. Mugambi and A. Nasimiyu-Wasike (Nairobi: Acton, 1999), 50.

dreams for fear that jealous relatives and neighbours will bewitch them. It is common to hear stories of people blaming their poverty and economic failures on witchcraft, family curses and angry ancestors.

The proliferation of religious practitioners within both Christianity and African Traditional Religions promising miraculous solutions to people's poverty shows that this fundamental world view has not changed and continues to affect economic life.

Ironically, despite its leading role in education and vocational training, Christianity is also responsible for poverty in Africa. This effect comes from the two main Christian world views on wealth in Africa. The traditional Christian view regards riches with suspicion, as things of this world to be avoided in the present because they will be enjoyed in future in heaven. This tendency to separate spiritual and material things can end up seeing poverty as something good, or at least as something to be tolerated. By contrast, the neo-Pentecostal world view regards poverty as a curse and riches as a sign that one is blessed or approved by God. Poverty and riches are seen as reflecting a person's spiritual condition, which results in people being preoccupied with attaining a spiritual condition that will bring material success. Moreover when riches are seen as a sign of faith and spirituality, compassion for the poor is easily replaced by despising them as people without faith who therefore deserve their poverty. This neo-Pentecostal link between faith and wealth is similar to the African traditional view of the poor as cursed or lacking good luck.

Public theology must critically engage with the theological beliefs that promote poverty in traditional Christianity and the theological beliefs that undermine the value of work in neo-Pentecostalism. Public theology must pay serious attention to religious world views on economic reality because "poverty thrives on unhelpful convictions, distorted perceptions and ideological (theological) justifications."[24]

A consumer culture

The consumer culture is a serious cause of poverty in modern Africa. Many people spend more than they earn and are heavily in debt. In South Africa, for example, the mass media are filled with advertisements for new technology, vehicles, furniture and clothes at seemingly affordable monthly payments which make it attractive to enter into debt. There are also many companies

---

24. K. Nürnberger, "The Task of the Church Concerning the Economy in a Post-Apartheid South Africa," *Missionalia* 22, no. 2 (1994): 131.

that offer easy credit. The returns on savings and investments are not nearly as attractive as the lure of easy money. For example, getting a R2,000 loan with very minimum requirements is far more exciting than putting money in a savings account that will only earn 3 percent interest per annum. The materialistically oriented modern world encourages people to consume more than they invest in creating wealth.

Sin

We should not discount the relationship between poverty and sin or someone's spiritual condition. Even though there are many Christians who are poor and non-Christians who are rich, in *some* cases there is a correlation between spiritual salvation and material poverty, so addressing material poverty must start by addressing the person's spiritual condition. For example, people who are impoverished by addiction or a superstitious world view may need to experience spiritual relief and gain a new perspective that frees them to pursue an economically viable life.

Liberation from the power of sin or the power of fear can boost a person's economic well-being. A relationship with God that makes a poor person aware that they are created in God's image and are loved and valued by God may prompt that person to shun drunkenness, gluttony and laziness (Prov 23:21) and to live a productive life that expresses the full extent of his or her identity with Christ and being indwelt by the Holy Spirit.

A right view of God and a right relationship with God can lead to right views about one's self, other people and material things in ways that empower poor people to meaningfully engage their material poverty. Therefore in Christian theology, human poverty is both a spiritual and material issue, which means that human poverty cannot be adequately addressed without addressing the attendant spiritual issues.

Dislodging Poverty in Africa

How can public theology play a role in dislodging poverty in Africa?

- *By exercising a critical prophetic role that promotes life.* Public theology needs to be a prophetic eye and voice in society that promotes God's life-affirming shalom. It must be on the alert for and speak out against socio-economic injustices that hinder the poor and powerless from experiencing God's abundant life. It must do so in the full awareness that religion can be used either to promote poverty or to work for its eradication. Africa has seen many uses of religion, including Christianity, to suppress, disempower and impoverish the poor. Christian public theology can avoid being a tool of death by maintaining a critical prophetic voice stimulated by God's hatred of injustice, his preference for the poor and marginalized, and his desire to give abundant life to his people. To speak authoritatively and usefully, public theologians must have a sound knowledge of God's word and also of socio-economic and political reality. This implies that theological training should also aim to develop a sound grasp of socio-economic and political issues.

- *By defining poverty in a manner that enables the church to engage it.* Public theology must define poverty in a way that enables the church to constructively engage it. Poverty must not be defined abstractly, making it difficult to clearly understand what poverty is and who the poor are. Simplistic and abstract definitions must be replaced by clear and practical definitions. If poverty is defined as a lack of ability to participate in economic life, a primary response to poverty must include liberating, empowering and enabling the poor to be participants in economic life. There is need to recognize that the poor are human beings bearing the full image of God who need to be challenged, equipped and empowered to live out their being in the image of God.

- *By adopting a holistic, multidisciplinary approach.* Related to the above point, public theology must adopt a holistic, multidisciplinary approach to development. It needs to make clear that it is not just people's hunger or homelessness that needs to be dealt with but all the aspects on which poverty thrives including sin, lack of a spiritual relationship with God, flawed relationships with other people, gender issues, poor knowledge of economics, lack of skills and education, ecological issues, and lack of knowledge about diseases and investments and savings. A multidisciplinary approach means that the task of addressing poverty cannot be left to pastors and theologians alone because they do not possess all the needed knowledge and skills. A multidisciplinary approach is a collaborative and consultative effort that can only thrive if the church works as a body. Technical experts must be incorporated, and the priesthood of all believers must be honoured in addressing poverty.

- *By being informed by sound eschatological hope.* Ultimately, public theology must engage poverty from an eschatologically informed perspective. Poverty must be engaged in the light of God's promise of a glorious future in heaven. As Moltmann affirms, hope of the kingdom of God "calls people out of their apathy and pessimism to active participation in the movements for liberation."[25] Engagement with poverty that is informed by sound eschatology will not pursue a utopia in this present world and will avoid promoting materialism. It will also realize that, while goodness and justice must be pursued, in this fallen world they may not be achieved. But whatever is not achieved in this world, God will perfect in his coming glorious kingdom.

Conclusion

This chapter has outlined a public theological understanding of poverty that can lead towards finding multidisciplinary approaches to engaging with poverty in Africa. As public theologians, we are challenged to play a prophetic role, defining poverty in a way that enables the church to engage with it, adopting a holistic multidisciplinary approach, and engaging with poverty in light of God's promised eschatological hope. Public theology must challenge the status quo to enable the redemption of the poor from poverty.

Questions

1. What is the theological and biblical basis for fighting poverty?
2. How can theology distinguish between realities and myths about the root causes of poverty in Africa in a way that leads to meaningful solutions?
3. What should public theology do to address the problem of poor and corrupt national economic leadership?
4. How can theological and pastoral training enable socio-economic and political literacy that leads to meaningful responses to poverty in Africa?
5. Given that governments and other funders are addressing poverty by investing more on science, technology, engineering and mathematics (STEM) than in humanities, what role can theology play?

Further Reading

Bedford-Strohm, H. "Poverty and Public Theology: Advocacy of the Church in Pluralistic Society." *International Journal of Public Theology* 2, no. 2 (2008): 144–162.

---

25. J. Moltmann, *Ethics of Hope* (Minneapolis: Fortress, 2012), 36.

Kakwata, F. N. "Strategies for Dealing with Sin in Relation to Poverty." *Stellenbosch Theological Journal* 2, no. 2 (2016): 273–294, http://www.scielo.org.za/scielo.php?script=sci_arttext&pid=S2413-94672016000200015.

Myers, B. L. *Walking with the Poor: Principles and Practices of Transformational Development*. Maryknoll, NY: Orbis, 1999.

Speckman, M. T. *A Biblical Vision for Africa's Development?* Pietermaritzburg, South Africa: Cluster, 2007.

Speelman, W. M. "The Franciscan *Usus Pauper*: Using Poverty to Put Life in the Perspective of Plenitude." *Palgrave Communications* 4, no. 1 (2018), https://www.nature.com/articles/s41599-018-0134-4.

Tangonyire, R. C., and L. K. Achal. *Economic Behaviour as If Others Too Had Interests*. Bamenda: Langaa RPCIG, 2012.

10

Rural Community Development

Olo Ndukwe

Urbanization is proceeding rapidly in Africa, but we should not forget the many Africans who still live in rural contexts. To give you an idea of their circumstances, let me describe one not-untypical village in Nigeria. It has a population of fewer than a thousand adults who farm and fish. There is no access road, no health facilities, no electricity, no access to potable water and only a primary school. The inhabitants of this village are among the poorest of the poor.

Their poverty is not only a matter of a lack of material goods or even of physical health, though many of them are malnourished and suffer from chronic diseases. A deep-rooted ideological poverty shapes their entire worldview, that is, the way they think, act and understand the world. They have limited access to information, services, labour organizations and opinion-leaders and policy makers, and they see themselves as weak, isolated, powerless, voiceless and oppressed, with no hope of bettering their circumstances. They have very low self-esteem.

With no hope of education, young women give birth to two or more children before they leave their teens. Some of them are unmarried and live with their parents, while others have been forced into marriage to men who are old enough to be their fathers. Meanwhile the ambitions of the illiterate and unemployed young men often centre on getting regular supplies of marijuana or other drugs and on the number of children they can father. Peasant farmers celebrate acquisition of several illiterate and dependent wives and concubines as a sign of progress in life. In such a climate, there is little respect for human dignity, and immorality of all kinds flourishes. Those who seek employment or a meaningful education face daunting challenges.

Such communities exist in close proximity to many of our rural theological colleges, and it is from these villages that many of our students come. I know this by experience, for I serve in the Hugh Goldie Lay/Theological Training Institution Arochukwu (HGLTTIA) in Abia State in south eastern Nigeria. HGLTTIA is the foremost theological training institution of the Presbyterian Church of Nigeria (PCN) and trains ministers, evangelists and laypersons for the PCN and other churches. Our students come from different denominations, from various ethnic groups and from the various social strata of Nigeria. They are resolute that the Lord has called them into the ministry, but many of them are drawn from the poorest of the poor and are reliant on others to help them achieve their dreams.

Given this context both within and outside the institution, it is not surprising that HGLTTIA is very much concerned with and committed to practical involvement in public theology and community development as indispensable aspects of its visionary theological enterprises.[1] It is doing everything in its power to strive for academic excellence and to send students into the larger society where they can use their higher thinking skills and creativity to serve the church, their communities, their country and the kingdom of God.

Teaching Public Theology in a Context of Poverty

Traditional methods of teaching theology tend to be one-dimensional in that they focus on conveying information and developing analytical reasoning skills. Theological students are assumed to spend their time studying texts about God, the church and so forth. But there is now a shift away from the type of theology that simply analyses what the church believes to an approach that stresses that theology is something to be done, not just something to be learned. In this approach, God is seen as a missional God and as the creator and redeemer of the earth, the one who calls his people to take part in what he is doing. This shift has "profound effect on the church's view of its own mission and, as such, on development."[2]

---

1. "About Hugh Goldie," Hugh Goldie Lay/Theological Training Institution Arochukwu (HGLTTIA), https://www.hughgoldie.edu.ng/. Accessed September 2019.

2. Jurgens Hendriks, "A Change of Heart: Missional Theology and Social Development," in *Religion and Social Development in Post-Apartheid South Africa*, eds. Ignatius Swart, Hermann Rocher, Sulina Green and Johannes Erasmus (Stellenbosch: Sun Media, 2010), 278–279.

At HGLTTIA we became convinced that we had to see our role not just as teaching theology but as practising theology if we were to participate in the mission of God who lives and works in community, who loves all he has created, and who has given us a responsibility to care for his creation and all who inhabit it. We could no longer see our role as limited to preparing people to serve in the church. Rather, we began to see the church as

> the community that exists for others . . . [and] must share in the secular problems of ordinary human life, not dominating but helping and serving. . . . Ministry includes both the church's proclamation of the gospel and the church's efforts to foster reconciliation in societies . . . prompting prophetic action on behalf of justice and freedom, and sustaining believers in their solidarity with the poor and their struggle against the powers of evil and injustice.[3]

We accordingly set out to develop an approach to public theology that constitutes a transformational-developmental Christian witness whose goal is the *shalom* (holistic peace and prosperity) of society. Our goal is to produce church leaders and a church that can be described as a reliable partner-in-progress with the government, NGOs, and civil society as well as a facilitator, enabler and catalyst of nation/community building, social transformation and development in order to alleviate the pain of the poor and other victims of society who suffer because of stereotypes or whose human dignity is not respected. This approach has four key features, namely advocacy, conscientization, a process of confession and summoning to action, and community development.

Advocacy

Advocacy is a political process in which an individual or group attempts to influence public policy and resource allocation decisions in a particular context. Advocacy may be motivated by moral, ethical or faith-based principles, or simply by a desire to protect an asset or interest. Among those who follow Jesus, advocacy should never be self-serving or self-promoting. Christ's self-emptying life, death, resurrection and ascension should constantly remind us that we must not be seeking our own good but the good of others, and that

---

3. Daniel L. Migliore, *Faith Seeking Understanding: An Introduction to Christian Theology* (Grand Rapids: Eerdmans, 2004), 259.

we should be doing so in the context of a community of faith. We should be helping the church to be a voice for the voiceless.

Advocacy should be a central task of Christian theological enterprises in rural Africa where people lack a clear understanding about their rights as citizens. The few who do know their rights find it hard to speak up for them. Poverty often renders them voiceless and powerless. In such contexts, the church has to have a prophetic witness and must seek to be a voice for the voiceless, advocating on their behalf while simultaneously helping them take more responsibility and exercise more control over the decisions that affect their lives. Advocating for people may also involve helping them to acquire the skills they need to access available information. Thereafter they may need guidance on how to use the appropriate media to influence others, especially government officials and the general public, in order to affect particular policy decisions.

Conscientization

Conscientization involves arousing people's awareness of the power structures within a given environment and of how these structures fall short of what God desires for human beings and for his creation. "Conscientization refers to a type of learning which is focused on perceiving and exposing social and political contradictions . . . [and] taking action against oppressive elements in one's life as part of that learning."[4] The goal is to help end the culture of silence in which the socially dispossessed internalize negative images of themselves, images that are projected on them by those in power. However, conscientization is not only for the poor; it is also needed by the rich and powerful who need to learn to look at reality from the perspective of the poor.

The whole process of conscientization calls for spiritual renewal and conversion that confronts and identifies the outer expressions of inner corruption and self-centeredness and insists that the powers of corruption, of moral disintegration and of undisguised evil have to be overcome if our societies are to flourish.

Conscientization should have an impact on public opinion, that is, on the pattern of thinking of the whole society that governs people's attitudes and behaviour. The change in public opinion should, in turn, lead to reformation.

---

4. Medhat Fam, "Paulo Freire's Approach to Education," https://www.academia.edu/37432024/Paulo_Freires_approach_to_Education.

A process of confession and summoning to action

The increased awareness generated by conscientization and the drive to action that is part of advocacy come together in a process of confession and summoning to action (also known as a *processus confessionis*). This process involves a call to individuals and churches to engage in a committed process of recognition, education and confession regarding things like economic injustice and ecological destruction.

We tend to associate the term "confession" with confessing our own sin, but that is only part of the meaning. Here the term is used to refer to something more like "a confession of faith," that is, a general statement of some point of Christian teaching on which Christians are in agreement. In the context of public theology, we are speaking of an agreement that a certain state of affairs falls short of what God wants and that as Christians we are committed to setting things right.

By speaking of this as a "process," we are acknowledging that such agreement does not happen overnight. It involves a long process of conscientization and formal and informal education of believers until they all come to agreement on what is wrong – even if they may disagree on what steps should be taken to set things right.

This type of reflection and public confession is indispensable for Christian witness for it sounds a wake-up call to the church to live up to its identity and mission by dealing meaningfully with deep-rooted issues of immorality, juvenile delinquency, insecurity, consumerism and ideological poverty in rural communities. When Christians take this type of stand against human degradation, they are offering a practical demonstration of their concern for the well-being of their neighbours.

Community development

As those who follow Christ and have embarked on a process of confession, we should recognize that communities being trapped in poverty is not only an affront to God's love for all but also poses a spiritual problem for those in the community. Christ promises abundant life to those who follow him. We are wrong to assume that this promise applies only to abundant spiritual life and has no relevance to the day-to-day lives of poverty-stricken Christians. If the church does not address their desperate need, they will question the meaning of the "abundant life" which the church preaches and will lose their remaining shreds of self-respect. They will feel themselves to be failures even as Christians.

It follows that when we do and teach public theology in this type of context, we must also engage in community development, a process that involves taking charge of the conditions and factors influencing a community and working to change the quality of life and commitment of its members for the better. In community development, we work to empower the poor, celebrate their human dignity and help to create opportunities for them to participate meaningfully in delivering their communities from the deprivation trap in which they find themselves. This is not a case of coming in to deliver aid; it must involve a "bottom-up" process in which the people themselves are drawn in so that they take part in the process and become empowered.

In 1948 the United Nations defined community development as "a process designed to create conditions of economic and social progress for the whole community with its active participation and fullest possible reliance upon the community's initiative."[5] It can also be described as "a way of strengthening civil society by prioritising the actions of communities and their perspectives in the development of social, economic and environmental policies. It seeks the empowerment of local communities"[6] as they become committed to self-initiated development of their societies.

In some communities racked with ideological poverty, the community may not be ready to show initiative and actively participate in development and will need gentle encouragement and role modelling. But it is vitally "important to help the people to understand that they have the power within themselves to solve their own problems, that the experiences they have gone through and the processes which they have learned are tools in solving any problem that may confront them."[7]

When we do and teach public theology in such contexts, we must not lose sight of this need for facilitation and enablement so that Christians and the church can serve as catalysts in the development of rural communities. We should not focus solely on the mobilization of community resources and community organizations to get them involved in pre-planned projects. It is more important that we focus on issues of powerlessness, decision making and empowerment, paving the way for discussion of what the community actually

---

5. https://canadianglobalresponse.ca/portfolio/community-development/.

6. https://www.unisa.ac.za/static/corporate_web/Content/About/Service%20departments/DCCD/Documents/career_community_socialwork_unisa_2018.pdf.

7. Burkey (1993) quoted in epigraph to Francis Theron and Ntuthuko Mchunu, "The Development Change Agent: Contextualizing the Agency-Beneficiary Partnership," in *Development, Change and the Change Agent: Facilitation at Grassroots*, eds. Francois Theron and Ntuthuko Mchunu, 2nd ed. (Pretoria: Van Schaik, 2016), 1.

needs if it is to find relief and release from the deprivation trap. Those who work in community development will find themselves debating issues like centralization versus decentralization, scrutinizing the role of bureaucracy and of NGOs, and emphasizing social enterprise, empowerment and ownership in terms of control over community resources and sustainable development.[8]

Doing Public Theology in a Rural Context

It is not enough simply to teach public theology; we must also do it. This was borne in on us very strongly as we looked at the rural poverty around us and at the material and ideological poverty of our students. Our Christian witness and education demanded that we take action.

> Christians believe in a God who loves each person and who wants us to seek justice for all those near and far. Thus God's love and mercy are universal, present and accessible to all people in all cultures. Christians believe that we humans can see the universal love of God in creation, experience it in the sustaining grace of providence, know it in Jesus Christ and hope for its fulfilment in the coming Kingdom where all the peoples can bring their gifts and find final healing.[9]

Christians long to see the coming of God's kingdom in the public world of history, and doing public theology is a living witness to the goodness and loving kindness of the living Lord who became flesh for us and for our salvation. At HGLTTIA, we set about doing public theology in terms of the parameters discussed above. I will describe our actions not so much to provide a blueprint for others as to stimulate others to creative thinking about what can be done in their contexts.

Doing advocacy

Advocacy was clearly needed in our rural area of Nigeria where politicians only put in an appearance during election campaigns. The local people are well aware of this pattern, and during a recent election some of them drove the politicians away, calling them liars and thieves who come only to plead for

---

8. Hennie Swanepoel and Frik de Beer, *Community Development: Breaking the Cycle of Poverty*, 5th ed. (Cape Town, South Africa: Juta Academic, 2012), 36–40.

9. Max L. Stackhouse, "Reflections on How and Why We Go Public," *International Journal of Public Theology* 1 (2007): 426.

votes but abandon the people once they are in power. Advocates are needed to pressure local and state government representatives to pay real attention to the plight of rural people, who currently live with fear and uncertainty about how politicians will treat them. Christians need to take a lead in this process.

But it is not enough for outsiders to advocate on behalf of people; the people also need to learn to advocate for themselves. They need to be helped, as was said above, "to understand that they have the power within themselves to solve their own problems, that the experiences they have gone through and the processes which they have learned are tools in solving any problem that may confront them."[10]

However, the ideological poverty of these communities left them powerless to do so, and thus the management board of HGLTTIA appealed to Tearfund to partner with us in a process of church and community mobilization (CCM), which is described in detail later in this chapter.

A similar ideological poverty afflicted the theological students who came from these communities. They saw themselves as dependent on others to supply all they needed at the college. A corollary of this was that they had little concept of financial management and spent whatever money they received. They tended to see those who were sponsoring their studies at HGLTTIA as equivalent to money-making machines, and they accepted money from family members, friends, fellow church members and others and spent it without regard for those who had sacrificed on their behalf. Lured by consumerism, they felt free to indulge in consumer goods.

The college leadership felt that the students' inordinate consumerism was ungodly, for it was an abuse of the grace of God and of the kindness of God-fearing human beings. They also recognized inordinate consumerism and ideological poverty as being like two midwives who deliver, nurture and sustain corruption in the church and in the larger society.

Knowing the importance of advocacy and given our definition of it as a political process in which an individual or group attempts to influence public policy and resource allocation decisions in a particular context, the leadership set out to influence resource allocation decisions in the context of the college community. They wanted to advocate that recipients of God's grace should end the culture of wasting God's gifts, time, life and other resources.

Reviewing the advocacy tools at their disposal, the leaders decided that the best approach would be to teach about the problem of consumerism in classes on public theology and to preach against consumerism in sermons.

---

10. Theron and Mchunu, "The Development Change Agent," 1.

They would illustrate both lectures and sermons with stories that showed the evils of inordinate consumerism and its link to ideological poverty. Students would be urged to use the resources they had productively.

This sustained advocacy campaign was very effective. Students started to think more carefully about how they used their resources, and many became entrepreneurs rather than consumers. They learned that they could take action to meet their own needs, and some of them can now support themselves and even help friends, family members and their churches.

A side effect of this advocacy campaign has been a marked decline in student complaints that they have limited access to information, services, labour organizations, opinion-leaders and policy makers. They have learned how to acquire and maintain their own communication devices and are beginning to feel empowered to advocate for their communities.

Doing conscientization

Theological colleges have a responsibility to help their students, who are future leaders, to take their place as the salt of the earth and the light of the world. Thus HGLLTIA has not only modelled public opinion formation and reformation in our advocacy against consumerism, but we have also sought to raise awareness of other problems that had simply been taken for granted.

We found that our students' opinions were shaped less by their Christian beliefs than by their immediate situations, general social and environmental factors and their pre-existing knowledge, attitudes, and values, which were often deeply affected by their ideological poverty. Many of them only became aware that their values were less than Christian when their public theology courses brought these patterns to consciousness, and the students began to rethink their attitudes and values. A similar situation applied in the rural communities around us.

For instance, some of our students and many members of the community saw nothing wrong with teenage girls being forced into marriages with men old enough to be their fathers. They saw such marriages as the only alternative to the girls becoming single mothers of two or more children while still in their teens. They did not think that the girls should have more schooling. The girls, too, saw little point in schooling and (often tacitly) preferred to be with the peasant farmers and commercial motorcyclists who judged their own progress in life by their number of wives or concubines and their offspring. In other words, the thinking of most of the people in the village, and even of those who went from the village to the seminary, was not shaped by biblical values.

To address this issue in the college and community and to make people more aware of issues of sexual abuse, the college and Tearfund encouraged the formation of community action groups (CAGs). "The CAGs are made up of 10–15 people who come together to help individual survivors. Members might include community leaders, health workers, faith leaders, school teachers and trusted police staff. Tearfund and its partners can train such members on ways of supporting survivors and local services available."[11] The work of these CAG groups has brought awareness to the issue and has been a wake-up call to the college and to the church, preparing the way for a more general confession that certain behaviours are unbiblical and prompting the community to take action against them.

As regards consumerism, the public theology course encouraged students to reflect on their own attitudes to resources and consumption and made them aware of how the surrounding culture promotes similar attitudes. Their growing understanding helped to transform them from inordinate consumerists into wealth creators and job creators. As a result of this conscientization, the grudges and animosities that inordinate consumerists or dependents often hold against their "money-making-machines" is becoming history. This too signals spiritual growth within the community. The congregations pastored by conscientized graduates (and even students) attest to the difference their new attitudes make to the entire economy of their congregations.

Embarking on a process of confession and summoning to action

The college leadership made a point of embarking on a process of recognizing what is wrong about consumerism and ideological poverty for themselves (conscientization) and of educating students and others to bring them to recognize these as evils (advocacy and conscientization). The goal was to bring the whole college community to the point that they would all agree that consumerism is fundamentally incompatible with the Christian faith (confession) and take appropriate action to combat it (community development). Such a process can be followed in colleges and churches in regard to any part of the church's work against human degradation. These activities are a demonstration of Christian concern for the well-being of our neighbours.

---

11. "Community Action Groups," Tearfund learn (n.d.), https://learn.tearfund.org/en/resources/publications/footsteps/footsteps_101-110/footsteps_106/community_action_groups/.

This process of confession and summoning to action has proved indispensable in HGLTTIA's efforts to deal meaningfully with deep-rooted issues in the community. It has, for instance, revealed that Christian witness in the forms of formal and informal education against human degradation is a practical demonstration of Christians' concern for the well-being of the neighbour and a response to those who question the meaningfulness of teaching Christian theology and the purpose of the church.

Doing community development

Doing public theology in the context of a poverty-stricken rural community involves being committed to supporting active democratic life by building up, encouraging and promoting the self-confidence of disadvantaged and vulnerable people and allowing their voices to be heard. These activities should not be seen as alternatives to godly spiritualty, reflection and practice but as manifestations of godly spirituality. So our students are encouraged to help their church communities to "go public" with their concerns and to ensure that church members

> are actively committed in serving the Lord and at the same time seeking to rule their areas of daily endeavours with godly ethics, for the Lord and to his glory and excellence (2 Pet 1:4) through Christ-centred community groups, organizations and networks; and by providing opportunities for all persons irrespective of their creedal affiliations to develop to their fullest potentials through education, training and motivation while creating the enabling environment for everyone to become a God-fearing somebody in his/her community development.[12]

To help students encourage community development in their own congregations after graduation, HGLTTIA has modelled what such development may look like. Their approach grew from the recognition that most students relied on the sacrifice of family members and friends for their fees and upkeep in the institution. They were passive recipients of charity. There was almost no talk about how to invest any of the money in fund-generating ventures, nor about how to make use of the abundant natural resources in the environment of the college. Whatever money the students could get hold of was

---

12. Olo Ndukwe, "Doing Theology in a Knowledge Society Today: A Nigerian Christian Public Theological Reflection," *Science Journal of Sociology and Anthropology* (14 April 2017).

simply spent. Their focus was on consumerism and acquiring goods, not on generating income. This attitude reflected their ideological poverty, the value system they had internalized and the expectations of their communities and of the college. It did not stand them in good stead when they graduated and embraced the challenges of rural ministry. It was also an attitude that the college administrators found troubling, as it was out of line with the goals and ideals of the institution as it sought to help its graduates, students and staff to embrace and engage a normative integrated world view as meaningful spiritualty.

The management board accordingly set out to demonstrate to all that public theology is not reducible to a discipline or to mere talk but also involves action. Staff members were challenged to become facilitators, enablers and catalysts of community development by finding something that they could do or encourage students to do using the available resources.

This substantive approach to community development, influenced by Tearfund's CCM, has proved very successful. Students have learned practically how they can generate funds and contribute meaningfully to growing the economy of their congregations and communities when they leave the college. The fruit that has been born and is still being borne constitutes meaningful grounds for celebration.

How did we go about this? To start with, the management board of HGLTTIA decided not only to teach theology courses but also to offer courses in information technology (IT) and to teach skills like photography, baking and farming to staff and students. They also worked to secure a donation that enabled staff and students to acquire laptops at very subsidized prices. They encouraged people to use these laptops not only for their academic work but also for income generation, using their own creativity and the knowledge and skills they had acquired at HGLTTIA to serve the church, their communities and in the final instance the kingdom of God.

In an attempt to demonstrate the wise use of funds as an aspect of public theology as a lived, living and liveable historical reality, the management board used some of the funds generated from the sales of the laptops to purchase desktop computers for HGLTTIA and lay the foundations for an IT building, which was completed in 2014 after we received a grant to complete the building and equip the centre.

Today, HGLTTIA can boast of staff members, graduates and students who are making their living with thriving ministries through the intellectual and material empowerment of the public theological vision of the institution. For instance, some staff and students have set up commercial business centres that type and bind students' theses, term papers, and the like. In addition, the Students' Union Government (SUG) now has a functional commercial business centre, which is also generating money for the Union. There is no longer a scarcity of photographers or videographers on campus or among our graduates. A Christian home video album and a Christian musical video album are now serving the Nigerian public, courtesy of the "Goldie Theatre" and the "Goldie Kids."

Other students and staff members took up farming, and today farm products such as Goldie Bee Honey are being sold to the school community and the larger community. Others turned to merchandising. Today, they take great pride in the Goldie Bookshop which imports and distributes good books as well as works produced under copyrights which the institution secures from oversea publishers. The SUG has set out to encourage an initiative to produce good quality ladies handbags as well as ladies and gents slippers. All of these projects have, as said before, benefitted the students by empowering them so that they no longer see themselves as paupers dependent on handouts and are even able to give to others.

The management board of HGLTTIA also recognizes its responsibility to do public theology in the surrounding impoverished communities. It has thus set out to work with Tearfund to use its approach to church and community mobilization (CCM) in our south eastern Nigerian rural context. The management board has also recently agreed to partner with Arochukwu Presbytery to appoint a pastor trained by HGLTTIA in a church in the rural community. The goal is to help the community grow in self-reliance, self-respect and self-esteem; make wise use of their God-given resources; and engage in self-development without rejecting useful external collaboration. Through the CCM process the villagers will also start to learn how to hold their corrupt leaders accountable for their evil practices.

This approach fits well with the understanding of public theology as something that strives to draw from a godly ethos to strengthen the capacity of human beings with a view to transforming them into citizens who are concretely committed to any God-centred effort to increase human knowledge and enhance human skills and productivity. The projects also show how public theology seeks to stimulate the innovativeness, creativity and resourcefulness of those with godly ethics in order to transform their communities into places that more closely reflect the revealed will of God and advance his kingdom.

Church and Community Mobilization (CCM)

The approach to church and community mobilization developed by Tearfund does not offer a "quick fix" for impoverished communities. Instead, it involves a five-step process that may take longer than some other approaches but produces far deeper change.[13]

- *Church awakening* involves motivating the church to understand its role and relationship to the immediate community. Bible study in small groups helps to stir the church into beginning to engage with the community and steer it towards actions that will help it to deal meaningfully with its poverty. The church thus starts to influence the life of the community by acting as salt and light in the community.

- *Church and community description* helps the church and the community to embark on a process of self-discovery as regards their spiritual, physical, economic and social lives and to begin to determine the strategies needed to effect transformation.

- *Information gathering* is a process that enables the church and community to gather detailed information on the issues they face and the available opportunities for addressing them.

- *Information analysis* helps the church and community to gain a true and full picture of their problems in order to inspire them to take action from an informed position.

- *Decision making* is the state at which the church and community determine the best options for change, design the most appropriate actions and take the necessary actions to move towards the better future they have envisioned.

Conclusion

In this chapter, I have been talking about practising public theology in a rural context. However, the principles laid out here can be used in any local context. Public theology presents a visionary approach to and focus on Christ-centred community development and sustenance which embodies a set of core theological values and social principles including respect for human dignity,

---

13. For more detailed information, see "Church and Community Mobilisation in Africa," Tearfund, https://learn.tearfund.org/~/media/files/tilz/churches/ccm/2017-tearfund-ccm-in-africa-en.pdf; and "Mobilizing Churches and Communities," Tearfund learn, https://learn.tearfund.org/en/themes/church_and_community/mobilising_churches_and_communities/.

human rights, social inclusion and respect for diversity, as well as specific skills and a knowledge base rooted in reflection on and pursuit of godliness. In short, public theology is about being committed to actions that help people recognize and develop their ability and potential with a view to organizing themselves to respond to problems and needs of common interest with a concrete Christ-centred ethos.

Let me conclude by quoting Daniel L. Migliore's description of the diaconal model of the church:

> The church is a servant community that is called to minister in God's name on behalf of the fullness of life for all of God's creatures.
>
> According to this model the church serves God by serving the world in its struggle for emancipation, justice, and peace. Dietrich Bonhoeffer defined the church as the community that exists for others. "The church," he wrote, "must share in the secular problems of ordinary human life, not dominating but helping and serving." This model of a church for others, a church that is servant rather than the master of the world . . . plays an important role both in the emphasis on the church's mission of reconciliation in the midst of conflict and in the call to the church to participate in the struggle for the liberation of the oppressed.[14]

Questions

1. What are the obviously wrong and unbiblical issues in your community that are never mentioned or spoken about?
2. How will you go about being an advocate and raising consciousness about these specific issues?
3. What specific steps can you take to develop the community in which you serve?
4. What will the process of confessing and summoning to action mean in your community today?
5. If we accept the argument that poverty is rooted in broken relationships with God, self, others and creation, what should leaders do to enable human flourishing on the African continent?

---

14. Migliore, *Faith Seeking Understanding*, 259.

Further Reading

Hendriks, H. J. *Studying Congregations in Africa.* Wellington: Lux Verbi, 2004.

Myers, Bryant L. *Walking with the Poor: Principles and Practices of Transformational Development.* Maryknoll, NY: Orbis, 2011.

Ndukwe, Olo. "Consumerism: The Backbone of Ideological Poverty in Nigeria." *Science Journal of Economics* (21 January 2013). https://www.sjpub.org/sje/sje-164.pdf.

Njoroge, Francis, Tulo Raistrick, Bill Crooks, and Jackie Mouradian. *Umoja: Facilitator's Guide.* Teddington, UK: Tearfund, 2009. https://learn.tearfund.org/~/media/files/tilz/churches/umoja/umoja_facilitators_guide_-_jan2012.pdf?la=en.

Swanepoel, Hennie, and Frik De Beer. *Community Development: Breaking the Cycle of Poverty,* 6th ed. Cape Town, South Africa: Juta, 2016.

Tearfund. *Mobilising Churches and Communities,* n.d. https://learn.tearfund.org/en/themes/church_and_community/mobilising_churches_and_communities/.

11

Education

Samuel Peni Ango and Ester Rutoro

Nelson Mandela said, "education is the most powerful weapon which you can use to change the world."[1] This is true universally, but especially so in Africa which has the world's highest birth rate with the result that more than 60 percent of the population is under the age of 25. The demand for schooling is high, and most African parents say that they value education and want their children to receive a good education. But the realities on the ground are dire. So before we can look at what public theology has to say about education, we need to understand what the problems are and why Africa's levels of education are so low.

The State of Education in Africa

Many countries in sub-Saharan Africa are failing to provide students with a high-quality education that can equip them to meet the demands of the ever-changing global, social, economic and technological environment. Without such an education, it will be difficult for Africa to meet the goals of *Agenda 2063*. A number of factors contribute to this situation.

Many children are not in school

The sight of children walking to school in the morning is a familiar one across Africa, but there are many children who do not join in that walk. Africa as a

---

1. Nelson Mandela in a speech given at Madison Park High School in Boston, 23 June 1990.

continent has the world's highest rate of children who are out of school, or in other words, not enrolled in school. UNESCO offers the following statistics for Africa:

> Over one-fifth of children between the ages of about 6 and 11 are out of school, followed by one-third of youth between the ages of about 12 and 14. According to UIS data, almost 60% of youth between the ages of about 15 and 17 are not in school.
>
> Without urgent action, the situation will likely get worse as the region faces a rising demand for education due to a still-growing school-age population.[2]

Many children who are in school are receiving a substandard education

UNESCO reports that "in Sub-Saharan Africa less than 7 percent of students in late primary school are proficient in reading," while only 14 percent are proficient in mathematics. These results have dire implications for their future job prospects.[3]

The following data highlight these findings:

1.   There are twelve countries in Africa – namely Malawi, Zambia, Ivory Coast, Ghana, Benin, Nigeria, Chad, Ethiopia, Congo, South Africa, Namibia and the Comoro Islands – in which 30 percent or more of children do not meet a minimum standard of learning by grades four or five.

2.   In countries such as Ethiopia, Nigeria and Zambia, over half of in-school students are not learning basic skills by the end of primary school.

3.   A global competitiveness report released by the World Economic Forum ranks South Africa last out of 140 countries in the quality of education offered.

4.   The fact that only 53 percent of year 12 students who sat for math exams in 2014 achieved above 30 percent, and only 35 percent

---

2. "Education in Africa," UNESCO (n.d.), http://uis.unesco.org/en/topic/education-africa.

3. Mariama Sow, "Figures of the Week: Africa, Education, and the 2018 World Development Report," Brookings: Africa in Focus (6 October 2017).

achieved above 40 percent. . . . 25 percent of South African schools do not even offer mathematics in grades 10 to 12.[4]

School infrastructure is often inadequate

The reasons the students are learning so little in school are often related to the poor physical conditions in the majority of schools and the low levels of investment in education. Leaders do not see these issues as a priority because their children can attend elite private schools where conditions are much better. In poorer schools, classes may be very large and the classrooms inadequate, and there is often an acute shortage of appropriate teaching and learning materials. These conditions are sometimes exacerbated by economic and political instability, corruption and environmental disasters which affect both the material aspects of schools and the mental health of the learners. It is difficult to learn when one is hungry, or scared of being abducted, or has spent the night hiding in the bush to avoid attacks. Political disturbances in politically volatile environments mean that schooling may be interrupted for long periods of time, and many students never return after a protracted absence.

Most teachers are undermotivated

There are many good and committed teachers in Africa. But there are others who have become demoralized by the poor conditions in which they work, and others who see teaching purely as a source of income and lack any commitment to their students, and may in fact abuse them. Economic challenges mean that most teachers have had to struggle to get a good education, and their teacher training has left them ill equipped to adopt new approaches towards effective teaching or to use new educational technologies, assuming such are even available in their schools.[5] African researchers have identified a lack of spiritually formed Christian teachers, poor teacher training, poor welfare for teachers, frequent strikes, cultism (gang violence) and corruption as leading to falling standards of education.[6]

4. Jagriti Misra, "10 Facts about Africa's Education Crisis," The Borgen Project (8 July 2017).

5. G. Bethell, *Mathematics Education in Sub-Saharan Africa: Status, Challenges and Opportunities* (Washington: World Bank, 2016).

6. See Y. Adebisi and I. Ononye, "Untold Stories of Suffering in Government Boarding Schools," *Saturday Independent* (20 October 2018): 18–19; F. W. Nguru, "Development of Christian Higher Education in Kenya: An Overview," in *Christian Higher Education: A Global*

The Need for New Perspectives

Irresponsible development and poor leadership have resulted in Africa facing crises on all fronts – social, cultural, economic, environmental and political. We now have to deal not only with regional political and economic conditions but also with the global effects of climate change, pollution and environmental degradation. Meanwhile cultural changes have resulted in increasing drug abuse, violence and destruction of societies.

The rapid social, political and economic changes that have transformed the structure of our societies have profound implications for our education systems. These implications go both ways, for the relationship between education and society is bidirectional. On the one hand, social changes inevitably affect our education systems; on the other hand, our education systems inevitably affect our society. Education shapes students who then shape the world beyond the classroom.[7] If we are to get the type of repositioning and transformation that Africa needs to reach the goals of *Agenda 2063*, we need a kind of education that focuses on building character and solving problems.

For too long, Africa and other developing countries have relied on what Paulo Freire calls the "banking system of education," where learners' minds are seen as empty vessels into which the instructors pour knowledge.[8] Learners are simply passive recipients of other people's ideas. What is needed is a problem-solving system of education in which learners take an active role and teachers facilitate learning rather than being the source of all learning.

The United Nations has recognized that we cannot continue to educate the way we did in the past, so goal 4 of its 2030 Agenda for Sustainable Development is to "ensure inclusive and equitable quality education and promote lifelong learning opportunities for all."[9] This statement of the goal is followed by a list of sub-goals, including the following:

Reconnaissance, eds. J. Carpenter, P. L. Glanzer, and N. S. Lantinga (Grand Rapids: Eerdmans, 2014); and A. Babalola, "The Dwindling Standards of Education in Nigeria: The Way Forward," First distinguished lecture series, Lead City University, Ibadan, Nigeria, 2006.

7. H. A. Giroux and P. McLaren, "Teacher Education and the Politics of Engagement: The Case for Democratic Schooling," in *Breaking Free: The Transformative Power of Critical Pedagogy*, eds. P. Leistyna, A. Woodrum, and S. A. Sherbton, 301–331 (Cambridge: Harvard Educational Review, 1996).

8. Paulo Freire, *Education for Critical Consciousness* (1967; New York: Bloomsbury Academic, 2013), 126.

9. United Nations, "Transforming Our World: The 2030 Agenda for Sustainable Development," Sustainable Development Goals Knowledge Platform, 21.

4.1 By 2030, ensure that all girls and boys complete free, equitable and quality primary and secondary education leading to relevant and effective learning outcomes. . . .

4.4 By 2030, substantially increase the number of youths and adults who have relevant skills including technical and vocational skills, for employment, decent jobs and entrepreneurship. . . .

4.7 By 2030, ensure that all learners acquire the knowledge and skills needed to promote sustainable development, including, among others, through education for sustainable development and sustainable lifestyles, human rights, gender equality, promotion of a culture of peace and non-violence, global citizenship and appreciation of cultural diversity and of culture's contribution to sustainable development.[10]

When reading these goals, it is important to remember that education is not just about imparting knowledge of certain facts or skills in basic literacy and numeracy. Education also affects students' social, attitudinal, emotional and psychological make-up and shapes their world view. It is instrumental in building character and training in conduct that leads to successful lives. Successful lives are even more likely if learning involves more than just doing what the teacher says and involves the students in thinking for themselves and discovering how to come up with innovative ways to solve problems.

Thus one of the primary aims of any education system should be to nurture thinking skills in order to help individuals realize their full potential.[11] Those students who develop these skills will be able to adopt an analytical and evaluative attitude towards their own performance and the performance of the society around them.[12] It is thus imperative that educators adopt teaching methods designed to encourage students' critical thinking skills including their problem-solving skills, research skills, skills in creativity and innovation and questioning and reasoning skills.

We need to offer our students an education that is carefully planned and implemented in ways that serve the economic and social objectives of Africa and advance the common good – which is a key principle of public theology.

---

10. United Nations, "Transforming Our World," 21.

11. M. Karakoc, "The Significance of Critical Thinking Ability in Terms of Education," *International Journal of Humanities and Social Sciences* 6, no. 7 (July 2016): 81–84.

12. L. Silva Almeida and A. H. Rodrigues Franco, "Critical Thinking: Its Relevance for Education in a Shifting Society," *Revista de Psicologia* 29, no. 1 (2011): 178–195.

As Christians, we would also say that the ultimate goal of education is to nurture the minds and hearts of students for meaningful service to all of God's creation.[13] God has given these students abilities, and we should not allow them to go to waste!

Given the importance of faith in Africa, a faith-based perspective should guide the development of an African education system. Such an education system will value not only sustainable development and the development of critical skills but will also nurture honesty, integrity and a God-fearing spirit. All of these are important if we are to protect God's creation for present and future generations and achieve the goals of *Agenda 2063*.

A Warning

We must be careful not to worship education or assume that if we put more effort into education, it will automatically deliver positive results. This becomes all too clear if we examine some African education systems that look good on paper but for a variety of reasons have not resulted in the envisioned socio-economic and moral transformation. Take the case of Zimbabwe, a country that has made great strides in achieving high levels of literacy. At independence in 1980, the Zimbabwean government was one of the most proactive in Africa in putting education at the centre of its national agenda. It set about abolishing all colour and gender barriers in the provision of education by a) establishing a system of free and compulsory primary and secondary education; b) abolishing sex discrimination in the education system; and c) identifying education as a basic human right and striving to ensure that every child had an opportunity to develop his or her mental, physical and emotional faculties.[14]

As a result of these policies, Zimbabwe attained one of the highest levels of literacy on the African continent, with a literacy rate of over 92 percent.[15] However, the focus on education did not produce the anticipated social and economic growth and transformation. Corruption and the effect of politics on the economy have meant that despite its high levels of literacy, Zimbabwe is going through one of its worst periods economically. Those graduating from

---

13. E. Gabriel, C. Woolford-Hunt, and E. M. Hooley, "Creating a Christ-Centred Climate for Educational Excellence: Philosophical, Instructional, Relational, Assessment and Counselling Dimensions," *Catalyst* 23, no. 2 (2016).

14. R. Zvobgo, *The Post-Colonial State and Educational Reform in Zimbabwe, Zambia and Botswana* (Harare: Zimbabwe Publishing, 1996).

15. Southern African Development Community (SADC), Zimbabwe Country Report, SDC Secretariat, 2018, 410.

the education system often lack the skills needed in the Zimbabwean economy, and there is a shortage of professionals because many university graduates left Zimbabwe as the economy declined.[16] The quality of education offered in Zimbabwe has also been affected by high teacher–pupil ratios, a lack of relevant resources, a shortage of textbooks and classrooms and instructional and assessment methodologies that do not instil critical skills in the learners.

Consequently people have resorted to all sorts of ways of making a living. Extensive trade in foreign currency on a parallel market has devastated the Zimbabwean economy and resulted in a shortage of cash, low levels of income, runaway inflation and prices for basic goods being beyond the reach of many people.

Zimbabwe's story shows that a government may achieve high levels of literacy but not achieve the expected benefit from an educated citizenry. The socio-economic conditions there have resulted in an educated citizenry resorting to using their skills in unethical ways. All this makes it clear that education on its own is not enough to fix Africa's problems, but without education, there will be no progress at all.

Biblical Perspective on Education

Recognition of the importance of education dates all the way back to prehistoric times, although naturally the education offered has taken different forms in different contexts and periods. The Bible has quite a lot to say about education, beginning with the instruction to Israelite parents to teach their children what God had taught them (Deut 11:18–19).

The book of Proverbs is particularly rich in references to education and learning because it is intended as a guide to living, one that holds to the principle, "Start children off on the way they should go, and even when they are old they will not turn from it" (Prov 22:6). In other words, education should start when children are young and should instil the right values while they are in formative stages of development. Proverbs also urges people to value education more highly than wealth:

> Choose my instruction instead of silver,
>   knowledge rather than choice gold,
> for wisdom is more precious than rubies,
>   and nothing you desire can compare with her. (Prov 8:10–11)

---

16. SADC, Zimbabwe Country Report, 416.

Those who make this choice will find that education when used wisely produces sound judgment that leads to prosperity and honour and a rich inheritance (Prov 8:17–21) – all things that are desperately needed in Africa.

The writer of the book of Ecclesiastes was also a man who valued education, for he says "I applied my mind to study and to explore by wisdom all that is done under the heavens" (Eccl 1:13). While much that he saw left him disillusioned, he still believed that an educated mind and wisdom are more important and more long-lasting than wealth: "For wisdom is protection *just* as money is protection, But the advantage of knowledge is that wisdom preserves the lives of its possessors" (Eccl 7:12 NASB).

In exploring "all that is done under the heavens," the writer of Ecclesiastes would also have researched the science of his day. Mathematics, science and technology are areas that are often neglected in African schools. But they are part of God's creation that students need to learn about, and Christians urgently need to develop expertise in these areas.[17]

Finally, we should not forget that teachers carry a heavy responsibility. James was speaking to the church when he wrote, "Not many of you should become teachers, my fellow believers, because you know that we who teach will be judged more strictly" (Jas 3:1), but his words also serve as a warning to Christians entering the teaching profession. As teachers, they are role models for their students and point the way to knowledge. They are responsible for giving all their students the right type of education in the correct way.

Teaching Methods

The type of teaching that will transform Africa includes inspiring students to live for greater purposes, combining academic and community-mindedness and engaging both the intellect and spirit of the students. Moreover, teachers should attend to the all-round needs of students – mental, spiritual and vocational – and focus more on learning than on just passing on information. Effective teachers know how to use students' preferred learning styles, help them learn by giving clear instructions and adopting a variety of methods, and

---

17. For more on this topic, see the chapter on science, as well as the chapters on economics, media studies and the environment. Christians must not just talk about these disciplines; some must become practitioners.

use questions to engage students.[18] But what sort of methods should they use to achieve this goal? Are some methods especially suited to Christian educators?

Contemporary methods

The Bible does not explicitly teach any one educational theory or methodology. This means that Christian teachers are free to study and use the diversity of teaching and learning methods developed by secular educators. Every useful educational approach must be engaged with and creatively adapted to each teacher's classroom. If teachers refuse to do this, they will continue to offer the type of education that has failed Africa and will not be preparing their students for life in Africa in the twenty-first century, with its new technological and social challenges.

African methods

Teachers in Africa do not have to use exactly the same methods as their counterparts in Western countries. Africa has had its own educational traditions, and teachers need to think creatively about how they can make use of these in contemporary schools. Are there any elements of the educational model followed in initiation schools that could be transformed and used in contemporary classrooms? Can traditional rites of passage and festivals be drawn on when looking for methods of teaching? What about teachers using African drama, song and dance, such as the Gule Wamkulu of Malawi or the Ozidi Saga of the Ijaw of Nigeria, to integrate African artistic expression into Christian teaching and learning? At the elementary school level, could students learn their multiplication tables better if they were taught using toyi-toyi chants and dance steps? How can African folklore, such as proverbs, folk tales, riddles and jokes, be used to enrich teaching and learning? We need African teachers who will draw on the richness of their heritage and their God-given creativity in the classroom, and we need African school principals and administrators who will not shut down the creativity of their teachers without careful consideration of the reasons why a teacher wants to adopt a different approach.

---

18. George Janvier, *A Vision for Teaching* (Bukuru: Africa Christian Textbooks, 2018), 175–177.

Christ's methods

As they consider both new and old approaches to teaching, teachers would also do well to consider the teaching style of Jesus Christ who was one of the greatest teachers ever known, as evidenced by the impact he had during his time on earth and down through the centuries.[19] Samuel Ango has suggested that "Christian educators ought to engage students in dialogue, reflection, critical thinking, and action . . . essential steps which Jesus took with Nicodemus an intellectual, Jesus' disciples who were ignorant fishermen, or the Samaritan woman."[20] Jesus answered their questions, asked them questions and engaged them in critical dialogue which often led to critical action.

Questioning

African teachers tend to answer questions from students directly, or to ridicule a student who asks what the teacher wrongly defines as "a stupid question." Jesus seldom responded like this. Rather, when people asked questions, he did not provide straight answers but threw the question back to the questioner, encouraging them to work out the answer for themselves. We see this in the way he responded to a question from an expert in the law:

> "Teacher," he asked, "what must I do to inherit eternal life?"
>
> "What is written in the Law?" he replied. "How do you read it?"
>
> He answered, "'Love the Lord your God with all your heart and with all your soul and with all your strength and with all your mind'; and 'Love your neighbour as yourself.'"
>
> "You have answered correctly," Jesus replied. "Do this and you will live." (Luke 10:25–28)

The learner was not fully satisfied with this answer, which affirmed what he already knew. So he asked another question, "And who is my neighbour?" (Luke 10:29). Once again, Jesus did not answer the question directly. Instead he told the parable of the good Samaritan, and then asked his questioner to respond

---

19. T. Mumuni, "Critical Pedagogy in the Eyes of Jesus Christ's Teachings: A Historical Study," *International Journal of Development and Sustainability* 7, no. 1 (2018): 340–354. See also L. Fønnebø, "A Grounded-Theory Study of the Teaching Methods of Jesus: An Emergent Instructional Mode" (PhD Dissertation 369, 2011), Digital Commons @ Andrews University Dissertations.

20. Samuel P. Ango, "Educating for Justice and Righteousness in Nigerian Society: Applying Freire's Pedagogy of the Oppressed," *International Journal of Christianity and Education* 22, no. 2 (2018): 108.

to what he had heard: "Which of these three do you think was a neighbour to the man who fell into the hands of robbers?" (Luke 10:36).

Jesus was using a questioning technique to get those around him to think for themselves. When the man answered Jesus's question saying, "The one who had mercy on him," he was also answering his own question. All that Jesus had to add was, "Go and do likewise" (Luke 10:37).

Questioning is the cornerstone of training in critical thinking because it requires the learner to move beyond memorizing facts supplied by the teacher. By asking questions, the learner is challenged to analyse what is actually going on beneath the surface and develops the ability to assess situations independently.[21]

Problem solving

The use of questions leads naturally to the use of problem-solving methods as learners are challenged to find their own solutions to particular problems. This challenge is not set merely by telling a student to "solve it yourself." Rather, the teacher must ask the right questions and supply the right examples so that students gradually learn how to think for themselves and become able to ask the right questions, identify problems, define the problems and design appropriate interventions to solve the problems on their own.

Jesus used problem solving when teaching his disciples and other people who followed him. For example, when he saw a large crowd approaching, he turned to a disciple and asked him, "Where shall we buy bread for these people to eat?" (John 6:5). Similarly, when the Pharisees dragged a woman caught in adultery before him, Jesus set out to make the Pharisees reflect critically on their own practice and solve the problem they had set for him for themselves. So instead of answering their question about what should be done to her, all he said was, "Let any one of you who is without sin be the first to throw a stone at her" (John 8:7).

Jesus put his questioners in a situation where they had to use their own thinking skills to decide what the right course of action was for each of them as individuals. This is the type of situation that evokes problem-based learning. Such learning can be used in all areas of the curriculum and is characterized by asking thought-provoking questions that stimulate critical thinking. It equips learners with the ability to find innovative ways of dealing with daily challenges and more complex issues.

---

21. Karakoc, "The Significance of Critical Thinking."

Research-based learning

As the problems students are asked to solve become more difficult, they will be forced to start engaging in research, which can be done by individuals or by groups of students working together. Ideally, research-based learning will help students develop intellectual curiosity and persistence, as well as skills in teamwork.[22]

You may ask what evidence of research-based learning there is in the Bible. In response, we can point to the description of the Messiah as one who "will not judge by what he sees with his eyes or decide by what he hears with his ears" (Isa 11:3). This implies that the Messiah looks beyond surface issues and investigates more deeply before making a judgment – which is exactly what researchers are called to do.

Similarly, when Jesus asked his disciples, "Who do people say I am?" (Mark 8:27), he was conducting an opinion survey in order to get the disciples to reflect on which opinion was closest to the truth. This is how research-based learning helps to develop critical thinking skills.

Encouraging students to explore their environment, identify problems, investigate the problems, come up with possible solutions and implement the solutions leads to high levels of student engagement in the process of education and equips them with skills they can use for the rest of their lives for their own benefit and the benefit of their communities. In this approach, learners are not passive recipients of knowledge handed down from above but are actively and collaboratively involved in constructing and communicating knowledge.

The African Christian Leadership Study provides a good example of research-based learning in Africa. Theological students in three countries in Africa were involved in researching who people identified as strong, positive leaders and were then asked to conduct structured interviews with those leaders to identify the key ingredients for successful Christian leadership in Africa. The results of this research project have been published and widely distributed.[23]

Conclusion

The education offered on the African continent should be able to impart lifelong skills that empower citizens to be creators of wealth who can create

---

22. H. Dekker and S. W. Wolff, "Re-Inventing Research-based Teaching and Learning." Paper presented at the European Forum for Enhanced Collaboration in Teaching, Brussels, 5 December 2016.

23. Robert J. Priest and Kirimi Barine, eds., *African Christian Leadership: Realities, Opportunities, and Impact* (Carlisle: Langham Global Library, 2019). For more information about the study, go to https://www.africaleadershipstudy.org.

sustainable societies. They should no longer simply rely on others to offer them employment but should be entrepreneurs, creating employment for others. At the same time, their education should inculcate the moral principles, integrity and respect for human rights that will empower them to stand up to corruption and abuses and build the Africa envisaged in *Agenda 2063*.

Questions

1. Research which of the reasons for the failure of education in Africa exist in your community. What actions can your church or you as an individual or as a teacher take to address one or more of these issues?
2. Listen to the education being given in your church or in a school in your community. Can you identify examples of the use of questioning, problem-solving and research-based learning? Can you suggest ways in which these techniques could be used to promote better learning in your community?
3. Can the education system and the church work together to provide ongoing education to people in your community who have moved out of the school system? Is such education needed?
4. What are the existing African models of education in your community that can be adapted for use in schools and churches?

Further Reading

Ango, Samuel Peni. "Educating for Justice and Righteousness in Nigerian Society: Applying Freire's Pedagogy of the Oppressed," *International Journal of Christianity and Education* 22, no. 2 (2018): 99–111.

"Education in Africa." UNESCO Sustainable Development Goals. http://uis.unesco.org/en/topic/education-africa.

Freire, Paulo. *Teachers as Cultural Workers.* Boulder, CO: Westview, 2005.

Karakoc, M. "The Significance of Critical Thinking Ability in Term of Education." *International Journal of Humanities and Social Sciences* 6, no. 7 (July 2016): 81–84.

Laal, M. "Lifelong Learning: What Does It Mean?" *Procedia: Social and Behavioural Sciences* 28 (2011): 470–474. https://core.ac.uk/download/pdf/82367162.pdf.

Mumuni, T. "Critical Pedagogy in the Eyes of Jesus Christ's Teachings: A Historical Study." *International Journal of Development and Sustainability* 7, no. 1 (2018): 340–354. https://isdsnet.com/ijds-v7n1-23.pdf.

United Nations. "Transforming Our World: The 2030 Agenda for Sustainable Development." Sustainable Development Goals Knowledge Platform. https://sustainabledevelopment.un.org/post2015/transformingourworld/publication.

12

The Environment

Ernst Conradie

A cross the African continent, environmental concerns threaten the livelihood of rural communities and urban populations alike, as well as having a major impact on plant and animal life. Such issues are widely covered in the news and intuitively recognized everywhere. A list of ten of these issues would include loss of biodiversity, climate change, deforestation, desertification, overfishing, pollution of water supplies (due to mining, oil, etc.), rapid population growth, soil erosion, municipal waste management and escalating water shortages. Each of these issues needs to be understood in terms of the history of colonialism, globalization, industrialization and urbanization.[1] Readers may want to add to this list or give priority to some more than others given particular local contexts.

Such environmental problems clearly require both prophetic and pastoral reflection within Christian communities. They influence the lives of people on a daily basis, for they affect the conditions in which people live and work, the food they eat, the water they drink, the air they breathe. They shape our relationship with the land, with one another, with animals, with what is visible and what is invisible. Environmental problems shape conflicts between people over land, water and scarce resources and the movements of people. Environmental issues therefore require attention in the public sphere and, accordingly, are on the agenda of public theology.

---

1. For discussion of these issues in the South African context, see Klaus Nürnberger, *Prosperity, Poverty and Pollution: Managing the Approaching Crisis* (Pietermaritzburg: Cluster, 1999).

This much should be clear. However, when we reflect on "public theology and the environment" we should think carefully about what we mean by each of those words. Each of them is open to misunderstanding. So let us investigate these concepts more closely.

Environment

The word "environment" literally means one's surroundings, what one finds all around oneself. The environment includes plants and animals, soil, water, mountains, rivers and clouds and other people, as well as buildings, furniture, cars, cell phones, paper, advertisements, plastics and waste. So it is helpful to distinguish between the biophysical environment, the social environment, the economic environment (resources) and the political environment. These dimensions are interrelated in multiple ways. Land (biophysical environment) is regarded as a resource for growing food (economic environment) that sustains communities (social environment), but growing food can also degrade the soil (biophysical environment). Conflict over land and water requires mediation (political environment) and influences families (social environment). Conflict can lead to further destruction of land (biophysical environment).

The word "environment" is often used as a rough synonym for ecology, land, world, earth, nature or creation. This is understandable, but it may be helpful to distinguish between these terms:

- *As indicated above, the "environment" refers to one's surroundings.* It is helpful to bring issues close to where one lives and works. However, the word may become rather self-centred so that tension can emerge between my environment and your environment. I might not want something in my backyard but may not be overly concerned about your environment or global issues that seem far away. Environment is also an anthropocentric term – centring around human beings and their needs – so that animals are treated as merely part of our environment and not as co-creatures that are also made by God.

- *"Ecology" is best used with reference to the functioning of ecosystems* and the multiple ways in which organisms interact with each other and with inorganic elements (water, air minerals, energy). From an ecological perspective, we human beings rely heavily on other forms of life. We cannot do without them, but they can do without us and might even do much better without us.

- *"Nature" is a slippery concept because it can refer to the biophysical environment*, but then often excludes human beings – ignoring the obvious fact that human beings form part of nature. We are one form of life alongside many others. We are mammals to be more precise, even if we may be quite special.

- *"Land" can be used in an anthropocentric way to refer to "my" land or the land of a people.* However, indigenous African knowledge maintains that we belong to the land more than it belongs to us. We inherit the land from our ancestors and borrow it from future generations. Indeed, the land belongs to God, not to us in the first place.

- *"Creation" is a religious term that confesses that the whole earth belongs to God as its creator.* Creation indicates that the world is not an autonomous entity but that its origin, life and destiny are in the hands of its creator.

The word "environment" is often used in two contrasting ways, referred to as the "green agenda" and the "brown agenda." The green agenda is associated with nature conservation and addresses issues such as the preservation of wilderness areas, endangered species, animal poaching, cruelty to animals, invader species and, in general, the impact of mining and industry, industrialized agriculture and urban sprawl on the habitats of plants and animals. The brown agenda is associated with the impact of ecological degradation on people. Examples include the plight of workers on farms, in mines and in factories and the living conditions of people in informal settlements (squatter camps) in cities. In fact, many of the problems experienced by the urban poor such as sanitation, access to drinking water, housing conditions, air pollution, health concerns, scarcity of firewood, overcrowding and so forth are environmental issues, even if not framed in that way. The brown agenda is typically focused on issues of justice and domination on the basis of race, class, gender and age. In general, the poor, women, children, the elderly and the disabled are victims of environmental injustices.

People supporting the green agenda are often accused of being more concerned about plants and animals than about their fellow human beings. People supporting the brown agenda are often accused of being anthropocentric, that is, thinking that the whole world exists to serve human beings and their needs. There have been attempts to integrate the green agenda and the brown agenda because they clearly cannot be completely separated. South African theologian Steve de Gruchy proposed an "olive agenda" to show how concerns about the land and its people are intertwined.[2] Nevertheless, the distinction is helpful to understand conflicting perceptions over environmental issues.

Another way of framing the debate concerns whether problems are caused by overpopulation or overconsumption. People in the highly industrialized countries of the global North are often concerned about population growth and associated environmental issues such as deforestation, endangered species, soil erosion and squalor. They point the finger at India, Brazil and Africa. By contrast, many in the global South suggest that overconsumption is the primary problem. They point the finger at the luxurious lifestyles of the majority in the global North and affluent minorities in the global South and the associated environmental problems such as industrial pollution, toxic waste dumping and especially climate change. Although both overpopulation and overconsumption clearly contribute to environmental destruction, their relative weight remains disputed. Christian communities in Africa may be right to criticize the environmental impact of affluence, but they should then be wary of seeking to copy such lifestyles tacitly or explicitly.

A final comment on the environment is important here. It may be true that environmental problems are not necessarily very high on political, social or church agendas. Many would say that economic growth to address poverty and inequality, job creation to address unemployment, education and training to address inequality, health care to address diseases like HIV/AIDS and malaria, safety to address crime and corruption or peace to address violent conflicts should receive top priority. However, each of these problems has an environmental dimension. Take the migration of people as an example. Migration may be caused by political conflict, but such conflict is often over scarce resources including land, water and oil. Moreover, climate change already has an impact on food security that will become worse in decades to come. It is best to regard the biophysical environment as "transversal," that is, as being a dimension of everything else, in the same way that religion, culture, language, gender, health, politics and the economy are a dimension of everything else. One may say that although everything is political, politics is not everything.

---

2. Steve de Gruchy, *Keeping Body and Soul Together: Reflections by Steve de Gruchy on Theology and Development*, ed. Beverley Haddad (Pietermaritzburg: Cluster, 2015).

Public

The environment is of public concern. It is not merely a private matter, as if what I do with the environment around me has no impact on others. In public theology a distinction is usually made between three publics, namely the church as the primary public from which Christian theology emerges and to which it is accountable (e.g. in terms of ministerial training); the academy where theological truth claims have to be discussed in relation to other disciplines; and then society as the place the impact and significance of Christianity becomes evident – for the better hopefully, but often also for the worse given the track record of Christianity and its contested ties to colonialism.

The church

Environmental issues are being addressed in the church in multiple ways. There is a widespread movement around eco-congregations that recognize that congregations are situated in a particular environment and have an impact on that environment. Consider the role of buildings, land, church graveyards, the use of electricity and other forms of energy, paper, transport and so forth. There is an obvious need for responsible stewardship here.

The liturgy may be regarded as a way of seeing the world around us from God's perspective. Not surprisingly, the environmental dimensions of each aspect of the liturgy have been explored. A movement started by the Ecumenical Patriarch of Constantinople and supported by the pope and the World Council of Churches seeks to introduce a Season of Creation as part of the liturgical year.

Pastoral care also has an environmental dimension. It does not help to be concerned about a person's medical, psychological and spiritual health if that person lives in a toxic environment. Such situations call for prophetic witness. Indeed, there are pastoral (priestly), prophetic and royal (stewardship) aspects of the churches' environmental responsibility.

The academy

Discourse on ecotheology has been thriving in the academy since the 1970s in all the major geographical contexts around the world, typically in different ways, depending on particular concerns. An increasing number of African theses and publications focus on the environment. All the traditional subdisciplines of Christian theology have become involved, including biblical exegesis, church history, doctrine, ethics, practical theology and its many subsidiary disciplines and missiology.

In the academy expressions of ecotheology enter into conversation with many other disciplines that go beyond the traditional conversation partners such as the biblical languages, history, philosophy, sociology and psychology. There is now also a need to engage with the so-called natural sciences, economic and management sciences, health sciences and so forth.

Society

Society may be subdivided into the different spheres of politics, state administration, business and industry, law, education (of which the academy forms part), media, sport and civil society (of which churches form part). Environmental concerns need to be explored in all these spheres of society. However, the role of Christianity in the public sphere is highly contested. In fact, Christianity itself stands publicly accused as one of the root causes of the environmental crisis. This accusation was first made in a famous essay by the American historian Lynn White titled "The Historical Roots of our Ecologic Crisis" published in 1967.[3] White argued that "Christianity is the most anthropocentric religion the world has seen" and that it "bears a huge burden of guilt" for environmental degradation.

This critique has often been repeated in secular discourse. There are many who accept the validity of the argument intuitively, especially since those Western countries where Christianity has traditionally been dominant are the countries typically accused of causing environmental degradation. It is not necessary to debate the validity of this thesis here. It does not apply to the African continent in the same way, but it cannot be avoided because of the ties between Christian mission and colonialism. The impact of Christianity on environmental destruction is widely discussed in all forms of Christian theology, including postcolonial/decolonial theologies.

"And"?

"Public theology and the environment" sounds like a set pair such as church and society, theology and religion, text and context, gospel and culture, creation and salvation or God and world. But these pairings obscure two related problems.

---

3. Lynn White, "The Historical Roots of our Ecologic Crisis," *Science* 155 (1967): 1203–1207.

The first is that if one tries to represent the pair with circles or blocks, the "and" seems to suggest that these are two separate entities that stand in relation (or tension?) with each other. But the reality is that one of these can also be included within the other, or vice versa. For example, is it not better to speak of the church as one organization *in* civil society, alongside others, that seeks to contribute to the wellbeing of society? But would that not reduce the church to less than it is, namely a sign of God's coming reign? To domesticate the church in this way may lead to the inverse problem, namely that society becomes embedded in the church so that the church comes to accept apartheid, ethnic identities or a consumerist culture. Likewise one may argue, as some do, that God is not separate from the world but that the world lives, moves and has its being *within* God. Or is the Christian message better understood that God in Jesus Christ came to dwell *among* us and through the Spirit lives *within* us, so God's dwelling place is the earth, as it is in heaven?

Following this line of thinking, one may suggest that public theology does not exist alongside the biophysical environment but is embedded within it. If humans as God's creatures form part of nature, then whatever humans do, including their culture and their (public) theology, forms part of nature too. It is precisely when we start thinking of theology as something separate from the environment that it can become ecologically destructive.

Things may be different as regards some other ethical themes addressed in public theology such as poverty, HIV/AIDS, gender or violent conflict. But even here it may be better to say that "the church has AIDS" than to speak of "the church and AIDS," as if AIDS is somehow separate from the church. Likewise, one may speak of the "church of the poor" instead of the church and poverty. Whether this language is theologically appropriate remains open for discussion.

A related set of problems is best understood with reference to ecumenical discourse on what is termed "ecclesiology and ethics." The early ecumenical movement focused on six main themes, namely, church unity, mission, "faith and order," "life and work," worship and theological education. These streams converged in the establishment of the World Council of Churches, but they retained their own identity. "Ecclesiology and ethics" is shorthand for the tensions that emerged between discourse on "faith and order" and on "life and work." The former focused on issues of doctrine and church order that divide churches all over the world. The latter focused on the witness of Christians in society wherever they live and work.

Ecclesiology and ethics are obviously related to each other. What the church is cannot be separated from what the church does. However, it is quite possible to emphasize the one more than the other. If "ecclesiology" is emphasized, then the church becomes centred on itself, its authenticity, doctrines, leadership, rituals, finances and so forth, and it can easily become irrelevant to the world around it. If "ethics" is emphasized, the church seeks to be relevant to society by addressing all the problems in society, including environmental problems. However, the church can then easily be reduced to just another organization in civil society.

In Africa the church undoubtedly plays a very significant role in civil society. It is very large, has millions of followers who meet regularly, and has strong leadership that is generally trusted by local people and a code of conduct shaped by the church's sacred texts. The danger is that the church can lose its distinctiveness if it begins to do what all other organizations do, trying to copy them. The gospel is then watered down for the sake of societal influence. Ecclesiology and ethics then stand in tension with each other. The "and" hides such tensions. One may say that at the local level, issues of "ecclesiology" are often dominant, while issues of "ethics" are emphasized at large ecumenical gatherings of church leaders.

These distinctions are relevant when talking about public theology "and" the environment. When addressing environmental issues such as deforestation, environmental justice (e.g. related to toxic pollution) or climate change, churches often merely repeat what is said in secular discourse. Perhaps they add some religious flavour to it, but there is little that is distinctive about the churches' role in this regard. But this does not mean that we should dismiss the church's contribution. It is sometimes necessary to stand up for justice and peace alongside others, including people of other living faiths. Doing so is already a form of witness. However, the question remains whether the church can contribute something distinctive to addressing such problems. If churches can do something that no other organizations can do but fails to do so, that would be a form of sloth. Often this failure boils down to not taking their own message seriously, not believing that the gospel can make a difference in healing the wounds of the world, including environmental destruction. In this way God's work of creation is separated from God's work of salvation – the first and the second articles of the Christian creed – with the danger of both becoming irrelevant. This is a huge challenge: environmental problems such as climate change are so overwhelming and so hard to address that it seems arrogant to suggest that an old message, the gospel of salvation in Jesus Christ through the work of the Holy Spirit, can make a difference.

Theology: Five Inadequate Approaches

There is no one approach to ecotheology. Globally and within the African context, ecotheology is characterized by a conflicting plurality of positions and approaches. It may not be possible to prescribe only one legitimate approach, but it is important to recognize some inadequate theological trends. A booklet published by the South African Council of Churches identifies five such trends.[4] Each contains an element of truth, but when this truth becomes isolated from other aspects of the Christian faith and disconnected from the context of Christian witness, the resulting form of Christianity becomes radically distorted.

- *Mastery theology*: This theology is typically based on the divine command in Genesis 1:28 to "subdue the earth" and to "rule over it." It also builds on Psalm 8, which portrays human beings as the "crown of creation" (v. 5). Accordingly, this theology suggests that God has created the entire universe for the sake of human beings. We may therefore use natural resources for our benefit as we deem appropriate. Sometimes such a mastery theology is softened into a theology of dominion or stewardship in order to emphasize our human responsibility to use such resources wisely and frugally. However, immense power and authority is still attributed to human beings. There can be little doubt about the need to exercise responsibility, especially given the impact of human-induced climate change. Nevertheless, the way in which the place of humanity in God's own creation is understood is arrogant, makes little cosmological sense and is easily abused to endorse unsustainable practices.

- *Escapist theologies*: Many Christians resist the reduction of the Christian faith to the social agenda of the church and emphasize the spiritual more than the material, the soul more than the body, heaven more than earth and the life to come more than this life. This thinking can lead to a form of escapism where present realities are not addressed. The Christian message of redemption in Jesus Christ is understood as salvation *from* the earth and not as the hope for the salvation *of* the whole earth. The God who redeems us has little to do with the God who created the world. Yet Christian hope

---

4. South African Council of Churches, Climate Change Committee, *Climate Change: A Challenge to the Churches in South Africa* (Marshalltown: SACC, 2009).

provides inspiration for Christians to work for the coming of God's reign on earth as it is in heaven.

- *Inculturation theologies in the context of consumerism*: Christians are not called to avoid that which is worldly. They may embrace various expressions of culture. This is especially the case when African cultures are portrayed as inferior. In such a context, there is a need to affirm culture. However, Christians also need to be vigilant and guard against any easy identification of the gospel with a particular culture. When a church becomes a carbon copy of the consumer society in which we live, it loses the critical edge of the gospel in the context of climate change. It is extremely easy to adapt the gospel to fit a society geared to meet the needs, wants and desires of religious consumers. In doing so, we merely conform to the thought patterns of this age (Rom 12:2), an age of selfishness and greed.

- *Blaming theologies*: The Christian notions of sin and forgiveness of sins are sometimes criticized for being too general. Some say that we are all equally guilty, and the gospel of forgiveness is therefore proclaimed to all. But in saying this they fail to acknowledge or even comprehend the ways in which domination in the name of gender, race, class, education, sexual orientation and species is deeply embedded in our societies. They do not see that the victims of society tend to become psychologically numbed by decades of oppression and internalize the idea that they are "inferior" citizens. In response, other Christians have suggested a distinction between those who are sinners and those who are sinned against. Jesus of Nazareth called sinners to repentance but showed mercy to the victims of society. Yet even this approach includes an unhelpful tendency to view victims as purely innocent and to always attribute problems to forces from the outside that are beyond our control – for example, colonialism, imperialism, racism and apartheid – and never to accept responsibility for the ills of society. Moreover, all too often people are both victims and perpetrators, as in the case of gangsterism and marriage trouble. In the context of consumerism, we have to be aware of the ways in which our rampant desires have fuelled the economy and spiralled out of control. Although the consumer class have led the way in this regard, those who belong to the lower middle class also desire that which they do not have. When it comes to the love of money, it may well be true that those who have the least love it the most.

- *Prosperity theologies*: The prosperity gospel flourishes on an element of truth, but also systematically distorts that truth. The element of truth is gratitude for God's blessings – including very concrete, material blessings such as rain at the right time, bread on the table, protection on the roads, success with one's studies, deliverance in times of crisis and enough income to live on. Sometimes money is indeed the way in which God blesses people. For those trapped in poverty, refraining from behaviours like alcohol and drug abuse, visiting prostitutes, borrowing money and gambling, and at the same time engaging in honest hard work, spending money frugally and being committed to the needs of one's family may well lead to increasing material prosperity. Who would deny that this kind of prosperity is a concrete sign of God's blessings? However, the prosperity gospel may be misused to legitimize a sense of upward social mobility and even to encourage overt displays of affluence. In many cases the underlying assumption is that if you give your best to the Lord (via the coffers of the local congregation), you will receive rich blessings from God. Thus such blessings become signs of the authenticity of your faith (and of the pastor's leadership). If you do not receive such blessings, your faith is at fault. In such instances charismatic leadership often becomes abusive. That is when the prosperity gospel too easily gives a divine blessing to institutionalized selfishness and greed.

Theology: Five Better Approaches

In response to such inadequate theological trends, I have elsewhere identified five better theological approaches that are found in the African context and beyond.[5]

Responsible stewardship

The dominant approach among evangelical Christians emphasizes the need for responsible stewardship. It critiques mastery theology but retains the emphasis on responsibility. Often this approach is associated with nature conservation, but the emphasis may also be on virtues such as cultivating a love of nature, a frugal use of resources or wisdom in economic decision making.

The concept of stewardship has been especially attractive among Reformed and evangelical Christians, while notions of priestly service may also be found among Orthodox, Catholic and Anglican Christians. Human beings

---

5. This section draws extensively on Ernst M. Conradie, "Christianity and the Environment in (South) Africa: Four Dominant Approaches," in *Christian in Public: Aims, Methodologies and Issues in Public Theology*, ed. Len Hansen (Stellenbosch: SUN Press, 2007), 227–250.

are portrayed as occupying a unique position within ecosystems. They alone are created in the image of God; they are powerful but sometimes abusive managers of the land and are called to exercise their responsibility with wisdom and restraint. This call is supported through an exegesis of texts such as Genesis 1:27–28, Genesis 2:15 and Psalm 8. The ecological wisdom embedded in the Bible and the Christian faith is thus emphasized. The problem is not the nature of the divine command but a lack of human obedience to it.

This approach has considerable strengths. One of the core elements of the metaphor of stewardship is its emphasis on human responsibility. Another strength is related to the recognition that God often acts in the world in and through human agency. Nevertheless, in Christian ecotheology the metaphor of stewardship has been the subject of an ongoing controversy. It should be noted that this approach assumes a strong form of anthropocentrism, and that its rhetoric is aimed at those in positions of relative power and authority. It is sometimes difficult to escape the impression that this approach continues to operate within a colonial paradigm where the emphasis is on proper management on the basis of prior subjugation. The approach can therefore easily fall in the trap of mastery theology as sketched above.

Restoring land

A second approach places emphasis on restoring ancestral land. The focus here is on the living conditions of impoverished rural communities throughout Africa. Problems around deforestation, overgrazing, soil erosion, desertification and the depletion of water resources are addressed. The emphasis is on water harvesting, sustainable agriculture and tree planting projects – for firewood, building and fencing material, fruit supplies, animal fodder, medicinal purposes, restoring the water table and the symbolic value of planting hardwood species for coming generations. This work is done through a wide range of community development projects under local leadership, sometimes supported financially from external sources.

This approach may find expression in a somewhat romanticized longing for precolonial times and for rural communities that are unspoilt by the forces of Westernization, urbanization, industrialization and consumerist greed. The degradation of ancestral land is regarded as the result of colonial conquest, while the impact of sustained population growth tends to be underplayed.

Such an approach is typically supported through a retrieval of the ecological wisdom in traditional African culture and religion. In virtually all such contributions, the harmonious relationship of humanity and nature in pre-industrial cultures is praised and celebrated in songs and legends. There is a sense of wonder at the fecundity of life, the land and all the creatures that live from it, and the cycles of the seasons. There is an almost overwhelming emphasis on notions of interrelatedness, mutual dependence, reciprocity, ecological balance, wholeness, the integrated web of life and, especially, *community*. The world exists as an intricate balance of parts. Human beings must recognize and strive to maintain this cosmic balance. Everything from hunting to healing is a recognition and affirmation of the sacredness of life. Where the ecological balance and the ancestral world are disturbed, human communities and other creatures suffer.[6]

This approach is epitomized by a number of significant earthkeeping projects. Here theological reflection typically follows from an involvement in (Christian) earthkeeping. Such projects are typically rural, which begs the question why these projects have seldom been replicated in urban contexts in Africa. How can such projects come to terms with the pervasive influence of the forces of globalization, urbanization and consumerism within urban Africa? How can one resist new forms of colonialism without romanticizing and longing for precolonial times?

The strength of this approach is clearly its ability to draw on traditional ecological wisdom from within the African context. From a Christian theological perspective, one also has to address questions about the continuity and discontinuity between African Traditional Religion and culture and the message of Christianity. There is sometimes a tendency to deal with traditional ecological wisdom extensively and to add a final section on Christianity without much attempt to explore the differences between the two. Nevertheless, interesting examples of African reflections on forms of worship, the liturgy and the sacraments have emerged from within this approach.

Sustainable development

A third approach places emphasis on the need for sustainable development. This is the preferred approach of entrepreneurs, industry leaders and politicians

---

6. See especially Emmanuel Asante, "Ecology: Untapped Resource of Pan-vitalism in Africa," *AFER: African Ecclesial Review* 27 (1985): 289–293; Samson K. Gitau, *The Environmental Crisis: A Challenge for African Christians* (Nairobi: Acton, 2000); Gabriel Setiloane, "Towards a Biocentric Theology and Ethic – via Africa," *Journal of Black Theology* 9, no. 1 (1995): 52–66; and Harvey Sindima, "Community of Life," *Ecumenical Review* 41, no. 4 (1989): 537–551.

who are concerned about environmental degradation. They argue that given the increasing human population, higher consumption patterns and the prevalence of poverty in Africa, the only way forward is through economic growth, job creation and development. The problem of economic scarcity needs to be addressed through the more efficient extraction of resources.

This approach builds on a long legacy of development discourse captured in the proverb that it is better to teach people how to fish than to supply them with fish. The problem is the assumption that indigenous knowledge has been lost and must be retrieved through innovative education and training. Moreover, financial resources are required to obtain a fishing rod and other gear, and to make sure that these comply with international regulations. A permit may be needed to gain access to the fishing waters where there are other powerful players. Once all of this is in place, one may be confronted with the problem of overfishing: the fish which are caught become smaller and smaller.

Those who hold to this approach agree that the environmental impact of economic activities has to be acknowledged and overcome through better education and training, technological sophistication, available capital and more efficient management systems. In other words, development needs to become more sustainable.

The idea of *sustainable* development serves as an important corrective to expansionist notions of economic growth. However, this idea may sometimes amount to little more than an emphasis on economic growth, qualified by a few environmental cautions. It may simply be greenwashing global capitalism, a euphemism for "business as usual." When faced with a choice between development and a sustainable environment, the interests of developers and entrepreneurs – who can often provide short-term economic gain in terms of employment – regularly seem to receive priority.

Some regard the concept of sustainable development as a contradiction in terms: development assumes economic growth, (relying on an increasing use of natural resources) and since infinite economic growth is impossible on a finite planet, sustainable development is ultimately impossible. Several Christian critics have also argued that such "development" has failed to bridge the gap between the affluent in the centres of economic power and the impoverished on the economic periphery.

In response to such criticisms, it may be possible to redefine the notion of sustainable development. However, it is difficult to escape from the legacy of discourse on the notion of "development." As long as there remains confusion on the aims and methods of development, merely labelling something "sustainable" does not address the underlying problems.

Environmental justice

A fourth approach is more prophetic in nature and calls for environmental justice. This approach is typically aligned with liberation theology, black theology, feminist theology and postcolonial/decolonial theologies. It is a response to the impact of environmental degradation on people. There is concern over the working conditions in factories, mines, farms and offices. The living conditions of the urban poor are examined in terms of the health hazards of air pollution from nearby industries, vehicles or the burning of coal; toxic waste from nearby industries; unsafe drinking water; noise pollution from airports and highways; overcrowding, a localized form of overpopulation; a lack of basic infrastructure, sanitation and hygiene; a high incidence of contagious diseases; inadequate waste disposal; the visual ugliness of stinking and rotting garbage in many poor neighbourhoods; regular flooding or landslides; deforestation following the cutting of trees for firewood; and the struggle for political control over ever scarcer resources. The focus of this approach is on the victims of environmental degradation: the poor, women, children, the elderly, people of colour and refugees. Concern for the victims of environmental injustices at the micro-level is often coupled with a critique of the macroeconomic roots of environmental degradation. The root causes of environmental degradation are related to neo-liberal capitalism, the exploitative and wasteful consumption of natural resources and the excesses of consumer culture.

In general, the struggle for environmental justice seeks to challenge the abuse of power that results in poor people having to suffer the effects of environmental damage caused by the greed of others. "Environmental racism" refers to the ways in which people of colour typically suffer more under the impact of environmental degradation than others. Environmental degradation is therefore not a separate concern from poverty, deprivation and economic exploitation, but often a manifestation of these ills. It is important to seek to understand the interconnectedness of the different manifestations of violence whether political, military, industrial, domestic, gendered, racial, ethnic or structural.

Calls for environmental justice typically draw on core Christian themes and seek to express Christian convictions within the public sphere. Concepts such as liberation, healing, reconciliation and reconstruction may be used and applied to human communities and the larger community of life. But the dominant themes are economic and restorative justice, human rights, including environmental rights for humans, and the formation of a human rights culture.

The values promoted include ecological wholeness and interrelatedness, justice and reciprocity.[7]

Ecofeminism

A final approach, which is perhaps not as prominent as some of the others, is ecofeminism. It argues that the logic of patriarchal oppression is similar and structurally related to the abuse of ecosystems for human interests. Domination based on gender has been expanded to include domination based on species. Ecofeminists typically argue that such domination is legitimized through a system of what is called "inter-locking dualisms." This means that the binaries of female and male, nature and culture, animal and human, brain and mind, body and soul, matter and spirit, earth and heaven and so forth are linked to each other. In each case the latter is regarded as "higher" than the former. Women's bodies, especially black women's bodies, thus become a site of struggle where such domination plays itself out. The rape of women and the rape of the earth are closely linked.

Ecofeminists resist such binaries and explore embodiment as a key for valuing what is natural, material, bodily and earthly. They use rich symbols, myths and rituals, not least in relation to traditional African rain-making dances. Ecofeminists typically plead for an appreciation of relationality that is not based on domination but on mutual respect, mutual support and reciprocity.[8]

Current Fermentation

The variety of approaches to theological reflection on the environment has created a climate of ongoing fermentation. Community-based organizations, non-governmental organizations and faith-based organizations are in an ongoing quest for a new vision of a sustainable society. A variety of metaphors are being explored, including stewardship, indigenous ecological wisdom, sustainable development, environmental justice and embodiment. In

---

7. See for example Diakonia Council of Churches, *The Oikos Journey: A Theological Reflection on the Economic Crisis in South Africa* (Durban: Diakonia Council of Churches, 2006); Ecumenical Foundation of Southern Africa, *The Land Is Crying for Justice: A Discussion Document on Christianity and Environmental Justice in South Africa* (Stellenbosch: EFSA, 2002); also SACC, *Climate Change.*

8. For African forms of ecofeminism, see Mary N. Getui and E. A. Obeng, eds, *Theology of Reconstruction: Exploratory Essays* (Nairobi: Acton, 1999); Musimbi R. Kanyoro and N. J. Njoroge, eds., *Groaning in Faith: African Women in the Household of God* (Nairobi: Acton, 1996).

ecumenical discourse there is also widespread appreciation for the metaphor of the whole household of God. Here it is pertinent to note the distinction between house and home. If heaven is not our true home, then the earth may be our God-given house. However, given the many injustices, this house is not yet our home.

In African women's theology a further distinction is suggested between a house, a home and a hearth where cooking is done amidst much conversation and laughter. The metaphor of the household of God is perhaps best understood as a verb referring to house-making and housekeeping. This metaphor may be a way that African theology can contribute to wider ecumenical thinking on the environment. Such metaphors can also break down the binary opposition between the private and the public that still exists in public theology. The domestication of women's concerns needs to be resisted. Instead, the private may serve as a lens to understand matters of public concern.

Questions

1. What evidence of environmental degradation do you see in your community or in nearby communities? What options are there for addressing this degradation?
2. Are environmental organizations working in your community? If so, how can your church partner with them? What distinctive elements will you bring to this partnership?
3. Do you see any evidence of the inadequate ecotheologies identified in this chapter in your community? If so, what can you do to help people develop a more adequate ecotheology?

Further Reading

Ayre, Clive W., and Ernst M. Conradie, eds. *The Church in God's Household: Protestant Perspectives on Ecclesiology and Ecology*. Pietermaritzburg: Cluster, 2016.

Conradie, Ernst M. *Christianity and Earthkeeping: In Search of an Inspiring Vision*. Stellenbosch: SUN Press, 2011.

Conradie, Ernst M., David N. Field, et al. *A Rainbow over the Land: Equipping Christians to Be Earthkeepers*. Edited by Rachel Mash. Wellington: Bible Media, 2016.

Moyo, Fulata, and Martin Ott, eds. *Christianity and the Environment*. Blantyre: Christian Literature Association in Malawi, 2002.

Mugambi, Jesse N. K., and Mika Vähäkangas, eds. *Christian Theology and Environmental Responsibility*. Nairobi: Acton, 2001.

13

Science

Danie Veldsman[1]

We know that the whole creation has been groaning as in the pains
of childbirth right up to the present time.

Romans 8:22

Groaning for Africa – The Need to Act Now

In our conference rooms, lecture halls, government chambers, church gatherings, open air meetings, protest actions and many other communal spaces all over Africa, as well as in numerous publications ranging from official documents and research papers to leaflets and brochures, we hear and read the urgent cry that we in Africa need action now. This message is reinforced by *Agenda 2063*, which states: "Present generations are confident that the destiny of Africa is in their hands, and that they must act now to shape the future they want."[2] The document ends with the slogan: "Agenda 2063 is gaining momentum. . . . It is time for action: Be part of the transformation!"[3]

There are very good reasons for the emphasis on *now* and *action*. Most African countries are challenged by a vast spectrum of social, economic and ecological ills springing from the historical effects of colonization and from bad and corrupt governance, economic injustices, the almost unlimited

---

1. My understanding of public theology is somewhat different from the one used elsewhere in this book, in that I work from the position that all theological reflection should be public, that is, we as Christians and theologians need to interact openly with the world and be able to explain our reasoning when we make statements about what we know.

2. African Union, *Agenda 2063: The Africa We Want* (2015), https://au.int/sites/default/files/documents/36204-doc-agenda2063_popular_version_en.pdf, 1.

3. *Agenda 2063*, 22.

power of external transnational corporations and environmental destruction by deforestation, soil erosion, desertification, wetland degradation, insect infestation and the like.

The need for *action now* is also emphasized in the 2018 *Africa Sustainable Development Report* which highlights six themes: clean water and sanitation, affordable and clean energy, sustainable cities and communities, sustainable consumption and production, life on land and, finally, science, technology and innovation (STI).[4] The authors argue that "the development of science, technology and innovation (STI) is vital for the achievement of the SDGs [sustainable developmental goals] and *Agenda 2063*. However, a robust STI system requires a sound infrastructure and a vibrant innovation system that connects the science community and researchers to the private sector and government."[5] They thus urge African governments and NGOs to "strengthen the science, technology and innovation ecosystem and leverage investments in research and development by building institutions that coordinate government, the private sector and the science community."[6]

The same stress on strengthening the sciences is found in the call to action in *Agenda 2063*, which urges that we "catalyse education and skills revolution and actively promote science, technology, research and innovation, to build knowledge, human capital, capabilities and skills to drive innovations."[7]

Nor are only secular sources emphasizing the urgent need for action now. So does Pope Francis in his letter *Laudato si*, in which he urges Christians not to put faith and the sciences in opposition to each other but to give equal importance to both and to learn from the most advanced scientific insights as well as from the most ancient spiritual sources of wisdom in the Bible and church traditions.[8]

The United Nations, the African Union, and the pope have all spoken to the effect that urgent action is needed now and cannot be undertaken without the help of science and technology. Clearly it is important that we as African Christians heed their words.

In this chapter, we will pay particular attention to how we think and feel about the place and role of the sciences in shaping the future we want for

---

4. United Nations, *Africa Sustainable Development Report: Towards a Transformed and Resilient Continent*, United Nations Economic Commission for Africa (2018).

5. United Nations, *Africa Sustainable Development Report*, xvii.

6. United Nations, xix.

7. African Union, *Agenda 2063*, 14.

8. Pope Francis, *Encyclical Letter Laudato si of the Holy Father Francis on Care for Our Common Home* (Vatican City: Vatican Press, 2015).

Africa.[9] Is science merely a Eurocentric luxury that we can do without? Or may Africa's problems be the result of our lack of engagement with the sciences? Or are the sciences actually at the root of many of Africa's problems since they have affected traditional thinking and world views in ways that have resulted in societal displacement and disruption? Or does the problem rather lie with religious world views that have nurtured hostility towards the sciences?

These questions have to be addressed if we are to come to terms with the place and role of the sciences in working towards an Africa that we want to live in and the future we want for our children. Can engagement with the sciences contribute to remediating our deep conviction, rooted in experience, that all is not well?

Groaning with Africa – The Need for Discernment

Before we can clearly address the role of the sciences and technology in Africa, we need to consider a number of questions. If we ignore them, they will be used as arguments against us or will become stumbling blocks that will derail our motivation for action.

Are the sciences purely a racist product of the West?

In South Africa, students are demanding the "decolonization of science" using the slogan "science must fall."[10] They argue that science as a whole should be scrapped and started again in a way that accommodates non-Western perspectives and experiences. But they are wrong to assume that the scientific knowledge taught in our classrooms and pursued in our laboratories is solely a product of Western modernity. The historical roots of many scientific

---

9. Note that "the sciences" is shorthand for a vast range of fields of knowledge with very different methodologies. The natural sciences, for example, can be divided into the life sciences (or biological science) and physical science. Physical science is subdivided into branches such as physics, chemistry, astronomy and earth science. Within each of these disciplines are sub-disciplines with their own methods. The use of "science" to cover all of these fields is similar to the way we use the word "theology" to cover different religions and different traditions within one religion (e.g. Roman Catholic, Protestant, Charismatic and Pentecostal theology). Because the terms "theology" and "science" are so broad in their embrace, we need to be clear about the context in which and from which we use them. We all speak from somewhere for some reason to someone.

10. The slogan was inspired by Cape Town University students who used the slogan "Rhodes must fall" in their campaign against the legacy of the imperialist Cecil Rhodes. For more on "science must fall," see Rohan Deb Roy, "Science Must fall? Why It Still Needs to Be Decolonised," *The Citizen* (9 April 2018).

achievements in medicine, maths, engineering and astronomy are non-European. Algebra, for example, was developed in the Middle East, as its Arabic name indicates, and its ancient inventors Ctesibius and Hero were based in Alexandria in Egypt.

However, very often those who protest against science as a Western artefact are actually protesting not science as such but the misplaced arrogance of those scientists who claim that matter alone matters and that Western civilization with its scientific approach to the world is superior to all cultures that do not share that approach. Such scientists promote Western reasoning and look down on African reasoning.

A Presbyterian scholar from Malawi has noted the harmful effects of the West's cultural imperialism, propagated by schools and churches, as it introduced new ways of thinking and living to Africa:

> Nature was reduced to mathematics or transformed into quantitative physical phenomena which could be grasped by rationality. Nature was purely other and merely material to be subjugated and manipulated. It had only instrumental value, determined by the extent to which people could use it. With this vision of nature in place, the stage was set for the rise of materialistic philosophy and its attendant manner of life. This way of life has captivated much of Western civilization ever since and has been exported to all places this civilization has gone in its quest of material resources and to fulfil its expansionist philosophy.[11]

Sindima argues that the original, pre-Christian African concept of "bondedness, the interconnectedness, of all living beings" was based on a holistic worldview in which the spiritual and material realms were closely related, and he urges that it is time to return to this model.

> For some time the people of Africa have been influenced by a cosmology inherited from the West: the mechanistic perspective that views all things as lifeless commodities to be understood scientifically and to be used for human ends. Yet these people have an alternative way of looking at the world, an alternative cosmology, which can better serve their needs for cultural development and social justice in an ecologically responsible

---

11. Harvey Sindima, "Community of Life: Ecological Theology in African Perspective," in *Liberating Life: Contemporary Approaches in Ecological Theology*, eds. Charles Birch, William Eaken, and Jay B. McDaniel (Maryknoll, NY: Orbis, 1990), 137–138.

context. This alternative way might be called a life-centered way, since it stresses the bondedness, the interconnectedness, of all living beings.[12]

A related example of the harm done by Western modes of thought relates to ecology and comes from a West African theologian who grew up in Ghana.

> The village in the North of Ghana where I grew up was located close to a forest and a river. In the forest from ancient times onwards the ancestors lived, therefore it was sacred. In the river there lived the spirit of the water; therefore it was sacred as well. Then people of my village became Christians. Now there were no ancestors any more in the forest and also there were no spirits any more in the river. The taboos were disintegrating and disappearing. Instead the people started to make use and exploit both the forest and the water of the river for their own purposes. Today next to this village there is no forest left anymore and the river – it turned into a cesspool. Who has done a major mistake here? And for what reason?[13]

Both these examples show that imposing an "other and strange" way of thinking on a new context can destroy or harm the very fibre of a society and its connectedness to nature. If the sciences are to be taken seriously, this is surely not the way to go.

When we advocate for the sciences in Africa, we will have to do so with open eyes and hearts, seeing both the value of engaging with the sciences and the problematic implications and entrenched dangers of Western models of science and rationality that make unfounded claims to be universally valid. Such claims are based upon the objectification and scientific domestication of the natural environment – thus they tend to lead in practice to actions that do not respect the very context they wish to serve.

This awareness is vital to us as Christians and as Africans whose eyes and hearts have been opened to see and feel different realities and so can grasp the idea of different ways of understanding reality. These different understandings of reality are not merely theoretical abstractions; they are deeply intertwined with our daily lives and experiences, as well as our emotions.

---

12. Sindima, "Community of Life," 137.

13. Cited in an unpublished paper presented at a 2018 UNISA seminar by Cornel du Toit.

Is science in conflict with faith?

The relationship between the science and theology has been messy in many parts of the world. So it is important that we find constructive ways of engagement. Let us start by acknowledging that both parties involved – science and theology – have contributed vastly to the current emotional messiness between the two. Both have often, to use a football metaphor, played offside. By this I mean that they have made statements and claims in the past that could not be supported or that were outside their scope. Let me explain.

Theology was once known as "the queen of sciences," and some theologians assumed that the "royal" status of their discipline meant that the Scriptures reveal all there is to know about the physical world and about biology. But they erred in treating the Bible as a scientific handbook and in assuming that they could decide what could be regarded as (true) knowledge about everything and anything.

The Bible is not a scientific handbook. It is a library of books spanning a long historical period and various contexts. It contains books in many different literary genres – historical stories, wisdom sayings, psalms, parables, fables – each of which must be respected and read according to its literary genre and within its historical context. It is not for us to turn the texts into something we want them to be to match our convictions.

Moreover, as believers we have been entrusted with two books by which we can get to know more about God and his creation. These two books are Scripture and nature. God has given scientists the ability to "read pages" from the book of nature and tell us about the depth, width and height of God's fine-tuned and glorious handiwork. As believers we do not have a monopoly on knowledge of the physical and biological worlds. That we must leave to the scientists. However, we are not to leave them alone! It is our task to tell the world from the biblical passages that our God is the creator (though not how he created) and the redeemer. We are to share from Scripture in a responsible, interpretative manner how the purpose of all that exists is to be understood, what values should be respected and pursued, and how we should treat one another and the world, which is God's creation.[14]

Christians' tendency to interpret our world as if the Bible were a scientific handbook and we were the self-appointed judges of truth has contributed

---

14. The most celebrated paradigm relating scientific and theological reflection is probably the one presented by the American physicist-turned-theologian Ian Barbour in *Religion in an Age of Science* (New York: Harper Collins, 1990), namely, conflict, independence, dialogue and integration.

intensely to the emotional messiness that we are currently experiencing. However, scientists also play offside when they claim that their scientific activities allow them to make claims about the purpose (or purposelessness) of all that is, about values (or the non-existence of values), or even to make bold claims that God does not exist. When scientists say such things, they are being untrue to their own methodologies which are based on observation and experimentation. Scientific methodologies specifically say that scientists can only make assertions on the basis of what they can observe and can repeat through experimentation. How then, we can ask the scientist, can you make a true statement about the existence or non-existence of God whom you cannot observe or control for experimentation?

Since both parties have been guilty of playing offside, the relationship between scientists and theologians has been deeply damaged and laden with misplaced accusations and claims. We need both parties to engage with one another in a constructive manner, with each side respecting the other for its specific contribution to getting to know the world that we live in together, the stuff that we are made of and the purpose of all that is.

We also need to refute the three popular but mistaken perspectives on the nature of scientific and theological activities in relation to each other.[15]

- *Error 1*: The sciences work only with facts whereas theological reflection works only with feelings. This assumption that theological reflection does not work with "facts" can be refuted by pointing out that the Bible is a historical document that recounts Israel's religious history. Christianity begins with the historical figure of Jesus of Nazareth who lived in Israel.

- *Error 2*: The sciences are objective, and theological reflection is subjective. This assumption can be refuted by pointing out that many scientists have some personal interest in what they choose to study. Moreover, scientists have to agree (reach consensus) on the way to study the thing they are interested in (e.g. under a microscope) and the methods to be used when studying it. Subjective concerns can creep in at all these points. Thus both scientists and theologians have to acknowledge that an element of subjectivity is unavoidable in their work.

- *Error 3:* The sciences deal with things that can be seen, whereas theology concerns things that cannot be seen. This assumption can be refuted by

---

15. For a good discussion of the three mistaken perspectives, see John Polkinghorne and Michael Welker, *The End of the World and the Ends of God: Science and Theology on Eschatology* (Harrisburg, PA: Trinity Press International, 2000), 1–16.

pointing to fields of science like quantum physics where the objects studied can only be seen when wearing theoretical "spectacles."

We must consciously put these mistaken perspectives behind us in order to bridge the deep divides between scientists and theologians. Otherwise our engagement with each other will only contribute further to the already existing messiness and to all kinds of misplaced suspicions.

Is technology neutral and used only for good?

The public face of the sciences is technology – and a very powerful face it is! Yet in spite of its wide-ranging developments and applications, technology is in no way neutral or simply innocent. That is why Pope Francis included the following strong warning in *Laudato si*:

> Many problems of today's world stem from the tendency, at times unconscious, to make the method and aims of science and technology an epistemological paradigm which shapes the lives of individuals and the workings of society. The effects of imposing this model on reality as a whole, human and social, are seen in the deterioration of the environment, but this is just one sign of a reductionism which affects every aspect of human and social life. We have to accept that technological products are not neutral, for they create a framework which ends up conditioning lifestyles and shaping social possibilities along the lines dictated by the interests of certain powerful groups. Decisions which may seem purely instrumental are in reality decisions about the kind of society we want to build.[16]

More often than not, technology serves the very specific interests of transnational companies and organizations, or of those in powerful positions. In many societies, technology has brought about deep divisions between the haves and the have-nots. There are also the never-will-haves, who are excluded from technological developments and fall further and further behind. A statement such as the following declaration of the Parliament of World Religions highlights what is at stake:

> Today we possess sufficient economic, cultural, and spiritual resources to introduce a better global order. But old and new ethnic,

---

16. Pope Francis, *Laudato si*, para 107.

national, social, economic, and religious tensions threaten the peaceful building of a better world. We have experienced greater technological progress than ever before, yet we see that worldwide poverty, hunger, death of children, unemployment, misery, and the destruction of nature have not diminished but rather have increased. Many peoples are threatened with economic ruin, social disarray, political marginalization, ecological catastrophe, and national collapse.[17]

Indeed, we see greater technological progress than ever before yet even greater misery, economic ruin and ecological catastrophes. Or as Jeffrey Shaw alarmingly puts it: "The whole massive complex of technology, which reaches into every aspect of social life today, implies a huge organization of which no one is really in control, and which dictates its own solutions irrespective of human needs or even reason."[18]

Does technology reach "into every aspect of social life today"? Yes, and deep into the very fibre of all aspects of our lives! In many countries in Africa, technological advances and applications have been very fruitful and constructive – think of the benefits that mobile phone technology has brought to Africa. But technology has also been disruptive, not least in the barriers it has introduced between the young and the old. In many countries in Africa, the insensitive, misplaced, short-sighted, arrogant application of technology has also brought about much pain, suffering, displacement and ecological destruction by those in power who are mostly pursuing their own interests. It follows that "The importance of technology in our time can hardly be overestimated. Technology is ubiquitous and all areas of life are influenced by it, such as work processes, mobility, relationships (especially the realm of communication), leisure activities and health."[19] For these issues not to become insurmountable stumbling blocks, we will have to act with discernment.

---

17. Hans Küng, "Declaration toward a Global Ethic," Parliament of the World's Religions (1993), https://www.global-ethic.org/declaration-toward-a-global-ethic/.

18. Jeffrey Shaw, "Illusions of Freedom: Thomas Merton and Jacques Ellul on Technology and the Human Condition," *Religion and Theology* 25, no. 1 (2018): 152.

19. Björn Schwenger, "'Heresy' or 'Phase of Nature'?: Approaching Technology Theologically," *European Journal of Theology* 25, no. 1 (2016): 44.

Groaning Together – Acting for Africa

Having groaned for Africa and groaned in discernment, it is time to groan together and act to create "an integrated, prosperous and peaceful Africa, driven by its own citizens and representing a dynamic force in the international arena."[20] Our goal should be that of *Agenda 2063*, which is that by 2063

> African countries will be amongst the best performers in global quality of life measures. This will be attained through strategies of inclusive growth, job creation, increasing agricultural production; investments in science, technology, research and innovation; gender equality, youth empowerment and the provision of basic services including health, nutrition, education, shelter, water and sanitation. . . .
>
> Africa's human capital will be fully developed as its most precious resource, through sustained investments based on universal early childhood development and basic education, and sustained investments in higher education, science, technology, research and innovation, and the elimination of gender disparities at all levels of education. Access to post-graduate education will be expanded and strengthened to ensure world-class infrastructure for learning and research and support scientific reforms that underpin the transformation of the continent.[21]

How we act now will determine the destiny of Africa.

But how should we act as regards the place and role of the sciences? What should we do? It is not possible to give an easy and quick answer to this question. If such an answer is given by anyone, distrust it immediately. It is most probably a shallow or deep cover-up for their own interests! However, we cannot ignore this difficult question; we will have to work through it now for the sake of Africa's future.

The most that can be offered in this chapter are some important guidelines for our thinking:

- *We must acknowledge our responsibility to identify and name the most important issues that must become the priorities for our community.* For example, are the most important issues in our context clean water and sanitation, deforestation, medical care, economic injustices, bad

---

20. African Union, *Agenda 2063*, 1.
21. African Union, *Agenda 2063*, 3.

governance or poverty? Taking responsibility for what "is not well" is itself a witness that we are accepting our identity as co-creators with God.

- *We must acknowledge our responsibility to be well informed on these issues.* Being well informed involves valuing the contribution the sciences can make. It must be clear from the outset that we are willing to pull together and combine our best theological convictions with the best scientific insights. Together, science and theology can move and be moved in wholesome directions! We should heed the words of Albert Einstein: "Science without religion is lame, religion without science is blind."[22] The South African theologian Klaus Nürnberger formulated this important insight differently: "Faith needs science to be credible; science needs faith to be responsible."[23]

- *We must either create or make use of societal platforms and networks within which actions can be decided on, formulated and launched.* Doing so may involve working with institutions such as government departments, churches and organizations; using technologies such as television, mobile phones and the Internet; and organizing mobilization through protest actions, awareness campaigns and the like. We must also seek creative ways to create communication channels that support the voices of those within our communities who have historically been excluded from platforms and networks. Their voices need to be heard because they often articulate the most urgent or neglected issues that should be acted upon.

- *We should act on the basis of information and data, but also with a clear understanding of the ethical implications of our actions.* Although scientists and theologians may not always agree on these matters, we must be willing to put all our cards on the table of open engagement and dialogue that will focus on the outcomes and ethical implications of our actions. At times, disagreements may relate to worldviews. Those with a Western-orientation should ask where am I "speaking from" on this issue? Those with an African orientation should ask who are we as community "speaking to" on this issue? When these "speakings" come together, they can create a much stronger voice!

---

22. German-born theoretical physicist (1879–1955) who developed the theory of relativity. The quotation comes from his essay "Science and Religion," in *Ideas and Opinions* (New York: Citadel Press, 1956), 26.

23. Klaus Nürnberger, *Regaining Sanity for the Earth* (Pietermaritzburg: Cluster, 2011), adapted from the cover text.

Say, for example, our problem is with the water supply. Are we simply going to ask the community to pray for rain, or are we going to build a dam? Or are we willing to both pray for water and build a dam? If we decide to build a dam, have we taken time to become informed about how it will affect the environment? This is obviously an oversimplified example. There are many other examples that are much more complicated involving medical matters, agricultural methods, intercultural relationships, societal values, sexuality, etc.

However complicated the matter or issue, this must be our guiding question: What kind of society are we shaping through our actions? This question is crucial because it opens up a spectrum of values. Does the outcome respect creation as a whole? Does it respect nature as a partner? How does it celebrate and enhance our connectedness to all that is, to bondedness? And as they discuss these issues, both the scientists and the theologians should be asking themselves the same self-critical question: Are we playing "offside" in acting upon the issues at hand?

These basic guidelines need to be an integral part of our thinking as we prepare for actions that will affect Africa's destiny. Note, however, that these are not the final guidelines – we need to work together to formulate clearer and broader guidelines for our own contexts.

Conclusion

Our journey in this chapter has taken us along the path of groaning for Africa, groaning with discernment, and groaning together. It is of the utmost importance that this journey should continue as we as believers seek to address the all-is-not-well groans of Africa. We will have to work on and cultivate constructive and friendly relationships with the sciences, taking great care not to simply serve our own interests but rather those of our communities.

Working with scientists, we must seek to help them direct their work in wholesome directions despite the current messiness. We must do so with an acute awareness of the ethical implications and outcomes of our every action and taking great care that we are not playing offside. We must act for a better future in Africa, but we must act with great care in voicing the earth's praise to God and simultaneously the concerns and needs of those without a voice in our societies.

As we act, we will discover and discern together in our conference rooms, lecture halls, government chambers, church gatherings, open air meetings, protest actions and many other communal spaces all over Africa how the groaning and cries can turn into healing and joy, into determination and wisdom and into constructive engagement as witness to the good story of God in Africa.

Questions

1. What was your personal opinion on the role of the sciences in your context before you read this chapter?
2. Would you agree that theological reflection needs the sciences to be credible and that the sciences need theology to be responsible?
3. Can you identify the current messiness of the science-theology relationship in your specific context?
4. What do you make of the accusation that both theologians and scientists sometimes "play offside"?
5. Can you relate to the call for action? What are you going to do about it?
6. What guidelines for action do you think should be added to the few already listed?

Further Reading

Agbiji, Obaji M. "Religion and Ecological Justice in Africa: Engaging 'Value for Community' as Praxis for Ecological and Socio-Economic Justice." *HTS Teologiese Studies* 71, no. 2 (30 April 2015): 1–10. http://dx.doi.org/10.4102/HTS.V71I2.2663.

Clayton, Philip. "Theology and the Physical Sciences." In *The Modern Theologians*, edited by D. Ford, 342–356. Oxford: Blackwell, 2005.

Conradie, Ernst, and Cornel Du Toit. "Knowledge, Values, and Beliefs in the South African Context Since 1948: An Overview." *Zygon* 50, no. 2 (2015): 455–479.

Deane-Drummond, Celia. "Theology and the Biological Sciences." In *The Modern Theologians*, edited by D. Ford, 357–369. Oxford: Blackwell, 2005.

Ellis, George. "Why the Science and Religion Dialogue Matters." In *Why the Science and Religion Dialogue Matters: Voices from the International Society for Science and Religion*, edited by F. Watts and K. Dutton, 3–26. West Conshohocken, PA: Templeton Foundation Press, 2006.

Nürnberger, Klaus. *Informed by Science: Involved by Christ.* Pietermaritzburg: Cluster, 2013.

——. *Regaining Sanity for the Earth.* Pietermaritzburg: Cluster, 2011.

14

Health

Daniel Rikichi Kajang

Health is like truth in that it has no colour, no tribe and no religion and affects every social class. The laws or constitutions of most democratic societies spell out that everyone has a right to the highest attainable standard of physical and mental health, and assign responsibility for the provision and maintenance of health services to various branches of the civil service. Unfortunately, for all the brave words in various African constitutions, Africa is struggling with major health care challenges. Christians need to stand up, take notice and work to address these issues.

Health Care in Africa

While most Western nations focus on both health care and health maintenance or wellness, most African nations are still at the level of "disease care" and are struggling to provide very basic health services. According to a 2017–2019 World Bank Report, the African continent accounts for less than 2 percent of global health funding, even though Africans make up 16 percent of the global population and carry 26 percent of the global disease burden. By 2050, Africans may well account for more than 50 percent of global population growth. This growth represents both a great opportunity and a ticking time bomb should we fail to fix our health systems quickly.

Currently, African countries import about $17.3 billion worth of drugs each year. Think how many jobs would be created if those drugs could be manufactured here! But the lack of facilities to produce such drugs is not the only economic effect of Africa's poor provision of health services. The World

Health Organization has established that there is a strong link between the health of the people and a nation's gross domestic product.[1] It estimates that nearly 630 million years of healthy life were lost in 2015 due to the diseases burdening its forty-seven member states in Africa, amounting to a loss of more than US $2.4 trillion from the region's annual GDP.

While these economic figures are very important in showing the stunning scope of Africa's health issues, we must see these figures not just as financial statistics but as a snapshot of the suffering that millions endure. Demographic studies reveal that in some regions, almost half the children die before the age of five due to malnutrition, accidents and diseases such as malaria, diarrhoea, pneumonia, tetanus, whooping cough, measles, polio and tuberculosis. Much of this suffering could be relieved by public health programmes, but African countries are among those with the lowest public spending on health in the world.

The fact that people are suffering and dying from conditions that can be prevented or cured cries out for theologians and the church to work to enhance the capacity of the health sector for the sake of the well-being of all Africa's citizens. We need to be asking theological and practical questions: What does the Bible say about issues of health and the causes of sickness? What has been the role of the church in the provision of health care, and what has been its impact on Africa? What should the church and individual Christians be doing today to promote better health care in their regions?

While health is not the meaning or purpose of human life, it is the source of strength for life. There can be no doubt that health outcomes across the board in Africa would improve if the church were to become deeply involved with relevant stakeholders to promote health and wellness programmes and so demonstrate the love of Christ in practical ways.

Defining Health

Like the concept of poverty, the concept of health has sometimes been interpreted in simplistic terms. There are actually a number of different definitions of health, and the definition we adopt will affect our attitude to health care and our understanding of what we as Christians can do to promote health care. The simplest definition of health is a negative one: One is healthy if one is not ill. In this case, restoring someone to health simply involves removing

---

1. World Health Organization, *A Heavy Burden: The Indirect Cost of Illness in Africa* (Brazzaville: WHO Regional Office for Africa, 2019).

the disease in a process that begins with a correct diagnosis followed by a correct treatment for that disease. This approach to health care is common in the health systems in African countries.

By contrast, a positive model of health does not focus merely on the absence of illness but on living in a way that actively promotes health. This approach to health care encourages people to take responsibility for their own present and future health and also addresses lifestyle issues and environmental factors affecting health. Using this definition, even those who have chronic diseases or permanent disabilities can be encouraged to strive for specific health goals as achievable targets.[2] This second definition is based on the World Health Organization's definition of health as "a state of complete physical, mental and social well-being and not merely the absence of disease or infirmity."[3] This definition explicitly states that to be healthy means something more or something different from just not being ill. A healthy individual is someone who enjoys life and experiences well-being.

With this understanding of health, we cannot assess the health of a group or of the general population simply by collecting statistics about morbidity (illness) and mortality (death). Nor can we judge the health of a nation simply by counting the number of medical personnel and hospitals. Rather, a nation's health is determined by a broad range of public policies not only at the national level but also at the local and community levels. These policies may be government policies, or they may be policies put in place by corporations or by communities (and churches).

The most fundamental determinants of people's health are meeting their basic needs for food, shelter, clean water, a safe environment and peace. Health is also affected by broader environmental issues such as a sustainable ecosystem, by communal issues such as good social networks, and by individual issues such as a sense of self-esteem and a feeling that one has some control over the conditions of one's life.

The many overlaps between health concerns and poverty serve as reminders that there are deep inequities when it comes to access to the prerequisites for health. The poor, unemployed and undereducated frequently lack the power to access the fundamental economic and social determinants of health. Therefore any strategy for improving the health of a nation or a community

---

2. Bridget Hathaway and Flavian Kishekwa, *Included and Valued: A Practical Theology of Disability* (Carlisle: Langham, 2019).

3. World Health Organization, *Constitution of the World Health Organization: Basic Documents*, 45th ed., Supplement (October 2006).

should include a focus on improving the health of the least healthy members of that society.

Traditional African Understandings of Health and Health Care

Africa has a long tradition of healers who have accumulated experience in fighting disease and related problems.[4] They have expertise and knowledge of herbal remedies and medicinal plants, as well as insight into the psyche of their community and its culture and beliefs. Debates are raging as to what role this traditional medical knowledge should have in modern health care delivery. Some argue that it has outlived its usefulness and should be discarded, while others consider it a useful resource for health care delivery. Certainly there are many, including many Christians, who still choose to consult traditional healers.

Unlike Western medicine, which tends to concentrate on physical aspects of human life and disease, African traditional healers do not treat diseases in isolation from the person. They are aware of the need for harmony between the spirit, mind and body, and so they delve into the root causes of the disease, which may be physical or spiritual. When in doubt, they resort to divination in order to ascertain the cause of the disease and the right treatment to give. They identify the spiritual causes of diseases as cosmic influences, witchcraft and attacks by evil spirits. They also recognize that a disease may be the result of some sin on the part of the sufferer, or may be brought on by the pangs of a guilty conscience. The treatments they prescribe may include performing certain rituals and making use of charms or amulets or herbal remedies.

Western medicine is increasingly in agreement with traditional medicine that some sicknesses can be related to a person's mental and emotional condition. If someone is very discouraged, very fearful, very angry, or in other ways mentally disturbed, their mental state may reduce their resistance to germs so that they become physically ill. Because mental distress is often caused by a bad relationship with another person, African traditional healers have not been wrong to investigate this aspect of illness when making a diagnosis.

Christians who wish to consult a traditional healer should do so in full awareness that God forbids the use of witchcraft, divination and consulting the dead for answers (Deut 18:10–12). There is also no need to consult a witchdoctor if one suspects that one is suffering because of some spell or

---

4. J. O. Mume, "The African Traditional Doctor's Concept of Public Health," in *Principles and Practice of Public Health in Africa*, vol. 1, 2nd ed. (Ibadan: University Press, 1996): 6–10.

curse, for these can all be broken by the power of Jesus, who is more powerful than all the forces of evil.

Before consulting traditional healers, Christians would be wise to consult mature Christian elders in the area about the religious beliefs of the healers and their reputation. Where did they learn their craft? Was it from a reliable herbalist, or have they just set up on their own without training? Have their remedies proved to be safe and effective in the past, or have they had serious side effects? The safely of medicines provided by a government or church dispensary will have been tested by scientists. Such medicines are generally safe if they are taken in the right way and in the right amounts as prescribed by a qualified health practitioner. There is less security when taking traditional medicine.

General Biblical Understanding of Health

It is important to consider what the Bible has to say about health in both the Old and the New Testaments and to weigh how the Bible agrees and disagrees with traditional African views and how Christians today respond to health issues. In particular, we should consider how the biblical perspective should inform our response to health issues as individuals and as churches.

Old Testament understandings

At creation, the human body was perfect and healthy, but after the fall, death entered the world and diseases multiplied. So in a general sense, we can say that sickness occurs because of the sin of Adam and Eve. In that sense, sickness is always a result of sin.

Later, God reminds the Israelites that "if you listen carefully to the LORD your God and do what is right in his eyes, if you pay attention to his commands and keep all his decrees, I will not bring on you any of the diseases I brought on the Egyptians, for I am the LORD, who heals you" (Exod 15:26). Here too God is saying that sickness can sometimes be a result of sin.

But it is important to note that Scripture does not say that every sickness is a direct result of a sin. For example, the physical sickness Satan brought into Job's life was not related to any specific sin that Job had committed, for God himself said that Job was blameless (Job 2:3, 7).

Job's story ties in well with African traditional beliefs. A Western doctor would have ascribed Job's skin disease to some bacterial or viral infection, but readers of the Bible know that it was Satan or his demons who brought Job into contact with the germs that caused his sickness. Similarly, King Saul had serious mental health issues that made him violent, but these issues were caused by a combination of his jealousy of David and the work of an evil spirit (1 Sam 18:10–11). Both emotional and spiritual issues were at work, and healing would not come if both were not addressed.

There is also harmony between the traditional African medicine and the Bible as regards the relationship between the health of the body and the state of a person's mind. The Bible contains verses like this one: "The human spirit can endure in sickness, but a crushed spirit who can bear?" (Prov 18:14). Another verse says, "A heart at peace gives life to the body" (Prov 14:30). This holistic understanding of health is sometimes ignored in modern Western medicine with its focus on germs, bacteria, viruses and pills.

When it comes to the specifics of what the Bible has to say about health, it can be instructive to read the Old Testament and note the attention paid to issues of diet and hygiene. While some of the dietary commands had religious roots and were set aside in the New Testament (see Peter's vision in Acts 10:9–16), it is clear that God is concerned about our eating habits. He wants us to eat well, for he promised the Israelites a land where there would be abundant food, symbolized by the description of it as "a land flowing with milk and honey" (Lev 20:24). But he condemns overeating and gluttony, warning that "a companion of gluttons disgraces his father" (Prov 28:7) and, "If you find honey, eat just enough – too much of it, and you will vomit" (Prov 25:16).

Regarding hygiene, the Israelites were told to "designate a place outside the camp where you can go to relieve yourself. As part of your equipment have something to dig with, and when you relieve yourself, dig a hole and cover up your excrement" (Deut 23:12–13). Today we call this "sanitary waste disposal," and its benefits are widely understood but not always practised – especially in poverty-stricken areas. History is filled with epidemics of typhus, cholera and dysentery that are linked to the careless dumping of human waste into streets and rivers, or feeding human waste to animals that are then eaten. Burying human waste breaks the life cycle of many parasitic organisms that spread disease. This simple practice is much more effective, and less expensive, than treating disease after it breaks out – and God put this principle in the Bible thousands of years before science understood its benefit!

Tattoos and cuttings on the flesh were also forbidden in the law (Lev 19:28). This may have been for religious reasons, but it would also have avoided a possible source of infection. Today, we know that unless strict health procedures are followed, tattoos and body-piercing can transmit diseases like hepatitis B, hepatitis C, syphilis and HIV/AIDS.

The Bible also includes rules about quarantine. People who touched a dead or diseased animal or person – or even garments or secretions from a sick person – were to bathe and wash their clothes and avoid contact with others (Lev 13–15; Num 5:2). Contaminated garments were to be washed or burned – important sanitizing principles that are still followed today. Dwellings that showed signs of mould or that had harboured sick individuals were to be cleaned, repaired or destroyed to prevent the spread of disease. Porous vessels that came into contact with unclean animals, reptiles and insects were to be broken (Lev 11). The Israelites would not have known it at the time, but such vessels can harbour harmful bacteria. People showing signs of some sicknesses were to be isolated – *quarantined* – until examined by a priest and declared well. Some of the practices might still be relevant today in regions where highly infectious diseases like Ebola are present.

And Ebola is only one of a number of newly-emerging killer pathogens that are gaining a foothold throughout the world. Other viral diseases such as Lassa fever and hantavirus, which are spread by rodents, and Rift Valley fever, which is spread by contact with the blood, body fluids, or tissues of infected animals can also be contained through preventive measures. Applying the principles of hygiene and quarantine could do much to help us fight diseases today.

New Testament understandings

Satan and his demons afflicted Job and Saul in the Old Testament, and in the New Testament the Gospels include examples of demons afflicting people with physical and mental problems. Thus it is not unreasonable to assume that demons will seek to attack people's health for evil purposes. But this is not to say that the activities of demons can be controlled by witches, sorcerers and secret societies, as is often claimed in Africa. True, there are some who attempt to manipulate demons, but demons are more powerful than any human being, and the only ones who can control them are God and the holy angels. During his time on earth, Jesus demonstrated his personal authority over Satan and demons. We need to remember that Jesus continues to protect his people today, so Christians have no need to live in fear of sorcery and witchcraft.

We should also note that in the Gospels not every disease is spoken of as having a spiritual cause, so we should be careful not to blame every sickness on witches or demons. It is likely that most of our sicknesses are simply the result of our coming into contact with the germs, often by drinking unsafe water or eating contaminated food. This contamination can come from our own hands which touch many things that may transmit germs, including money, door handles and other people's hands. That is why it is important to wash hands before eating. Sicknesses are also transmitted when we breathe in germs that are spread by coughing or sneezing.

Nor should we assume that every disability or illness is a result of sin. Jesus explicitly said that this was not the case with the man born blind (John 9:1–3). And Paul makes no mention of sin when he speaks of the serious illness of his close helper Epaphroditus (Phil 2:25–30). However, some diseases do arise from personal sin, as Jesus suggested when he healed the man who had been sick for thirty-eight years and warned him, "See, you are well again. Stop sinning or something worse may happen to you" (John 5:5–14). James implies something similar when, after saying that sick Christians should call for the elders of the local church to pray for them, he adds, "If they have sinned, they will be forgiven" (Jas 5:15). But note that "if" – yet another reminder that not all sickness is a result of sin.

The most obvious examples today of sicknesses that are directly related to sin are diseases associated with sexual immorality such as HIV/AIDS and syphilis. However, we should not forget that an innocent person can be infected with these diseases by a sinning spouse, and that HIV can also be acquired through blood transfusions and other mechanisms that involve no sin. We should not leap to conclusions as soon as we hear of a diagnosis. Nor should we use the link to sin as an excuse to shun those who have these diseases. Jesus associated with all kinds of people, including those who were shunned as "sinners" (Luke 5:30), and he reminded those who judged others as sinful on the basis of their circumstances that they too needed to repent (Luke 13:1–5).

Regardless of the reason for sickness, God is merciful, and in most situations, he grants healing in response to prayer and the use of appropriate medicines. In some cases, he grants healing without the use of any medicine, but we should not assume that will be the case. A Christian who is sick should seek for the best medical help available.

What are we to make of Jesus's own health? We are not told whether he ever caught a cold or suffered from a migraine. We do know, however, that he experienced suffering and human weakness, that he wept at the news of the death of his friend Lazarus, and that in his anguish at Gethsemane "his sweat was like drops of blood falling to the ground" (Luke 22:44). Some have argued that Jesus's willingness to endure suffering indicates that suffering may be redemptive and should not be avoided. But this belief is something that we can apply only to our own suffering; we must not use it as an excuse to avoid relieving the suffering of others. The Gospels often speak of Jesus's healing ministry and his compassion for the blind, the sick and the lame (Luke

7:22). His parable of the sheep and the goats makes it clear that he expects his followers show the same concern for others (Matt 25:31–46).

The New Testament also makes it clear that faithful followers of Jesus may endure ill health. We have already mentioned Ephaphroditus's illness (Phil 2:25–30), and Paul may have suffered from chronic health conditions. In his letters, he speaks of his "thorn in the flesh" and of illness and possibly problems with his eyesight (2 Cor 12:7–10; Gal 4:13–15). Strikingly, Paul says that he prayed to have the "thorn" removed, but his request was denied. His experience refutes the arguments of those who claim that people are not healed because they lack faith. We must not take the promise that "the Lord will raise them up" in James 5:13–15 as implying that this "raising" will always involve restoration of full physical health.

Some of Jesus's disciples were indeed given the power to heal (Luke 10:9), and in Acts 3:1–10, a lame man was healed "in the name of Jesus Christ of Nazareth." Paul explicitly mentions that Christ gives the gift of healing to some but not to all in his church (1 Cor 12:9, 28, 30). James shows how this ministry may have been exercised when he instructs the sick to call for church leaders to pray for them and to "anoint them with oil in the name of the Lord" (Jas 5:14).

Theological Categories of Health and Healing

When talking about healing, it is important to start with the assumption that all healing is ultimately divine healing and to acknowledge that God may choose to use a variety of methods for healing our diseases. We should not dare to tell God what to do by insisting that we will accept only miraculous healing.

We also need to acknowledge that it is possible for some healings to be counterfeits. For example, if demonic powers cause some illness, the illness may be cured by a traditional healer's use of witchcraft. Satan can afflict a person with sickness and can remove that sickness in order to deceive people and persuade them to believe in the power of divination and witchcraft instead of trusting in God for true and perfect healing through Christ.

Here are some of the possible ways in which God may bless and heal:

- *Through drugs, surgery, natural substances or other interventions.* The idea that using medication and undergoing surgery reveals a lack of faith is not supported in the Bible. Luke, who travelled with the apostle Paul and was the author of the Gospel of Luke, was a professional doctor who would have prescribed medicines (Col 4:14). Paul suggests that his friend Timothy take a commonly used medicine for stomach trouble (1 Tim 5:23). Healing through medical means is part of God's gift to us, for it is God who gives doctors and scientists the insight they need to develop medicines and surgical techniques. A Christian who is sick should seek for the best medical help available.

- *Through prayer and deliverance.* God has the power to heal the sick in response to prayer. We see this in the biblical accounts of the healing of Hezekiah and Dorcas (2 Kgs 20:1–7; Acts 9:39–40). Jesus also performed many miracles of healing, and so did the apostles (Acts 3:1–9; 5:16; 14:8–10). But such healings do not appear to have been common at all times in biblical history. Long stretches of Scripture contain few records of healings, even by godly men like Old Testament prophets. When praying for healing, Christians should be encouraged to examine themselves to make sure that there is no open or hidden sin that may be bringing God's judgment on them (Ps 19:12–14). These may be sins of the heart such as resentment, bitterness, jealousy or hatred. Broken relationships can crush the human spirit, and so relationships have to be restored if a person is to be truly healthy. We should remember that Jesus told his followers that if they want God to answer their prayers, including their prayers for healing from sickness, they should forgive anyone they are angry with before praying to God (Mark 11:25; see also 1 Pet 3:7). Those whose hearts are filled with wrong attitudes may remain sick despite taking the prescribed medicine. This having been said, we should remember the case of Job and not accuse those who are not healed though prayer of harbouring unrepented sin.

- *Through granting health.* God gives some people the gift of health so that they do not endure much sickness. Sometimes this gift is given to people who take responsibility for their own health by exercising and avoiding poor dietary choices and addictions. But such people should also recognize that God in his grace has spared them from exposure to hazardous environments and harsh social and economic conditions that would damage their health, regardless of how responsible they tried to be. Those who enjoy the blessing of good health should use it to further the work of God.

- *Through divine life.* All who live on earth will eventually die. If they do not die in an accident, some illness will eventually take their life. But in the new Jerusalem, believers in Christ will enjoy perfect health, for "there will be no more death or mourning or crying or pain" (Rev 21:4).

Health and the Church Community

Churches should be known as places for positive health, not merely for the healing of disease. If the church is to glorify God, then Christians must begin to show evidence of God's gifts of spiritual, physical, mental, emotional and social healing. We should hold one another accountable for choices that will negatively affect our own or someone's health and prevent us or them from participating fully in service to God and society.

Our understanding of health should also reflect the love of God and motivate us to be present to one another in health, sickness and suffering. When Christians fall sick and need care, the church community should acknowledge the illness so that the one who is sick may be restored to health. However, what is even more important is that the community should help the one who is sick to remain part of the church community even if their health is not restored. A healthy Christian is not one who is not ill; rather, a healthy Christian is someone who lives in reliance on Christ and his community – the church – even while facing the realities of illness and death. It is this faithfulness to Christ that makes Christian suffering different. Thus those who are suffering should not be seen as cursed by God; some of them may be closer to God than we who are healthy!

Christians should be taught both to seek medical care and to pray in all cases of sickness. If the sickness is severe or if no medicine is available, they should call for the elders of the local church to come and join them in prayer for the one who is sick (Jas 5:14–16).

The church is a community that can sustain us and help us care for our bodies. Such community is essential, for a life lived in isolation can be meaningless and full of existential loneliness. But as we share in the suffering of others, as we open ourselves to their needs, we realize how much we have and how little we really need (Deut 15:10–11).

Health and the Local Community

In colonial times, health services were directed primarily towards protecting the health of colonial civil servants and the employees of large corporations. But there were also missionary doctors and nurses working in remote areas across Africa. They were the first to begin training their African staff in Western medicine, and they started rehabilitation programmes for the chronically sick and disabled, especially those suffering from leprosy, polio and eye disease.

When African countries gained their independence in the 1960s, they often took over the missionary hospitals as well as the government hospitals. But the health care systems they inherited were fragmented and not fully adapted to each country's needs. Most African countries had no medical schools to train doctors and dentists. Health services were available primarily to reasonably well-off urban dwellers or those in public service or regular employment, and even in big cities the rates of immunization of pre-school children were often very low.

The ability of the new governments to administer the health system was severely constrained by factors such as a low revenue base and bad governance. These conditions have continued, and there is plenty of scope for the church to step in and play a role in health-related issues for the benefit of society — as we should do if we are to obey Christ's command to love our neighbours.

Church involvement in community health care would be welcomed by many, for the failure of public health systems has affected the quality of life, and epidemics of preventable diseases still lead to loss of lives, especially in rural communities. Millions still suffer from malnutrition or die from diseases like malaria, meningitis and cholera. Every day in Africa, women die in childbirth, and children die because their parents cannot access health care. Hypertension, diabetes and coronary heart disease are increasing at astronomical rates while medication is in short supply.

Public theology cannot solve all these problems. But what we can do, in obedience to the teaching of Christ, is work to help churches develop a comprehensive agenda to promote the health, safety and wellbeing of the communities in which they operate. They will find that health care is often central to spreading the gospel of hope that presents Christ as the ultimate healer.

Strategies for Improving Community Health Care

Given that the focus of African medicine is still largely curative (a negative definition of health), there is plenty of scope for the church to promote positive health by supporting basic preventive measures, and particularly environmental health measures. Devastating illnesses like typhoid fever, dysentery, cholera, malaria and tuberculosis flourish in communities that lack clean water and have poor sanitation, poor housing and poor feeding. African governments need to be encouraged to focus on preventive medicine and especially environmental health, and to allocate money to such services. But African governments cannot do all of this on their own. The church needs to do what it can to be part of the solution.

There are certain key strategies that can be used as we work towards better health for all, namely developing a process, setting public policy and encouraging community participation. Ideally Christian leaders within the health care field should be the leaders here, but local input is crucial, and where there are no Christian medical professionals, churches may take the lead.

- *Developing a process.* Too often churches simply adopt some random issue related to health and tackle that. While such efforts can be useful, it is also important to develop some ongoing process to ensure that the health status of the community remains an ongoing concern and to ensure that the whole community is fully involved in defining its health problems and developing solutions to them. Those in charge of the process must enjoy strong community support and be people of integrity who have the trust of the whole community. Given that African communities may be divided along religious and cultural lines, it may be good to have representatives from different groups come together to work out the process to be followed. These representatives should work out what issues are important to the community and the sequence in which they should be addressed.

- *Setting out a policy.* Once a process for contributing to community health has been identified and specific problems and solutions have been agreed on by the community, it is time to start work on specific policies to deliver the required services. Ideally, any policy agreed on should involve a blend of government initiatives and community initiatives and should involve different groups in the community, from teachers to business women to church leaders. The policy should be one that will unite and not fragment the community. Examples of such policies include, say, a concerted attempt by all groups of leaders to encourage vaccination or to promote a clean-up of polluted water sources or to raise funds to acquire mosquito nets to distribute to all.

- *Involving the whole community.* Because true healing occurs only in community, without community healing is incomplete. So the representatives of the various groups who developed the process and agreed on the policy must work hard to involve members of their communities in delivering the health care and in maintaining positive health. The goal must be to help people gain increasing control over illness and improve their health.

Human Resources and Health Care

Many Christians enter the health care field with high ideals, but their morale is often sapped by the low remuneration for their work, the poor motivation of some of their co-workers, and the widespread corruption that manifests itself in the illegal sales of drugs and other hospital supplies, right down to the level of the sheets and towels intended for the patients. These issues affect health professionals across Africa and result in a constant brain drain as qualified health practitioners leave Africa to pursue lucrative jobs elsewhere.

How can theologians respond to this issue? On the one hand, we need to speak out against the increasing professionalization of health care and the tendency to see it as a job rather than as a vocation. There is real need for people who understand that the value of care goes beyond technical expertise. Believers working in health care should be encouraged to sacrifice the comforts of life in the West or in urban areas in order to care for Africa and rural Africa. This sacrifice is similar to that expected of the early missionaries and is what Christ himself did in his incarnation.

However, we cannot ask people to make huge sacrifices if we do not at the same time address the mismanagement and corruption issues that cause those who start off with idealistic commitment to give up and leave. We need to encourage Christians and communities to work out ways to promote good governance and accountability to ensure there is no corruption in the use of funds allocated for the health sector and to eliminate waste.

Conclusion

Leaders, policy makers, politicians, church leaders and local churches need to start talking about what they are doing to make health care available to all citizens. Achieving *Agenda 2063* will depend on strong health systems that not only promote health and prevent diseases but also strengthen the capacity of both the public and private sectors to provide sustainable health services to all. The involvement of the church in this process is biblical and imperative. A healthier Africa will be a happier Africa, and a happier Africa will be a productive Africa for the gospel of salvation through Christ.

The public theologians' role in promoting public health should be to encourage Christians to think about health in terms of physical, mental and social wellbeing and not simply in terms of disease. They should also encourage churches to use their own initiative in defining and promoting healthy living in their communities.

To sum up: Churches should not think that the only way they can contribute to the health of a nation is by deploying medical staff or building hospitals and clinics. Churches can also contribute by engaging in activities that promote health, teaching ways to prevent illness, and offering rehabilitation to all who need it.

Questions

1. What are the top health and wellness concerns in your community? How are these related to social and environmental conditions, and what resources do you have to address them?
2. Try to formulate a customized health and wellness programme for your church. What criteria will you use to judge whether you are achieving your goals and health targets?
3. How can we better formulate and communicate health policies to key stakeholders?
4. How can you as a church work with those of other traditions, including traditional healers and Muslim healers, to improve the health of your community?
5. If there is mining activity in your region, does it have health implications that need more attention?

Further Reading

Gwatkin, Davidson R., Adam Wagstaff, and Abdo S. Yazbeck, eds. *Reaching the Poor with Health, Nutrition, and Population Services: What Works, What Doesn't and Why*. Washington, DC: The World Bank, 2005. http://siteresources.worldbank.org/INTPAH/Resources/Reaching-the-Poor/complete.pdf.

Hathaway, Bridget, and Flavian Kishekwa. *Included and Valued: A Practical Theology of Disability*. Carlisle: Langham Global Library, 2019.

Sofoluwe, G. O., R. Schram, and D. A. Ogunmekan, eds. *Principles and Practice of Public Health in Africa*, vol. 1, 2nd ed. Ibadan: University Press, 1996.

15

Human Rights

Kajit J. Bagu (John Paul)

Public theology in Africa should embrace the task of teaching about human rights and advocating for them. This is a task to which the church is called both by its theological beliefs and by the need to address the harm caused by the neglect of human rights. From slavery to the horrors of colonialism and racism, the persecution of foreigners in xenophobic attacks, the abuse of vulnerable women and children, and the killing of people of different faiths or ethnic identities, Africa has suffered and still bleeds from the abuse of human dignity and rights.

Theology and Human Rights

Theology and human rights are intimately connected, given that theology is the study of how God is at work in this world. The first example of God being at work in this world is found in Genesis 1, which tells how God created the world. The account culminates in the creation of human beings in God's own image and in his granting them dominion over creation with a mandate to multiply. God thus endows all human beings with rights and dignity (Gen 1:27–28; see also Jas 3:9). All discussion of human rights and public theology must take the fact that all human beings are made in God's image as its starting point.

It is because human beings are made in God's image, albeit flawed after the fall, that God has taken action to reveal himself to them. One of the key moments in this revelation was his gift of the Ten Commandments, written on two tablets of stone (Exod 20:1–17). In these commandments, God sets out our human obligations to God and to our neighbours, or in other words, to other human beings. We are to act in ways that uphold human rights and human dignity and are not free to abuse others emotionally, physically or materially.

Jesus summarized the commandments as "Love the Lord your God with all your heart and with all your soul and with all your mind" and "Love your neighbour as yourself" (Matt 22:37–40). His second command repeats what he had said earlier in the Sermon on the Mount when he propounded what is known as the golden rule: "In everything, do to others what you would have them do to you" (Matt 7:12). This rule implies that if you and I wish to be given our full human rights and to be treated with full human dignity, we must grant these same rights and dignity to everyone else. We are not allowed to reserve some rights for ourselves and exclude them for others. What this means for us in the church is that when we teach about human rights, we must do so in comprehensive terms rather than falling into the historical trap of teaching human rights in a way that is riddled with inconsistencies and exclusions.

When a young man asked Jesus, "Teacher, what good thing must I do to get eternal life?" Jesus's reply pointed him to his obligations towards humanity: "You shall not murder, you shall not commit adultery, you shall not steal, you shall not give false testimony, honour your father and mother, and 'love your neighbour as yourself'" (Matt 19:16, 18–19). These words, with their reference to the Ten Commandments, are a reminder that those who want to be saved should uphold the human rights and dignity of others. Christians need to be convinced that every human person is equally human in the eyes of the Creator and that all Christians should frown on anything that is segregated, discriminatory and dehumanizing.

Human rights in Africa must be seen as belonging to Africans as human beings created by God rather than as a Western construct that is gradually being imported into Africa. Public theologians in Africa must make human rights a tool for the pursuit of the Africa God wants.

Human Rights in Africa

Much of the contemporary discussion of rights has taken place in the West, but we should not forget that ideas of human dignity and rights are found in every culture and place, including Africa. As the Ugandan scholar Mahmood Mamdani says, "it is difficult to accept that human rights was a theoretical notion created only three centuries ago by philosophers in Europe."[1] In different

---

1. Mahmood Mamdani, "The Social Basis of Constitutionalism in Africa," *Journal of Modern African Studies* (1990): 360.

cultures, these rights may have been expressed differently, but all cultures recognize the need to prevent human beings from abusing other human beings. This fact alone testifies to the universal omnipotence and omniscience of God Almighty who imbued every human community with his image and likeness and with the concept of human dignity and rights.

When it comes to differences between approaches to human rights in the West and in Africa, it is probably safe to say that Western approaches tend to be individualistic and increasingly secular, whereas African approaches tend to be more communal and religious. In much of Africa the concept of *ubuntu*, "I am because we are," expresses a communitarian affirmation of the human rights of each member of the community to exist and thrive.

Human Rights in History

While all cultures, both Western and African, have some understanding of human rights, it is also true that all cultures have a terrible record when it comes to upholding those rights. The West's implicit claim to be the guardian of human rights is rightly greeted with some scepticism given that in the past its expression of these rights was often discriminatory and exclusionary. Westerners were categorized as superior and all others, including Africans and disfavoured groups like the Irish and Roma, were categorized as "inferior" and so excluded from the enjoyment of full human dignity and rights.

The irony of recognizing human rights while at the same time justifying their abuse has accompanied moves to establish human rights throughout history. We see this clearly when we look at the historical progress of human rights in the centuries prior to the issuing of the Universal Declaration of Human Rights (UDHR) in 1948.[2]

Human rights pre-1948

One of the first political statements of human rights was the Magna Carta, signed by King John of England in 1215. This document limited the power of the English king, but the human rights it established applied only to English nobles.[3] The American Declaration of Independence in 1776 and the French

---

2. The UDHR was proclaimed on 10 December 1948 as a universal standard for human rights following the atrocities of the Second World War.

3. See William Sharp McKechnie, *Magna Carta: A Commentary on the Great Charter of King John* (Glasgow: James MacLehose & Sons, 1914).

Declaration of the Rights of Man and of the Citizen in 1789 extended human rights to ordinary men – but not to women, Native Americans, Africans or other non-European peoples.[4] Slavery and other forms of dehumanization were justified on the basis that Africans were mere savages, barely human and fit only to be beasts of burden. This restriction of who counted as a "man" when it came to human rights inspired the protest slogan of African-Americans over a century later: "I am a Man."[5] It was a statement of defiance expressing the desire to be acknowledged as someone who counts as a human being whose human dignity is fully recognized.

The exclusion of non-Europeans from Western notions of human rights and dignity was at one time so pervasive that in 1537 Pope Paul III issued a papal bull titled *Sublimus Deus* blaming Satan, "the enemy of the human race," for inspiring the belief "that the Indians of the West and the South, and other people of whom we have recent knowledge should be treated as dumb brutes created for our service" and strongly asserting that "the said Indians, and all other people who may later be discovered by Christians, are by no means to be deprived of their liberty or the possession of their property, even though they are outside the faith of Jesus Christ."[6] However, European societies ignored this injunction and slavery flourished right through to the eighteenth and nineteenth centuries. And after the formal abolition of slavery throughout the British Empire in the 1830s, colonialism took hold in Africa as the next stage of dehumanization.

The West's eyes were only fully opened to the poisonous nature of assumptions of racial superiority when they saw its fruits in Europe during the Second World War when the Nazi and Fascist ideologies inspired the invasion of "inferior" nations like Poland, France and Russia and the attempts to enslave their peoples and exterminate all Jews. The death of millions shocked the world and resulted in a strong movement to recognize the innate dignity and rights of all human beings. The result was the Universal Declaration of Human Rights (UDHR) signed in 1948, three years after the end of the war.

---

4. The concept of "man" in both the American and French declarations of human rights was consistent with slavery and other forms of dehumanization, since non-Europeans were typically "Moors," "Negroes," "Indians," etc., who were categorized as "barbarians" or "savages."

5. This reference to "man" was echoed by the American Civil Rights Movement. See for instance Steve Estes, *I Am a Man!: Race, Manhood, and the Civil Rights Movement* (Chapel Hill: University of North Carolina Press, 2005).

6. Pope Paul III, "*Sublimus Deus*: On the Enslavement and Evangelization of Indians" (1537), Papal Encyclicals Online, https://www.papalencyclicals.net/paul03/p3subli.htm.

Human rights post-1948

Even after the issuing of the Universal Declaration of Human Rights, not all rights were available to all, as can be seen in the various statements of human rights that continued to be issued. For example, in 1966 the United Nations accepted the International Covenant on Civil and Political Rights (ICCPR). The rights mentioned in that document are known as first generation rights and are the types of individual rights favoured by Western societies. At the same time, the United Nations accepted the International Covenant on Economic, Social and Cultural Rights (ICESCR) that enshrines what are referred to as second generation rights. The relegation of these rights to secondary status meant that they were less likely to be enforced.

The separation of civil and political rights from economic, social and cultural rights reflects Western individualism. It also favours the economic and political interests of Western societies while opening up non-Western societies to social, economic, cultural and political influences, domination and control by the West.[7] While individuals can insist on their freedom of expression, right to own private property and other rights under the ICCPR, they find it more difficult to demand the rights to housing, education and health care enshrined in the ICESCR. We see this separation of rights in most African countries. In Nigeria, for example, chapter 4 of the 1999 Federal Constitution sets out the civil and political rights that are enforceable by high courts.[8] However, economic, social and cultural rights are treated as "fundamental objectives and directive principles of state policy" – in other words, they are aspirational but not enforceable.[9]

In 2007 the United Nations adopted the Declaration on the Rights of Indigenous Peoples (UNDRIP) that addresses the rights of the most excluded, oppressed and dehumanized sections of humanity. Indigenous peoples have been denied the right to language, culture, ancestral homelands, self-determination as indigenous people, identity and the indigenous knowledge and memory upon which the ways of life of countless communities and cultures depend. Denial of these third generation rights has the effect of stripping them of the right to exist except as colonial subjects. They have to speak the colonial languages and be educated in foreign (largely Western or Arab-Islamic) ways.

---

7. See for instance the perspectives expressed in David Beetham, "What Future for Economic and Social Rights?" *Political Studies* 43 (1995).

8. These are contained in sections 33 to 45 of Nigeria's 1999 Constitution.

9. The fundamental objectives are contained in sections 13 to 24 of Nigeria's 1999 Constitution which is also Part II of the Constitution.

They are denied ancestral territories and are instead consigned to arbitrary territorial and political locations in accordance with foreign colonial methods and mappings.

The Western states most guilty of physical and cultural genocide against indigenous peoples were the most vociferous opponents of the UNDRIP, while the long-oppressed indigenous peoples of South America were among the most enthusiastic supporters of its passage. When it came to voting, four countries voted against UNDRIP (the USA, Canada, New Zealand and Australia), while eleven countries opposed it by abstaining, among them three African countries: Nigeria, Kenya and Burundi. In the case of Nigeria, the British-empowered Fulani group claim to be of North African or Middle Eastern descent (Flora Shaw writing in 1905 described them as "a partly white race"[10]). The Tutsis in Burundi also have an immigrant and "different race" narrative. Both groups tend to oppose the idea of indigenous people's rights. In Kenya, the powerful Kikuyu and other dominant groups tend to obscure the existence of more than forty other identities. It should not be surprising that these African countries also have indicators of repression against indigenous peoples. In Nigeria, for instance, the APC government of President Muhammadu Buhari set up a "True Federalism" Committee that proposed to eliminate the indigene concept and the federal character from Nigeria's constitution.[11]

Ultimately, historical accounts reveal that human rights are still imperfect and a work in progress. The multiplicity of charters of rights bears testimony to the reality that there is something deeply troubling about the way human beings treat others. Even the theology of human rights is still a work in progress. As Christians, we should be asking what did God intend regarding human dignity when he made human beings in his image and likeness? Or to put it another way, did God intend human beings to have rights and dignity?

Human Rights as a Tool for Transformation

The Africa God wants is an Africa where every person is recognized, respected and conferred with all the rights that accompany the fact that they are human. These rights should not be restricted by age or sex but should apply to every

---

10. Flora L. Shaw, *A Tropical Dependency: An Outline of the Ancient History of the Western Soudan, with an Account of the Modern Settlement of Northern Nigeria* (London: James Nisbet, 1905), 21–22.

11. See Ahmed Nasiru El-Rufai et al., *Report of the APC Committee on True Federalism* (Nigeria: APC Adhoc Committee, 2018).

human being across their whole lifespan, from conception to natural death. The notion of segregating rights and making some enjoyable by selected members of society to the exclusion of others must be condemned as morally reprehensible. No human being is less human than another in the eyes of the Almighty, and public theology aimed at forging a desirable Africa must envision a comprehensive, inclusive and transcendent idea of human rights. This concept is best expressed by Pope John Paul II in his 1993 encyclical *Veritatis Splendor* (The Splendour of Truth):

> Even though intentions may sometimes be good, and circumstances frequently difficult, civil authorities and particular individuals never have authority to violate the fundamental and inalienable rights of the human person. In the end, only a morality which acknowledges certain norms as valid always and for everyone, with no exception, can guarantee the ethical foundation of social coexistence, both on the national and international levels.[12]

If teaching about human rights in Africa is to be faithful to what God intends for humanity as a whole, and for Africa in particular, it must work to erase the idea of first, second and third tiers of human rights which leads to segregation of rights. It should instead aim to build a comprehensive, interdependent and inclusive consciousness about human dignity and rights.

The inclination to treat human dignity and rights as comprehensive has been bolstered by voices from the African continent and elsewhere that speak of our "interdependence" rather than of segregated rights. For example, the 1986 African Charter on Human and Peoples Rights (ACHPR) clearly states that "civil and political rights cannot be dissociated from economic, social and cultural rights in their conception as well as universality and that the satisfaction of economic, social and cultural rights is a guarantee for the enjoyment of civil and political rights."[13] The charter covers civil, political, economic, social and cultural rights as well as the rights of indigenous peoples. Its title deliberately encompasses both human rights and peoples' rights in an attempt to eliminate the segregation written into Western accounts of human rights.

In 1993, the World Conference on Human Rights also backed a comprehensive, interdependent approach to human rights:

---

12. Pope John Paul II, "*Veritatis Splendor*, The Splendour of Truth" (Rome: Vatican, 1993), 97.

13. Paragraph 7 of the preamble to the ACHPR, http://www.humanrights.se/wp-content/uploads/2012/01/African-Charter-on-Human-and-Peoples-Rights.pdf.

All human rights are universal, indivisible and interdependent and interrelated. The international community must treat human rights globally in a fair and equal manner, on the same footing, and with the same emphasis. . . . Democracy, development and respect for human rights and fundamental freedoms are interdependent and mutually reinforcing.[14]

The same voice is heard in *Agenda 2063*[15] and in the 2007 UNDRIP, which represents the ultimate attempt to break down the destructive divide that seeks to perpetually dehumanize peoples of non-European descent within the rights framework. The struggle to have the UNDRIP proclaimed was drawn out, hotly contested and full of intrigues unworthy of human beings made in the image and likeness of God. The strong opposition to the inclusion of indigenous peoples as bearers of rights within the proper indigenous context bears the marks of evil. Such efforts are part of the same dehumanizing school of thought as the older efforts to dehumanize those who are different in some way. They are rooted in enslaving, colonizing and genocidal legacies that contemplate and pursue the elimination of various communities and identities across the world because they are indigenous to a place and bearers of their own distinct identities and cultures.

Africa's indigenous peoples are communities whose ancestral roots and existence are tied to the continent of Africa. They include every indigenous identity as well as groups like the San and Pygmies who are marginalized by dominant groups and experience "discrimination and contempt . . . dispossession of their land and the destruction of their livelihoods, cultures and identities."[16] African Christians need to hear the message so strongly affirmed in the preamble to UNDRIP: "All doctrines, policies and practices based on or advocating superiority of peoples or individuals on the basis of national origin or racial, religious, ethnic or cultural differences are racist, scientifically false, legally invalid, morally condemnable and socially unjust."[17]

---

14. World Conference on Human Rights, "Vienna Declaration and Programme of Action," (Vienna, 1993), articles 5 and 8.

15. United Nations, *Agenda 2063*. Aspiration 3 of the Agenda envisages "respect for human rights," which must be seen in the light of the African Charter.

16. See African Commission on Human and Peoples Rights (ACHPR) and International Working Group for Indigenous Affairs (IWGIA), *Indigenous Peoples in Africa: The Forgotten Peoples? The African Commission's work on indigenous peoples in Africa* (Banjul: African Union, 2006).

17. United Nations Department of Economic and Social Affairs: Indigenous Peoples (2007), *Declaration on the Rights of Indigenous Peoples* (UNDRIP), 3.

Many of the conflicts and mass atrocities afflicting Africa today are rooted in the practice of applying and pursuing a segregated notion of human dignity and rights. Where government policies, institutions and basic structures are crafted to apply human dignity and rights through a discriminatory approach, it is only logical that dehumanizing and discriminatory tactics will also be employed, often with dire consequences. We must be aware of these dangers as we craft our public theology.

Human Rights and Identity

Identity is one aspect of being human that can facilitate inclusion or exclusion as regards human dignity and rights. But what is identity? In the Western framework it is conceived in individual terms, but in Africa and beyond it has a more communal sense. We as Africans and as Christians need to wrestle with this issue.

From the Christian theological viewpoint, God created humanity as male and female, and every person, male and female, is made in God's image and likeness. Each person is individually known and recognized by God, so each individual is entitled to full human dignity and rights. However, a communal or group sense of identity is often crucial to the way an individual is empowered to enjoy his or her individual rights. It is this context that makes the second and third generation of rights so fundamental and essential to human dignity in the African context.

To give one example, the right to freedom of expression belongs in the first generation of civil and political rights. However, given Africa's colonial and neo-colonial past, how is a person of Ijaw identity from the Niger Delta region of Nigeria supposed to exercise their right to freedom of expression as an Ijaw person if his or her right to use their indigenous language is denied by the country's official language policy? They are compelled to speak English, or use an interpreter, or be silent! The first generation rights are meaningless without the other rights categorized as second or third generation rights.

If God has decreed a plurality of languages and identities in the world and sustains the bearers of those identities, it is wrong to adopt policies or programmes that directly or indirectly seek to silence, eliminate or distort those diverse languages and identities. It is unfortunate that some in the past have used the name of Christianity to pursue policies that seek to eliminate particular identities, for example, by making African communities abandon their identities and languages in order to profess the Christian faith.

If God deemed it fit to make every visitor in Jerusalem hear the apostle Peter in his or her own language (Acts 2:5–12) and did not seek to compel new Christians to abandon their own identities and languages and adopt a Jewish identity, it must be contrary to God's will for Christians of a different era to do the direct opposite by working to eliminate a convert's indigenous language and identity! Dehumanization cannot be a morally legitimate path for evangelization.

In projecting an interdependent and inclusive pedagogy of human rights in Africa, every Christian as a public theologian should emphasize the fact that any segregation of human rights in Africa is evil and tantamount to denying the humanity of Africa's peoples as individuals as well as their communal identities.

Human Rights, Sexuality and Public Theology

The Western evolution of human rights has resulted in the concept currently including elements of atheism and rejection of God, which is why caution is needed as human rights may be hijacked and used to derail public theology. As theologians, we must never forget that human beings are fallen, morally weak and inclined to sin, and so can pervert even what is good. Even the language of human rights, which is good, can be subverted in ways that directly contravene the divine intention for humanity and human dignity. To be true to its calling, public theology must support human rights while maintaining an acute consciousness of the limits imposed by our knowledge of God's revealed will.

The most resounding example of a clash between secular and Christian understandings of human rights involves same-sex or gay rights and same-sex marriage. Here, there is a secular perspective on the scope of human rights and sexuality with which Christianity cannot agree. God created human beings as male and female in his image and likeness, and in Leviticus 18:22 he expressly prohibits same-sex relations: "Do not have sexual relations with a man as one does with a woman; that is detestable."

The language of human rights should not be subverted to mutilate God's will in relation to human sexuality. Individual identity includes definite sexual identities, and a marriage should be between a man and a woman. Sexual identity is tied to individual identity and can never be mutilated within a theological context.

But does this mean that those who are homosexual or lesbian or any of the other shades of sexuality have forfeited all their human rights? As theologians, we can label their behaviour as sinful while also acknowledging that God does not reject sinners but loves them and calls them to himself. We must also acknowledge that sin does not deprive a human being of their divinely ordained human rights – if it did, there would be no scope for even speaking of human rights, for we all sin. Like us, gay and lesbian people have human rights. They too can grow into the image and likeness of God. We should not revoke all their human rights any more than we revoke those of others in the congregation who sin.

Human Rights and Cognitive Justice

It is well known that modern Africa is still shackled by the nation-states imposed on it by the Berlin Conference of 1884/85. Although a few details have changed since colonial times, many realities are structurally the same as they were in their colonial heyday, with violent, dehumanizing and destabilizing results that afflict Africa daily. Makua Matua insists that because the very idea of a nation-state is a Western concept, "the post-colonial state, the uncritical successor of the colonial state, is doomed because it lacks basic moral legitimacy."[18] Mutua is not alone in making this point. It is this lack of basic moral legitimacy that drives African states' contempt for human rights and human dignity. Until this problem is addressed, initiatives like *Agenda 2063* are unlikely to succeed in their transformative task. This is why cognitive justice peacebuilding (CJP) and plurinational constitutionalism (PC) are important political, philosophical and constitutional concepts for Africa to grapple with as we move towards 2063.

The cognitive justice proposition advocates the remaking of Africa with the aim of forging morally legitimate socio-political constructs derived from the free and informed democratic expression of Africa's numerous indigenous identities and communities. This goal is best reflected in the plurinational constitutional idea. The idea is about returning to Africans, or rather Africans taking back, the prerogative of choice that was stolen by the colonial project and never returned.

Cognitive justice plurinationalism involves a blending of political philosophy and constitutional theory into a new line of thinking that offers a path to a better Africa.[19] It takes the general idea of cognitive justice as discussed by academics and forges a political and philosophical conception of justice designed to inspire constitution making and political remaking of

---

18. Makau Mutua, "Why Redraw the Map of Africa: A Moral and Legal Inquiry," *Michigan Journal of International Law* 16 (1995): 1116.

19. Kajit J. Bagu, *Peacebuilding, Constitutionalism and the Global South: The Case for Cognitive Justice Plurinationalism* (Abingdon, UK: Routledge, 2019).

Africa and the global South. The goal is to have a better world in which the full human dignity of all is acknowledged as all identities are recognized and treated as equal. It seeks to have this recognition embedded in Africa's constitutions, which should be transformed from nation-state frameworks into plurinational frameworks in which every identity dignified as a nation is constitutionally recognized and protected.

What distinguishes this approach from others is its stress on the "cognitive" element, that is, on the way of life, cultures and worldview through which people of various identities make sense of the world in their own language in their ancestral homelands. It seeks equal recognition and treatment of diverse knowledge systems and their bearers or identities so that a knowledge system and its bearers are not in practice rendered non-viable or reduced to a dead group for mere historical and data reference. One way to do this is to adopt a plurinational constitutional order that makes every living indigenous language in Africa an official language in its ancestral homeland, alongside other regional or state-wide languages of intercultural official communication. The aspiration to self-determination would be satisfied if states were conceived of as consisting of many nations, each recognized in the constitution, with the necessary structures, developmental infrastructure and empowerment on a case-by-case basis. These ideas give a hint of the cutting-edge innovative and reformative potential in this approach.

Theologians need to work hard to undo the harm done by the dehumanizing classification of Africans as "inferior" over the last 500 years, and they will find CJP-PC a cutting-edge conceptual and reform tool as they address this deadly legacy and seek to shape a better Africa where every identity is conceptually and practically imbued with full human dignity. CJP-PC will help them to explain the meaning of Jesus's golden rule – "In everything, do to others what you would have them do to you" (Matt 7:12) – in the context of human rights and politics. In doing this, they will have to emphasize four concepts:

- *Human dignity*, that is, the connection between the human dignity of every individual member of a community – the child, the widow, the stranger, the prisoner, the vulnerable, etc. – and the dignity of the whole community.

- *Intercultural translation*, which means that other cultures are not rejected but are seen as something one should seek to understand. Most crucially, each identity should learn to see those with different identities through the same dignifying lens as the one through which it sees itself.

- *Equal constitutional recognition* of all identities and languages and cultures.

- *Openness to a plurality of approaches* when solving problems or organizing society structurally. There is no one right way to do something.

The new perspective introduced by CJP-PC results in a call to love and cooperate with those of other identities rather than to suspect them, hate them and engage in unhealthy competition.

Cognitive justice peacebuilding is thus "the equal recognition and treatment of different identities in democratic constitutional society, with the aim of fostering peace through the elimination of legal, political, institutional, structural, social and economic inequality of different identities, whether such inequality be direct or indirect, express or implied, visible or invisible, and whether contemporary or historical."[20]

Cognitive justice provides a suitable conceptual, philosophical, institutional and structural template for building a desirable Africa in which human dignity and rights are conceived and taught using an interdependent, inclusive pedagogy. The old wineskin of the colonial nation-state has a way of corrupting every new wine poured into it. Let there be new wine-skins of plurinational state orders for the new wine of transcendent and comprehensive human dignity and rights through cognitive justice.

Conclusion

Sunday Bobai Agang rightly insists that we must go beyond praying about what we have identified as being wrong to taking relevant action to redress it: "public theology calls us to apply our minds to the problems that face Africa. We are called to look closely at the problems, going beyond the surface issues to the underlying causes rooted in social structures and prevailing worldviews."[21]

The pursuit of the Africa we want will be strengthened when we grasp that human rights are interdependent and inclusive. The duty to promote and defend human dignity is a central tenet of theology. However, the evolution of human rights in the Western tradition has resulted in a tendency to segregate human rights into categories, which always leads to dehumanization and abuse of those excluded. We see this tendency at work in the Africa we have today. Yet while human rights constitute a valuable tool in advancing a desirable Africa,

---

20. Kajit J. Bagu, "Plurality, Peacebuilding and Islam: Gülen Optimism and the Cognitive Justice Prism," in *The Hizmet Movement and Peacebuilding: Global Cases*, eds. Mohammed Abu-Nimer and Timothy Seidel (Lanham, MD: Lexington, 2018), 249.

21. See chapter 1, "The Need for Public Theology in Africa," 3.

the public theologian must be cautious not to mutilate theology by advocating human rights perspectives that subvert the divine will.

Although positive developments towards interdependence in treating human rights are seen in the African Charter, UNDRIP and *Agenda 2063*, there is still much that needs to be done to give Africa the leverage needed to forge its future in accordance with the divine will, so that the full human dignity of every individual and communal identity is respected. It is with this in mind that I have put forward the cognitive justice proposition which aims at fostering cognitive justice peacebuilding for the remaking of a morally legitimate, just, peaceful and sustainable Africa.

Questions

1. Is your personal human dignity sufficiently protected by the human rights law and practices in your country? If not, what changes would you suggest need to be made, and how can you go about advocating for those changes?
2. How does your concept of your own human dignity and rights compare to those of people belonging to communities or identities other than your own within your country? Are they treated as your equals, inferiors or superiors?
3. After reading this chapter, try to apply the biblical and historical lessons learned to your current context. What rights are being affirmed or denied, and to whom? Are there other rights that should also be considered?
4. Can you identify an indigenous African community and undertake an outreach to educate them about their human dignity as willed by God and about their rights under the UNDRIP? How will you go about doing this?
5. In what ways would you propose that your country's constitution be remade in accordance with cognitive justice peacebuilding and plurinational constitutionalism so that every identity is recognized as a nation in the build up to 2063?

Further Reading

African Commission on Human and Peoples Rights (ACHPR) and International Working Group for Indigenous Affairs (IWGIA). *Indigenous Peoples in Africa: The Forgotten Peoples? The African Commission's Work on Indigenous Peoples in Africa*. Banjul: African Union, 2006. https://www.iwgia.org/en/resources/publications/305-books/2545-indigenous-peoples-in-africa-the-forgotten-peoples-the-african-commissions-work-on-indigenous-peoples-in-africa.

Anaya, S. James, and Siegfried Wiessner. "The UN Declaration on the Rights of Indigenous Peoples: Towards Re-Empowerment." *The Jurist* (3 October 2007). https://www.jurist.org/commentary/2007/10/un-declaration-on-rights-of-indigenous-2/.

Bagu, Kajit J. *Peacebuilding, Constitutionalism and the Global South: The Case for Cognitive Justice Plurinationalism.* Abingdon, UK: Routledge, 2020.

McCorquodale, Robert, ed. *Human Rights.* Abingdon, UK: Routledge, 2003; reissued 2018.

16

Gender

Esther Mombo

If theology in its most basic sense is the study of God, then public theology is the study of God as it pertains to issues in the public sphere. If something is a public issue, public theology has something to say about it – and thus it also has to say something about gender, for gender permeates all spheres of life and affects everyone from birth to death. This point is clear from the first question we ask when we hear that a child has been born: is it a boy or a girl? As human beings we think in terms of these categories and have done so since God created the first man and woman.

But what does it mean to be male or female? This is where the concept of gender comes in. Gender is related to biological sex, but it primarily has to do with society's assumptions about males and females. In many African societies, a boy child is valued more highly than a girl child, and men have higher status than women.

These differences in status and value are closely linked with the social roles assigned to men and women. These culturally defined roles affect access to productive resources outside the home and decision-making authority. While there are differences in the specifics of these roles, in Africa men are generally regarded as responsible for productive activities outside the home, while women are expected to be responsible for reproductive and productive activities within the home. This perspective shapes our understanding of many issues and permeates all spheres of life, including our social, religious, political and economic life. So understanding gender is important for understanding our own communities.

The Importance of Gender Issues

Gender issues are increasingly prominent in the wider society around us. Yet some Christians choose to dismiss the topic of gender, suggesting that it is a modern idea that is being imported into Africa by foreign (feminist) powers. But to deny the need to think about gender implies that African cultures have no flaws in regard to gender issues. Yet we know that no culture is perfect. All cultures are both good in that they bind communities together and harmful in that they do not always serve the needs and interests of all people equally. Cultures can oppress those who are defined as "other." This oppression is widely recognized in racism and tribalism – why should it not also be recognized in gender issues, which also involve distinct groups of people?

Research has shown that our understanding of gender has deep roots in our traditional cultures and that some gender problems in Africa predate the coming of Islam and Christianity to Africa and the colonial era.[1] There are many situations in which men and women have not been treated equally and where rigid enforcement of stereotypes means that those who do not fall in line with the culturally assigned gender roles struggle to find a place in the community. We need to accept that discussions around gender are here to stay and that they are important because they bring to light deep-seated gender inequalities.

As Christians we are called to have our thinking transformed, and this includes our cultural thinking. We need to learn to discern what needs to be cherished and what needs to be changed in our cultures. We also need to work for the transformation of our communities into places that are better for both men and women, both of whom are made in the image of God.

There are others who acknowledge some gender issues in Africa but complain that things have been taken too far and that men are now at a disadvantage. For three years in a row I have had to listen as children's choirs sing "The Lament of a Boy Child." Here are some stanzas from this song, translated from Kiswahili:

> On her birthday a girl is allowed to celebrate with a big party;
> A boy has a smaller party.

> When school starts, girls go shopping and have pocket money;
> A boy's pocket money is reduced because he is told he does not
>   need much money at school.

---

1. Mercy Amba Oduyoye, *Introducing African Women's Theology* (Sheffield: Sheffield Academic Press, 2001), 24.

When a girl is punished, she is allowed to cry;

When a boy is punished and he cries, the punishment is increased
   because boys are not supposed to cry.[2]

This song implies that boys are neglected and discriminated against while girls are given all the opportunities – they have more money and more opportunities academically and socially. It resorts to hearsay and stereotypes as it argues that this discrimination must stop and that both girls and boys should be treated equally.

Similar reasoning may also underlie the recent growth in manhood-affirming programmes for young men and boys. These programmes are often modelled on the traditional initiation camps where boys were circumcised and given instruction by elders as they moved on to another stage in life. The goal is to welcome boys into the manhood club where they are no longer children and understand what it means to be a man, and not a woman. Sometimes these programmes are run by church-based organizations or NGOs and given names like "Unleash the Man Within" and "Man Enough." It is claimed that a ten-week course will allow young men to experience manhood in a different way and to take their "rightful" position in the family, church and society. Using the Bible, the training provides an understanding of masculinity that is based on power and authority. A man is defined as the provider, protector and priest for his family. His leadership in the home is extended to the society around him. While there is much that is good in such training, it is disturbing that it reinforces gender stereotypes and roles.

These stereotypes are also present in the many wedding sermons that stress rigid gender roles and hierarchical structures in marriage. More time is devoted to the husband's authority and the need for the wife to show respect and obey him than to mutual love and respect. The woman's place is perceived as in the private sphere while the man's place is in the public sphere. There is often a marked disconnect between the reality in society and the sermons and speeches given during the wedding. Such sermons justify gender inequality and create space for violence within the marriage.

Given these concerns, it is important that we pay attention to how the Bible is used and abused when we talk about gender issues.

---

2. The poem entitled "The Lament of a Boy Child" was sung in Kiswahili by the boys of St Paul's Primary School at three graduation ceremonies (2014, 2015, 2016).

The Bible and Gender

The Bible has had such an influence in Africa that it is quoted on all kinds of occasions – religious, economic, social, cultural and political. For example, in the 2017 general elections in Kenya, the leaders of the opposition used the narrative of Moses and the Israelites crossing the Red Sea to the promised land. When they did not win the election, they argued that when they reached the Red Sea, they found it was infested with crocodiles. Even though there is no mention of crocodiles in Exodus, the narrative was one that people could identify with and was used to legitimize the party and explain its defeat. Similarly, people will quote the Bible when discussing gender issues without much concern for what the Bible actually says in context. They simply use the Bible to legitimize culturally constructed gender roles. They ignore the fact that the Bible was written in a culture that was both androcentric and patriarchal, and they also ignore the fact that the principles laid out in Scripture undermine this world view.

That comment about the Bible in the last sentence may startle some readers, so let me explain what I mean. First, I am not denying that the Bible was inspired by God. But even those who hold to a very high view of Scripture acknowledge that God worked through human agents and that the writers' individual personalities and interests shine through their writing. It is also true that the Bible's human authors were probably all men. Only two of the thirty-nine books in Old Testament are named after women: Ruth and Esther. None of the twenty-seven New Testament books is named after a woman.

The story of the Bible also focuses largely on the public life of the people which was dominated by male figures such as kings, warriors, priests and prophets. We hear little about the private space that was occupied by women, and only a few women are mentioned by name. Thus the subject matter of the Bible is more masculine than feminine, reflecting the male-centred world of the time.

Yet as we read both the Old and New Testaments, we become aware that gender issues do emerge there too. Because this chapter is short, it is impossible to deal with all these issues here, and I will have to focus only on some key issues relating to gender and creation and gender in the ministry of Jesus.

The account of creation in Genesis 1 emphasizes the equality of men and women and makes no mention of any hierarchy or difference. Both male and female are made in the image and likeness of God, both are responsible for ruling the earth, both are blessed and both are responsible for being fruitful (Gen 1:26–28). The man and the woman are fully equal. However, Genesis 2 introduces a difference in the way human beings were created. In this account, both the man and the woman were created from a single human, but the man names the woman, which indicates that he has authority over her (Gen 2:21–23). Yet at the same time, in Genesis 2:24 we are told that a man is to leave his father and mother and cleave to his wife, which is not the case in most cultures of the world. It is usually the woman who leaves her parents and cleaves to the husband. Clearly we need to think carefully about some aspects of gender in light of our current realities.

The incarnation, life and ministry of Jesus give us another lens for looking at gender issues. The society in which Jesus became incarnate and lived for thirty-three years was a patriarchal one in which both women and men had gender-constructed roles. The men we encounter in the Gospels are portrayed as kings, leaders, priests, Pharisees and Sadducees. They are shown engaged in occupations like fishing.

While men are shown to have roles in the public sphere, women's roles are in the private realm. And yet there is no one portrayal of women in the Gospels. While some women are portrayed as carrying out roles typically determined by gender such as nurturing and caring, other women are portrayed with traits that are not typically regarded as feminine. We see resilient women like the woman with the flow of blood and the Syrophoenician woman. A Samaritan woman has a long theological discussion with Jesus. There is the woman who anointed Jesus, and Martha and Mary who hosted Jesus and his disciples. Other women are daring and follow Jesus to the place of his death and wake up early to visit his burial site.

There can be no doubt that Jesus taught and performed his miracles in a patriarchal context, yet it is also clear that he endeavoured to empower women. For example, he broke social norms by touching an "unclean" bleeding women and a dead girl (Mark 5:21–43), by appointing both men and women as his followers (John 4:1–42), and by sending both men and women to spread his message (Matt 28:1–10). He also challenged the gender stereotypes that denounced sexual unfaithfulness on the part of women but not when it was done by men (John 8:1–11). In doing so, he refused to subscribe to a gender discriminative worldview and interpretation of the law. Jesus's way of dealing with the gender issues of his time was to introduce a transformative way of thinking, bringing to the centre those who were marginalized and empowering them to have a voice.

The early church maintained Jesus's radical transformative stance towards women for a while. The church was founded as a community where distinctions of gender, class, race and ethnicity were not tolerated. Peter quoted the Old Testament in support of their approach:

In the last days, God says,
> I will pour out my Spirit on all people.
> Your sons and daughters will prophesy,
> your young men will see visions,
> your old men will dream dreams
> Even on my servants, both men and women,
> I will pour out my Spirit in those days,
> and they will prophesy. (Acts 2:17–18)

In the Acts of the Apostles, the church is shown as a community that attempted to do away with all oppressive social categories. The members of the new community were known as children of God regardless of their gender role. This point emerges clearly in Paul's letter to the Galatians: "So in Christ Jesus you are all children of God through faith, for all of you who were baptized into Christ have clothed yourselves with Christ. There is neither Jew nor Gentile, neither slave nor free, nor is there male and female, for you are all one in Christ Jesus" (Gal 3:26–28).

Elsewhere in Paul's letters he teaches that in Christ we have attained a freedom that should not be denied or compromised by any social system. He acknowledges the ministry of women and men, and even the ministry of women in preaching the gospel. In his letter to the church in Rome, for instance, he mentions ten women – Phoebe, Priscilla, Mary, Junia, Tryphena, Tryphosa, Persis, the mother of Rufus, Julia, and the sister of Nereus (Rom 16:1–15). Paul describes these women in different ways and speaks of their roles as deacons, co-workers and apostles in the ministry of preaching the gospel. In his letter to the church in Corinth, Paul also shows that he recognizes the equality of the genders in marriage when he states that both spouses have conjugal rights. The wife has authority over the man's body, and the man has authority over the woman's body (1 Cor 7:4). He does not regard marriage as a must for all and insists that both men and women have a right to give up marriage in order to serve God (1 Cor 7). This idea went against the norms of Paul's time and the norms of Africa, where being single is often frowned on or looked down upon.

It is true that there are places where Paul seems to contradict some of what has been said above about his views on gender equality, as when he discusses women's clothing and their leadership (1 Cor 11:1–16; 14:33–35). But when we look at the context, it is easy to see why Paul reintroduces ideas of hierarchy and traditional roles. He was writing within the Greco-Roman empire, and Christians knew they would face persecution if they violated too many social norms. In the surrounding culture, there was a great fear of "free women" and a great stress on hierarchy. These cultural norms affected the structure of the church. Just as it did with the issue of slavery, the early church chose not to challenge the existing system of relationships at that time, although that is not to say that the early church endorsed slavery or the oppression of women.

Public Theology and Specific Gender Issues

Today there is still fear of the empowerment of women and the marginalization of men (see the examples above). It is thus important that we address these concerns. The place to begin is by acknowledging that male supremacy is entrenched in our social, political and economic systems and that men are eager to preserve the status quo. One reason for this situation is the belief that men are stronger than women and so women should depend on men for survival. Male leadership is thus viewed as the only legitimate leadership and is thought of as protective for women. These beliefs may have had some foundation in an era when women were constantly pregnant and men had to hunt for food and defend new mothers and babies from attack by wild animals, but they no longer apply today. Instead, these patriarchal beliefs have often become toxic and are the basis for violence against women and the exclusion of women from leadership roles where mere physical strength is not a requirement.

Gender violence

Newspapers are filled with stories of gender-based violence in the domestic and public spheres. Statistics show that one in every four women around the world has been beaten, abused or coerced into sex during her lifetime. Men and boys also experience sexual violence, especially in conflict countries and in situations where their gender identity conflicts with gender norms. It seems as though gender-based violence is now normalized.

Recently, many movements have been formed to address gender violence (e.g. Me Too; My Dress, My Choice; Time's Up; and Thursdays in Black). But theologians and the church have often remained silent. They are happy to speak out about political, economic and cultural issues, but they leave it to women to talk about gender-based violence. This is wrong. Gender-based violence should be discussed by both men and women, and it should be a keen concern of public theology. Gender violence needs to be something that is addressed from the pulpit.

Gendered leadership

Many still assume that male leadership is the only legitimate leadership. This applies in society in general, and it also applies in the church. While some women are now being ordained, this is happening in the face of barriers that do not apply to men. For example, women may be barred from some forms of leadership because they are single, widowed or single mothers. Men who are single, widowed, or who have fathered children out of wedlock face far fewer obstacles.

In most parts of Africa, women face the additional hurdle of ethnicity. Leaders are often chosen based on ethnic criteria. For a man, it is not a major problem if his wife is of a different ethnicity. But a woman who marries a man of a different ethnicity forfeits her original ethnic identity without being fully accepted into her husband's ethnic group. This constitutes a barrier to leadership because both groups are suspicious of her ethnic identity and regard her as an outsider. It is time that we ask how this linking of gender and ethnicity relates to the fact that in Genesis it is the man who is told to leave his parents and cleave to his wife.

Given the link between leadership and education, it is no surprise that men outnumber women in African universities. However, the imbalance is even greater in theological institutions, where men vastly outnumber women. The result is that in our churches women largely occupy the pews and men occupy the pulpits. If the church is really committed to inclusive leadership, it needs to deliberately reach out and offer training to more women.

But gendered leadership does not only refer to who leads but also to how they lead. Within society and within the church, we often see domineering male leadership that allows little space for female leadership. Male leadership often depends on the use of power *over* people rather than power *with* people, which is what women prefer. Leadership models based on domination and subjugation are not in line with the teaching of Jesus Christ and do not reflect the way Jesus related to the men and women of his day.

The impact of the unequal power relations of men over women has been to increase inequality. Women hear the message that they are not equal to men and are not called by God to use the gifts they have been given by God. They are relegated to roles and responsibilities within the private sphere of the home where their contributions are undervalued and largely unrecognized.

Gender identity

We assume that every child that is born is either a boy or a girl. However, it sometimes happens that a child is born with both male and female biological features, or with neither. It can be difficult to determine whether such a child is male or female. Cultures differ in how they respond to such children. In some indigenous cultures, children of indeterminate sex were regarded as two-spirited and given a distinct or separate status. In others cultures, such a child was killed at birth.

Today, there is considerable debate about how we should respond to those whose physiology, chromosomes or hormones mean that they do not fit in the categories of male and female in terms of their biological make-up or gender roles. The debate is complex, but the one point on which Christians should agree is that these people are human beings, and as such they are also made in the image of God and are loved by God. We should respond to them with respect, listen to their concerns and treat them with kindness.

Conclusion

Our understandings of gender roles are profoundly shaped and maintained by our cultures. This is inevitable because our culture is a major framework of meaning that guides how our relationships are formulated and lived out. Culture is about our way of living, loving, eating, playing and worshipping. Culture is different for different people, groups and times, but it is always present. No human being can exist without a culture of some kind.

Sometimes we forget that culture is not static. It changes over time. For example, women are now showing that they are capable of performing roles that were previously restricted to men, and are claiming these roles. Understandably, this change is stressful. For some it represents a step into the unknown, while for others it represents a loss of things to which they felt entitled. This stress explains why some people look for ways to deny female empowerment, claiming that it goes against our culture.[3] But culture cannot be absolutized. We need to recognize that in some respects our traditional culture may have harmed women (and thus also men). Rigid understandings of gender do not allow us to exercise the gifts given to each of us by God.

We need to grasp the truth that all human beings are created in the image and likeness of God (Gen 1:26–28). This truth applies to the whole human community. The group identified as male does not represent God on its own. Rather, God is represented by both genders existing together in mutuality rather than hierarchy.

---

3. Musimbi Kanyoro, "Culture," in *Dictionary of Third World Theologies*, eds. V. Fabella and R. S. Sugirtharajah (Maryknoll, NY: Orbis, 2000), 62–63.

When we grasp this truth, we will also grasp the need to challenge the rigid gender norms embedded in our understandings of masculinity and femininity. These norms are largely stereotypes and are very unfair to both genders. We will set about dealing with gender issues in the same way that Jesus dealt with them in his day through transforming marginalized individuals by acknowledging them and giving them a place in society.

Questions

1. We tend to focus on God as our father. But are there also ways in which God is like a mother? Should we talk of these things too? Why?
2. What is the understanding of gender roles in your community? Are there any people who do not conform to the expected cultural roles? How are they regarded within the community? How does your church's response to them align with the way Jesus responded to men and women?
3. What scope is there for women to exercise leadership in different areas of your church?
4. What can you do to address gender violence in your community?
5. How can we encourage both girl children and boy children to use the skills God has given them without being trapped by gender roles?

Further Reading

Dube, Musa W., ed. *Other Ways of Reading: African Women and the Bible*. Atlanta: SBL; Geneva: WCC, 2001.

Mouton, Elna, Gertrude Kapama, Len Hansen, and Thomas Togom. *Living with Dignity: African Perspectives on Gender Equality*. Stellenbosch: SUN, 2015. https://pdfs.semanticscholar.org/f106/9f46cd9bcc4d3d5d825cd0a6bc4a9c64399e.pdf.

Oduyoye, Mercy Amba. *Daughters of Anowa: African Women and Patriarchy*. Maryknoll, NY: Orbis, 1995.

Tearfund. *Silent No More: The Untapped Potential of the Worldwide Church in Addressing Sexual Violence*. Teddington, Middlesex: Tearfund, 2011. https://www.wewillspeakout.org/resources/silent/.

17

Migration and Human Trafficking

Babatunde Adedibu

Migration is not a new phenomenon. It has been part of the human story for more than six hundred thousand years, since human beings left the Rift Valley in Africa and moved into the rest of the world. Migration simply means moving from one place to another.

Migration is also deeply embedded in biblical history, for Abraham became a migrant when he left Ur, and his descendants became immigrants in Egypt and later fled that country as refugees seeking a promised land. Many centuries later, they experienced forced migration and lived as exiles in Assyria and Babylon. They went on to experience the hardships of returnees, as recorded in the books of Ezra and Nehemiah. Migration also played a key role in the growth of the New Testament church as Christians scattered by persecution linked up with the Jewish diaspora across the world, taking the gospel with them. Clearly, migration is not purely negative, although times are often hard for migrants.

Today the same factors that drove earlier migrations are still at work: war, ethnic conflicts, natural disasters and economic opportunities. However, the twentieth century ushered in a new dispensation in international migration with the rise of nation states and the issuing of passports and visas to control the movement of people across borders. The result has been increased focus on issues of identity and belonging and increased difficulties for migrants. The politicization of migration has led to claims that countries need to "crack down" on migration in order to maintain their sovereignty.

Yet the reality is that most cities and nations are now melting pots of ethnicities and cultural diversity, even if the church has not yet fully recognized this change. In this chapter, we will discuss why people migrate, the benefits and serious drawbacks of migration and the crimes of those who exploit migrants. We conclude with a challenge to Christians and the church to rethink how they relate to migrants and to help all migrants achieve their full potential.

Push and Pull Dynamics in African Migration

Migrants leave their homes partly because they are pushed out and partly because they are pulled by what other places have to offer. There is no clearer illustration of the strength of these push and pull dynamics in African migration than the harrowing pictures of those drowned when flimsy boats capsized as they attempted to cross the Mediterranean Sea from Africa to Europe. These men and women were young and healthy. What drove them to leave their homes, cross the vast Sahara and undertake such a dangerous journey? The push factors must have been very strong.

For African young people, these push factors include grinding poverty, which is endemic in some regions. People who see no hope of escaping poverty may set out in hope of finding better circumstances elsewhere, either for their own sakes or in the hope of being able to send money home to relieve the distress of their families. Their poverty is often an indirect result of corruption at all levels of government that deprives them of services, education and aid. Many who want to use their skills are thwarted by incessant demands for bribes and forced payments to various groups. There is also the failure of African governments to address issues like environmental degradation and climate change. Those who can no longer eke out a living from their family's land must either migrate or starve. Unemployment and an absence of hope for change in the foreseeable future are strong push factors.

Other migrants may come from regions where they could survive as farmers or business owners but find their lives totally disrupted by political instability, civil wars and ethnic and religious crises. Driven from their homes, or living with the knowledge that it is only a matter of time before their homes and their very lives will again be threatened, it is not surprising that many of them seek to find a more peaceful place where they can flourish. When they hear of places that offer educational opportunities, better social amenities and infrastructure, security and more professional opportunities, the pull factor combines with the push factor and they set out as migrants.

It is important to distinguish migrants whose motives are purely economic from those who are forced to migrate by persecution or some ethno-religious crisis. The latter group have the right to apply for asylum and refugee status under the 1951 Refugee Convention of the United Nations, which has been ratified by 145 states. This convention sets out the rights of migrants and the legal obligations on receiving nations to safeguard them. States are required to have an effective clearing system for migrants at the various ports of entry in order to identify who qualify as refugees and who do not. However, many states still lack adequate systems.[1]

Pros and Cons of Migration

Many today assume that most migration occurs as people from the global South move to the global North. But this is not the case. The majority of migrants in the global North come from the global North, and the majority of migrants in the global South come from the global South.[2] Thus migration is not synonymous with movement from developing countries to developed countries; it takes place everywhere and is a universal phenomenon. Within Africa, we see migration from rural areas to the cities and from struggling regions to more prosperous regions, both within one country and across international boundaries.

When those who migrate are skilled professional workers, there is often talk of a "brain drain" which is said to contribute to the ongoing problems of their places of origin. Studies have shown that Burundi loses a lot of its top talent to migration, as do Algeria, Mauritania, Chad and Guinea.[3] However, we must beware of overly simplistic responses to brain drain. Academics who have left have become part of the international African diaspora, and their work has resulted in the emergence and sustenance of institutional collaboration with universities in their former homelands.[4]

A World Bank Report also noted that the positive effect of the African diaspora on African exports is higher than the average effect of migration on exports at the world level.[5] Disapora migrants are able to overcome the major challenges of African trade such as institutional weakness, information costs

---

1. For more on issues relating to refugees, see chapter 18, "Refugees and Stateless People."

2. United Nations Department of Economic and Social Affairs: Population Division. *International Migration Report 2017* (ST/ESA/SER.A/403), 1.

3. Klaus Schwab, *United Nation's World Economic Forum's Global Competitiveness Report 2014–2015* (Switzerland: World Economic Forum, 2014).

4. Jacky Kaba Ahmadu, "Africa's Migration Brain Drain: Factors Contributing to the Mass Emigration of Africa's Elite to the West," in *The New African Diaspora*, eds. Isidore Okpewho and Nkiru Nzegwu (Bloomington: Indiana University Press, 2009), 109.

5. Schwab, *United Nations World Economic Forum*.

and a lack of integrity. Moreover, these migrants not only contribute to their host countries; they also contribute to the economy of their country of origin through the money they send home to their loved ones.

Migrants in the African diaspora are playing a major role in churches worldwide. For example, the Redeemed Christian Church of God (RCCG), which was founded in Nigeria, is now present in 198 countries. It can even be said that African worshippers are bringing new life to dying churches in the West.

It is, however, important to note that many migrants do not reach their destination. They often have to cross other countries in order to get there, and some choose to remain in those countries or are forced to do so by circumstances such as illness or a lack of money to continue their journeys. Others are detained in migrant camps like those set up in Libya which are similar to prisons.

Migrants are not always warmly received in the countries to which they go. The differences in culture and language cause strains, as does the perceived competition for employment between migrants and the receiving country's nationals. Migrants are also perceived as putting a strain on the social, health and infrastructural facilities of the host country. These perceptions have resulted in xenophobic and racial attacks on migrants in both African and Western countries, resulting in the destruction of their possessions and in some cases the loss of life.

We should not dismiss these concerns out of hand, for it is true that immigration changes the social, political, economic and cultural tapestry of any society. This fact has led to the politicization of migration by leaders who claim to be exercising their sovereign right to determine issues affecting their country. The question we as Christians face is how we are to respond to such changes.

One of the other major problems associated with migration is the emergence of human trafficking. This problem is so vast that we will discuss it under a separate heading.

Human Trafficking

The rise in African migration has been accompanied by a rise in human trafficking, particularly in West and Central Africa. Such trafficking is not a new phenomenon – it is following in the footsteps of those who trafficked slaves in Africa, which is why human trafficking and modern slavery are often spoken of as twin evils.

In order to understand and combat human trafficking, we first have to agree on what it is. That explains the importance of the international agreement known as the Palermo Protocol which was signed in December 2000. This UNICEF document defines human trafficking as follows:

> Trafficking in Person shall mean the recruitment, transportation, transfer, habouring or receipt of persons, by means of threat or use of force or other forms of coercion, of abduction, of fraud, of deception, of abuse of power or of a position of vulnerability or of the giving or receiving of payments to achieve the consent of a person having control over another person, for the purpose of exploitation. Exploitation shall include at a minimum, the exploitation of others or other forms of sexual exploitation, forced labour or services, slavery or practices similar to slavery, servitude or the removal of organs.[6]

The broad scope of the Palermo Protocol definition of human trafficking reflects the wide variety of forms it may take. It is not necessarily confined to trafficking across international borders and can also include things like forcing young women into the sex trade or into domestic slavery.

Migrants are particularly vulnerable to trafficking because of the push factors that create their need to flee, including anarchy, failed states, ethnic or religious crises, civil wars, natural disasters, political instability, economic crises or poverty. People who are struggling to deal with new social, economic, political or geographical circumstances are easy targets for those who desire to exploit them. Many migrants use human traffickers or smugglers for at least one stage of their journey to their desired destination, particularly on routes that are conflict prone or pass through dangerous zones that are under the control of religious fundamentalists. Human traffickers can also provide the required local intelligence to navigate border checks, particularly in regions where there are restrictions on crossing international boundaries or where the political, economic or religious status of the migrants makes it impossible for them to use or procure the required travelling documents. In places like Libya, smugglers travel alongside their clients. Their knowledge of the Sahara is essential for immigrants seeking to cross its vast expanse with inadequate resources.

---

6. UNICEF, "Trafficking in Human Beings, especially Women and Children," UNICEF Innocenti Resource Centre (2003), 3.

The smugglers' motives may be mixed. Some may actually want to help the migrants reach their destination, but others are more interested in the money that can be made from desperate migrants.

Migrants find smugglers through social and community networks and rely mostly on personal recommendations. The fee for the smugglers services may be high: it can cost as much as US $2,000 to travel to Khartoum in Sudan and then on to Libya.[7] Once a destination and fee have been agreed on, the smugglers use a network of contacts to get their clients from one point to another across various terrains. Many migrants lose their lives in transit, dying in the desert or drowning in the Mediterranean as they are transported to Europe in overloaded boats that capsize or are swamped by waves. Still others fall prey to gangs who rape and abuse them.

For those migrants who do reach their destination, their dependence on their traffickers may turn their dream into a nightmare. Many migrants live in exploitative and dehumanizing conditions and experience intimidation and harassment by the authorities and by their traffickers. Women may be trapped and forced to work as prostitutes to repay the cost of their trafficking to Europe. However, through the Palermo Protocol and the work of various governments and pressure groups, legislation is now in place in many European countries to address the issue of human trafficking within their jurisdictions. But many migrants are unaware of the legal protections available to them, or are reluctant to risk contacting the authorities because of their past experience with officialdom and because they are in the country illegally. Their fear increases their vulnerability.

Discouraging Migration

The phenomenal loss of life that accompanies irregular migration has led to calls for strong measures to discourage migration. Many countries have launched information campaigns to dissuade irregular migrants from setting out on their risky journeys. Before discussing these campaigns, it is important to note that no campaign will be truly effective unless we also understand the drivers of migration and address them by remedying the evils that lead people to make desperate choices.

Official information campaigns stress the hazards of the journey, the likelihood of dying en route and the lack of welcome by the receiving countries,

---

7. Heaven Crawley, Franck Duvell, Katharine Jones, Simon McMahon, and Nando Sigona, *Unravelling Europe's "Migration Crisis"* (Bristol: Policy Press, 2008), 91.

but they have proven ineffective. Prospective migrants do not trust the message because of the vested interest of those who direct the campaigns. Moreover, the severity of the political persecution, religious crises and economic conditions in the country of origin may mean that the perceived benefits of successful migration far outweigh the risks involved.[8]

There is an urgent need for credible ways to discourage young people from embarking on journeys that lead to death rather than new life. The United Nations High Commissioner for Refugees (UNHCR) has provided practical guidelines on how both governments and non-government organizations can go about doing this.[9] These guidelines are summarized as follows by Evie Browne:

- Information campaigns are most effective when they target the entire community rather than only potential migrants, since decisions to leave a home country are generally based on, and supported by, a family or community.
- Information campaigns must not discourage legitimate refugees or asylum seekers. Raising awareness about legal migration opportunities, where they exist, can increase the effectiveness of information campaigns.
- Mass media campaigns, using radio or television, can address large audiences of different profiles and backgrounds.
- Discussion sessions and theatre productions may reach fewer persons, but they offer a more in-depth opportunity to discuss, exchange ideas and persuade individuals to change their minds.
- "Catch-phrase messages" are useful for attracting the attention of the audience and providing information on complex matters in a direct and memorable manner. The language of these messages can also be tailored to the culture of the audience.
- Real-life testimonies can render information more accessible and intelligible.
- Using celebrities or high-profile individuals to convey messages can help establish trust, reach the target audience, and raise difficult and sometimes contentious issues.[10]

---

8. Evie Browne, "Impact of Communication Campaigns to Deter Irregular Migration," *Governance and Social Development Resource Centre Helpdesk Research Report 1248*, University of Birmingham (2015), 2.

9. UNHCR, "Chapter 10: Information Strategy," in *Refugee Protection and Mixed Migration: The 10-Point Plan in Action* (Geneva, 2011).

10. Browne, "Impact of Communication Campaigns," 4.

Churches and Christian groups may want to think about how some of these recommendations can be adapted for use in their settings. For example, producing a mass media campaign is expensive, but social media platforms may be more effective and are far cheaper to set up. Churches and NGOs can also join forces to encourage political and economic leaders to address the factors that prompt migration and develop policies on how to provide for migrants.

Caring for Migrants

Christian work should not be limited to discouraging migration. We also have to work to help those who are in the process of migration and those who have reached their destination. These migrants have to cope with major change as they try to adapt to a new culture where they may not know the local languages. They may be dismissed by some as ignorant interlopers, but we as Christians need to acknowledge their human dignity and offer them kindness. Doing so is not optional for us but mandatory, for the Bible commands us to love our neighbours and our enemies. We should point those who deny that migrants are our neighbours to Christ's parable of the good Samaritan in which he establishes that we are to be neighbours to anyone who needs help.

We also need to remember that in Genesis God ordered Abraham to leave his home and become a migrant, a migrant through whom all nations would be blessed. Contemporary migrants too can be sources of blessing and should be treated with dignity and respect. We should also respond to them with empathy, as many have faced life-threatening situations that have left physical and emotional scars.

The law of Moses commands that strangers or migrants be shown love, granted protection and treated fairly (Lev 19:33–34; Deut 24:17). The practical outworking of this care is demonstrated in the book of Ruth, where a Moabite migrant becomes part of King David's family tree and thus an ancestor of Christ. Job specifically mentions care for strangers as one of the good things he has done (Job 29:16). In the New Testament, Christ commends caring for strangers as being equivalent to caring for him, and he promises blessing to those who care for those who cannot care for themselves (Matt 25:34–36; Luke 14:12–14). Paul commanded the Roman Christians to practise hospitality (Rom 12:13), as did Peter in 1 Peter 4:9. So did the writer of the letter to the Hebrews, who specifically mentions showing hospitality to strangers (Heb 13:2–3).

A statement put out by the World Council of Churches makes the point clearly:

We are told: "Do not forget to entertain strangers, for by so doing some people have entertained angels without knowing it" (Heb 13:2). Churches can be a place of refuge for migrant communities; they can also be intentional focal points for intercultural engagement. The churches are called to be one to serve God's mission beyond ethnic and cultural boundaries and ought to create multi-cultural ministry and mission as a concrete expression of common witness in diversity. This may entail advocating justice in regard to migration policies and resistance to xenophobia and racism.[11]

Although the rising tide of religious terrorism and xenophobia might make us sceptical or fearful of welcoming strangers from different cultural and social backgrounds, our recognition of the dignity and humanity of migrants requires us to show practical love to the displaced, poor, and economically disadvantaged.

Questions

1. What are the push and pull factors affecting migration in your region? What concrete steps can you take to reduce the effect of the push factors?
2. What information does your community have about the dangers of informal migration?
3. What could you do to affirm the human dignity of migrants in your community?
4. Are there ways in which those who have migrated from your community and found success can be encouraged to help potential migrants in the community, whether by helping them avoid human traffickers or by making it possible for them to remain in the community?
5. Is there any legislation in your country that addresses the challenges of human trafficking?

Further Reading

Basumatary, Songram, ed. *Migration in Perspectives: Towards the Age of Migration from the Margins*. New Delhi: Gurukul, 2018.

Castles, Stephen, Haas de Hein, and Mark J. Miller. *The Age of Migration: International Population Movements in the Modern World*. New York: Guilford Press, 2013.

---

11. World Council of Churches, Jooseop Keum, ed., *Together towards Life: Mission and Evangelism in Changing Landscapes* (Geneva: WCC Publications, 2013), 26.

Crawley, Heaven, Franck Duvell, Katharine Jones, Simon McMahon, and Nando Sigona. *Unravelling Europe's "Migration Crisis."* Bristol: Policy Press, 2008.

IOM Staff. *Human Trafficking in Eastern Africa: Research Assessment and Baseline Information in Tanzania, Kenya, Uganda, and Burundi.* Nairobi: International Organization for Migration. 2008. https://publications.iom.int/books/human-trafficking-eastern-africa.

Padilla, Elaine, and Peter Phan. *Christianities in Migration: The Global Perspectives.* New York: Palgrave Macmillan, 2016.

Synder, Susanna. *Asylum Seeking, Migration and Church.* Farnham, UK: Ashgate, 2012.

18

Refugees and Stateless People

Benaya Niyukuri

L eave the country and get a ration card!" This was the message to Burundians as gunshots forced them to leave their homes. Confined to refugee camps, they were allowed no access to the outside world and had to eat food they would not have chosen for themselves. They were vulnerable, homeless, jobless and stateless. This was my experience, and it is the experience of all refugees. It affects us socially, psychologically, physically, emotionally, mentally, economically and even spiritually. Yet as a student of theology, I have found meaning amidst the dilemmas caused by my own homelessness, joblessness and statelessness. In this chapter, I seek to integrate my personal story with public theology in order to help Christians think about how they should relate to the refugees in their countries.

Ethnic Conflicts in Burundi

Burundi achieved independence from Belgian in 1962. The first prime minister was Prince Louis Rwagasore, the hero of independence, who was Tutsi but led a multi-ethnic party. However, he was assassinated within weeks of winning the election. Burundi was plunged into ethnic violence.

The first post-independence election in 1964 was won by Pierre Ngendandumwe, a Hutu, but many Tutsis could not accept being ruled by a Hutu prime minister, and he too was assassinated in January 1965. The Hutu's angry response to his assassination was violently put down. The following year, Captain Michel Micombero, a Tutsi army chief, launched a successful coup and proceeded to abolish the monarchy and proclaim Burundi a republic. All political parties except his own were banned. Hutu protests resulted in more Hutu deaths.[1] Micombero set out to remove all Hutus from the army and the government. Then in 1972, he launched a "selective genocide," focusing especially on Hutus who had any education. Some 300,000 Hutus died, and many more fled to neighbouring countries.[2] "The conflict produced one of Africa's most prolonged refugee situations, in which over 200,000 Burundian refugees have lived in three designated settlements in western Tanzania, known as the Old Settlements, for 36 years. This refugee population is distinct from those groups of refugees who arrived later and were hosted in refugee camps in north-west Tanzania."[3]

In 1972, my Hutu father was a school principal and so was on the list of those to be killed. By God's grace, he managed to escape and fled to Zaïre, the current Democratic Republic of Congo. However, four of his brothers who were teachers at other schools were killed.

Captain Michel Micombero continued ruling the country with an iron fist until 1976 when he was overthrown by Colonel Jean-Baptiste Bagaza, another Tutsi. In an attempt to promote national reconciliation, Bagaza banned any references to people's ethnic identity. His policies persuaded some Hutu that it was safe to return from exile. But in 1987, he too was overthrown in a coup. His successor, Major Pierre Buyoya, continued his predecessor's development plans but lifted the ban on referring to people's ethnic identities. The next year, fierce ethnic conflict erupted in two districts in the north. Buyoya's intervention to separate the warring parties caused widespread loss of life.

In 1992, the United Nations persuaded President Buyoya to introduce multiparty democracy. The first democratic elections in 1993 saw President Melchior Ndadaye elected as the first Hutu president. Three months later, Ndadaye was assassinated by the army which was still controlled by Tutsis. Angered by the death of Ndadaye, the Hutus took up arms, and the resulting civil war led to thousands of deaths and to many people becoming refugees.[4] The war ended only after the Arusha Peace Agreement was signed on 28 August 2000.

---

1. Rene Lemarchand, *Burundi: Ethnic Conflict and Genocide* (Cambridge: Cambridge University Press, 1996), 69–70.

2. Bridget Johnson, "A History of Hutu-Tutsi Conflict," Thoughts.Co (7 May 2019).

3. Jessie Thomson, *Durable Solutions for Burundian Refugees in Tanzania* (2008), https://www.fmreview.org/sites/fmr/files/FMRdownloads/en/protracted/thomson.pdf.

4. Lemarchand, *Burundi*, 119.

When President Ndadaye was assassinated on 21 October 1993, I was away from home in a boarding school. Fearing what would follow, my friends and I decided to flee. I put on three pairs of trousers and pulled a large pair of jeans on over them. I also put on three shirts, and my friends did the same. However, some of our schoolmates saw what we were doing and reported us. Soldiers came and assembled us all in the dining hall. They intimidated us, asking why some of us had put on more than one set of clothing. We took off all our extra layers for fear of being searched and tortured.

Early the next morning, we slipped out of the school and set off on a long journey without even knowing which direction to take. Along the way, we met some people who advised us not to walk during the day. They hid us in a house and slaughtered a goat to feed us. Then at around four in the afternoon, we set out to walk to Tanzania. We reached the river that marked the border at midnight and joined the large group of refugees gathered on the far side of the river.

We spent some time there, only returning home when we saw some prospect of peace. But I could not return to my boarding school, for there were grenade attacks on students. So I decided to attend a school near my home. But schooling was not easy because of the ongoing fighting between rebel groups and government forces. Men took turns mounting watch around the village while women and children slept. At the least sign of suspicious activity, those on watch would wake everyone to flee the place. It was very difficult to study after such disturbed nights.

In 2001, I decided it was time to flee to far away Namibia and apply for asylum. But I found that life as an asylum seeker was not easy either. Food supplies were limited, and I was unemployed and confined to a refugee camp.

All of this background explains why I am qualified to speak about the problems faced by refugees. My subsequent training in theology has helped me to reflect on what the Bible has to say about these problems and on how the church can help refugees.

Refugees and Asylum Seekers

Before the Second World War, there was no clear, universally accepted definition of who qualified as a refugee and no obligation on other countries to accept them. Since 1951, however, a refugee has been defined by the United Nations as someone who owing to well-founded fear of being persecuted for reasons of race, religion, nationality, membership of a particular social group or political opinion, is outside the country of his [or her] nationality and is unable, or owing to such fear, is unwilling to avail him [or her]self of the protection of that country; or who, not having a nationality and being outside the country of his [or her] former habitual residence as a result of such events, is unable or, owing to such fear, is unwilling to return to it.[5]

This definition has also been expanded over time to include people who flee generalized violence in their regions.

Anyone who claims to be a refugee is subjected to careful scrutiny to determine whether they meet the criteria laid down by the United Nations High Commissioner for Refugees (UNHCR) as well as international or regional eligibility criteria. While the decision about their status is being made, the person is often referred to as an "asylum seeker" rather than a refugee.[6]

The UNHCR allows countries to set up their own procedures for processing refugee claims, insisting only that these procedures must be fair, efficient and non-discriminatory. Those making the decisions need to be fully aware that "a wrong decision might cost the person's life or liberty."[7] That is why officials need to be trained so that they have special skills, awareness and expertise in issues related to asylum. These skills include the ability to work with qualified and impartial interpreters, familiarity with cross-cultural interviewing techniques and knowledge of the special techniques required when interviewing women, children and "survivors of sexual abuse, torture or other traumatizing events."[8] Christians who want to work with refugees would do well to seek to develop these skills themselves.

One very important issue is confidentiality. Any information shared by an asylum seeker should remain strictly confidential. "No information should be shared with the authorities of the applicant's country of origin, nor should such information be released to any third party without the express consent

---

5. United Nations High Commissioner for Refugees (UNHCR), *Refugee Status Determination: Identifying Who Is a Refugee,* Self-study module 2 (Geneva, 2005), 5, https://www.refworld.org/pdfid/43141f5d4.pdf.

6. United Nations High Commissioner for Refugees (UNHCR), *UNHCR Protection Training Manual for European Border and Entry Officials: 3 Who Is a Refugee?* (Brussels: UNHCR Bureau for Europe, 2011), 4.

7. UNHCR, *Refugee Status Determination,* 112.

8. UNHCR, 114.

of the individual concerned."[9] Breach of confidentiality may put the asylum seeker's life at risk. This means that Christians must exercise caution even when requesting prayer or any other support for particular refugees.

Asylum seekers are entitled to expect to be informed about any decision on their refugee status in writing and to be told the reason if their refugee claim is rejected. Those whose claims have been rejected should not be deported immediately but should be allowed to appeal the decision before a body that is independent of the one that made the first decision.[10]

The process of applying for refugee status can be long and stressful, and so can add to the suffering of refugees. The process is especially painful when refugee status is denied.

Once a person is accepted as a refugee, "they will be entitled to a number of important rights and benefits as well as assistance and protection measures which, taken together, constitute what is known as 'international refugee protection'. Refugees also have certain obligations towards the host State, notably that of abiding by the laws of the host country."[11]

The Challenges Faced by Refugees

Whether granted refugee status or not, refugees and asylum seekers face challenges while living in the countries of asylum. They often find themselves confined to refugee camps and endure stigma, unemployment and poverty, all of which may lead to frustration, deep depression and nostalgia for their past.[12]

Stigma

The terms "asylum" and "asylum seeker" now have "overwhelmingly negative connotations in the minds of policymakers, the public and the media, especially in the more prosperous regions of the world."[13] It is assumed that refugees are

---

9. UNHCR, 118.

10. UNHCR, 118.

11. UNHCR, 4.

12. Lisa E. Baranik, Carrie S. Hurst, and Lillian T. Eby, "The Stigma of Being a Refugee: A Mixed-Method Study of Refugees' Experiences of Vocational Stress," *Journal of Vocational Behavior* 105 (2018): 121.

13. Jeff Crisp, *Beyond the Nexus: UNHCR's Evolving Perspective on Refugee Protection and International Migration*, New Issues in Refugee Research, Paper No. 155 (UNHCR: Geneva, 2008), 2.

passive and reliant on aid.[14] As a pastoral therapist, I have encountered this stigma when I strive to support people in need of my counselling skills. Fellow pastors have discouraged people from making use of my services, saying that as a refugee I am the one in need of support.

Confinement

Host countries often see refugees as a threat to their existing social structure and to their social resources and infrastructure. They also fear that refugees will take jobs from nationals and generally increase the cost of living.[15] So they seek to minimize expenses related to security, health, education and social services for refugees[16] and confine refugees in overcrowded camps, often located in isolated places with few natural resources. There the refugees face shortages of food, water and fuel and endure other abuses.[17]

Yet, the fears that lead to the confinement of refugees are often unwarranted. Refugees have the potential to be self-reliant and productive, thereby contributing significantly to the economy of host countries, provided that they are allowed access to land, the labour market and freedom of movement.[18] Where refugees have been encouraged to use their skills, they can be self-employed and can create jobs for locals as well as contributing to the tax base. Entrepreneurial and agricultural schemes also enable refugees to be less dependent on aid. This has been evident in countries like Malawi, Mozambique and Zambia where refugees have managed to live in towns with freedom to do business. Refugees have been prosperous enough to make significant contributions to the economy while also providing for their families and employing locals.

Unemployment

Refugees face many challenges when it comes to finding work. They have difficulty finding jobs because employers prefer to hire locals. Those who do find work are often exploited because people expect them to work for less

---

14. Baranik et al., "Stigma of Being a Refugee," 126.

15. Sarah Deardorff Miller, *Assessing the Impacts of Hosting Refugees*, World Refugee Council Research Paper No. 4 (2018), 1.

16. Miller, *Assessing the Impacts*, 1.

17. Baranik et al., "The Stigma of Being a Refugee," 121.

18. Miller, *Assessing the Impacts*, 3–5.

than locals and to put up with worse working conditions. Many refugees are underemployed in the sense that they work fewer hours than they would like or in jobs that do not match their qualifications. Their education and experience in their home countries is often undervalued or discounted. That is why we hear of medical doctors working as taxi drivers.

A lack of proper documentation makes the problem of unemployment even more acute. The types of documents given to refugees are not acceptable in most sectors in the countries of asylum. I can vouch for this from my own experience, for I have struggled to find employment despite having high education qualifications. Far too many job offers come with the requirement "the applicant must be a citizen," indicating that a refugee is not eligible for the advertised post. This situation "causes poverty, financial problems, and inability to afford life in the country of asylum."[19]

Discrimination

Discrimination has been identified as a major cause of anxiety, depression and sleep disturbances among refugees.[20] This discrimination may take the form of physical abuse and harassment or of being treated differently from nationals. It results in poor relationships between refugees and locals, as well as limited networking opportunities, social isolation and a lack of social support.[21]

Language issues are often grounds for discrimination. Having a foreign name, being unable to speak a local language and having a foreign accent when speaking English or French are treated as signs of inferiority. For example, some people make fun of me when I try to speak a local language in Namibia. Others respond in English when I greet them in a local language. My accent betrays me, and people refer to me as an *ombwela*, an Oshiwambo word that means "stranger, one unable to speak the language."

Discrimination also results from refugees' lack of knowledge of the surrounding culture, which makes it difficult for them to blend in. Rather than helping them, citizens of the host culture look down on them as they struggle to deal with unfamiliar legal, administrative, economic and social practices.

---

19. Baranik et al., "The Stigma of Being a Refugee," 117.
20. Baranik et al., 126.
21. Baranik et al., 121.

Statelessness

Every person in the world has the right of citizenship,[22] yet there are currently more than ten million people who are "not recognized as a national of any country."[23] This situation results from "gaps in and between the nationality laws of States, . . . the protracted marginalization of specific groups within a society, or from stripping individuals or groups of their nationality."[24] People thus often end up stateless because of racial or ethnic discrimination. Gender discrimination enhances statelessness among women because they sometimes "lose their citizenship upon marriage to foreigners, and are unable to pass on their citizenship to their children."[25]

Statelessness is a problem because people who are stateless lack identity documents and so face a range of problems. For example, they cannot vote in elections; they cannot obtain travel documents or qualify for employment; and they cannot benefit from many government services in their countries of residence.[26] These services can include education and health care.

Refugees in the Bible

The Bible is full of accounts of people who had to move from their homes to settle in other places. Some of them were being sent into exile; others were escaping natural disasters or famine, or fleeing from political strife, violence or persecution.

> It started with Adam and Eve as they were sent from the Garden to wander, to start again in a new place. Noah and his family were also called, like Adam and Eve, to leave sin behind and begin society in new ways and in a new place. Some of the descendants of Noah built cities; and it was in the city of Ur that Abraham was born, yet God sent Abraham and Sarah out to occupy new land.[27]

---

22. Article 5 of the 1948 Universal Declaration of Human Rights.

23. Marilyn Achiron, *Nationality and Statelessness: Handbook for Parliamentarians* (2014), 3. UNHCR.

24. Achiron, *Nationality and Statelessness*, 5.

25. Indira Goris, Julia Harrington, and Sebastian Köhn, *Statelessness: What It Is and Why It Matters* (2009), 5.

26. Goris et al., *Statelessness*, 5.

27. Christian Churches Together, *What Does the Bible Say about Refugees and Immigrants?* (2013), 1.

Abraham's great-grandson Joseph found himself in Egypt, where he had to live and adjust to a new culture after being sold by his brothers. Later on, Joseph's father (Jacob) and his brothers and their families joined him in Egypt as refugees due to a famine that had ravaged their land.[28] Their descendants endured oppression in Egypt until they fled to the promised land. Centuries later, the people of Israel and Judah were carried into exile by the Assyrians and the Babylonians. Jesus himself became a refugee when his parents fled with him to Egypt while he was still a baby to escape King Herod's slaughter of new-born babies in Bethlehem.[29]

The Bible reminds God's people of their ancestors' experience of being refugees as it urges them to treat refugees as they themselves would like to be treated. "When a foreigner resides among you in your land, do not mistreat them. The foreigner residing among you must be treated as your native-born. Love them as yourself, for you were foreigners in Egypt" (Lev 19:33–34). They had learned a lesson that would keep them from treating others as they had been treated when they were strangers.[30] Foreigners were not to be oppressed or denied justice as had happened to the Israelites in Egypt.

Those foreigners who wished to participate in Jewish festivals, or in other words to adopt the Jewish faith, were expected to take this change in belief seriously. For example, they could not celebrate Passover like a Jew unless they and their household were circumcised to confirm their full membership in the nation (Exod 12:48). However, all foreigners were expected to join the rest of the nation in having a day of rest on the Sabbath (Exod 20:10) and in fasting on the Day of Atonement (Lev 16:29); to obey the regulations on where and how sacrifices were to be offered (Lev 17:8–9; 22:18–20); to abstain from eating blood and the flesh of animals torn by wild beasts (Lev 17:10, 15); and to refrain from blasphemy and obey the laws (Lev 24:16–22). These regulations are in accord with the modern requirements that refugees must obey the laws of their host country.

The Israelites were also commanded to make sure that the foreigners among them had food to eat: "When you reap the harvest of your land, do not reap to the very edges of your field or gather the gleanings of your harvest. Do not go over your vineyard a second time or pick up the grapes that have fallen. Leave them for the poor and the foreigner" (Lev 19:9–10). This instruction was meant to remind the Israelites of the poor people, immigrants and refugees

---

28. Christian Churches Together, *What Does the Bible Say*, 1.

29. Christian Churches Together, 1.

30. John Schultz, *Commentary to the Book of Leviticus* (Bible-Commentaries.com, 2002).

living among them who did not own land and depended on leftovers from the local fields. Besides leaving such leftovers for the poor, the Israelites were also instructed to offer a special tithe from their crops to support strangers, Levites, orphans and widows:

> When you have finished setting aside a tenth of all your produce in the third year, the year of the tithe, you shall give it to the Levite, the foreigner, the fatherless and the widow, so that they may eat in your towns and be satisfied. Then say to the LORD your God: "I have removed from my house the sacred portion and have given it to the Levite, the foreigner, the fatherless and the widow, according to all you commanded. I have not turned aside from your commands nor have I forgotten any of them." (Deut 26:12–13)

The reason the Lord urges his people to love foreigners is that he loves them. We know from John 3:16 that God loves the whole world, but there is already a hint of that truth in Deuteronomy 10:18–19 where the Israelites are told that God "defends the cause of the fatherless and the widow, and loves the foreigner residing among you, giving them food and clothing. And you are to love those who are foreigners, for you yourselves were foreigners in Egypt." We are called to feel compassion for those who suffer because this is how God reacts to their suffering.

The same care for foreigners that was part of the law in the days of Moses continues in the time of the prophets. The prophet Jeremiah delivered this message to the rulers of Judah and to the people around them: "This is what the LORD says: Do what is just and right. Rescue from the hand of the oppressor the one who has been robbed. Do no wrong or violence to the foreigner, the fatherless or the widow, and do not shed innocent blood in this place" (Jer 22:3). Writing at much the same time, the prophet Ezekiel, who was in exile, had a vision of the future when God would restore the nation of Israel. It is striking that his vision of the healed nation is not nationalistic. These are the instructions he relays from the Lord:

> "You are to distribute this land among yourselves according to the tribes of Israel. You are to allot it as an inheritance for yourselves and for the foreigners residing among you and who have children. You are to consider them as native-born Israelites; along with you they are to be allotted an inheritance among the tribes of Israel. In whatever tribe a foreigner resides, there you are to give them their inheritance," declares the Sovereign LORD. (Ezek 47:21–23)

If God prohibits discrimination against foreigners living among his people, then by what right do churches discriminate against people of other ethnic groups? And should not our countries offer refugees the same rights as the native-born as well as the same justice if they fall foul of the law?

Jesus did not specifically discuss his follower's responses to strangers, but he spoke of God's love for the world and sent his followers out to reach the world. They are to become strangers on his behalf as they travel to "all nations" (Matt 28:19). Persecution resulted in some of his first followers becoming refugees, but they "preached the word wherever they went" (Acts 8:1–4). People would have missed great blessing if they had refused to receive these refugees or had confined them to refugee camps. This is probably part of what the writer of the letter to the Hebrews had in mind when he said, "Do not forget to show hospitality to strangers, for by so doing some people have shown hospitality to angels without knowing it" (Heb 13:2). In fact, their hospitality may have been extended to one who is even higher than the angels. Listen to Jesus's words in the parable of the sheep and the goats:

> Then he will say to those on his left, "Depart from me, you who are cursed, into the eternal fire prepared for the devil and his angels. For I was hungry and you gave me nothing to eat, I was thirsty and you gave me nothing to drink, I was a stranger and you did not invite me in, I needed clothes and you did not clothe me, I was sick and in prison and you did not look after me."
>
> They also will answer, "Lord, when did we see you hungry or thirsty or a stranger or needing clothes or sick or in prison, and did not help you?"
>
> He will reply, "Truly I tell you, whatever you did not do for one of the least of these, you did not do for me."
>
> Then they will go away to eternal punishment, but the righteous to eternal life. (Matt 25:41–46)

In this parable the righteous include those who offer hospitality to refugees.

Serving Refugees and Stateless People

If we admit that the Bible calls on us not to reject strangers, including refugees and stateless people, then the church must respond to that call. But how should the church respond? In the first place, we should respond to people's immediate needs for food and shelter. When we cannot help them ourselves, either because we are far away from the location of the refugee crisis or do not have the resources to respond, we should pool our resources with those of aid agencies that can carry out the task.

But we cannot leave the entire response to refugees in the hands of aid agencies. If we do this, we run the risk of solidifying the barriers between "them," the refugees who need care, and "us," the host nation, and such distinctions feed into xenophobia and alienation. The result is refugees being confined to camps filled with other refugees and being denied rights in the country to which they have fled. The camps may be places where refugees' immediate suffering is relieved, but they are not places where their long-term needs can be met and where they can recover from the traumas they have endured.

Here is where Christians as individuals have to step up and befriend and help refugees, seeing them as fellow human beings. Churches too have to reach out to the refugees within reach of their communities, welcoming them as people who will not take from the church and community but will bring blessing to the church and the community by using the skills and gifts that God has given them. Some churches have even deliberately set out to have refugees serving alongside local church members on various committees and in leadership so that the church is aware of the actual needs of refugees in their community, rather than making assumptions about what those needs are. Church leaders too have to interact with community leaders and government officials to ensure that fair and humane guidelines and laws are in place for refugees.

By taking these actions, we can affirm the human dignity of refugees, help to meet their need for family, provide charity, show solidarity and offer spiritual service.[31] Let me explain what these have meant in my life as a refugee.

Affirming human dignity

The people who drove me away from my home regarded me as less than human, not worthy to live. On the road as a refugee, I was hungry, scared and stripped of most of my possessions. Once I reached the safety of a refugee camp, I found that I was reduced to merely "another refugee." There was no place for me in the wider community because I was stigmatized, rejected and denied employment and other benefits because of my refugee status. Is it surprising that at times I felt as if I were worthless and that life was not worth living?

What has restored my human dignity? Theologically, it is the knowledge that I am a human being created in the image of God, regardless of what my

---

31. This section relies heavily on Sandie Cornish, "Welcoming Christ in Refugees & Displaced Persons: Discussion Guide to the Pastoral Guidelines," Social Spirituality (2013), 2.

oppressors may call me. It is also the knowledge that I am one of those whom Christ loves and for whom he died. But I have also needed more day-to-day assurance of my human dignity from other people. I have received this when people have taken the time to know my name, talk with me and listen to me, when my skills and education were acknowledged, and when I was given responsibilities rather than handouts.

Being a family

Refugees and stateless people usually leave their families in their countries of origin. Sometimes family members are killed in war or refugees are separated from them and no longer know where they are. I found myself alone as a young man, having left my family behind, and I suffered from loneliness and the loss of family company and support. This isolation can lead some refugees to join gangs which offer a sense of community. But the church should become a Christian family for refugees. On the theological level, all believers belong to the family of God, but on the day-to-day level, churches need to help by creating opportunities for refugees to interact with people of all ages and to share meals and celebrations with local families. I am grateful to those who "adopted" me into their family as a son or a brother.

Offering charity

Charitable deeds are very important because refugees and stateless people desperately need food and shelter and guidance as they navigate the web of government regulations and the everyday matters of life like getting medical help, getting children into school and even mastering the language. Once they have found shelter, they need to be helped to acquire basic kitchen equipment so they can cook for themselves and bedding so they can sleep well at night. Some may need warm clothes if the nights are cold. This care should not be restricted to members of the Christian family. In Nigeria, some Christian groups offer care to both Muslims and Christians who have suffered in the ongoing violence there.

Showing solidarity

Acknowledging my human dignity is one thing. Standing in solidarity with me is another. It is a public statement that human beings "all form one human family, in spite of our national, ethnic, and cultural differences, and that we are also dependent on each other."[32] Solidarity means challenging xenophobia. It means the willingness to stand with refugees and stateless people in their suffering and powerlessness and to advocate on their behalf. People show solidarity when they speak up on behalf of refugees even though this may expose them to the scorn of others in the community. They take upon themselves the shame of the refugee and so are acting like Christ, who in the incarnation came to stand in solidarity with human beings and deliver them.

Meeting spiritual needs

Even though refugees and stateless people need help meeting their material and social needs, spirituality is also a very important area of their lives that should not be neglected. Refugees should be provided with opportunities to worship with others from their own group and with the local community. They need to hear God's word preached, which is a source of comfort; they need pastoral counselling as they deal with trauma; and they need to sing about their sorrows as well as about the God who hears them. In my suffering as a refugee, I was aware of a huge spiritual hole that needed to be filled. I had so many questions to ask about God's part in my plight. Yet my suffering and questioning drew me closer to God as I wrestled with him in prayer, meditation and lamentation. I ended up writing and reciting poems related to the suffering we endured as refugees. I shared these poems with those around me, whose songs, like mine, were dominated by lament. People in refugee camps spend so much time in prayer, pleading with God to intervene in their suffering. The church should provide a place for them to pray and also a place where they can minister both to their fellow refugees and to the non-refugees around them. Then refugees will be able to say with Paul,

> Praise be to the God and Father of our Lord Jesus Christ, the
> Father of compassion and the God of all comfort, who comforts
> us in all our troubles, so that we can comfort those in any trouble
> with the comfort we ourselves receive from God. For just as we
> share abundantly in the sufferings of Christ, so also our comfort
> abounds through Christ. (2 Cor 1:3–5)

---

32. Cornish, "Welcoming Christ in Refugees," 2.

Conclusion

Paul wrote the words above at a time when he was in similar circumstances to many refugees:

> We were under great pressure, far beyond our ability to endure, so that we despaired of life itself. Indeed, we felt we had received the sentence of death. But this happened that we might not rely on ourselves but on God, who raises the dead. He has delivered us from such a deadly peril, and he will deliver us again. . . . Then many will give thanks on our behalf for the gracious favour granted us in answer to the prayers of many. (2 Cor 1:8–11)

May the church in Africa be active in praying for those who are refugees and stateless; may it be moved to take action on their behalf and to stand in solidarity with them; and may the church in Africa end up praising God for the blessings that refugees and the stateless bring to those who are willing to receive them. This rejoicing will be a foretaste of the reward promised to those who offer the powerless even a cup of cold water, even if that is all they have to give (Matt 10:42).

Questions

1. Are there refugees in your area? If so, what is your church doing to serve them on all four dimensions outlined above?
2. What is the attitude to refugees among the people in your area? What can your church do to change these attitudes?
3. Are there local, regional or national government regulations that make life unnecessarily difficult for refugees? If so, how can you advocate for improvements to these regulations?

Further Reading

Baranik, Lisa E., Carrie S. Hurst, and Lillian T. Eby. "The Stigma of Being a Refugee: A Mixed-Method Study of Refugees' Experiences of Vocational Stress." *Journal of Vocational Behavior* 105 (2018): 116–130.

Crisp, Jeff. *Beyond the Nexus: UNHCR's Evolving Perspective on Refugee Protection and International Migration.* New Issues in Refugee Research. Research Paper No. 155. Geneva: UNHCR, 2008. https://www.unhcr.org/research/working/4818749a2/beyond-nexus-unhcrs-evolving-perspective-refugee-protection-international.html.

Miller, Sarah Deardorff. *Assessing the Impacts of Hosting Refugees.* World Refugee Council Research Paper No. 4, 2018. https://www.cigionline.org/sites/default/files/documents/WRC%20Research%20Paper%20no.4.pdf.

Rupen, Das, and Brent Hamoud. *Strangers in the Kingdom: Ministering to Refugees, Migrants, and the Stateless.* Carlisle: Langham Global Library, 2017.

19

Interfaith Relations

Johnson A. Mbillah[1]

The continent of Africa is known for its vast religious landscape, with most Africans being deeply religious people. Christianity and Islam joined the primordial African religions, commonly referred to as African Traditional Religions, thus producing Africa's triple religious heritage. This triad of religious pillars was then transformed into Africa's rainbow of religions with the addition or growth of other faiths such as Judaism, Hinduism, Sikhism, Jainism and the Baha'i faith.

In the recent past, Africa's rainbow of religions has extended further into a mosaic of religions, as variants of the religions above joined "the pioneer religions" in seeking to attract African followers. Today new religious movements parade themselves all over the continent. Given these developments, there is no doubt that religion plays a pivotal role in shaping the actions and/or inaction of many Africans.

The growing religious plurality in the African continent means that Africans have multiple identities. In the past, for example, people spoke primarily about their ethnic identities. In the present situation, however, someone might say, "I am Kenyan, a Kikuyu, and a Christian of the Presbyterian denomination." Another might say "I am Ethiopian, an Oromo and a Muslim," possibly adding that he or she belongs to the Tijaniyya Sufi fraternity. This maze of possibilities for defining an African's identity can be enriching and rewarding if harnessed properly. Equally, however, the multiple identities can be troublesome and destructive if not harnessed properly.

---

1. This chapter is taken from *African Theology on the Way: Current Conversations*, edited by D. B. Stinton (London: SPCK, 2010). Reproduced with permission of SPCK through PLSclear.

In this chapter we reflect on what the churches in Africa must do to ensure that the mosaic of religions are appropriately harnessed to bring about collaboration and cooperation in attending to human needs and concerns. We also advocate for what the Programme for Christian-Muslim relations in Africa (PROCMURA) calls constructive engagement with other religious groups for peace and peaceful coexistence for the holistic development of the human family. This entails seeking ways to celebrate our common humanity in the spirit of our God-given inalienable rights and freedoms, and being responsible for our actions or inactions. We shall not shy away from issues that may be seen to be controversial in interfaith engagements, but rather highlight them and raise questions for further reflection.

The chapter addresses three key issues, as follows:

- the churches and interfaith relations in Africa;
- the essence of interfaith collaboration and cooperation;
- thorny issues in interfaith relations: what shall we do?

The Churches and Interfaith Relations in Africa

Religious diversity has existed throughout the ages. Our Christian understanding of God, made clear by his self-revelation in Jesus Christ, affirms that religious diversity never came about without God's knowledge. We cannot say that God brought about our religious diversity, but certainly it arose with his knowledge, at best with his permission and at worst against his will. Whatever the case may be, religious diversity has been part and parcel of the entire human family, including the African religious heritage.

Christian theology states that God grants human beings the freedom to choose the religious path that they wish to tread, but they are responsible for the choices that they make. With this understanding, the churches in Africa must be tolerant of the religious variety around them since this diversity is bound to continue until the end of time. A credible question for the churches to ask, therefore, is not how to eradicate religious diversity (for that may mean attempting to eradicate the God-given freedom of human beings), but how to relate constructively with others in this religious diversity.

The churches in Africa, like elsewhere in the world, inherited a certain stream of Christian tradition that discouraged relationships with peoples of other faiths. In some cases it was virtually taboo to do so. Many have asked, "What has belief got to do with unbelief?," or "What has Christianity got to do with 'paganism'?" The common, traditional Christian approach to religious variety has been to bring those outside the household of Christ to Christ – to convert them. More recently, an emerging trend has essentially advised, "Leave them alone; let us relate and not convert lest we give the impression that Christianity is true and the other religions false." These two approaches, as well as other emerging trends, have created different camps within Christianity as far as interfaith relations are concerned.

The two main camps ("convert them by all means" and "leave them alone") need to face the existential reality as it is, and not as they would imagine or wish it to be. For the truth of the matter is that those who see conversion as the ultimate or only objective of interfaith relations have to answer the crucial question: What happens if that objective is not achieved? In other words, if you present the gospel to a person of a different faith who decides to remain in his or her faith, what do you do to still remain friends and good neighbours as narrated in the story of the good Samaritan (Luke 10:25–37)?

For those who are anti-conversion, the question also remains as to whether conversion is in essence an activity of the human person or of the Holy Spirit. If it is of the Holy Spirit, as demonstrated in the story of Cornelius (Acts 10:1–48), for example, who are they to limit the activity of the Holy Spirit? In any case, the reality of the African religious environment shows that significant numbers of people are converted from one faith to another, just as many people choose to remain within their original faith.

What Christian proponents of interfaith relations advocate is that we talk with, and not just about, people of other faiths. We do so because of our faith in Christ who challenges us on what merit there is if we love only those who love us (Luke 6:32). In other words, what merit is there if we take for neighbours only those with whom we share a religion?

Interfaith relations in the African way

In many African societies, especially at grassroots levels, families live together in the same households with interfaith and intra-faith differences. They eat together, work together, celebrate the diverse religious festivals together, share in the joys of birth and the sadness of death, and jointly work towards the development of the community. This phenomenon, which may be described as practical theology brewed in the African pot, demonstrates long-standing African spirituality that focuses on existential matters over dogma. Thus the bedrock of African religiosity is to "live and let live" with religious diversities in harmony.

Therefore, engaging in interfaith relations in Africa today is not a matter of introducing anything new. Rather, a central concern is how to curb the growing intolerant religious spirit that blows around the world, including in parts of Africa such as Nigeria and Sudan to a greater extent, and in other countries to a lesser extent. To put it another way, we need to revitalize our societies, which were previously tolerant of religious diversity, and protect them from the wave of religious intolerance that would rather see us live by the law of the jungle: "eat or be eaten."

To engage effectively with people of other faiths, churches in Africa must first put their own houses in order regarding intra-faith relations, or relations among the various Christian religions. Only then can they agree on the way forward in interfaith relations for peace, harmony and human development. What this means in practice is that all church denominations in Africa must be encouraged to get involved in interfaith relations so as to build bridges of understanding for harmonious relationship.

Interfaith relations from a position of faith

"Interfaith relations" means "faith meeting faith," or people of one faith meeting others of another faith. In practice it is not, and should not be, a meeting aimed at compromising or watering down the beliefs of any faith with the hope of finding a mean and concluding that all faiths are the same. Of course, if all faiths were the same, there would be no need for interfaith relations.

Recently, some international interfaith relations meetings seemed to suggest, whether overtly or covertly, that Christians should do away with their cardinal belief in the uniqueness of Christ since this may be offensive to those of other faiths. Therefore, the charge goes, Christians who hold this belief may hinder the success of the interfaith meeting. This challenge raises the issue of context in interfaith relations. The undisputed objectives of interfaith relations, namely peace, harmony, development and sharing our common humanness (*ubuntu* in South Africa), are noble and must be vigorously pursued. However, historical experiences and cultural differences mean that interfaith relations from one continent, region or country cannot be exported wholesale to another continent, region or country. They may be shared in other areas, to enrich or inform, but they should not be transposed as if they were the norm everywhere.

The present situation, in which some Christians imply that biblical truth should be watered down to enhance interfaith relations, is not acceptable to many Christians in Africa and elsewhere. It will be a disaster for interfaith relations if those from any faith attempt to explain away their cardinal doctrines for the sake of peace and harmony. The quest for peace and harmony among faiths is possible only if we are able to acknowledge that there are major differences in our belief systems. Instead of agonizing over them, we must accept our differences and seek to live harmoniously despite them.

Perhaps the best illustration of how we need to approach interfaith relations in Africa comes in conversation between Dr Nnamdi Azikiwe, the first president of Nigeria, and Alhaji Ahmadu Bello, a premier and saurdauna of Sokoto in the mid-1960s. The two leaders met to discuss growing tensions between coalition partners in the central government (the Northern People's Congress and the National Council of Nigerian Citizens). These tensions brought into the open divergences between the majority Muslim north and the majority Christian south which were degenerating into ethno-religious antagonism. In the cause of dialogue to restore some understanding, Dr Azikiwe is quoted as having said to Ahmadu Bello, "Let us forget our differences." Abmadu Bello replied, "No, let us understand our differences. . . . By understanding our differences we can build unity in Nigeria."[2] This short conversation between the two leaders indicates the real grounds for carrying out interfaith relations in Africa: accepting our differences in peace, not in pieces.

Having set out the principles under which interfaith relations have to take place in Africa, I will now turn my attention to areas of collaboration and cooperation to improve the human condition in the continent.

The Essence of Interfaith Collaboration and Cooperation

It is important for Christians to collaborate and cooperate with those of other faith communities in Africa to address issues of common concern. However, if we are to scratch where it itches the most, we must put the interface between Christianity and Islam high on our agenda. These two religions command the largest following in the continent. They have also shown throughout history and at the present time that they are the best at building peace and stability in the continent (and the world at large). Yet they can equally be the worst at creating or fanning conflicts and strife.

As missionary religions that have succeeded in gaining adherents in Africa, Islam and Christianity may produce greater tensions to come if their

---

2. Ibrahim Gambari, "The Role of Religion in National Life: Reflections on Recent Experiences in Nigeria," in *Religion and National Integration in Africa: Islam, Christianity, and Politics in the Sudan and Nigeria*, ed. John O. Hunwick (Evanston, IL: Northwestern University Press, 1992), 98.

respective adherents are not proactive in collaborating and cooperating to improve human conditions across the continent. To this end we would like to briefly outline key areas that the churches in Africa need to explore carefully in pursuing collaborative interfaith actions.

Peace and peaceful coexistence

Success stories of interfaith cooperation have emerged in Sierra Leone and Liberia, where religious leaders took ground-breaking initiatives that contributed immensely to restoring peace. What is not adequately recognized is that in the case of Liberia, there were attempts to publicize the war as one between Christians and Muslims. Fortunately, the Christian leaders of the country worked hard to defuse the tension that was generated. They teamed up with Muslim leaders so that together they formed an interreligious council to work towards peace in the land.

This example clearly indicates that interfaith collaboration is possible only when there is peaceful coexistence between and among faith communities. Religious leaders can be agents of peace in the continent only when they are themselves at peace with one another. Faith communities involved in violent conflicts have no moral ground whatsoever to mediate in other conflicts, such as those that are ethnically or politically motivated.

In Africa, people of faith continue to listen to their religious leaders and, in most cases, take directives from them. Therefore religious leaders of all faiths must capitalize on this advantage in order to collaborate for peace in a continent yearning for peace.

Our programmes for peace must seek to consolidate peace in peaceful situations, and to promote peacebuilding in situations of strife. The programmes must also be continual, to avoid the situation of churches only cooperating with other faith communities in times of tension. Rather, peace is a process that must be worked at all the time.

Religious rights and peace

The most difficult aspect of interfaith relations for peaceful coexistence in Africa is that of religious freedoms and rights. The religious rights claimed by some can be viewed as a violation of others' religious rights. Nowhere is this more evident than in Nigeria and the Sudan, where the introduction of the *shariah* (Islamic law) in its totality contributed in large measure to violent conflicts between Christians and Muslims.

The irony of such situations is that both parties, Christians and Muslims, argue in defence of their God-given rights. Muslims argue that it is their God-given right to introduce the *shariah* in its totality to govern themselves, while Christians argue that it is their God-given right not to live under the *shariah*. Similarly, faith communities in Kenya, Tanzania, and to some extent in Uganda have to deal with debates on entrenching *khadi* (Muslim) courts in their respective country's constitution. These are issues that can and do divide religious people, especially Christians and Muslims.

In the churches' bid to work for peace with people of other faiths, issues such as those mentioned above are bound to arise from time to time and to poison relations. Therefore, the critical question is not so much how to prevent such issues from emerging, but how to deal with them when they do arise.

One of the most important areas of PROCMURA's work is fostering a spirit of understanding between Christians and Muslims. The aim is to ensure that when conflicts occur between them, they are addressed in a non-violent manner. The churches must always look to Jesus Christ who is himself the Prince of Peace (Isa 9:6), and who is recorded as having said "Blessed are the peacemakers, for they will be called children of God" (Matt 5:9). Insofar as it is possible, let us work hard to ensure that we live peaceably with all our neighbours (Rom 12:18).

Other areas of collaboration and cooperation

There are several areas that require appropriate interfaith cooperation, especially if these are concerns across the religious divide. Two such issues are the HIV/AIDS pandemic and what has come to be known as female genital mutilation. In view of the devastating impact these continue to have across Africa, it is crucial for Christians and Muslims to work closely together in addressing them.

Since some issues are more sensitive and controversial than others, it is advisable for interfaith relations to first approach those that are less controversial. This lays a foundation for then tackling those issues that are more thorny.

Thorny Issues in Interfaith Relations: What Shall We Do?

In the introduction to this chapter, we noted the multiple identities of African people. We now explore how these multiple identities, as they relate to faith, create divided loyalties and thus lead to the segmentation of African societies.

The formation of the African Union signifies that Africa's diversity, which includes religious diversity, should not stand in the way of Africans being united. Churches must carefully examine three main areas for interfaith action towards justice, peace and development of the continent: politics, African identity, and Christian mission and Muslim *da'wah*.

Politics

In the realm of politics, there is now a widespread tendency to categorize African heads of state according to their religious affiliations, especially Christian and Muslim. This is a dangerous trend which can easily lead to "religious tribalism," where adherents of one religion or another vote for presidential or parliamentary candidates because they share a religion and not because the person is competent to govern.

The forefathers and foremothers of Africa's modern political landscape identified themselves as African irrespective of their religious affiliations. In this light, Leopold Senghor, a devout Catholic, could be voted in as the president of Senegal, a predominately Muslim country. Not long ago, President Bakili Muluzi, a Muslim, was elected as president of Malawi, a majority Christian country. If this noble trend is to continue, interfaith programmes must embark on political education that emphasizes unity of purpose and development among Africans despite their belonging to different faith communities. Politicians must likewise be cautioned against religio-partisan politics.

African identity

From PROCMURA's experience, one crucial issue is the question of African identity in relation to the universality of the Christian and Muslim faiths. The fact that Africans have multiple identities can evoke the question as to whether they are African Christians and African Muslims, or Christian Africans and Muslim Africans. In other words, which aspect of an African's identity takes priority over other aspects or calls for greater allegiance? For example, after the events that took place in the United States on September 11, 2001, Christians and Muslims in Africa took sides with those involved in the conflict, to the extent that violent confrontations erupted in some parts of the continent.

Christianity is a universal religion that recognizes all its followers as belonging to the body of Christ. Likewise Islam teaches the universal *umma* (community) to which Muslims all over the world belong. It is truly unfortunate that this sense of universal belonging found within both faiths then creates negative perceptions towards those of the other faith, especially on the basis of conflicts occurring elsewhere in the world. In the case above, political conflicts between the West and the Arab world have set Africans against each other.

Therefore interfaith relations in Africa must ensure that the universal nature of Christianity and Islam is viewed constructively. We must avoid conflicts that arise from making alliances with those with whom Africans share faith, even if they are far away, and enemies of those who live close by but do not share the same faith. Rather, our common humanity as people of faith, both in Africa and beyond, should be harnessed to bring about peace and development instead of antagonism and destruction.

Christian mission and Muslim da'wah

Christian mission, including witness and evangelism, and its near equivalent in Muslim *da'wah*, are imperatives for the two faiths. The question therefore is not whether Christian mission and Muslim *da'wah* should be carried out, but how they should be done so as to avoid polemics, stereotypes and derogatory remarks about the other. This is an important area for establishing positive interfaith relations.

It must be said that any form of mission or *da'wah* that does not transform lives for the better, but rather provokes tension and conflict, should be regarded as a deformation of these faiths. Is it not possible, for example, for Christian and Muslim religious leaders in Africa to establish a guiding ethic for recommending their respective faiths without defaming the other? This would seem to be a crucial priority for interfaith relations.

Conclusion

This chapter has examined interfaith relations in Africa, particularly between Christians and Muslims. The focus has been on what the churches in Africa must do to engage constructively with Muslims for peace and peaceful coexistence for the holistic development of the human family.

In conclusion, we must underline that the future of interfaith relations in Africa rests on our theological institutions. Ecumenical and denominational theological colleges and seminaries need to incorporate interfaith relations in the theological formation of priests and pastors. This will help the future leaders of our churches to critically examine our inherited theologies, so as to construct an African theology of interfaith relations.

Questions

1. What are some of the key challenges to interfaith relations, according to Johnson A. Mbillah and to your own experience?
2. Do you think that engaging in interfaith relations means that you must compromise, or water down, your own religious beliefs? Argue your case in relation to Mbillah's view.
3. Why is peacebuilding so foundational in interfaith relations?
4. Explain the three thorny issues in interfaith relations that Mbillah identifies. What relevance do these issues have to your own experience of interfaith relations?

Further Reading

Azumah, John. *My Neighbour's Faith: Islam Explained for Christians*. Jos, Nairobi, and Carlisle: HippoBooks, 2008.

Azumah, John, and Lamin Sanneh, eds. *The African Christian and Islam*. Carlisle: Langham Monographs, 2013.

Conteh, Prince Sorie. *Traditionalists, Muslims and Christians in Africa: Interreligious Encounters*. New York: Cambria Press, 2009.

Sanneh, Lamin. *Piety and Power: Muslims and Christians in West Africa*. Eugene, OR: Wipf & Stock, 2015.

20

The State

Theodros Assefa Teklu

Modern state building projects in colonial and postcolonial Africa focus on establishing an efficient central state structure that functions under the rule of law and in compliance with requirements of transparency and accountability. African states have, however, by and large struggled to achieve this and instead have inefficient, corrupt, and dysfunctional systems and structures. Some states are taking active steps to address these problems, and Christians want to be supportive. But how can we do this? What is the relationship between public theology and the state?

Before we can explore this relationship, it is important that we understand the fundamental characteristics of a state – what it is and what it should do.

What Is the State and What Should It Do?

In the field of political and social theory, offering a precise definition of the state is not a straightforward matter, but for the purposes of this chapter we will regard a state as an entity characterized by territoriality, sovereignty, constitutionality/legality, bureaucracy, legitimacy, and nationality/citizenship.[1]

---

1. This characterization is based on Max Weber's definition:

   A compulsory political organization with continuous operations will be called a "state" insofar as its administrative staff successfully upholds the claims to the monopoly of the legitimate use of physical force in the enforcement of its order. . . . [it] possesses an administrative and legal order subject to change by legislation, to which the organized activities of the administrative staff, which are also controlled by regulations, are oriented. This system of orders claims binding authority, not only over members of the state, the citizens, most of

- *Territoriality.* The first characteristic feature of states is that they have clearly defined territories. Without a geographic base, no state can exercise its sovereignty and operate effectively. War often breaks out when the territorial integrity of a state is transgressed by another state or states.

- *Sovereignty.* The idea of sovereignty implies the absolute authority of a political community.[2] Authority is not absolute when there are competing forces within a single territory. For this reason, historically, the emergence of the modern state in Europe involved the pacification of the regional nobilities that fragmented power. Today in democratic countries, the idea of sovereignty is associated with the general will of the people or citizens of a state and with institutions that carry out executive, legislative and judicial tasks. However, some argue that sovereignty and democracy are not good in that they represent the tyranny of the majority.

- *Constitutionality/legality.* Without law, a state and its political order cannot exist or function properly. Because law-making cannot be arbitrary, it must be governed by certain laws in the constitution, which establishes "the laws about making laws"[3] and legitimizes the state and its authority. Both the obligations of the state towards its citizens and of citizens to the state are set out in the constitution. Constitutional power is not the rule of authorities but the rule of law which goes with the exercise of impersonal power and demands publicly accepted and transparent procedures.

- *Bureaucracy.* Bureaucratic administration is carried out in accordance with fixed rules and procedures and official documents (files) and involves hierarchies with various levels of expertise.[4] The proper functioning of bureaucracy and the flourishing of just institutions are important for mass democracy and are considered signs of progress. Nonetheless, bureaucracy can be critiqued for happening at the expense of human beings who are

---

whom have obtained membership by birth, but also to a very large extent over all action taking place in the area of its jurisdiction. It is thus a compulsory organization with a territorial basis. *Economy and Society: Volume 1* (1922; New York: Bedminster, 1978), 54–56.

2. F. Harry Hinsley, *Sovereignty*, 2nd ed. (Cambridge: Cambridge University Press, 1986), 1, 26.

3. Christopher Pierson, *The Modern State* (London: Routledge, 1996), 17.

4. Weber, *Economy and Society: Vol. 1*, 220–221; *Economy and Society: Vol. 2* (New York: Bedminster, 1978), 956–963.

abused by the system and for the potential of bureaucrats to seek to increase their own wealth by disadvantaging others.[5]

- *Legitimacy.* Without legitimacy, that is, the acceptance by citizens of the authority of the state, no state can survive for long.[6] If the legitimacy of the state is seriously questioned or resisted by citizens, the sustainability of the state is questionable or endangered. To ensure that they have legitimacy, states seek to make their laws acceptable to all citizens, or at least to a majority of them, by claiming a basis in some kind of natural law, some divine mandate or the superior governance of a charismatic leader. The authority of the state rests "on a belief in the legality of enacted rules and the right of those elevated to authority under such rules to issue commands."[7] Thus legitimacy makes an appeal not only to rules but also to the belief of the people, including their religious beliefs and teachings (theology).

- *Nationality/Citizenship.* Nationality or citizenship is defined as "a status which, in principle, bestows upon individuals equal rights and duties, liberties and constraints, powers and responsibilities [within] the political community."[8] Citizenship rights are not identical to natural or human rights, which are universal. Unlike human rights, citizenship rights do not apply to everyone. Those excluded may be insiders – historically women and other oppressed groups – or outsiders such as immigrants. Consequently, David Held argues, "Citizenship is a double-sided process. In principle, its exclusion may empower individuals over and against the state. But, at the same time, it implies a strengthening of the authority and the obligation of the state's rule (now presented as the expression of the collective will of all the citizens)."[9]

This quotation shows the political nature of citizenship. The association of citizenship with where people are born (nativism) can exacerbate nationalism, that is, the identification of the state with a particular nation or ethnic core. In many parts of the world including Africa, issues related to citizenship can pose challenges as states have to manage very diverse populations.

---

5. Pierson refers to this behaviour as "rent-seeking," *Modern State,* 21–22.

6. Pierson, *Modern State,* 22.

7. Weber, *Economy and Society: Vol. 1,* 215.

8. David Held, *Democracy and the Global Order* (Cambridge: Polity, 1995), 66.

9. Pierson, *Modern State,* 29.

Statehood and Its Challenges in Africa

The above description of the essential elements of a state was developed in the West. So it is interesting to see how these characteristics play out in the construction of modern African territorial states in the aftermath of the colonial period.[10] What evidence do they show of territoriality, sovereignty, constitutionality/legality, bureaucracy, legitimacy and nationality/citizenship? And what factors play a role in the expression of these characteristics in Africa?

In traditional Africa, a multiplicity of ethnolinguistic groups were loosely held together through their subjection to a tribal leader, a kingdom or an empire. There were some cultural and historical convergences between them, but the idea of creating a common culture that demanded cultural integration or assimilation was unknown. However, after the scramble for Africa, the colonial system introduced a new kind of political geography that remains in place today. It is now common to find a single ethnic group scattered in two or more states, and some nations or ethnic groups do not have their own states.

The imposition of territorial boundaries that did not reflect existing social networks has led to the ongoing struggle of African states to transcend ancient ties of blood, language, region, religion, and custom and build a strong centre from which to modernize their societies.[11] There is often conflict between elites who seek to support the concept of the state with its authority and bureaucracy and common people whose sense of self is primarily related to their community rather than to the state as such. Regional elites may also seek to retain their traditional powers over against those of the national state, so further fracturing society.

The American anthropologist Clifford Geertz has spoken of this conflict in terms of "essentialism" versus "epochalism": the former is oriented to "the indigenous way of life" and the latter to "the spirit of the age."[12] No one can be purely essentialist or purely epochalist, but individuals will have a tendency or a bias towards one or the other. When large groups in society having conflicting biases, the result will be a state characterized by increasing unmanageability.

Because postcolonial African states came into being as a result of international recognition rather than on the basis of internally negotiated nation-building processes, they have proved to be weak, unstable and unable to

---

10. The difference between African states and their European counterparts has led some to distinguish between "genuine states" and "quasi-states" and to ask whether statehood is a relative concept.

11. Liah Greenfeld and Michael Martin, *Center: Ideas and Institutions* (Chicago: University of Chicago Press, 1988), 278.

12. Clifford Geertz, *The Interpretation of Cultures* (London: Hutchinson, 1975), 240–243.

defend themselves militarily against external threats. They struggle to manage their populations socially, economically and politically. One result of this has been that African states are highly dependent on the international system and are vulnerable to external pressures. This was evident during and after the Cold War, and in the political and economic demands imposed in the name of structural adjustment and the influence of transnational corporations.

Some states have simply collapsed under the strain and are now classified as failed states because they are unable to carry out the primary or minimum state responsibilities of providing their citizens with education, security and governance. Failed states are places of anarchy where "life is cheap and talk is loose."[13] Power is held by elites who control economic resources to extract the maximum benefits for themselves at the expense of the disadvantaged majority. To stay in power, these elites may try to engineer "a constitutionally sanctified one-party state" or dictatorship.[14]

Some states fail because of the intervention of foreign countries that work to destabilize them by triggering ethnic conflicts or supporting rebel groups. Sometimes this intervention is done in the name of religion, as can be seen with Boko Haram in Nigeria and Al-Shabaab in Somalia.[15]

Some have responded to the failure of African states by emphasizing the role of civil society, defined as the "set of diverse non-governmental institutions which is strong enough to counterbalance the state and, while not preventing the state from fulfilling its role as keeper of the peace and arbitrator between major interests, can nevertheless prevent it from dominating and atomising the rest of society."[16] Civil society is seen as counterbalancing or limiting the power of the state.

Others, however, oppose the idea of civil society as a solution to the abuse of state power in Africa, arguing that it is a neo-liberal ideological project of the West to "vilify" African states.[17] Nonetheless, developments that contribute to the decentring of the state and the limitation of its power are generally

---

13. Global Policy Forum, "Failed States: Where Life Is Cheap and Talk Is Loose," originally published in *The Economist* (17 March 2011).

14. Daron Acemoglu and James A. Robinson, *Why Nations Fail: The Origins of Power, Prosperity, and Poverty* (London: Profile Books, 2012), 149, 376.

15. Natana J. DeLong-Bas, *Wahhabi Islam: From Revival to Reform to Global Jihad* (Oxford: Oxford University Press, 2004), 265–279; Patrick Sookhdeo, *Unmasking Islamic State: Revealing Their Motivation, Theology and End Time Predictions* (McLean, VA: Isaac, 2015), 89–108.

16. Ernest Gellner, *Conditions of Liberty: Civil Society and Its Rivals* (Harmondsworth: Penguin, 1996), cited in Paul Gifford, *African Christianity: Its Public Role* (London: Hurst, 1998), 17.

17. Gifford, *African Christianity*, 17–20.

endorsed by African states as important for the promotion of human rights.[18] Yet these developments must be done with care. When state power is simply "privatized," the beneficiaries are often those who already occupy high positions within the state.[19] The result may be "state capture" or "shadow statehood" in which political authorities gain access to the wealth of the state through corrupt networks of personal deals.[20] In such a context, civil society – which exists between the individual and the state – can contribute to societal well-being and flourishing. What is needed is a public sphere approach rather than a state-centred approach.

The role of religion in the public sphere is particularly significant in this respect. The public sphere can be defined as a "social space – distinct from the state, the economy and the family – in which" citizens deliberate "about the common good."[21] Note that this "social space" is not so much a physical gathering of people but rather people exchanging opinions and beliefs and debating issues relating to their common social life. In other words, the public sphere is "communication, whether in words or actions."[22]

The shifting of "public life . . . from government to civil society"[23] offers an important opportunity for religion and its public teachings (or public theology).

The Three-fold Task of Public Theology

The three-fold task of public theology involves self-criticism, critique and construction. These dimensions should not be seen as watertight, for they may overlap in practice.

---

18. Claude E. Welch, "The Organisation of African Unity and the Promotion of Human Rights," *Journal of Modern African Studies* 29 (1991): 535–555.

19. William Reno, *Corruption and State Politics in Sierra Leone* (Cambridge: Cambridge University Press, 1995).

20. Reno, *Corruption and State Politics*, 22.

21. Eduardo Mendieta and Jonathan Vanantwerpen, eds., *The Power of Religion in the Public Sphere* (New York: Columbia University Press, 2011), 2.

22. Jürgen Habermas, *Knowledge and Human Interest*, trans. Jeremy J. Shapiro (Cambridge: Polity Press, 1987), 238.

23. Scott R. Paeth et al., *Shaping Public Theology: Selections from the Writings of Max L. Stackhouse* (Grand Rapids: Eerdmans, 2014), 252.

Self-criticism rather than subordination

Public theology needs to be able to reflect on itself in a critical manner and not simply assume that it is always on the right track. To understand why this is so important, we need to remember that there have been times when the relationship between theologians and the state has been one of subordination, so that public theology has effectively served the interests of the state. Such subordination is always inappropriate, but it is especially dangerous when the state seeks the aid of public theology to establish its legitimacy. Public theologians may then be coerced or manipulated into supporting unjust state structures and operations, as happened under the apartheid regime in South Africa. The South African anti-apartheid "Kairos Document" spoke of a theology that gives sanction to the state as a "State Theology" which offers a "theological justification of the status quo" and "blesses injustice, canonizes the will of the powerful and reduces the poor to passivity, obedience and apathy."[24]

Of course, the state does not produce state theology; Christians who misuse biblical texts and theological doctrines produce it. Romans 13:1–7 is the most misused Christian text in this regard, for it has often been used to assert the absolute authority of the state and the absolute requirement that Christians always obey it:

> Let everyone be subject to the governing authorities, for there is no authority except that which God has established. The authorities that exist have been established by God. Consequently, whoever rebels against the authority is rebelling against what God has instituted, and those who do so will bring judgment on themselves. For rulers hold no terror for those who do right, but for those who do wrong. Do you want to be free from fear of the one in authority? Then do what is right and you will be commended. For the one in authority is God's servant for your good. But if you do wrong, be afraid, for rulers do not bear the sword for no reason. They are God's servants, agents of wrath to bring punishment on the wrongdoer. Therefore, it is necessary to submit to the authorities, not only because of possible punishment but also as a matter of conscience.
>
> This is also why you pay taxes, for the authorities are God's servants, who give their full time to governing. Give to everyone

---

24. Gary S. D. Leonard, ed., *The Kairos Documents* (Kwazulu Natal: University of KwaZulu Natal, 2010), 9. For the full text of the Kairos Document, see https://kairossouthernafrica. wordpress.com/2011/05/08/the-south-africa-kairos-document-1985/.

what you owe them: If you owe taxes, pay taxes; if revenue, then revenue; if respect, then respect; if honour, then honour.

To understand this text, we need to understand the context in which it was written. In contrast to some Jewish people who were prone to violent resistance, Christians were to be submissive to the Roman state despite its serious flaws. Such behaviour was essential to minimize unnecessary persecution of the small minority group. This text does not mean that Christians cannot speak out against a government when they are closer to a majority or may even be represented in the government.

Moreover, in writing this command Paul was using a standard style of moral exhortation at the time that spoke in absolute terms but did not mean that this was the only possible form of right behaviour in all circumstances.[25] Sometimes uncritical obedience to and legitimation of states can hide the operation of an oppressive ideology.[26] Public theologians and Christians in general need to be aware of this danger.

Critique and confrontation

Fear of subordination must not lead Christians to attempt to refrain from any relation to the state. Rather, public theology should have a prophetic edge and engage in critique of the state and its institutions. The challenge of subordination should be countered by confrontation and critical engagement, not by retreating from the public sphere.

The requirement to critique the state flows from the fact that believers have divided loyalties and dual citizenship. The Accra Charter spells this citizenship out clearly: "By the virtue of the divine sovereignty we live our lives as members of the religious community, while as citizens we conduct our affairs as subjects of the state (1 Pet 2:13–14)."[27] Let us take a look at the verses cited: "Submit yourselves for the Lord's sake to every human authority: whether to the emperor, as the supreme authority, or to governors, who are sent by him to punish those who do wrong and to commend those who do right."

---

25. Craig S. Keener, *The IVP Bible Background Commentary: New Testament* (Downers Grove, IL: IVP Academic, 2014), 450.

26. Tinyiko Sam Maluleke, "Reflections and Resources: The Elusive Public of Public Theology: A Response to William Storrar," *International Journal of Public Theology* 5 (2011): 79–89.

27. Lamin Sanneh, *The Accra Charter of Religious Freedom and Citizenship* (Oxford: OMSC Publications, 2012), 7.

Here the apostle Peter is making the same point that Paul did about the need to obey the Roman state, and in a similar context. But the next verse adds an interesting perspective: "For it is God's will that by doing good you should silence the ignorant talk of foolish people" (1 Pet 2:15). The reason Christians are to obey the law is that they are serving God and promoting his kingdom. They are not merely servants of the state. Craig Keener puts it like this: "For Christians, freedom meant freedom to be God's slaves rather than slaves of sin; it meant freedom from the tyranny of the state but also freedom to uphold the laws of the state as God's servants."[28] Thus the text affirms our dual citizenship; it both encourages us to be submissive to the state and reminds us of our duty to the sovereign God.

Christians' dual citizenship means that they have different, and sometimes conflicting, convictions and loyalties. They participate in "public discussions of the secular state while living by narratives not shared by these polities."[29] The drafters of the Accra Charter made a similar point when they stated that our "citizenship, however, does not exhaust our status as moral persons, because the state cannot be a substitute for the Church as 'the edifice of human worth, freedom, and well-being.'"[30] Thus a Christian public theology cannot simply uphold the state; it must also issue a prophetic summons to action to correct what is wrong. In this sense, public theology must be confrontational.[31]

Constructive engagement at points of intersection

While the interests of the church and the state do not align perfectly, they are often not in complete contradiction. There are points where their interests intersect, so they can sometimes work together while each maintaining relative autonomy. However, before public theology can enter into this type of constructive engagement, it needs to tackle the task of determining what constructive contribution it can make in its current context. Content and context are both of great importance.

The task of constructing public theology begins by asking a contextual question: What is the time? Where are we today culturally, socially and politically? This reading of "the signs of the times" (Matt 16:3; Luke 12:56) is

---

28. Keener, *IVP Bible Background Commentary*, 691.

29. Rowan Williams, "Convictions, Loyalties and the Secular State," *Political Theology* 6, no. 2 (2005): 154.

30. Sanneh, *The Accra Charter*, 10.

31. Leonard, *The Kairos Documents*, 63.

important for public theology which should be prophetic, that is, relevant to the time and the life contexts.

Reading the signs of the times endows public theology with a prophetic edge that is attentive to structural injustice, poverty and the poor. For example, if a state fails to work to promote the common good of all its citizens, then the signs of the times clearly indicate the need to develop a state-critical public theology that asserts the rights of all people.[32] However, we also need to offer a vision of an alternative social order.

One surprising way to start presenting an alternate vision may be by lament. The African theologian Emmanuel Katongole draws attention to the theological potential of lament as a source of hope and activism and a way by which we enter into "the drama of God's saving engagement with the world, at the heart of which is the mystery of Christ's suffering, death and resurrection."[33] Lament enables us to imagine an alternative vision of a new society and a better future.[34]

Public theologies of hope are usually considered utopian, and hence impractical. However, a public theology of hope fosters practices of hope in the present. Here I wish to offer another example from the South African context, namely the theology of reconstruction as advanced by Charles Villa-Vicencio who uses the metaphor of exile to construct a theology of reconstruction, as also has the Kenyan Catholic theologian Jesse Mugambi.[35] A public theology of reconstruction is a nation/state building theology that is concerned with social renewal and focuses on democracy, human rights, constitutionalism and the rule of law.[36]

What matters in constructing public theology that engages the state is not only the content but also the context of communication. Public theologians need to attempt to translate religious truth or theology into a secular idiom so that it can be understood by the wider public, and they must engage in open

---

32. Leonard, 68.

33. Emmanuel Katongole, *Born from Lament: The Theology and Politics of Hope in Africa* (Grand Rapids: Eerdmans, 2017), 261.

34. Katongole, *Born from Lament*, 263.

35. Charles Villa-Vicencio, *A Theology of Reconstruction: Nation-Building and Human Rights* (New York: Cambridge University Press, 1992), 14. Cf. Jesse N. K. Mugambi, *From Liberation to Reconstruction: Christian Theology in Africa after the Cold War* (Nairobi: East African Educational Publishers, 1995); Jesse N. K. Mugambi, *Christian Theology & Social Reconstruction* (Nairobi: Acton, 2003); Valentin Dedji, *Reconstruction and Renewal in Christian Theology* (Nairobi: Acton, 2003).

36. Villa-Vicencio, *Theology of Reconstruction*, 52.

public debates in a rational manner.[37] As the well-known public theologian Max Stackhouse remarks, "Public theology . . . respects the delicate tissues of sentiment, civility, virtue, and awareness by which nonintellectuals all the time – and intellectuals most of the time – hold the fragments of their lives together."[38] Those communicating public theology that addresses the state should be cognizant not only of the local context but also of the "global civil society" in order to foster "a new catholicity and a new ecumenicity."[39]

"Catholicity" means "universality," and is important given the ecclesiastical or denominational divides that have become the norm today. Although the church and its social teachings or public theology may be shaped by the particular context in which the church is situated, Christians should not be forgetful of the universal church and the worldwide family of God. Without ecumenicity, that is, the willingness to work with Christians from other branches of the Christian family, Christian social action remains fragmented and powerless.

Who Does Public Theology in Relation to the State?

Public theology is a theology that faces the world. But it is rooted in the life of the church. It is directed to the world while grounded in the life of the church. Thus it cannot be divorced from the church and from its base community, that is, the believers who make up the congregation. Hence public theology should make sense to the church as a whole: to both its ministers (such as pastors) and its "lay" believers, even though they are not professional public theologians. They all need to share a common awareness that even the language of worship implies a public theology. For example, the proclamation "Jesus is Lord" may be a political act in that it affirms an authority higher than the state. We need to cultivate a growing awareness that even worship and liturgical activities reveal implicit public theologies.

All Christians thus need to apply what has been said in this chapter to themselves and to their own local churches. First, Christians need to be self-critical. It is all too easy to succumb to state ideology and become uncritically submissive to the state. Christians need to consciously seek to hold a critical distance from the state and to display godly wisdom in what they think and

---

37. Mendieta and Vanantwerpen, *Power of Religion*, 5. See also the works of Mugambi and Dedji cited above to explore African idioms for engagement.

38. Max Stackhouse, *Public Theology and Political Economy: Christian Stewardship in Modern Society* (Lanham, MD: University Press of America, 1991), 14.

39. Paeth et al., *Shaping Public Theology*, 253.

do. As dual citizens, their primary loyalty should be to God and then to the state. Second, Christians must be critical of the state whenever they find the state's dealings with its citizens are unjust and inhumane. Without such a critical stance, God's sovereignty over all spheres of life is lost, and the state becomes the absolute untouchable power. And last, Christians can seek to become involved in the development of public theology, in the construction of a theology of hope for their communities, and in its public communication in the spheres of life in which they are engaged.

When we set out to do these things and have a self-critical, state-critical and constructive stance, we will be working towards a public theology that fosters the transformation of Africa from the Africa we do not want into the Africa we long for.

Questions

1. In view of the basic features of modern states outlined in this chapter, what are the failures of the state in your own particular national context?
2. What common goals could public theology and the state have? What differences exist between them?
3. How ought we to respond to those who claim that theology must not be involved in political matters related to the state?
4. After reading the signs of the times in your own national context, what shape must the public theology you wish to construct assume?
5. In a pluralistic context with many religions or faiths, how could Christian public theology have a hearing?

Further Reading

Katongole, Emmanuel. *Born from Lament: The Theology and Politics of Hope in Africa.* Grand Rapids: Eerdmans, 2017.

Mugambi, Jesse N. K. *Christian Theology and Social Reconstruction.* Nairobi: Acton, 2003.

Musana, P., A. Crichton, and C. Howell, eds. *The Ugandan Churches and the Political Centre: Cooperation, Co-Option and Confrontation.* Uganda: National Ecumenical Publishing Consortium; Cambridge: Cambridge Centre for Christianity Worldwide, 2017.

Sanneh, Lamin. *The Accra Charter of Religious Freedom and Citizenship.* Oxford: OMSC, 2012.

Villa-Vicencio, Charles. *A Theology of Reconstruction: Nation-Building and Human Rights.* New York: Cambridge University Press, 1992.

21

Police and Armed Forces

Sipho Mahokoto

Africa is a beautiful continent where many good things happen. It is also a continent that can be proud of its identity, heritage, culture and shared values, especially the values associated with *ubuntu*.[1] This is the Africa we want, a place that values care and respect for one another.

But there is another side to the continent. Africa is also plagued with corruption, war and terrorism. Leaders abuse their power, and the police and armed forces are often either the instruments or the perpetrators of these abuses. What hurts the most is that it is our own governments that are violating people's rights and dignity. It is our own governments that inflict physical pain on us and steal from us.

In this chapter, we will look at what public theology has to say about the use and abuse of state power, that is, the power of the police and the armed forces, and consider how the church and individual Christians can respond to such abuses.

The Reality of Abuse of State Power

Many of those in political leadership in Africa have little regard for constitutional government, the rule of law or the needs of those they lead. Their prime concern is to promote their own interests, as can be clearly seen

---

1. *Ubuntu* is the African understanding that a human person is a person through other persons. No one exists in isolation; rather, we embrace our diversity and care for each other. From a Christian perspective, *ubuntu* means that we see Christ through the eyes of others, and not merely on our own.

from the way some politicians and their friends grow wealthy in office. The mechanisms by which this may be done have been exposed in the hearings related to "state capture" in South Africa. Politicians who are only interested in their own well-being cling to power and rig elections to give their exploitative governments an air of legitimacy. Their abuse of the democratic process is an example of an abuse of state power, for it often requires that the police work alongside complicit officials.

Those who publicly challenge the abuses of those in power expose themselves to danger. If they are in official positions, they are likely to lose their employment. If they are activists, journalists and demonstrators, they are likely to be beaten, teargassed, imprisoned, raped and even murdered. The fact that these actions can be done with impunity is an indication of the abuse of state power. If you need an example, you need look no further than Zimbabwe where the armed forces and police have tortured and killed thousands of civilians in their war against dissidents and where there has been state-sponsored violence during election campaigns and throughout the land reform movement.[2]

The contempt of leaders for the rule of law and democratic processes means that in some quarters it is accepted that the only way to depose leaders is by a revolt, or coup d'état. While these violent revolts are not as common as they were in the first years after Africa threw off colonialism,[3] they are still happening today, as evidenced by the coup in Zimbabwe in 2017 and the failed coup attempt in Gabon in 2019. Other regions of Africa are roiled by uprisings that often also result in the abuse of power by private militias, so that civilians suffer at the hands of the state and the rebels.

It is not surprising that coups are often led by the military, who have the power denied to civilians and the training to organize actions. However, even when these military leaders are acting with honourable intent to restore order and solve political and economic challenges, the governments that result from coups generally fall into the hands of those who are power hungry, and the situation repeats itself.

Meanwhile ordinary soldiers are often underpaid or unpaid, and they resort to violence to have their needs met. They have the tools of violence, the willingness to use them, and the favour of a government that is being propped

---

2. L. Sachikonye, *When the State Turns on Its Citizens: 60 Years of Institutionalised Violence in Zimbabwe* (Harare: Weaver Press, 2011), 148.

3. See chapter 18, "Refugees and Stateless People," for an account of what happened in Burundi.

up by military force. Soldiers can thus use violence with impunity and are often more feared than respected. The same is often true of Africa's police forces. They are widely regarded as corrupt, open to bribery and serving only the elite. The poor have little respect for them, which undermines respect for the law in general.

Theology and State Power

We should not think that Africa's situation is unique. Very similar circumstances prevailed in the New Testament era when Herod and his sons were engaged in coups and countercoups and put down revolts with great bloodshed, while Roman soldiers felt free to abuse Jewish civilians. This situation continued in the early centuries of the Christian church when Roman emperors were regularly overthrown in coups, the soldiers of the vast Roman army exercised power as they saw fit, and Christians were persecuted by the authorities and by mobs. So Christians of that era also wrestled with questions of state power. What were the legitimate uses of such power? Should Christians obey abusive governments? Could Christians serve in the army, or in the police force of that day, or should they refuse to be involved with organizations that use violence?

We can trace at least three historical shifts in Christian thinking about the military, war and violence, all influenced by the context in which Christians were living at the time.

- *Pacifism and non-violent resistance to power.* The early Christians, who suffered extreme persecution for their faith, responded by advocating pacifism and non-violent resistance to power, as presented in the Sermon on the Mount. Their marginal social and political status meant that it was wise to avoid provoking the powerful political and military systems, and they did not want to attract unwelcome attention that might lead to even greater persecution.

- *Reflection on the right use of power.* After the Emperor Constantine adopted Christianity as the religion of the empire in AD 313, Christians enjoyed increased social status and political power. They came to have a much closer relationship to political rulers and governments and found themselves required to discern under which circumstances war and violence could be justified. How were governments to use the power of the sword that God had given them (Rom 13:4)? What forms of force or violence might be used to protect order, save lives and further so-called Christian values?

Moreover, Christians were now serving in the military, so a new set of ethical and theological questions had to be resolved.[4]

- *"Christian" violence.* Between AD 1096 and 1291 Christians in Europe were in the ascendency, and they went to war in the name of the Christian faith. Christian rulers and leaders in the church felt that it was justified to engage in war to conquer territories and destroy rivals in the name of Christ. These wars, known as the Crusades, have left a long history of bitterness in Muslim hearts.

These historical perspectives all influence our thinking on war, peace and military force as we continue to wrestle with the complex theological and ethical debates around what measure of force and violence Christians may use in protection of the common good. This issue is a clear example of why we as Christians need to reflect on the relationship between our beliefs and the systems and structures of power with which and within which we operate.

The Bible's teaching on attitudes to power

Although Christians may not yet have all the answers as regards the use of state power, some things are very clear. The first is that God wants those who are in leadership both in the church and in the state to lead by example and to be transparent and responsible in their leadership. They should imitate Christ in seeking to serve (Luke 22:25–26) rather than being like the thieves and robbers who seek "only to steal and kill and destroy" (John 10:10). These last words remind us that when the powerful use their positions, influence and power to serve their own interests, they are in fact stealing from those whom they are meant to serve, and especially from the poor and those on the margins of society. Thus they are breaking the seventh commandment (Exod 20:15). The arrogant contempt for others that accompanies corruption is incompatible with loving our neighbours as ourselves (Matt 22:39).

But knowing what leaders *are not* to do does not answer the question of what they *are* to do. Why does God give some people and institutions power and authority in society? Paul says that God does this so that they can punish those who do wrong (Rom 13:4). But Paul does not only describe state power in negative terms. He also says that "the one in authority is God's servant for your good" (Rom 13:4). So we can say that people are given power in order to

---

4. For more see, J. Daryl Charles and Timothy J. Demy, *War, Peace, and Christianity: Questions and Answers from a Just-War Perspective* (Wheaton, IL: Crossway, 2010), 108–109.

serve the common good of the community. In contemporary terms, we can say that institutions like the police force and the military are given authority and responsibility for safeguarding the freedoms, rights and well-being of society, and particularly of the most vulnerable and at risk members of society whose rights may be abused by the more powerful.

Sadly, corrupt leaders often use the power of these institutions not to serve others but to protect their own wealth, privilege and status. As a result, we find the police and the army being used to silence opponents and enforce obedience to unjust laws, or to the mere wishes of a leader. This use of power does not make for Christlikeness or create the stability for which Christians are to pray (1 Tim 2:1–4); it actually destabilizes the social order. The lack of stability may not always be evident on the surface, but it will eventually erupt in discord and revolution.

Theology and the proper role of the police and the army

If the police and armed forces fulfil their role by maintaining the safety and stability of a country and of its citizens and resources, they deserve respect for promoting the common good through upholding justice, good governance and fairness in the country. We can identify four criteria which should govern their actions: *accountability*, both to the people and to God; *service* rather than self-aggrandisement; *integrity* rather than corruption; and a desire for *reconciliation and respect* between those who differ rather than fomenting division and enmity.[5] These criteria apply to all who exercise state power, including all policemen and women and all soldiers.

While the police and the army are often seen as the perpetrators of injustice, we should not forget that they too may suffer from injustice within their own ranks. It is not unknown for them not to receive the pay they are due, which may lead them to extort money from civilians. Women in the forces often experience gender discrimination and are abused physically and psychologically and denied promotion.[6] Soldiers and police officers may be expected to carry out orders that they know are cruel, unjust or abusive. Yet out of fear for their own safety or that of their communities, they suppress

---

5. Peter Storey, "Banning the Flag from Our Churches: Learning from the Church-State Struggle in South Africa," in *Between Capital and Cathedral: Essays on Church-State Relationships*, eds. Wessel Bentley and Dion A. Forster (Pretoria: University of South Africa, 2012), 3.

6. E. M. Mathebula, "A Critical Analysis of the Crime Prevention Role of the Military Police Division in the South African National Defence Force (SANDF)," unpublished doctoral dissertation, University of South Africa (UNISA), 2018, 187.

their consciences and comply with unjust commands. Consequently, morale is low, and there are often suppressed feelings of discontent and division in the ranks. All of these issues make for corruption. There are many cases of former combatants or members of the police services being arrested for criminal activities such as robberies, ATM bombings and cash-in-transit heists.[7]

Yet it is also true that in many African countries where a high percentage of the population are members of the Christian faith, there are Christian men and women serving in the police and armed forces. These believers should be influencing the way these forces operate and should conduct themselves for the good of the nation and its citizens. They should be seeking to promote the ethical use of power and the responsible discharge of official duties. Sadly, there has been little evidence that this is the case.[8] This situation could be an indication that Christians and churches have not made an explicit connection between faith and life, and particularly between Christian belief and Christian ethics in everyday life. We shall consider what role the church might play in shaping and informing such views in the section that follows.

The Role of the Church in Relation to State Power

The church as an ecumenical body, as a denomination, as a local congregation and as individuals is very influential, and we should expect justice and accountability from our members, as well as from those in power.[9] We should remind ourselves and the rest of society that God requires us all to practice good governance, respect human rights and be accountable to God and the persons we are serving. We should also remind members of the public that they should expect accountability from those who hold public office or are employed in civil service. But we should not resort to violence or wilful destruction to back up our demands.

---

7. Andrew Faull, "Corruption and the South African Police Service: A Review and Its Implications," *Institute for Security Studies Papers* 150 (1 September 2007): 20.

8. Knox Chitiyo, "The Struggles for Zimbabwe, South Africa and SADC: Liberation War Theology and Post-Nationalism," *The RUSI Journal* 153, no. 3 (1 June 2008): 80–86. See also M. J. Manala, "'A Better Life for All': A Reality or a Pipe-Dream? A Black Theology Intervention in Conditions of Poor Service Delivery in the Democratic South Africa," *Scriptura: International Journal of Bible, Religion and Theology in Southern Africa* 105, no. 1 (1 January 2010): 519–531.

9. See the discussion on the ways in which Christians and the different expressions of the church bring about change in Dion A. Forster and Johann W. Oostenbrink, "Where Is the Church on Monday? Awakening the Church to the Theology and Practice of Ministry and Mission in the Marketplace," *In Die Skriflig* 49, no. 3 (2015): 1–8.

If we truly believe that we are called to be salt and light in society (Matt 5:13–16), we should take greater responsibility for shaping, informing and strengthening the values of transparency, accountability and service in society. We must not be content just to preach the word to "others" but must also apply it to ourselves. We must make sure that the household of God is administered in a proper way and that our members are trained to treat all with dignity. As churches, we should be training our members in what good governance and the wise use of power looks like in all spheres of life – in our churches, in our families, in our homes and in our communities and public institutions as well as in the military and police service. If we do not train our members to exercise good governance in our own environments, it will be very hard, if not impossible, for us to expect accountability and service from the police and the army. So we need to reflect, pray and study about how best to equip our own members to serve in local, regional and national government, in positions of leadership in other organizations, or in the military and police.

Yet at the same time we must not neglect our broader civic responsibility to hold all political leaders, business leaders, and figures of authority – including military leaders, police officers and members of the judiciary – to high standards of ethics and justice for the common good. Where we see the unjust use of power, or corruption in the police service or the misuse of military power, we should speak out against such abuses, safeguard the abused, stand for the oppressed and witness to truth and justice.

When we come to the practical details of how the church relates to state power, we can draw on the categories in chapter 20, The State, where the relationship between church and state is described in terms of subordination, confrontation and cooperation. Those categories apply to all aspects of governments, but how do they apply specifically to state power and the relationship between the state and the army and police?

Subordination

It is unfortunate that some church leaders become politically aligned with those in power, and having been co-opted, can no longer hold them accountable in any way. South Africa provides an example of how this can be done: President Mandela set up a National Religious Leaders' Forum (NRLF) to help with nation building and national reconciliation. However, when President Zuma came to power he largely ignored that group and preferred to work with the newly established National Interfaith Council of South Africa (NICSA). It was later discovered that this new interfaith structure was not established by impartial religious leaders but by a compromised process initiated by the government to serve the interests of the ruling political party.[10] As such, it failed to have a prophetic voice in response to corruption, state capture and the abuse of power by those in leadership positions.

Governments are happy to appoint church leaders who do not criticize them to chaplaincy positions at all levels of government offices. The result is an erosion of public trust in religious leaders and religious organizations,[11] the abuse of limited resources intended to serve the poor and needy[12] and even church participation in the persecution or betrayal of political rivals of the state or powerful political entities.[13]

Christians should be discipled, taught and supported in the conviction that our primary allegiance is to Christ and in the values of justice, fairness and dignity that are central to the person and ministry of Jesus Christ and his kingdom. This education and advocacy could take the form of policy engagement between Christian leaders or Christian bodies such as the All Africa Council of Churches or a national council of churches and political leadership. Christians could also take a more personal approach, such as visiting local commanders of military units or policewomen and men to encourage them to do what is just and right for society. This approach might require preaching, praying and sharing care with persons within the military or police force who feel pressured to compromise their values and commitments. What is evident is that Christians and the church have an important role to play in safeguarding against the subordination of integrity to corrupt persons and practices.

Confrontation

What is the church to do in situations where people are protesting against government policies? Should the church support the protesters, and even join them? In South Africa this issue came to the fore with the Marikana incident, where the police fired on unarmed striking mine workers, killing many. Many

---

10. Ernst M. Conradie, "Notions and Forms of Ecumenicity: Some South African Perspectives," in *South African Perspectives on Notions and Forms of Ecumenicity*, ed. E. M. Conradie (Stellenbosch: SUN, 2013), 13–15.

11. Dion A. Forster, "A Kairos Moment for the Methodist Church of Southern Africa? Engaging Nationalism and State Theology in the Democratic South Africa," *Methodist Review: A Journal of Wesleyan and Methodist Studies* 11 (2019): 1–23.

12. Daniel Jordan Smith, "Corruption, NGOs, and Development in Nigeria," *Third World Quarterly* 31, no. 2 (1 March 2010): 243–258.

13. Timothy Longman, "Church Politics and the Genocide in Rwanda," *Journal of Religion in Africa* 31, no. 2 (1 January 2001): 163–186.

church leaders spoke out and condemned the violence, calling on the police and the mine owners to negotiate with words and not with bullets. In October 2012, church leaders issued a formal statement which read in part:

> Although we became deeply aware of the woundedness of our nation and the cry of our beloved country, we firmly believed that the unity of believers in South Africa can create an enormous opportunity and be a beacon of hope. Church leaders further affirmed that we are a wounded nation facing poverty, distrust, racism and the breakdown of society which impacts negatively on the moral fibre of our country. For example, Marikana sent out a stern warning to us which shows that this is a Kairos moment requiring transformational leadership and action. We commit as Church Leaders not only to exercise a prophetic and lamenting role in addressing the issues and struggles in South Africa but to get actively involved in making a difference in the lives of the poor, sick and suffering in our land today and to play a role in effecting healing, reconciliation and wholeness. In the same breath we call on government to more seriously recognize that Religious bodies are key partners in bringing about change in South Africa. In as much as we helped in dismantling apartheid we are called to play a vital role in the reconstruction of our beautiful land. We need integrated efforts of people, groups and institutions in making a difference. In this, Christian leaders readily avail and commit themselves to these initiatives.[14]

Africa has a rich history of Christian leaders taking a stand for justice against powerful political, military and economic leaders. Some notable examples are Bishop David Gitari in Kenya[15] and Archbishop Desmond Tutu in South Africa.[16] There are also numerous examples of Christian communities, organizations and groupings taking a stand for justice and human rights, as the Black Sash women's movement did in response to apartheid in South Africa.[17]

---

14. National Church Leaders' Consultation Media Statement 16–17 October 2012. For the complete statement, visit www.nrasd.org.za or www.efsa-institute.org.za and request a copy.

15. David Gitari, "Church and Politics in Kenya," *Transformation* 8, no. 3 (1 July 1991): 7–17.

16. John Allen, *Rabble-Rouser for Peace: The Authorised Biography of Desmond Tutu* (New York: Random House, 2012), 2–6.

17. Jo MacRobert, "Ungadinwa Nangomso – Don't Get Tired Tomorrow: A History of the Black Sash Advice Office in Cape Town 1968 to 1980," unpublished PhD dissertation, University of Cape Town, 1993.

Wherever Christians see the rise of evil, the abuse of the helpless or the erosion of the dignity and rights of individuals or groups, we have a responsibility to witness for the truth and to advocate for the powerless and helpless. Doing so may mean that at times we are at odds with political, economic and cultural leaders. In the darkest period of South Africa's apartheid history, the church and individual Christians played a crucial role in protesting against military abuse, police brutality and the unjust deployment of military personnel to suppress political opponents and silence those who were working for justice and peace.

We sometimes forget that the word "protest" is derived from the Latin word *testari*, which means to witness or testify. As Christians we are called to testify to the truth, to what is good and right and pure (Phil 4:8). Protest can be an act of faithful Christian witness. At times protest may be within the structures of the military or the police, as when women and men have refused to bear arms in an unjust cause,[18] and at other times it may be a witness against the abuses of military or police power.

Cooperation

When it comes to responding to abuses of state power, it is important to keep in mind that many of the people who are deeply involved in corrupt action and in abuses belong to our churches. For example, during the Jacob Zuma administration in South Africa, a parliamentary census showed that the majority of parliamentarians belonged to the Methodist Church of Southern Africa.[19]

The church has a responsibility to nurture, shape, critique and inform our members who are in positions of responsibility and power in the government, the military and the police. These people do not stop being church members when they are outside the church building or when they wear their uniforms. It is vital that we reflect deeply and critically on the role and responsibility of these sectors of society and on what God and our Christian faith would expect of persons in such positions. It is only when we have developed sound, responsible, Christian theological insights into the conduct, expectations and

---

18. Merran W. Phillips, "The End Conscription Campaign 1983–1988: A Study of White Extra-Parliamentary Opposition to Apartheid," unpublished Master's thesis, University of South Africa, 2002.

19. Forster, "Kairos Moment," 11–13.

responsibilities of the military and the police that we will be able to support and guide them in their important task.

Two further points to consider are these. First, we should be encouraging our members to discern where and how their abilities and talents should be used in society. This may mean that some of them should be encouraged to serve in either the military or the police. We need Christian women and men to serve in these sectors of society. Even more, we need women and men who see such work as a calling in which they can honour God and achieve God's will in society. Second, the church should be helping to shape the values and practices of their members, and indeed of all persons serving in the military and the police, in ways that are consistent with the values of peaceful conflict resolution and the establishment of justice, reconciliation and freedom. What we believe as Christians imposes a public responsibility and has public consequences. Christians have an important role to play in shaping the values and principles that guide and form a nation.

Conclusion

Throughout this book, we have seen that one of the challenges we face in Africa is the disconnection between our Christian values and our social reality. Africa is the region in which Christianity is growing most rapidly on earth, yet that growth is not reflected in our societies. We are ignoring our responsibility to emulate the person and work of Jesus in our society and to seek to establish values and principles of justice, mercy and peace that are characteristic of the kingdom of God. It does not help that churches and church leaders only assume their prophetic role when challenges arise while doing very little to teach, disciple and lead the way towards a just society. The church must practice what it preaches.

The Scriptures call on us to identify with the poor and the marginalized. The church and faith leaders therefore have an obligation to stand against any person or institution that abuses its power and to stand in solidarity with those who suffer injustice, persecution or abuse. Christianity has an important role to play in modelling how power should be used for the common good rather than for the subjugation of dissent or for self-aggrandisement.

The police and military play a crucial role in protecting the vulnerable from violence and abuse, maintaining and establishing peace, working for law and order in society, and ensuring that crimes are not committed and that justice is sought for those who have been wronged. Christians and the church have a crucial role to play in shaping society's understanding of the role of the military and the police and in supporting the military and the police as they seek to carry out their duties with care, responsibility, and fairness.

We must commit ourselves to creating spaces where people in various regions in Africa are able to listen to one another and to the voice of God. Wherever possible, we should seek to avoid violent behaviour that shuts down dialogue, for it is only through deep dialogue, listening and courageous actions that we can find long-term solutions for Africa. The Africa we want demands that we become patient with one another and listen to each other in order to achieve the dream that God has for our continent and its people.

Questions

1. How can Christians and the church hold members of the military and the police services accountable for their role in society? What can you do to improve the accountability of any groups you are associated with?
2. What role do you think God has for the military and the police in establishing justice, security and peace in your context? What can you do to serve, encourage and help members of these sectors of society to fulfil their responsibility and mandate?
3. How should Christians respond when they encounter violence? What role could you or your church play in working for peace?
4. What advice and warnings would you give to a young person in your church who is considering a career in the military or the police force?

Further Reading

Charles, J. Daryl, and Timothy J. Demy. *War, Peace, and Christianity: Questions and Answers from a Just-War Perspective.* Wheaton, IL: Crossway, 2010.

Sachikonye, L. *When the State Turns on Its Citizens: 60 Years of Institutionalised Violence in Zimbabwe.* Harare: Weaver Press, 2011.

Sebahene, A. *Corruption Mocking at Justice: A Theological and Ethical Perspective on Public Life in Tanzania and Its Implications for the Anglican Church of Tanzania.* Carlisle: Langham Monographs, 2017.

Storey, P. "Banning the Flag from Our Churches: Learning from the Church-State Struggle in South Africa." In *Between Capital and Cathedral: Essays on Church-State Relationships,* edited by Wessel Bentley and Dion A. Forster, 1–20. Pretoria: University of South Africa, 2012. http://uir.unisa.ac.za/bitstream/handle/10500/6093/Bentley-11-07-2012.pdf?sequence=1.

Wink, Walter. *Engaging the Powers: Discernment and Resistance in a World of Domination.* Minneapolis: Fortress, 1992.

22

Land Issues

Dwight S. M. Mutonono

African history is fraught with painful memories of land disputes that have resulted in atrocities and unspeakable acts of violence. Like people in other parts of the world, the people of Africa need healing from sinful acts that have been perpetrated against them, and that in some instances they have perpetrated themselves. At the same time, the continent is wrestling with issues of climate change and environmental crises that pit farmers and herders against each other in battles for land and access to water. Those who join the steady stream of urbanization find themselves in competition for small parcels of land in Africa's teeming cities. Clearly, land is an important issue in Africa, so land issues need to be addressed as an important part of public theology.

This chapter will consider land issues primarily from a Zimbabwean perspective, because this is the situation I know best. However, the colonial history of Africa is shared, and the lessons learned in Zimbabwe can be applied in other African contexts.

After considering land issues from biblical and African traditional perspectives, I will turn to the colonial and contemporary systems of agriculture (commercial farming) and mining that were introduced to the continent. This will be done in the context of trying to understand the effects of globalization and the introduction of the concept of a nation-state to previously traditional systems. The chapter will conclude by proposing a holistic approach towards a public theology of land. But let me begin with some examples that will be used as the basis for the reflection in this chapter.

Examples to Reflect On

As I was driving to preach at a church in Glen View, a relatively poor area of Harare, Zimbabwe, the roads became progressively worse. Eventually they became so pot-holed that it was better to get off what remained of the jagged tarmac and drive on the dusty sides. Then I saw something that made me think deeply about what had been done to the country. I saw a young man, probably in his early twenties, cutting wood to be sold for cooking fires because the authorities were failing to provide electricity for the city. He was doing this outside a shopping centre where hundreds of vendors were selling their wares outside their darkened shops. I thought about that young man in his early twenties and wondered what the picture would be like, at least in physical terms, if he had not come into the world from the womb that bore him. Supposing that he had been in a Japanese womb, for example, and had been born in Japan. At age twenty, he would almost definitely not be cutting wood to sell by the roadside. His big mistake, it would seem, was coming out of the wrong womb.

This first example is probably linked to my second example, which is that the development trajectory of Zimbabwe took a serious downturn in the early 2000s due to violent land invasions that expelled white farmers and had serious negative economic ramifications for the country. Any analysis of Zimbabwe's economy will have to admit that from the early 2000s, or some will say from about 1997, it has nosedived, hitting world record levels of inflation in 2008. As I write this in 2019, we are again experiencing a resurgence of hyper-inflation.

The causes of this economic downturn are hotly disputed. Some blame sanctions and alienation by the international world. What cannot be denied is that the land invasions have failed to yield the envisaged economic prosperity for the country. A few have benefitted from them, mainly due to patronage relationships of some kind. The reality is that some of the white farmers who were expelled from Zimbabwe were given land in Zambia, and today, Zambia exports food to Zimbabwe.[1] The economic disparity between Zambia and Zimbabwe in the 1980s and 1990s would have made such a scenario unthinkable. Zimbabwe's economy was much stronger then, and Zambians would come to Zimbabwe to shop for basic necessities.

The third reflection point is that in the midst of all these problems, some Zimbabweans, especially those with political power, have become incredibly rich. For example, due to a divorce wrangle the assets of a man who served for

---

1. Al Jazeera English, *White Farmers Thrive in Zambia Years after Driven from Zimbabwe* (23 November 2017).

some time as minister of lands in Mugabe's government were revealed in court records. According to those records, he owned a hundred properties (houses, residential and commercial stands, and farms) and was estimated to have a net worth of over US $1.2 billion.[2] I have no personal agenda against this man, and the validity of these estimates will probably be disputed. There are several other examples that could be presented, but for the purposes of this chapter, this one example from court records is illustrative of the extent of the abuse of public office and the level of plundering that some have enjoyed. Keep these three examples in mind as you read the rest of this chapter.

Biblical Reflections

It is not a mistake that a person is born African. God has a plan and purpose for placing us in a specific historical and geographical context. God told Jeremiah that he knew him before he was conceived and placed in his mother's womb (Jer 1:5). So it is God who places us in our mother's womb, and it is God who fearfully and wonderfully forms us with our unique qualities (Ps 139). Our uniqueness is evident even in science's ability to identify us as individuals by our fingerprints or by iris scans.

Nor is relative poverty the only factor we should consider. While Africans are comparatively poorer in material terms than the Japanese, as alluded to in the earlier example, it should be noted that suicide "is now the single biggest killer of men in Japan aged 20–44."[3] A holistic analysis and comparison of life for a twenty-year old might reveal that, contrary to appearances, the poor young man cutting wood in Africa is happier than the rich young man in Japan.

The lie of modernity, which underlies colonial philosophy and culture, is that material development is the answer to all things and that the more economically prosperous a country, the happier its people. This is not entirely true, and we may need to rethink our definition of poverty. Bryant Myers defined it as rooted in four broken relationships, namely our relationship with

---

2. Elias Mambo, "Embattled Chombo's Vast Property Empire under the Spotlight," *The Zimbabwe Independent* (8 December 2017); Gosebo Mathope, "Zim's 'Most Corrupt Official' Reportedly Found with R140m Cash, 'Owned 100 Properties,'" *The Citizen* (20 November 2017); *The Zambian Observer*, "Ignatius Chombo; Zimbabwe's Finance Minister Net Worth Over $1.2 Billion," (27 November 2017).

3. Rupert Wingfield-Hayes, "Why Does Japan Have Such a High Suicide Rate?," BBC News Tokyo (3 July 2015).

God, with ourselves, with others and with creation.[4] By this understanding, Zimbabwean poverty is deeper than just material poverty.

The forcible acquisition of land in colonial times was not an expression of how God would have wanted others to treat Africans. They, like all human beings, are made in the image of God (Gen 1:26–28) and so are worthy of respect. Missionaries like David Livingstone, whose statue remains standing at the Victoria Falls, were not happy with how poorly the European colonial system treated the African people. "Livingstone opposed the white South African colonists' ill treatment of the Xhosa in the 1840s. One reason he moved northward into Central Africa was to avoid the areas dominated by European settlers, who burned down his mission station and library because they opposed British missionary efforts to assist the Africans."[5] Livingstone and other missionaries spoke out against what they saw as inhuman treatment of black people by colonial regimes that were driven more by greed than by biblical values. These regimes sinned against black people. Their spiritual poverty caused them to ignore or silence the missionaries' voice, resulting in low morals and ethics, and they treated Africans unjustly by taking their land.

The Bible makes three main points in relation to the issue of land.[6] First, *God owns the land* because he created it and gives it to whom he chooses (Ps 24:1). He gives and takes away land according to his sovereign choice, even allowing certain people groups to displace others. This displacement is not done in an arbitrary or capricious manner, but relates to the second point, which is that *God's laws govern life on the land*. In the book of Genesis, shortly after the first murder of a human being, we read words that describe what happened from a divine perspective: "The LORD said, 'What have you done? Listen! Your brother's blood cries out to me from the ground. Now you are under a curse and driven from the ground, which opened its mouth to receive your brother's blood from your hand'" (Gen 4:10–11). Notice that the Lord speaks of the blood and ground in anthropomorphic terms. The blood of Abel "cries out" from the ground that "opened its mouth" to receive it. It's like the land is crying out to God, saying, "I was not made for this! I am being violated! God,

---

4. Bryant L. Myers, *Walking with the Poor: Principles and Practices of Transformational Development*, rev. ed. (Maryknoll, NY: Orbis, 2011).

5. Dana L. Robert, *Christian Mission: How Christianity Became a World Religion* (Chichester: Wiley-Blackwell, 2009), 84.

6. For a list of Scriptures particularly relevant to the issue of land, see Dwight S. M. Mutonono and Makoto L. Mautsa, "Land," in *Africa Bible Commentary*, ed. Tokunboh Adeyemo (Nairobi: WordAliveGrand Rapids: Zondervan, 2006), 290.

do something about what has just happened to me!" Similar anthropomorphic language regarding land can be found in the book of Leviticus:

> Do not defile yourselves in any of these ways, because this is how the nations that I am going to drive out before you became defiled. Even the land was defiled; so I punished it for its sin, and the land vomited out its inhabitants. But you must keep my decrees and my laws. The native-born and the foreigners residing among you must not do any of these detestable things, for all these things were done by the people who lived in the land before you, and the land became defiled. And if you defile the land, it will vomit you out as it vomited out the nations that were before you. (Lev 18:24–28)

The sins committed on the land of Canaan caused the land to become defiled. The land was not created to host sinful acts, and its reaction to them is compared to the violent response of the human body when it ingests bad food or drink. The land in these examples is like a living organism that ingests whatever goes on in it. If what goes on is as it should be or as God intended, it is good and pleasing to the land, and the land responds by yielding its crops and produce. Conversely, the land can violently eject its inhabitants when they become intolerably wicked.

God and the land seem to be constantly in conversation. Sodom is a graphic example of this. God describes his visit to Sodom as a response to a great outcry that had led him to go down and see the reality on the ground (Gen 18:20–21). The word translated "outcry" is "a technical word for the cry of pain or the cry for help from those who are being oppressed or violated."[7] God therefore hears the cry of pain and suffering, the anguish of the oppressed in Africa.

The root of the pain and suffering Africa has experienced in colonial and postcolonial times is that people do not understand this second point of God's laws governing life on the land. To go back to Myers' analogy, material poverty results from spiritual poverty or a broken relationship with the God who owns the land and whose laws govern life on it.

The third point is *God wants land to benefit its inhabitants.* Human beings are commanded to manage the earth God gave to us all in such a way that the land enables human flourishing (Gen 1:26–28). In order to flourish, human beings require food for their stomachs, scope for their bodies to grow to full

---

7. Christopher J. H. Wright, *The Mission of God: Unlocking the Bible's Grand Narrative* (Leicester: IVP Academic, 2013), 359.

strength, and scope to use their brains to think creatively and rationally. God intended that the earth would provide all of these. His ideal is that there be no poor people in any given land (Lev 25:8–34; Deut 15:1–11). Deuteronomy 15:4 specifically says there need not be any poor in the land. When geographical areas are managed as they should be, or as closely aligned to God's original intentions as possible, human flourishing results. When they are managed badly, human suffering is the inevitable result.

The colonial regimes that came to Africa failed the continent because they did not properly represent or demonstrate what a just society run along biblical values would be like. The missionaries who came with them are often accused of being complicit with the colonialists who tried to subjugate all other peoples and establish the superiority of the white race. This accusation is not entirely true. Some missionaries were indeed more influenced by their context than by the Bible, and others misinterpreted the Bible and held wrong views of Africans as slaves and servants. But there were also those who were discerning enough to see the sin in their own culture and to point it out to their contemporaries, with varying levels of success. The fact that today, after the missionaries and colonizers are gone, Africa is one of the world's leading continents in terms of Christian demographics is testament to the fact that, despite their failings, missionaries did plant a true kingdom seed. Nevertheless, the colonial regimes did sin against the people of Africa, causing them much pain and suffering.

The colonial regimes' effect on African land will be considered in more depth later in this chapter, but here it is important to note that they failed to properly represent the God of the Bible in how they treated African land and people. Instead of working towards an environment where there would be no poor in the land, the colonists selfishly took the best land, subjugating and impoverishing the original inhabitants.

This colonial model has been perpetuated in postcolonial Africa. Sadly, the sins of the colonizers have been imitated by subsequent leaders who have shed innocent blood on the land and have not listened to their own prophets, leading to uprisings against them. Many of these leaders could be described in the words of former Zimbabwean prime minister Morgan Tsvangirai, who spoke of a corrupt government minister as being like "a greedy baboon trying to grab every cob from a farmer's maize field."[8]

Public office is a trust. In the modern world, we generally elect people into office and trust them to lead in the hope that they will use that trust to better the lives of those who elected them. Public officials should serve those

---

8. Mathope, "Zim's 'Most Corrupt Official.'"

who put them into office. At a higher level, however, public officials need to understand that it is God who has entrusted them with their position and that they are accountable to God for how they act. God is especially concerned for the poor and oppressed, and he hears their cries.

The articulated motive for expelling white farmers from Zimbabwe was a desire to right historical wrongs perpetrated against the black people of the nation. However, in supposedly righting those wrongs, innocent blood was shed, and atrocities were perpetrated against white people. As a young boarder at a high school in the early 1980s, I shared a dormitory with a white farmer's son. He had a recurring nightmare and would wake up screaming, "The terrs are coming! The terrs are coming!" Terrorists, or freedom fighters (depending on who was describing them) had come to his parents' farm, shot his father, brutalized others in his family and the farm workers and plundered the farm.

The white farmers who remained on the land up to the early 2000s were also forcibly removed with much bloodshed and pain to innocent white people. In *Stewards of Power: Restoring Africa's Dignity*, I highlight the testimony of a white Christian farmer who prayed for those who had invaded his land even as they beat him and his father-in-law. He survived, but his father-in-law did not.[9] Such suffering is also part of the outcry against the land, the cry of pain of the people on the land that is heard by God. The white farmers have gone to places like Zambia where they have been loved and accepted and the sins of their forefathers forgiven, and the land of Zambia is enjoying the blessing of God for it.

The cry of the young man cutting wood in the city of Harare, who had to become a street vendor just to stay alive, is also part of the outcry against the land. We hear all kinds of justifications and blame shifting for economic failure in the nation, but in truth what is needed are public officials who will lead with righteousness – rightness before God, or justice – in all they do and will not use public office for personal gain but to serve God and their fellow human beings with fear and reverence.

African Traditional Thinking

African traditional thinking is still operational in some parts of rural Africa, but the precolonial times represent its purer forms. In those times, life was not perfect. Humans are sinful, and any honest, unromanticized history will show

---

9. Dwight Mutonono, *Stewards of Power: Restoring Africa's Dignity* (Carlisle, UK: HippoBooks, 2018), 111–112.

that there was some good and some bad in Africa. For our purposes, however, we will consider the idealized use of land in traditional Africa.

In the best cases, African traditional land was used in the service of the people: "Selling or amassing land while others had none was considered a sign of unfaithfulness to God."[10] The food that was grown on the land was generationally passed down and was healthy food. It was well-suited to the soils, and a good crop rotation process was built into the culture. Today, many want to go back to the traditional foods, which are proving much better for the body than the foods that were introduced in colonial times and have become the modern diet.

Though the chief was wealthier than the rest of the community, this was not because he used his power to evict people and appropriate their land. He was wealthy because the people would give a certain portion of their produce to him so that in times of hunger, perhaps due to a bad rainy reason and low crop yields, his storehouse would have enough for the community. This arrangement was known as the king's storehouse, *Zunde raMambo* in Shona, and matches "Joseph's advice to Pharaoh the Egyptian king on storage of grain in preparation for the long famine."[11] John Ringson argues that this concept can be drawn on when arranging for the care of orphans and vulnerable children in modern Zimbabwe, which is failing to look after them as they were looked after in traditional Zimbabwe.

African traditional thinking on land involved relatively small-scale and subsistence-level farming. Families and clans would work their land to harvest enough to feed themselves until the next season. The granary would perhaps store enough to go through a season of drought, but not much more. Communities were mostly tribal. Farming at commercial levels to feed a nation was a concept that came with colonialism and modern ways of life.

After studying metaphors of leadership in various sub-Saharan languages, William Addai was struck by the fact that so many dialects associate sitting and eating with leadership.[12] In Shona, my own language, I found that people who have succeeded in life are described as *akagarika*, which literally means "he or she is now sitting." They are said to *varikudya na mambo*, meaning

---

10. Mutonono and Mautsa, "Land," 290.

11. John Ringson, "Zunde RaMambo as a Traditional Coping Mechanism for the Care of Orphans and Vulnerable Children: Evidence from Gutu District, Zimbabwe," *African Journal of Social Work* 7, no. 2 (2017): 54; Mutonono, *Stewards of Power*, 22–26.

12. William Addai, *Reforming Leadership Across Africa* (Accra, Ghana: William Addai, 2009).

"they are eating with kings." Connecting leading with eating is even part of slang. Young people use *chibuns* (literally "big buns") as street language for money and speak of their motivation for work as *trikuda kuluma*, which literally means "we want to take a bite." (You may want to look for similar metaphors in your own language.) Addai wonders whether these metaphors may explain why African leaders are more focused on consumption than production. In African thinking, good leaders sit and eat. Work is done so that one has something to consume, and success is to sit and eat an abundant harvest, often while being served by others. Consumption is not bad in itself, but a problem comes when people choose to eat by themselves, a modern phenomenon that is foreign to African values. At one time, those who ate alone were the most despised people in a community. So if production is for the sole purpose of consuming, then let us at least consume together. However, in this respect, African culture can also learn from other cultures. It is time to expect leaders to be producers who maximize resources rather than just consumers of resources.

At the religious level, it is necessary to enter a dialogue with African Traditional Religion on the issue of land. Both agree that ultimately the physical land has a spiritual origin and creator who is God to whom people must account for how they use the land. However, disagreement comes at the level of the continued ownership of land by departed ancestors as well as the ancestors' perceived role in causing fertility or famine, which leads to appeasing forms of worship. In African Traditional Religion, certain areas are also regarded as sacred and not to be used unless some appeasing rituals are done. These interreligious issues need biblical critique as part of public theology, as is discussed in chapter 19 on public theology and interreligious dialogue.

Colonial leaders ignored African traditional thinking on land, or relegated it to what were called communal areas or tribal trust lands. They introduced the colonial attitude towards land, which we also need to consider.

Colonial Land Use

The colonial powers came from the industrialized world, and they sought the raw materials that were abundantly available on African soil to enrich themselves. The most crude and violent example of this was in the Congo, which King Leopold of Belgium treated as his personal property. He subjected the people to forced labour, even amputating limbs if workers did not produce the required amount of raw resources in a given time frame. His brutality is clearly depicted in books by Adam Hochschild and Emmanuel Katongole.[13] Leopold created a culture in which African lives were disposable:

> Once this dispensability of African lives had been accepted and came to be accepted as part of the official, normal way of nation-state politics, postcolonial successors to the colonial project have had no qualms perpetuating the same wanton sacrificing of lives in pursuit of their political ambitions and greed. Thus, we see the same wasting of lives in the fighting in eastern Congo as with the LRA [Lord's Resistance Army] in northern Uganda. Similarly, a Mobutu or a Mugabe will never voluntarily step down from office in the national interest. Instead, he will readily sacrifice, waste, starve, and kill "his people" for his own political ambition.[14]

At the time of writing, Katongole's analysis of Mugabe might have been disputed. But history has shown Katongole to have been very perceptive and even prophetic.

The idea of the dispensability of African lives cannot be attributed entirely to colonial regimes. An honest study of precolonial African history will show that Africans were fighting among themselves, which made it easier for colonial powers to divide and rule. In Southern Africa, Shaka's history and the Ndebele wars illustrate some precolonial atrocities. However, the colonial regimes made the dispensability of African lives an intrinsic part of the way they led, and those who took over from them have maintained the culture. For example, in Zimbabwe the police and army operate as if the country is in a constant state of emergency. Even when there is no discernible external threat, roadblocks are common, and these are often monitored by menacing-looking people armed with large rifles. I remember the night I picked up a visitor from the United States on her first visit to Africa. Her first experience of Africa, coming from the airport, was my being stopped by two men with rifles at a roadblock on a dark street. She had never seen a roadblock manned by people with rifles in her life, for in the USA that would only happen if there were a terror alert. She describes this experience as one of the most frightening moments of her life; for me, it was just everyday life in Zimbabwe.

---

13. Adam Hochschild, *King Leopold's Ghost: A Story of Greed, Terror, and Heroism in Colonial Africa* (Boston: Houghton Mifflin, 1999); Emmanuel Katongole, *The Sacrifice of Africa: A Political Theology for Africa* (Grand Rapids: Eerdmans, 2011).

14. Katongole, *Sacrifice of Africa*, 17.

The colonial regime in Rhodesia instituted a state of emergency when it was under threat, with shops being bombed, national fuel storage facilities blown up and even civilian airplanes shot down. But after independence, the general populace of Zimbabwe found that this was how the army and police still operated. There have been a number of instances of violence against civilians by those who should be there to protect citizens and their rights.

What this means is that colonial regimes introduced a culture of subjugation of the people to the point of enslavement. African lives only had meaning and value in relation to utilitarian purposes. The colonists' real interest was not in the people but in becoming wealthy. They were greedy and ambitious, and they passed that attitude on to their African successors.

It is also important to understand that the colonies existed to serve their home countries, and produce from the colonies would go back to Europe by various commercial means. Produce from farming and mining had ready markets in Europe, which led to more advanced structures being set up in Africa. In place of the traditional subsistence farmer, the colonial regimes introduced the commercial farmer who would produce enough to feed a nation or a substantial portion of it. This production, of course, translated into food sold in shops and contributed to the national economy. Zimbabwe used to produce more than enough to feed itself, and industries were created to support farming and mining activities. The economic systems created were complex and interlinked, so tampering with one area would affect other areas. And that is exactly what happened in Zimbabwe with the land invasions.

The illustration of falling dominos explains what happened. All the dominos in the economic system began to fall, one by one, and the net effect was poverty for everyone. The failure of the Zimbabwean economy in recent times can be directly attributed to the collapse of farming after the land invasions which started in 2000. The commercial farms were broken up and parcelled out to people. At one point the government was offering forcibly acquired land to any who would apply for it. A number of people were given land in this way. Some of them were urban dwellers who had no idea how to run a commercial farm. Zimbabweans came up with a name for these new farmers who also held jobs in the city: "cell-phone farmers." Though many of them tried their best, they lacked the expertise to make the land produce anywhere near what the white farmers used to.

To add to the problem, the government ignored fundamentals of how commercial farming that feeds a nation should be run. The new farmers had no title to their land, so they could not use it as collateral to borrow money from banks.[15] But commercial farmers generally borrow money from banks to fund inputs to the farm and then pay back the loan after harvest. To avoid overdependence on the weather, commercial farmers build dams and incrementally add to their farming infrastructure by acquiring tractors, harvesters, irrigation systems and the like. Commercial farmers had done this for years. But the new farmers had no way to do these things. Mambondiyan quoted Eddie Cross, an economist and MP for Bulawayo South, as saying that "Mugabe's land reforms were intended to strip away security of tenure and replace it with political control – much like the old traditional systems when local chiefs controlled access to land."[16]

The traditional system of land tenure adequately describes the kind of thinking that dominated at the time of the land seizures. The new farmers who took possession of the land often operated with a rural-agrarian, traditional farming mindset. Several commercial farms became rural subsistence homesteads. It was sad to see farms that once produced enough to feed the nation lying fallow, with a few huts dotted here and there, and maybe a small section, enough to feed a family, being cultivated.

Mining was also adversely affected by the land seizures. The overall production from this sector plummeted, and even the Marange fields (MDF), which were first publicly mentioned in 2006, have been the subject of much looting. Zvaridza claims that MDF is "the biggest find of alluvial diamonds in the world covering an area of 60,000 hectares and with a value of over US$800 billion."[17] But he adds –

> The value chain of Zimbabwe's Marange diamonds has been dominated by officials who abuse power and public trust for personal gain. As mentioned, to enter the industry, one has to be highly connected in the ruling party; no fair considerations are made in allocating claims. The tax regimes are such that little revenue is directed to the treasury while most revenue flows to the police, army, CIO, and other ruling party faithful. . . . More than $2 billion realized from Marange diamond sales between 2012 and

---

15. Andrew Mambodiyani, "Bank Loans beyond Reach for Zimbabwe Farmers without Land Titles," *Reuters* (20 July 2016).

16. Mambodiyani, "Bank Loans."

17. Tawanda Zvarivadza, "Making the Most out of Zimbabwe's Marange Diamonds: Leaving a Lasting Positive Legacy for Distressed Communities," *Mine Closure 2015*, 10th International Conference on Mine Closure, Vancouver, Canada: InfoMine Inc., 1.

2013 has disappeared amidst outrageous salaries and benefits for executive officers running diamond mining ventures in Marange.[18]

Global Implications

Like most of Africa, Zimbabwe was introduced to the idea of the modern nation-state and its associated governance and economic systems through colonial influences. The country has moved from a traditional system into a modern world system dominated by Western world powers.

There are advantages and disadvantages to globalization. However, the reality is that the world as it is structured today is interdependent. Countries need each other. Zimbabwe has not been able to produce as it used to, and global markets that we once traded with have been lost. Assigning blame to other people for whatever goes wrong does not help in overcoming the problems. What does help is to directly face the issues, and the reality is that we as Africans need to learn to make God-given resources work for us.

Globalization requires nation-states to work with each other. Nations are in some respects like businesses, and business principles apply – people will buy where they get a good deal; the more stress-free, the better. International rankings such as indices of corruption or ease of doing business or human rights records are used by investors as they make decisions. Countries with low rankings are high risk. A person who wants to do business with such countries is likely to be crooked and therefore happy to operate in environments of low transparency and accountability. The implications for Zimbabwe and other African nations is that they first need to help each other by establishing trading blocs, and then they need to make Africa attractive to the rest of the world. Rwanda from about 2009 on is a good example of what can happen economically when a country deliberately works on improving its international rankings on various indices.

Conclusion

Christians need to have a sober and holistic perspective on the complexities surrounding land issues in the African context. This chapter has endeavoured to present such a perspective as it has looked at these issues

---

18. Zvarivadza, "Making the Most," 6.

in terms of biblical thinking, African traditional thinking and colonial and contemporary perspectives.

A biblical approach reveals that God is concerned with what happens on any given land because ultimately he owns all land, and he gives it to whom he wants. His laws govern life on the land, and he hears the cry of the oppressed and violated. Tokunboh Adeyemo asked the question, "Is Africa cursed?"[19] I agree with his argument that it is not, and there is hope for Africa. But Africa should know and understand that there is a God in heaven who hears the cry of the widow and the poor, and any people who cause an outcry against them to reach heaven are asking for trouble.

We should refer to African traditional thinking as we highlight that greedily taking everything and eating alone is despicable. Africans share, and as in biblical ideals, communal thinking will ensure that there are no poor in the land. The colonial example of greed and making African lives disposable or dispensable was their worst legacy to the continent, and it should not be followed. Finally, global realities require African countries to act in their own best interests. Countries are like businesses in this respect: international rankings matter. It makes no sense to invest in a place that is likely to result in losses because of an unstable environment. Investors will take their business somewhere else where there is less drama.

In closing, it is important for Christians in public office or operating in public capacities to understand that in this issue particularly, they need to be moral or ethical referees. They must be the voice of reason, the voice of conscience. Like Livingstone, they must be prepared to be prophetic voices that can if necessary be counter-cultural, and they must be prepared to face reprisals due to their stand for what is right. They need to be careful not to become entangled in land issues and thereby lose their voice. The referee should not get into the game and start playing too. In all land dealings, let the wisdom of the book of Proverbs prevail: "A good name is more desirable than great riches; to be esteemed is better than silver or gold" (Prov 22:1).

Questions

1. In Africa, public office tends to be seen as a place to eat rather than a place to serve, an attitude that easily creates a patronage culture. Do you agree or disagree with that statement? Discuss its implications.

---

19. Tokunboh Adeyemo, *Is Africa Cursed?* (Nairobi: WordAlive, 2017).

2. Leadership and land issues are historically related – in bad times and in good times. What is required from leadership to have a just land policy, and how do circumstances and societal changes effect land policy and farming practices?

3. Urbanization is a growing reality in every single African country. How is it going to affect land issues and farming practices in your region?

4. After independence from colonization, Africans have sought to manage conflict by creating negotiated ways of reparation. However, human selfishness and greed have a tight grip, especially regarding land. In what just ways can reparation be balanced with enabling human flourishing for all? How can people learn to care for others and share?

Further Reading

Chigumira, Easther. "Re-Peasantization under Fast Track Land Reform: Implications for Livelihood and Landscape Change, Sanyati District, Zimbabwe." PhD, University of Oregon, 2014. http://search.proquest.com/pqdtglobal/docview/1621504985/abstract/37E20BDE4F184120PQ/1.

Masengwe, Gift. *Land Reform and the Theology of Development: The Zimbabwean Fast Track Land Reform (FTLR) Program and Environmental Ethics* (Lambert, 2011). https://www.academia.edu/28848184/Land_reform_and_the_theology_of_development_The_fast_track_land_reform_programme_of_Zimbabwe_and_environmental_ethics?.

Mutonono, Dwight. *Stewards of Power: Restoring Africa's Dignity.* Carlisle, UK: HippoBooks, 2018.

Mutonono, Dwight, Simpson Munyaradzi, and Makoto L. Mautsa. "Land." In *Africa Bible Commentary*, edited by Tokunboh Adeyemo, 290. Nairobi: WordAlive Publishers; Grand Rapids: Zondervan, 2006.

23

The Media

Bimbo Fafowora and Rahab N. Nyaga

We may not be aware of it, but what we do, how we do it and what we say are all influenced by the media to which we and our communities are exposed. Information is power, and the media are now our sources of information.[1] Contrary to what you might expect, the media's power lies not mainly in the way stories are covered but in the way media choose what to highlight and what to ignore from the thousands of possible stories they could tell each day. What they choose to cover influences the importance placed on those topics and sets the agenda for public discussion.[2]

Print media like newspapers, magazines and books have been around for a very long time, and with the expansion of literacy, their reach has extended worldwide. In the twentieth century, print media were joined by electronic media like radio and television, which have been hugely influential because even the uneducated can receive and understand the messages relayed. A television programme may be in a language that is not understood, but the images are fascinating and may challenge local taboos. For example, in Africa it would once have been unheard of for a teenage girl to hug her father, but the Western culture depicted on the screen portrays this as normal behaviour. The power of visual media has led most of Africa to accept, adapt and practice formerly taboo interpersonal interactions.

---

1. Manuel Castells argues that power is no longer associated solely with military and economic strength but with the ability to control the information that shapes our identity and drives transformation and other socio-political processes. See M. Castells, *The Power of Identity: The Information Age: Economy, Society and Culture*, vol. 2, 2nd ed. (Oxford: Blackwell, 2004).

2. M. McCombs and D. Shaw, "The Agenda-Setting Function of Mass Media," *Public Opinion Quarterly* 36, no. 2 (1972): 176.

In Africa radio and television programming gradually changed from using only the colonial languages of English, French and Portuguese to using major regional languages like Kiswahili. Community radio then emerged, broadcasting religious, political and development messages in local languages. Since the 2000s, television has also been broadcast in African languages and has featured local characters. With the emergence of digital media in the twenty-first century, Africa was swept into real-time communication with the rest of the world. While Internet connectivity may still not be at the same level as in more developed countries, Africa has embraced the new digital era.

Media audiences in Africa today thus range from the uneducated who cannot read or write but who can listen to the radio, watch television and maybe use a mobile phone to those who appreciate the written word and radio and television broadcasts and who may be computer literate and use a mobile phone. And then there are the youth, many of whom are digital natives, so used to modern communication technology that they cannot imagine life without it.

Media, the Church and Public Theology

Public interaction in Africa takes place across a range of media – from traditional oral face-to-face communication to radio and television broadcasts, social media posts and video calls and conferences. It is thus important for Christians to think about the power of the media and about how this power can be used and abused. Christians who work in the media need to think about how their Christian faith should affect their work, and Christians who use media need to think about how their Christian faith should shape the ways they use it.

Our starting point when thinking theologically about the media is to recognize that they are a gift from God. The goal of all media is to communicate, and God himself is a communicator who communicates with us through creation (natural revelation) and through his word (special revelation). When God created human beings in his own image, he endowed them with the ability and desire to communicate. He also gave them the intelligence to learn how to use science and technology to enhance human communication in the ways we see today.

In the Bible we see God communicating with human beings through a variety of media (spoken, visual and written) and genres (poetry and prose). God also adapted his message to the eras in which he was speaking. This is supremely evident in Christ, who lived and communicated in a Jewish community as a Jewish man. If we seek to communicate God's message to the current generation, we need to be like him and use strategic, effective and culturally appropriate methods of communication that correctly instruct human beings and reveal God to them in a language that is meaningful to them. Today, this means that we need to use the media.

Like all of God's gifts, the media can be used and abused. The information they convey can shape people's beliefs, values, perceptions and behaviour both positively and negatively. In Kenya, for example, media broadcasts carry significant blame for the violence after the 2013 election.[3] Yet it is also through media coverage and appeals that Kenyans rally to assist victims of drought, floods and fire, or respond to appeals for medical funds.

Public theologians have a dual responsibility: they should both condemn abuse of the media and encourage and contribute to its healthy use. Carrying out this responsibility well calls for serious reflection on the nature of different media and how Christians can and have used them, the nature of media influence and the ethical responsibilities of those who work in media industries.

Public Theology and Various Forms of Media

The church in Africa has long used various forms of media as a means of fulfilling the divine mandate of preaching the gospel of our Lord Jesus Christ to all nations.

Print media and public theology

The invention of the printing press marked the first technologically driven venture into mass communication. It was immediately seized on by theologians who used it to print Bibles in a range of European languages and to disseminate the ideas that drove the Reformation in the sixteenth century. Printed books were the medium that transformed religious thought in Europe.

The rise of print media in Africa is closely connected with Christianity, for Western missionaries were eager to promote literacy so that Africans could read the Bible and other Christian literature for themselves. The missionaries were soon subordinated to colonists, who expected the print media to reflect

---

3. S. G. Kimotho and R. N. Nyaga, "Digitized Ethnic Hate Speech: Understanding Effects of Hate Speech on Citizen Journalism in Kenya," *Advances in Language and Literary Studies (ALLS)*, 7, no. 3 (2016): 189–200.

their point of view and support their interests rather than those of Africans and migrants like the Indians who had been brought to Africa as labourers.[4]

Today, African newspapers still tend to propagate the point of view of their owners. Some of them may be ardent supporters of the government in power, while others may be critical of it. Ideally, newspapers should follow the example of the newspapers in South Africa that took a strong stand against the abuses of the apartheid government and were equally critical of abuses by the ANC government that followed it. Their prophetic focus on exposing corruption made them unpopular with the authorities. In some African countries this type of journalism can be dangerous, and many journalists have "disappeared" or been murdered. Despite their biases and the opposition they face, newspapers remain an important source of current news in Africa, providing useful information on the political, economic, religious and social welfare of the nation.

Magazines have a longer shelf life than newspapers and often carry articles of a more enduring nature. These articles sometimes address issues that are relevant to public theology in that the opinions offered are persuasive and influence public behaviour. Christians should seize every opportunity to respond to such articles through the media to ensure that the Christian position is articulated in public forums. Some churches and religious organizations publish their own magazines or contribute articles to weekly or monthly magazines in which they may address the types of issues that concern public theologians. Such articles give the church a voice in the public arena and are useful as a public conscience to remind people of God's sovereignty over the affairs of all.

Books are even more enduring than magazines and allow for detailed discussion of topics in order to promote deeper understanding. The book you are currently reading, for example, aims to introduce you to the concerns of public theology and encourage you to take action and to read more so that you can become informed and apply your faith in all areas of your life.

Radio and public theology

Radio remains the most widely available mass communication medium in Africa, as well as the most affordable and the most trusted. In countries like Tanzania and Kenya, over 80 percent of the population get news and

---

4. R. Nyaga, D. Njoroge and C. Nyambuga, *An Introduction to Communication* (Nairobi: Oxford University Press, 2015).

information from the radio. Radio is particularly important in rural areas, where it can be used to supply quality instruction to schools with very limited teaching capacity. In areas without electricity or even mobile phone signals, battery-operated radios are lifelines as connections to the rest of the world. Information delivered by radio to those remote corners of Africa can mean the difference between life and death.

Radio can be used to mobilize and build a community as it fosters engagement and participation. For example, farmers, the sick and other groups with special interests can get real-time help through interactive call-in programmes and updates on current affairs, weather, crop conditions and food prices. Vernacular radio broadcasts mean that communities can now discuss issues in their mother tongues so that even the aged and uneducated can participate and share their wisdom. Thanks to vernacular radio my own mother, Rahab Nyaga, who is 85 years old and had little schooling, can understand the politics of the day, government directives and social concerns.

Radio is a medium that aligns well with the concerns of public theology in that it can be used to empower the poor and disadvantaged and give them a voice and access to those in positions of power. Radio is also a medium that Christians have long used for evangelism and preaching. Church services and devotional broadcasts are common, and a number of prominent African Pentecostal churches run their own radio ministries.

Television and public theology

Television presents people with images of places they have never been to and phenomena they have never experienced. Unfortunately, for a long time African television content was dominated by information about developed countries and their lifestyles. The few available programmes about Africa were through the eyes of colonizers, who painted a picture of a dark, savage, disease-ravaged Africa. Today, however, Africa tells its own story to the world, showcasing our rich cultural heritage and people's everyday struggles, failures and successes and offering theological discourses that resonate well with this very spiritual continent. Strangely, "it is Big Brother Africa, a voyeuristic spectacle of ordinary living which has [. . . provided] viewers in many African countries with knowledge of people in other countries in Africa and viewers in the UK with images of Africa which do not emanate from conditions of 'need.'"[5]

---

5. F. Harding, "Africa and the Moving Image: Television, Film and Video," *Journal of African Cultural Studies* 16, no. 1 (2003): 71.

Live television shows enable viewers to participate through asking questions and expressing their views. These broadcasts can be watched on smart phones, tablets and computers, extending their reach. Newsworthy events are shown around the world moments after they happen. Viewers who are not happy with the programming from a local TV station can now easily tune in to TV stations worldwide.

Television's combination of visual and audio communication gives it great emotive power. That is why politicians seek to control it in order to promote their own parties. Churches, and particularly Pentecostal churches, have also seen television as a powerful tool to spread the Christian faith.[6] Unfortunately, the power of television can also be toxic. We have witnessed the rise of a culture of celebrity pastors and speakers who use television not only to preach the gospel but also to publicize themselves. Often these supposed "men of God" or "women of God" operate without any oversight and are not accountable to anyone outside their own organization. They offer highly entertaining viewing and peddle a prosperity gospel that fills their pockets and fuels their celebrity lifestyle but does not advance the kingdom of God. Their message is not judged by its faithfulness to Scripture but by the preacher's wealth and social connections. Some of these pastors have fallen prey to sins ranging from sexual impropriety to alcoholism to abuse of power and fraud. We need to be concerned about these developments both because a celebrity culture undermines the humble message of Christ and because the behaviour of these celebrities can bring the entire Christian community into disrepute. Moreover, when the spotlight falls primarily on individuals, moral and ethical issues that are important for society as a whole languish in the shadows.

Social media and public theology

Social media platforms are the most recent arrival on the media scene. The term is used to describe computer software and applications that enable users to create and share content and establish social networks on the web. The impact of social media can be compared to the invention of the printing press in that they both transformed the nature of communication. With social media, the recipient is no longer a passive container into which an elite group of writers

---

6. J. Kwabena Asamoah-Gyadu, "Hearing, Viewing, and Touched by the Spirit: Televangelism in Contemporary African Christianity," in *Global and Local Televangelism*, eds. Pradip Ninan Thomas and Philip Lee (Basingstoke, UK: Palgrave Macmillan, 2012).

and directors can pour content; now the recipient can generate content and be an active participant in communication.

The power of social media has been enhanced by the widespread distrust of governments, which are regarded as self-serving, corrupt or controlled by the rich and professional politicians. People are now choosing to trust only those who agree with their own view of the world. In many places political debate no longer involves dialogue about ideas; instead, people merely vilify those who disagree with them. These tendencies can be given free rein on social media and lead not only to citizen protests but also to increasingly nationalistic/ethnic and reactionary politics.

This dramatic change challenges Christians and theologians who are used to dispensing ideas rather than interacting with others around ideas. They are also used to communicating from a distance through the written or preached word and may take time to recognize that "social media makes our comments and our relationships a bit more public." Stephen Holmes states,

> I see social media in part as a megaphone and in part as a tape recorder: It (at least potentially) amplifies anything we say so that many more can hear, and it captures what we say so that it can come back to haunt us.
>
> Both of these functions are ethically neutral in themselves, but might make us think hard about the ethics of our communication. If I know that this joke could be retrieved from Facebook any time in the next decade, would I still want to tell it? . . . Social media makes our comments and our relationships a bit more public. I think we should welcome that: it makes us more accountable in crucial areas of our lives.[7]

Theologians and Christians should welcome the opportunities social media platforms create to communicate with and interact with others.[8] This dialogue and interaction is closer to the way Jesus taught. But Christians need to remember that social media can also be a dangerous place, for ideas can be twisted or taken out of context, and bitter conflicts can result that bring no credit to Christ or his church. Thus we need to tread carefully when using social

---

7. Stephen Holmes, "A Theology of Social Media," EthicsDaily.com (3 December 2012).

8. For an example of how social media can be used, see the transformation of *Die Kerkbode*, which began as a newspaper for the Dutch Reformed Church in South Africa in 1849, but has recently become more of an online discussion forum adapted to social media communication and inviting the participation of readers on topical and controversial issues, https://kerkbode.christians.co.za/.

media to promote public theology. But tread we must, for we have a message that the world needs to hear. We should also show that we have heeded Jesus's warning to be wise as serpents and harmless as doves.

Given the wide range of social media platforms, it may be helpful to subdivide them into five categories:[9]

- *Blogs and vlogs* allow individuals to express their views on particular topics in short articles and to interact with those who respond to their ideas. A number of pastors and theologians maintain blogs that appear more or less regularly and may be automatically shared with those who subscribe to the blog. Christians in other professions might consider doing something similar to show how their Christian beliefs impact their professional lives as well as their daily lives. Vlogs are like blogs but are presented in the form of short videos in which the vlogger expresses their views or documents their personal life. The visual and audio aspects of vlogs make followers feel connected with the author. Vlogs can be used by Christians to deliver an almost face-to-face message including all the non-verbal aspects of communication like gestures and facial expressions.

- *Content communities* are places where users can share things like videos and podcasts by posting them online and inviting others to click on a link to go to that site.

- *Collaborative projects* are sites where many participants work together on the same project. The most famous example may be Wikipedia.

- *Social networking sites* like Facebook, LinkedIn, Twitter and Instagram are used for social communication. People and organizations can post their profiles here and invite others to see their posts and interact with them. Facebook is reportedly the most widely utilized form of social networking in Africa because of its large number of subscribers and ease of use.[10]

- *Virtual social worlds and virtual game worlds* are sites where users interact through personalized avatars and can do things that they would not or could not do in real life. Although virtual reality has not gone completely

---

9. A. M. Kaplan and M. Haenlein, "Users of the World, Unite! The Challenges and Opportunities of Social Media," *Business Horizons* 53, no. 1 (2010): 59–68.

10. Mookgo S. Kgatle, "Social Media and Religion: Missiological Perspective on the Link between Facebook and the Emergence of Prophetic Churches in Southern Africa," *Verbum et Ecclesia* 39, no. 1 (2018): 1–6. See also P. White, Fortune Tella, and Mishael Donkor Ampofo, "A Missional Study of the Use of Social Media (Facebook) by some Ghanaian Pentecostal Pastors," *Koers* 81, no. 2 (2016): 1–8.

mainstream, some Christian organizations in the Western world are already harnessing its potential to provide their clients with faith-based VR experiences such as personal devotions and church services.[11]

Influence of social media

The use of social media has soared with increasing Internet access and increasingly affordable mobile phone technology. Social media platforms are used by individuals and by communities to increase their visibility and present themselves in a favourable light. They are also used to reach out to and establish online and sometimes face-to-face relationships with people with similar interests.

Like all things human, social media can be a great good or a great evil, or a mix of both. The positive effects include the way it can enhance community by enabling people to stay in touch with friends and family and to share their interests and beliefs. Social media has also proved valuable in coordinating social action to help victims of disasters or to protest government policies.

In Africa, many churches have embraced social media and have their own Facebook, Twitter and Instagram accounts to contact their members and reach out to others. Christ Is the Answer Ministries (CITAM) in Nairobi, for example, has launched a CITAM Church Online. In 2019, their Facebook page claimed to have more than 50,000 followers. On that page, a message urges you to listen to the church's podcasts while you are stuck in traffic, exercising in the gym, shopping or just going about your daily schedule. Social media platforms give people an opportunity to be enriched with gospel messages wherever they are. The interactivity of these platforms allows Christians to comment on issues of public theology and join in discussions of them with other believers and theologians.

Social media can, however, be abused. People use Facebook pages to present positive images of themselves and hide anything negative in their lives. Others then have a false impression of who the person is and feel that their own life does not compare well. Some users resort to living on social media rather than interacting with friends face to face. Psychologists in the West speak of the great loneliness of many in the social media generation. The desire to look good on social media also plays into materialistic tendencies, which may

---

11. C. T. Casberg, "The Surprising Theological Possibilities of Virtual Reality," *Christianity Today* (11 November 2016). See also Jon Christian, "HTC Thinks Virtual Reality's Killer App Could Be Christianity: Christians Adapted Radio and Rock Music. Maybe VR Will Be Next," *Futurism* (16 December 2018): 6.

be exacerbated by some preachers who emphasize divine prosperity. These issues may account for the increased competitiveness and desire for material possession within the Christian fold.[12]

Social media can also be used to harass individuals in what is called cyberbullying. Such bullying can drive people to suicide. Christians, including pastors and theologians, must speak out against cyberbullying and emphasize the Christian values of love and respect. As Christians, we are to love our neighbours and our enemies, and love is incompatible with online attacks. We also need to work to repair the damage caused by such bullying, which undermines self-confidence.

Marketers use social media to interact with potential customers, increase brand awareness and boost sales. However, the constant bombardment of advertising plays into the development of a consumer mentality and a materialistic lifestyle. This message is something that churches and individual believers need to counter online and in their personal lifestyles.

Scammers and confidence tricksters use social media to target and defraud the vulnerable. These frauds may even be done under the guise of Christianity. Gullible Christians may forward posts encouraging others to donate to fraudulent causes. Ongoing education is needed to alert people to these dangers and to direct them where to look for confirmation if they suspect that a message is fraudulent. Christians need to be made aware that if they are easily deceived on the Internet, others will assume that they are easily deceived in their faith. So public theology must stress the importance of discernment.

Influence of fake news

Discernment is particularly important in an era in which information can be shared with the click of a button on social media. Sometimes, however, this information is tainted and constitutes fake news or false information.

The practice of spreading misinformation, disinformation or fake news has been in existence for a very long time – the first fake news was delivered by the serpent in Eden. The Old Testament prophets frequently denounced those who proclaimed "fake news" that brought disaster on the nation. Recent events in America have given fake news a prominent place in public consciousness, and

---

12. J. Kwabena Asamoah-Gyadu, "God Is Big in Africa: Pentecostal Megachurches and a Changing Religious Landscape," *Material Religion* (29 May 2019): 1–4, 6.

who is the Truth – must look for ways to curb the circulation of fake news and misinformation. A first step in doing so is to avoid being guilty of creating it. No cause is good enough to justify spreading lies against those who disagree with you. Satan is the father of lies, and as those who follow Christ and are commanded to love our enemies, we should not slander them. Before posting something on social media, check that it does not fall into one of the categories of false news identified above. A second step is to avoid propagating false news. Christians should not forward social media information that will inflame feelings against others or whose motives are suspect.

While these two suggestions are good in theory, they run into the practical problem of how to distinguish false reports from true reports. The answer is that we should check the facts before posting, develop media literacy and learn how to verify the sources of information that come to us on social media.[17] While individual Christians have a responsibility to do this, the responsibility weighs even heavier on Christians who work in the media and who have the power to decide what news to pass on across national and community networks.

Public Theology and Journalism

As has been pointed out, the greatest power of the media is not the way stories are covered but the way the media choose which of the thousands of stories received daily count as newsworthy, and what points they highlight. Media choices influence the importance placed on topics of public interest and set the agenda for what the public discusses.[18] Thus the agenda-setting power of the media can propel the public theology agenda, or in other words, direct Christians to the issues they need to address if their voice is to be heard in society.

Christians who work in the media may also use this agenda-setting power to bring about positive change. For example, if we want the African Union's *Agenda 2063* to flourish and change attitudes and mindsets, we need to work for a consistent and deliberate media focus on Africa's aspirations, highlighting and analysing salient issues and so encouraging community interaction and discussion, which will in turn affect policies and actions on the ground.

Christians in media can also seek to offer informed opinions about matters relating to religion. Too often, journalists who write about issues related to

---

17. For more see Richard Stengel, "We're In the Middle of a Global Information War: Here's What We Need to Do to Win," *Time* (26 September 2019): 36–39.

18. Nyaga, et al., *Introduction to Communication*.

religion have little understanding of the context and may misrepresent people's positions. Some seem to enjoy discrediting the church. A journalist who is rooted in the church and in theology should not reflexively leap to defend the church, for churches and believers are sometimes guilty of sin and of showing poor judgment. However, such a journalist could write with an understanding of the factors at work and the value system that Christians seek to uphold.

Christians in the media world must take seriously the role of the press as a watchdog to alert the public to societal ills, including corruption. In the past, repressive and dictatorial regimes made it difficult for journalists to write about any leader's abuse of office, mismanagement of funds and other forms of corruption. Media outlets were banned from publishing or broadcasting content deemed offensive by the government, and investigative journalists were harassed, intimidated or even killed for attempting to report on politically sensitive issues. Bribery and partisanship have sometimes led newspapers and TV stations to refuse to air stories that are against the interests of the powerful.

With the advent of the Internet and social media, journalists have far more ways to gather information without having to be physically present at the scene. They also have far more access to data because of the increasing use of information and communications technology by government departments and other groups. For example, it is now easier to gain information about bids on government contracts and other processes that are vulnerable to abuse.[19] The media know how to access this data, can engage reputable analysts to examine it and can then broadcast their findings on a wide variety of media platforms. It is time for them to speak out boldly against corruption.

There are specific agencies targeting corruption in Africa, but the problem is too deeply rooted to be dealt with by any one agency – whether governmental or private. A successful anti-corruption campaign requires concerted efforts from both the leadership and civil society, and it requires people to know what is going on and to be able to share information widely. That is where the media come in. Writing about the role of the Zambian media in the exposure and eventual conviction of former Zambian President Fredrick Chiluba, Peter Anassi asserted, "all the apparatus and organizations fighting corruption cannot succeed without the power of the media."[20] The media also helped to force the

---

19. John Carlo Bertot, Paul T. Jaeger, and Justin M. Grimes, "Promoting Transparency and Accountability through ICTs, Social Media, and Collaborative E-Government," *Transforming Government: People, Process and Policy* 6, no. 1 (2012): 78–91.

20. Anassi cited in Isaac Phiri, "Evolution of Anti-Corruption Journalism in Africa: Lessons from Zambia," *Global Media Journal – African Edition* 2, no. 1 (2008): 18.

resignation of South African President Jacob Zuma by exposing his association with the corrupt Gupta brothers.[21]

If representatives of the media in Africa act with professionalism and with fear of God and of the people, they have the power not only to end an era of widespread corruption but also to bring about positive changes. The onus is on practising journalists to view their profession as a higher calling that should be carried out without fear or favour.

Theologians should stand alongside journalists in the forefront of the fight against corruption by keeping abreast of information shared by credible media sources. Such information will help them to know the true state of the society and enable them to call out corrupt leaders while also proclaiming God's mind concerning corrupt leadership.[22] Churches can also reduce their emphasis on prosperity preaching and instead use their radio and television ministries to instil godly values and build Christian character.

Social Media and Social Activism

Like traditional media, social media sites can become instruments of mass propaganda in the hands of a powerful few and be used to spread government propaganda and fake news. However, social media can also be used to expose government propaganda through promoting a counter-narrative geared towards promoting truth and transparency in government. In so doing social media platforms are taking on the roles of traditional or mainstream media such as investigation, analysis, commentary, advocacy and mass mobilization.[23] Here are a few examples of social media sites where these things are happening:

- *I paid a bribe* (www.Ipaidabribe.com) is an Indian site encouraging Indians to report cases where bribes are extorted.

- *The Global Anti-corruption Blog* (https://globalanticorruptionblog.com) describes itself as "devoted to promoting analysis and discussion of the problem of corruption around the world. This blog is intended to provide a forum for exchanging information and ideas across disciplinary and

---

21. John Campbell, "South African Media Recognized for Exposing Zuma on Foreign Corruption," *Council on Foreign Relations* (12 April 2018).

22. P. M. Theron and G. A. Lotter, "Corruption: How Should Christians Respond?" *Acta Theologica* 32, no. 1 (2012): 96–117.

23. Roxanne Bauer, "How to Use Social Media to Fight Corruption," World Economic Forum (12 December 2014).

professional boundaries, and to foster rigorous, vigorous, and constructive debate about corruption's causes, consequences, and potential remedies."[24]

- *Corruption Watch* (https://www.corruptionwatch.org.za) is an accredited chapter of Transparency International (TI) that targets corruption in various sectors in South Africa.

- *Publish What You Pay* (https://pwyp.org) is the website for "the only global movement working to ensure that revenues from oil, gas and mining help improve people's lives. . . . Our shared vision is a world where everyone benefits from their natural resources – today and tomorrow."[25] This organization is active in countries like Togo, Ghana, Nigeria, South Africa, Kenya, Tanzania, Uganda, Zimbabwe, Democratic Republic of Congo and Madagascar.

- *Whistle Blowers* (https://www.whistleblowing.co.za) is a South Africa-based group that people can contact to report unlawful activities and unethical practices such as bribery and theft. Their services are offered to both local and international clients.

- Global Witness (https://www.globalwitness.org) "campaigns to end environmental and human rights abuses driven by the exploitation of natural resources and corruption in the global political and economic system."[26]

Governments too are seeking to use social media to fight corruption. For example, the Economic and Financial Crimes Commission is a law enforcement agency that investigates financial crimes in Nigeria. It uses social networking websites such as Twitter (@OfficialEFCC) and Instagram to create awareness about its activities and to help members of the public report financial crimes.

The above are only a few of many groups on the Internet who are advancing causes that churches and theologians can stand behind. The information gathered via social media can be used to prompt investigative reporting in mainstream media.

Public Theology, the Media and Entertainment

While journalists spend much of their time reporting news, others whose aim is primarily to entertain the public also work in the media. Here too

---

24. GAB, "The Global Anticorruption Blog," https://globalanticorruptionblog.com/about/.
25. "Publish What You Pay (PWYP): Who We Are," https://www.pwyp.org/about/.
26. "Global Witness: About Us," https://www.globalwitness.org/en/about-us/.

there is scope for informed Christians to apply their theology in the types of entertainment presented. They can set to work with the knowledge that what the media platforms carry, emphasize and glorify reaches many and is often taken as important and noteworthy. The impact of media is as great in regard to values as it is in relation to news. Christians working in the media should seek to promote shows that assert human dignity rather than humiliating people, that encourage people to make good judgments based on sound values and that encourage social control and restraint for the good of all.

Conclusion

The media have a key place in public discourse today and must be taken seriously by theologians, churches and laity who want to live out their faith in their communities. The media should be used, and not misused, by the church in Africa to propagate the values that truly represent and present Christ as the answer to the issues that plague humanity.

Questions

1. How can the church use the agenda-setting power of the media to propagate godly values and combat corruption?
2. How does passing on fake news and scams hurt the church? Is doing so also associated with apathy and disillusionment with Bible promises?
3. What is the place of "celebrity culture" in the church?
4. How can Christians curb the production and spread of various forms of fake news using faith-based approaches?
5. The increased use of social media among churches has drawn attention to some strange and questionable Christian doctrines. Discuss how this practice has affected theological convergence and divergence among believers.

Further Reading

Ihejirika, Walter Chikwendu. "Research on Media, Religion and Culture in Africa: Current Trends and Debates." *African Communication Research* 2, no. 1 (2009): 1–60. http://ccms.ukzn.ac.za/files/articles/ACR/Media%20and%20Religion%20in%20Africa.pdf#page=5.

Ireton, Cherilyn, and Julie Posetti, eds. *Journalism, Fake News and Disinformation: Handbook for Journalism Education and Training*. Paris: UNESCO, 2018. https://en.unesco.org/fightfakenews.

Nyaga, Rahab, Dorothy Njoroge, and Charles Nyambuga. *An Introduction to Communication*. Nairobi: Oxford University Press, 2015.

Thomas, Pradip, and Philip Lee, eds. *Global and Local Televangelism*. Basingstoke, UK: Palgrave Macmillan, 2012.

24

The Arts

Ofonime and Idaresit Inyang

What is the role of the arts in human life? This profound question has received many answers, but the one point that cannot be denied is that the arts have been present in human life since the earliest days, when prehistoric hunters scratched designs on rocks in Africa or told stories around the fire at night. But why do people do this? Why are they creative?

Creativity and the Image of God

For Christians, the immediate answer to the question of why people are creative is that people are made in the image of God, who is himself creative: "God said, 'Let us make mankind in our image, in our likeness, so that they may rule over the fish in the sea and the birds in the sky, over the livestock and all the wild animals, and over all the creatures that move along the ground'" (Gen 1:26). The words "let us make" imply a desire to give birth to something that had never existed before – the first human being. Creativity and the desire to make something new are part of the essence of God, the supreme creator of the universe. When he created human beings in his likeness, he endowed these with the same characteristics and made space for the arts to be part of his creation. Those who exercise their creative gifts are living out an important part of what it means to be a human being made in the likeness of God. Artists like to joke that they are the people closest to God!

Creativity and Communication

God's reference to "us" in Genesis 1:26 is also significant. It implies that God was involved in communication with others in his creative imagining. Thus the human ability to communicate is also part of our being made in the image of God. This ability can be seen as one of God's greatest gifts, for communication brings people together in a sharing process in which ideas and messages are exchanged and relationships are built. Without communication there can be no community.

Communication and creativity have come to represent the two cardinal activities in human history because everything revolves around them. To live in the world successfully is to learn to communicate with others while creating things to help you live more comfortably. Nothing that is made was not first imagined. And every product of the imagination only becomes functional when people start putting it to use and communicate its usefulness to others.

The process of communication involves a person who has something to communicate – a "message" – formulating it in a way that will be understood by the one who receives the message. That person, in turn, receives the message and formulates a response. Communication is thus a dynamic process in which both parties indicate whether they have understood or failed to understand what was being communicated and whether they agree or disagree with it.

Communication is always directed to a particular person or group and has a particular goal that the sender seeks to achieve. By this definition, the creative arts are a form of communication because the artist – whether a poet, actor, sculptor, writer, videographer, dancer or musician – is always seeking to convey some message and elicit some reaction from those who read, see or hear what has been produced. But in contrast to the verbal messages we usually receive, communication through the arts involves our other senses too.

Theology and the gospel also have a message that needs to be communicated in ways that the target audience will understand. More specifically, African public theology has a message that needs to be disseminated to Africans if the Africa that God wants is to emerge. Sometimes the best way to get this message across is not to imitate political leaders and thinkers by talking about best practices and sustainable development but to speak directly to the hearts, minds and souls of Africans through the instrumentality of the creative arts.

Mainstreaming the creative arts into African public theology will also check the elitism often inherent in the use of conventional communication channels that often reach only the elites in urban centres. We should not forget that much of Africa is still rural and that there are many people who are not formally educated and speak only local dialects. The creative arts can communicate across these barriers and use local idioms and familiar styles to take the holistic message of the gospel to people in remote areas and in different strata of society.

African Christians and the Creative Arts

The term "creative arts" covers all the various kinds of art that are used as instruments to display and create knowledge of nature and human nature. Our human creativity prompts us to apply our imagination to our environment, to objects and to our different experiences and transform them into messages that can be shared in the form of paintings, music, dance, drama, videos, films, poetry and so on. The arts thus become a vehicle for communicating ideas and emotions and a way of exploring and appreciating the nature of God and of human beings. Through the creative arts, we reveal who God is in our lives as individuals.

There are so many varieties of creative arts that it is impossible to discuss all of them in this short chapter. So here we will comment briefly on a few areas but will focus primarily on drama, because that is our area of expertise.

Painting and sculpture

Many African artists have long been creating works of art and sculpture that embed Christian imagery and themes. For example, Elimo Njau is a Lutheran artist from Tanzania whose work ranges from fresco painting to graphic design. He sees his art as an effective way of teaching the Bible through imagery. There are also African Christian sculptors such as Cornelio Manguma (Zimbabwe), Joseph Agbana (Nigeria) and Samuel Wanjau (Kenya). Mwabila Pemba (DRC) specializes in beaten copper works, and Kafusha Laban (DRC) uses coloured resin on glass as an economical alternative to stained glass. All these artists are widely acknowledged for using their art to project and share the gospel.

Songs and music

Music as a creative art can also contribute to African's understanding of public theology. The Bible is a great repository of musical compositions in psalms, songs, hymns and laments. People like David, for example, used their gifts in music for various spiritual and social functions, including lamenting their individual sorrows and the suffering of the nation as a whole.

Africa is blessed with a rich musical heritage that has to be tapped creatively to propagate the gospel. In churches, the singing of indigenous hymns and the use of indigenous instruments needs to be encouraged. But our thinking about how we use God's creative gift of music has to move beyond the hymn traditions and doctrinal musicality of church groups. The teeming population of African young people, like young people all over the world, is greatly drawn to music. Unfortunately, the immoral lyrics and lewd music videos that are so readily available use art to corrupt their minds.

Public theology needs to encourage Christians with gifts in music to tap into the multifunctional impact and therapeutic influence of music. Like David, we can use music to lament our sorrows and find healing in expressing them, as Katongole reminds us.[1] Good music is soul lifting, soothing, calming and reflective in nature. Youth are attracted to the beautiful things of life, and beautiful music with a good message is capable of reaching out to them. Youthful energy also needs positive expression, and Christian musicians need to find creative ways to engage this energy and direct it towards positive values. The Africa that God wants includes youth who fear God, grow in discipleship and take over the leadership of the future. We need to help Christian musicians promote that future.

Drama and theatre

The word "drama" comes from a Greek word that means "to do or perform," and the word "theatre" is said to have come from a Greek word meaning "a viewing place." Together, these definitions point to the fact that a theatrical production or a play involves an actor or actors doing something while observed by an audience.

There has long been a close connection between drama and religion. In fact, some scholars argue that the theatrical arts evolved from modes of worship in prehistoric times. Certainly in Africa, traditional religious festivals have long been celebrated with songs, dances, chants and rituals that encapsulate people's social and religious lives and represent the community's collective ethics and beliefs. Thus the role of the creative arts in connecting people to their spiritual or theological base long predates their use for entertainment.

The potential of the theatre to combine entertainment and instruction has also long been recognized. The medieval church in Europe drew on this

---

1. Emmanuel Katongole, *Born to Lament: The Theology and Politics of Hope in Africa* (Grand Rapids: Eerdmans, 2017).

potential by using drama for liturgical purposes, to teach illiterate Christians the faith, and to spread the word of God.

Drama is different from other art forms in that it uses live actors to portray human characters before a live audience. It thus draws in the audience both emotionally and intellectually as they see people who are in some ways like them acting and reacting to the events around them. That is why Shakespeare could speak of drama as holding "the mirror up to nature."[2] In other words, drama mirrors life. The audience watching this "mirror" see a reflection of what their society looks like, or should look like. As Inyang says, drama "opens societies and peoples to understand themselves using materials derived from daily observation of that society."[3] This function of drama was already well known to the ancient Greek playwrights who used plays to critique their societies.

By promoting reflection, drama also has the ability to promote introspection. Anyone who watches a drama engages with it. It creates an opportunity to examine one's values in light of the message of the performance. The fact that sight and memory have been involved enhances the duration of this effect, for what is seen and heard has more impact than what is merely read or heard. Fully aware of this impact, actors have used drama to spread the gospel and to challenge corruption and oppression.

The strong communicative effect of drama has also been recognized by governments around the world who have sought to use plays to promote their policies and educate people about epidemics like HIV/AIDS. Studies have shown that theatre and drama can be powerful tools for development advocacy and for bringing about behavioural change.[4] African playwrights like Wole Soyinka have used drama to arouse people's sociocultural and political consciousness by engaging with relevant issues in the fields of religion, economics and politics. Drama is particularly suited to consciousness raising because it is a flexible medium of communication and so can easily be taken to people at different levels – on the street, in the market and in schools, community centres, village squares, local churches and parks.

---

2. William Shakespeare, *Hamlet*, Act 3 Scene 2.

3. Ofonime Inyang, *Introduction to Theatre and Media Arts Practice: A Beginner's Guide* (Lagos: Bezeliel, 2016).

4. Zakes Mda, *When People Play People: Development Communication through Theatre* (Johannesburg: Witwatersrand University Press; London: Zed Books, 1993); Steve Ogah Abah, "Vignettes of Communities in Action: An Exploration of Participatory Methodologies in Promoting Community Development in Nigeria," *Community Development Journal* 42, no. 4 (2007): 435–448; Christopher F. Kamlongera, *Theatre for Development: The Case of Malawi* (Cambridge, UK: Cambridge University Press, 2009).

Christians should not neglect the world of drama, especially in light of the fact that the Bible can be described as theatrical. Every statement and scene description in the Bible, from Genesis to Revelation, seems to be shaped by a divine director so that it is fit for the stage or film making. Drama can reinvigorate this creative energy of Scripture in a performance context. Jesus himself made generous use of tales, storytelling and visual descriptions to drive home a point while teaching his disciples or other people gathered to listen to him.

It has even been said that theology

> is inherently theatrical, and it is so by the virtue of its object, mode, and goal. First, theology is theatrical because its object is the triune God who says and does things in the theatre of the world. God created this cosmic theatre, but he also performs the lead role. He does this not merely by speaking from the offstage, but by entering into action, preeminently by becoming flesh and dwelling among us as Jesus of Nazareth. Theology is a response to and a reflection on God's incarnate performance and his continual involvement in the world theatre as Spirit.[5]

We thus need to expand the place of theology beyond preaching from pulpits and create new or "other" types of pulpits that can bring visual character to the messages of the Bible through the creative arts. Because theatre is a very collaborative art, public theologians should come together with those who have dramatic gifts to develop plays and other dramatic productions using screen, radio or the stage that will not only be instruments for evangelism but will also serve to educate and enlighten people about issues affecting their society. Drama can be used to stir people's minds to think about what the Africa God wants actually looks like.

Note that not all the plays Christians produce must be "religious" works with overt moral messages. Christians in the theatre world can write and produce entertaining plays that are informed by Christian thinking and address real social issues without any overt mention of religion.

A number of African Christian artists are already using the medium of drama to propagate faith-based Christian messages by writing and staging gospel-oriented and value-based plays. Saviour Nathan Agoro, a Nigerian academic and seasoned Christian theatre practitioner and researcher, has

---

5. Wesley Vander Lugt and Trevor Hart, eds., *Theatrical Theology: Explorations in Performing the Faith* (Cambridge: Lutterworth, 2014), 2.

not only written plays himself but has also done extensive research on the evangelical underpinnings of drama and theatre in Africa.[6]

Mike Bamiloye, a Nigerian film actor, dramatist, producer and director, founded Mount Zion Drama Ministry and Mount Zion Television and used these ministries to tell stories about salvation, prayer, God's love and Christian values. We have staged plays with Christian subject matter within and outside the university environment in Akwa Ibom State and other parts of Nigeria. For example, in 2016 second-year students at the Department of Theatre Arts at the University of Uyo staged the play *Guest of the Dungeon* as a sensitization drama promoting Christian values among the student population.

Films, video, television and new media

Africa is already part of the digital world dominated by cinema and television screens and computer and phone screens. Viewers have access to a wide array of productions from overseas sources, some of which are unsuitable but are simply dumped in Africa. But viewers also have access to productions from local sources. Sites such as Netflix, YouTube, Amazon Prime and Hulu have a selection of faith-based productions showcasing the gospel, and some of those productions are by African artists. The Nigerian movie industry, Nollywood, has made movies about issues affecting Nigerian society and has gained tremendous local patronage as well as an enthusiastic response from the African diaspora.

Unfortunately, the intrusiveness and psychological influence of the digital world are drawing many away from positive values. For example, *Big Brother Africa* airs nationally and internationally and has become very popular with the young, although much of its message defiles and corrupts and is at odds with Christian values. Similarly, the reliance on witchcraft in many Nollywood scripts is spreading superstition and stimulating existing beliefs in witchcraft, often with disastrous consequences.

Social media, film and video productions have been used by those hostile to God to undermine the church. A clear case in point is the growing popularity of online bashing of churches and church leaders by self-appointed critics who pounce on the slightest mistake made by a church or its leader. It is true that some consider such criticism a form of citizenship journalism aimed at

---

6. See for example, Saviour Nathan A. Agoro, "A Study of Selected Themes in Christian Drama in Nigeria," (2002); Saviour Nathan A. Agoro, "The Notion of Christian Comedy," *Kiabara: Journal of Humanities* 17, no. 1 (2011).

checking the abuses prevalent in religious organizations, especially churches, and the misdemeanours and unbecoming conduct of preachers. But the openly deriding and abusive language employed in some of these critiques points to ulterior motives including a deliberate attempt to smear the image of the church and ministers of the gospel.

Some television talk shows, dramas and popular reality shows parade content that appears primed to attack Christianity and delegitimize belief in God and involvement in church activities while promoting extreme liberalism, new age philosophy, free thinking and spiritism to young audiences. Some films written and produced in Africa, including those of Nigeria's Nollywood, feature negative themes and project belief in voodoo, witchcraft and consulting negative powers for wealth and solutions to life's challenges. Such productions create a wrong impression and send the wrong message about Africa as a continent that is still steeped in diabolical practices. Putting these productions side by side with the growing incidence of atheism in Africa has rocked the long-held notion of Africa as a bastion of religion and religious practices and presents the contrasting and complex dynamics in the present state of our continent, which is clearly not the Africa that God wants.

The solution is not to turn our back on these media. The globalizing influence of visual media is here to stay, and the church should not turn away. African public theology should help those working in these media to envision how to propagate positive values in society using these new media channels. Creativity is needed if Christians are to deploy television, film, video and social media in strategic and Spirit-led ways to counter the onslaught of the kingdom of darkness on our continent and on the destiny of our young people.

Many churches today already livestream their services to reach wider audiences, but that is only a first step into the stream of media technology. Far more needs to be done. The youth are hooked on social media and technological devices for their interaction and gaming, so to connect with the youth, the church must find creative ways of integrating the gospel into these platforms. Mobile apps must be built and games with biblical themes must be developed to bring the gospel into play arenas filled with young people. Children also need to see programmes on the media channels that will attract their interest, teach them morals and promote their growth in the Lord. Cartoon networks dedicated to the gospel need to be established, and we need storybooks, playlets, novellas and action pictorials that portray the uniqueness of the gospel.

To reach youth and children, we will need to build new creative art outlets, retrain the personnel in some existing ones and rethink the whole concept of evangelism. Training institutions must begin to reimagine their programmes and curriculums so that the creative arts are included in the training of the church personnel and evangelists of the future.

African Artists and African Public Theology

After reading what has been said so far, some people might argue that much has already been done in using the creative arts to propagate the gospel. But the reality is that most of these efforts, though useful, lack the public orientation and focus on the wider society that is the hallmark of African public theology. Much work still needs to be done because the changing dynamics of African society require transformative strategies to reach the hearts of people.

African artists and transformation

Globalization and the various appurtenances of the globalism are here to stay. So rather than being overwhelmed by the flood of new philosophies and practices brought about by the changing landscape of the continent, we should pay attention to the word of God that urges us to be and act as the salt of the earth (Matt 5:13–20). As Christians, we should reflect deeply on what we see and use the capacity of art to influence society by producing gospel-promoting films, plays, music and art with themes that can affect the continent positively and give people a vision of the Africa that God wants. In doing so, we will contribute to the creation of that Africa.

In the past, there were some who condemned creative artistry as satanic, belonging to the devil, and therefore to be completely rejected by Christians. However, research has shown what artists already knew, namely that art is a form of communication ordinary people can easily understand. Therefore if we want ordinary Christians to think theologically about what it means to be salt and light in their communities, we need to tap into people's indigenous creativity. Local songs, dances, storytelling and folk narratives, games, proverbs and music can be used to reach people with the life-transforming message of the Scriptures. Films and videos in people's own languages can play a powerful role in reaching and discipling people who live in rural areas who have access to few other resources.

African artists: protesters or sycophants?

Earlier in this chapter we said that the dramatic arts mirror human experience. What aspects of human experience do they mirror in Africa? Do they show

Africa only as we would wish it to be, or as some authority wants us to see it? Or do they show Africa as it is, flooded with conflict in various forms? From Central to Northern and Southern Africa, and from the west to the east coast, social, economic and political organizations have been destroyed by political, religious and ethnic crises and conflicts, leaving a new culture of violence and a lack of respect for human life and its creator. No meaningful development can take place in the absence of peace, which is the basis for all development and progress in society and life.

How can the creative arts affect this dark scenario? Our answer would be that we can use art as an instrument to help people understand the world and our place in it in terms of the different roles we play in the world and society. Music and drama can become ways of speaking to political, religious, economic, educational and other issues and of seeking to create order in a chaotic world. Playwrights and musicians can promote public discussion or debates on these issues by creating awareness of them and paving the way for solutions through collective decision making and action.

Because the world is a place of tension, conflict and contradictions, writing and presenting dramas may involve both external and internal struggle. But creative artists are called to both participate in society and to confront society without fear. They are to use their gifts to expose problems and to call on those in power to restore balance to society. This call should go out to the powerful in both the state and the church – for Christian dramatists must look at issues in the church too. Art should be an instrument that always speaks the truth to people on all levels of society.

Over the centuries, music and drama have been used for entertainment and as a weapon. Like everything else on earth, they can be used for good and evil. Public theologians should speak out to encourage those who have artistic gifts to use them in ways that spread the message that God wants Africa to hear at this time. Dramatists and all other creative artists should use the arts to promote peace by exposing evil, suggesting ways forward and arousing the conscience and senses of the common people so that they will call for change. In this way, the church and the arts can collaborate in the task of nation building that can bring transformation to Africa.

Funding the Arts

Churches are often willing to support spending on medical services and education. They will offer their resources for these purposes and will call on the government to invest more money in hospitals, clinics, schools and preventive medicine. But when last did the church demand that the government also spend money to support the arts? Or when did the church offer support to creative artists from church funds – unless the artists were the musicians who lead in worship? We would argue that public theology needs to work to change this situation in both churches and in the allocation of government resources.

On the level of state funding, we should remind the state of the importance of freedom of expression without hindrance or manipulation. We should also remind legislators that the creative arts are part of our reflection of the image of God, and so they should be made widely accessible in our societies. To do this requires funding and the provision of the infrastructure needed if the arts are to thrive.

Money should be budgeted, allocated and spent on the arts as well as on the sciences. Both the arts and the sciences offer windows into the world that help us see what is happening around us. Literature, music, theatre, the visual arts, the media (film, photography, and television), architecture and dance reveal aspects about ourselves and the world around us and the relationship between the two.

Moreover, it is important not to separate the arts from education, for the arts can be powerful educational tools, as we have observed in our own work. So some of the money allocated to education should go to the arts.

What is this money needed for? Well, artists need to eat, but apart from that, successful teaching through the creative arts requires the use of materials and teaching aids. In drama, for example, money is spent on creating costumes, on makeup, on building scenery, on lighting and on sound systems. Some of these materials can be re-used, but different stories require different props if they are to be believable and appeal to young learners. If the church is serious about using the arts to teach Africans about the Africa God wants, then the church has to provide funding for the artists and also encourage the government to support the creative arts.

The same is true when it comes to creating a Christian presence in social media and on the Internet. Computers, servers and skilled operators need to be found and trained. The investment will be costly, but the rewards will be high.

Conclusion

In this chapter, we have seen that the arts and artistic expression are not merely about entertainment but about creating a space for dialogue. They contribute to the exchange of information and ideas and connect people through creative activities. As tools of public communication, the arts have the potential to contribute to building the Africa God wants. This potential is growing as the arts are becoming an increasingly important medium in contemporary society.

The arts' role as a mirror of society gives it the capacity to speak truth to power, to bring people together, to create a space for reflection and thinking and to promote societal development. So we need to think deeply about how music, painting, theatre or drama, photography, dance and oral narratives can be used to reflect and propagate positive themes and values and to showcase the Africa God wants and expects us to uphold in our different spheres.

The church in Africa should make extensive use of the arts to create appropriate messages that will build up Africa in the light of God's word and purposes. Artists in Africa should also seek to improve the spiritual state of the church by using their creativity to teach positive attitudes and lifestyles that reflect who God is. They should recognize the power of art to shape the culture of a society, that is, its ideas, values and beliefs. Those values and ideas reshape lives and will be passed on to the next generation.

To present the Africa God wants, we must take care not to use our creative tools to disseminate messages without values and knowledge of the existence of God. Such messages are capable of destroying our society and creating disharmony. Instead, we must become evangelists for the way God expects us to live in this season by presenting creative messages loaded with values in plays, films, and music.

In doing this, creative artists should see God as their model and take a cue from him by intervening in the world with light as the opposite of darkness. Now is not the time to be sitting contentedly in churches while the devil prowls about freely in our continent using the creative arts and the media.

Questions

1. Choose one of the creative arts. Discuss how it is already being used in the church and how its use could be creatively expanded outside the church doors. Then discuss how your church could consider funding this type of creative work.
2. Identify some work of art that has affected your nation for good (or bad, if necessary) in some way. Discuss how and why it did this and what we as Christians can learn from the creative techniques employed.
3. Create something yourself – a play, a song, music or a painting. Then talk about your experience of creating it and about the message it holds for

you. Ask the group what message they receive from your art. How does this experience affect your understanding of God as the creator?

4.   How should Christians respond to art that offends them?

Further Reading

Balthazar, Hans Urs von. "Real Enactment: The Role of Theology in Drama." In *Faithful Performances: Enacting Christian Traditions*, edited by Steven R. Guthrie, 13–32. Abingdon: Routledge, 2016.

Inyang, Ofonime. *Introduction to Theatre and Media Arts Practice: A Beginner's Guide.* Lagos: Bezeliel Books, 2016.

Okeke, Austin, and Eze Norbert. "Solo Drama as a Potent Tool for Rural Christian Evangelism." In *50 Years of Solo Performance Art in Nigerian Theatre 1966–2016*, edited by Greg Mbajiorgu and Amanze Akpuda. Ibadan: Kraft, 2018.

Vander Lugt, Wesley, and Trevor Hart, eds. *Theatrical Theology: Explorations in Performing the Faith.* Cambridge: Lutterworth, 2014.

25

Leadership

Maggie Madimbo

To reach the Africa God wants us to have, we need visionary leaders who can take people from where they are to where they are supposed to be. Not everyone has the gift of leadership, and not all who call themselves leaders think beyond tomorrow. Our task as Christians is to encourage leaders who will look beyond the present, who will think and dream about Africa's future and who can develop plans to fulfil the goals of *Agenda 2063*.

When looking for such leaders, it is important to begin by defining what we mean by "leadership." Yukl has defined leadership as "the process of influencing others to understand and agree about what needs to be done and how it can be done effectively, and the process of facilitating individual and collective efforts to accomplish the shared objectives."[1]

Note what this definition does *not* say: it does not say that the person doing the influencing has an official title that declares that they are a leader. Some leaders are officially recognized; others exercise great influence behind the scenes. Leadership is open to all who have the capacity to influence others in some way. This point is important because many who are not referred to as leaders can still look for opportunities to exercise leadership in some way in their churches, communities and places of work.

Note, too, that this definition refers to leadership as a *process* rather than a status and describes it in terms of *influence* rather than in terms of issuing

---

1. Gary Yukl, *Leadership in Organizations*, 8th ed. (Saddle River, NJ: Prentice Hall, 2002), 7.

orders. It can even be said that "without influence, leadership does not exist."[2] Moreover, this influence is exerted on *others*, for a leader requires followers.

Finally, the definition states that a leader uses their influence to get agreement on particular *objectives* (or goals or visions) and on how to achieve these. A true leader always has a future orientation. They have a clear mental image of where they want a group or a community to go and are aware of the big picture rather than focusing primarily on details. Leaders communicate their vision to their followers and help them make that vision a reality. Thus leadership involves setting and attaining goals.

Leadership is very important in any scenario where people have to work together. The success of all economic, political and organizational systems in any field depends on the effective and efficient guidance provided by the leaders of these systems.[3]

The Leadership Africa Has Had

One reason we currently live in the Africa we do not want is that the continent has been plagued with poor leaders. For too many of them, their only goal has been to remain in power and maximize the power and wealth of their own family and ethnic group. They have not served the interests of the nation or the broader community. Their pursuit of short-term personal benefits rather than long-term goals has impoverished us and led to war, insurgencies and widespread poverty and hunger.

But to say this is merely to state the obvious and to focus solely on the present. We need to dig deeper into the past if we are to understand Africa's traditional and current patterns of leadership and discern what we should hold on to and what we should change.

Precolonial models of leadership

Precolonial understandings of leadership centred on the concept of a king or chief who was both a community leader and a religious leader in that he represented the community in various religious ceremonies.[4] In Western

---

2. P. G. Northouse, *Leadership: Theory and Practice*, 4th ed. (Thousand Oaks, CA: Sage, 2007), 3.

3. J. Barrow, "The Variables of Leadership: A Review and Conceptual Framework," *Academy of Management Review* 2 (1977): 231–251.

4. M. Masango, "Leadership in the African Context," *Verbum et Ecclesia* 23, no. 3 (2002): 707–718.

models of kingship, the king came to be thought of as someone remote from the community, but the position of an African king or chief was very different. Their position was understood in terms of the African philosophy of *ubuntu*, which is based on the foundation that *umuntu ngumuntu ngabanye abantu*, literally "a person is a person through other persons."[5] *Ubuntu* emphasizes the common good and concern for each other's well-being. Thus a good leader was one who led with respect and concern for the welfare of the community as a whole. Such leadership was founded on humanistic principles of inclusion and service to the community.[6] As Masango puts it, "good leadership in Africa always shares life with others."[7]

In the precolonial era, leaders generally ruled over homogenous communities, unlike the situation today where a person may have to lead people from many ethnic groups. In the past, it was also accepted practice to bring gifts to the leader, who received no other salary and was expected to use his wealth for the benefit of the community. This traditional practice, rooted in communities where wealth was fairly evenly distributed, has changed so that today leaders sometimes demand exorbitant gifts, which only the wealthy can bring, to secure favours. The community who benefit from a leader's wealth are now often only his close family and sometimes members of his own ethnic group.

The previous paragraph uses the masculine gender when referring to a leader because kings and chiefs were generally male, even in matriarchal communities where women wielded considerable power behind the scenes. The role of queen mother was a powerful one in some regions of Africa.

Colonial and postcolonial models of leadership

The traditional model of leadership, even though not always practised in its ideal form, had many strengths. But this model was deeply affected and weakened by the colonial era, during which African communities were grouped into nations not on the basis of existing communal ties but on the basis of the whims and relative strength of European powers. The concept of a leader as

---

5. D. M. Tutu, *No Future without Forgiveness* (New York: Doubleday, 1999), 31.

6. R. Bolden and P. Kirk, "African Leadership: Surfacing New Understandings through Leadership Development," *International Journal of Cross Cultural Management* 9, no. 1 (2009): 69–86.

7. Masango, "Leadership," 320.

someone overseeing a cohesive, largely mono-ethnic community was destroyed on the national level.

Colonial leaders were appointed by the colonial powers and owed their primary allegiance to those powers rather than to the African communities over which they ruled. When colonialists delegated power to traditional rulers, they expected these rulers to support the colonial administration, and they removed the ability of communities to depose chiefs who failed to rule well. Because these chiefs were paid a salary by the colonial power, there was no longer any connection between how well a chief served his own community and his wealth. Gifts to honour the chief's service became bribes to secure his favour and corruption spread.[8]

Moreover the colonists tended to work only with male leaders, and so entrenched "a gendered power system," that is, "a network of social, political and economic relationships through which men dominate and control female labour, reproduction, and sexuality, as well as define women's status, privileges and rights in a society."[9] It was assumed that men were leaders and women were followers, and this view still influences people's thinking today.

After the departure of the colonial powers from Africa, many of the leaders who came to power modelled their leadership on the colonial style. No longer accountable to the colonial power, they acted as if they were absolute monarchs, accountable only to themselves, and they followed the colonial example of plundering their people's wealth. Their lack of accountability meant there was no means of removing them from power except by violent conflict, and Africa was plunged into decades of civil wars and coups d'état.

This pattern of bad leadership at the top filtered down through all levels of society, so that bureaucrats take bribes and some pastors and church leaders act like dictators. Many of the wealthy, who might be expected to be leaders in the community, serve only their local ethnic communities and focus on maintaining their power rather than on serving the entire community and the nation.

---

8. Liya Palagashvili, "African Chiefs: Comparative Governance under Colonial Rule," *Public Choice* 174, no. 3–4 (11 January 2018): 277–300.

9. F. Kalabamu, "Patriarchy and Women's Land Rights in Botswana," *Land Use Policy* 23, no. 3 (2004): 237.

Biblical Models of Leadership

Africa has had both good and bad leaders, and so did ancient Israel as we can see from the historical records in the Bible. Most of these leaders were male, although there are a few examples of women leaders. Some women like Deborah were acknowledged leaders (Judg 4:4–6), while others like Abigail took action and became leaders when circumstances required (1 Sam 25).

One such leader was Esther, who can serve as a model for all African leaders, male and female. She found herself in a position of privilege where it was easy to ignore what was going on around her. She could easily have missed the opportunity to intervene and avert disaster. But when she became aware that something was wrong, she sent out a researcher to find out what the real problem was, listened to her advisers and then took time to ponder and pray over the correct response. Africa is a continent in crisis and needs Christian leaders who, like Esther, will take time to research the root cause of the problems that Africa is facing. They will need to listen to what people tell them, seek God's face and listen for his voice if they are to bless Africa's peoples with leadership that delivers them from the bondage of poverty, fear and corruption.

An Old Testament metaphor for leadership that fits well with traditional African concepts is that a leader is a shepherd of his people (e.g. 2 Sam 5:2). This metaphor implies that a leader is responsible for the general welfare of the nation, just as a traditional leader was expected to care for his people. The Old Testament prophets spoke out loudly against those who abused their position as shepherds. The description of the conditions of those led by bad shepherds resonates with those in Africa who have endured the rule of equally bad leaders:

> Woe to you shepherds of Israel who only take care of yourselves! Should not shepherds take care of the flock? You eat the curds, clothe yourselves with the wool and slaughter the choice animals, but you do not take care of the flock. You have not strengthened the weak or healed the sick or bound up the injured. You have not brought back the strays or searched for the lost. You have ruled them harshly and brutally. So they were scattered because there was no shepherd, and when they were scattered they became food for all the wild animals. (Ezek 34:2–5; see also Jer 23:1–4)

Not all the leaders of Israel were rulers. Some of those whom God called to leadership were given a prophetic ministry. For example, God told the prophet Isaiah to "Comfort my people" (Isa 40:1). Others like Ezekiel and Jeremiah were called to denounce bad leaders, as we saw above. The words of the prophets leave no doubt that God cares when people are abused, and he calls on those who follow him to denounce corrupt leaders. God wants leaders in Africa who are willing to heed his voice and lead the people with wisdom and integrity, as David led the people of Israel (Ps 78:72).

In the New Testament, the apostle Peter paints a vivid picture of Christian leaders. While he was writing about leaders in the church, the same principles surely apply to those who lead companies, schools and hospitals. Leaders are to serve willingly. They must be motivated not by greed but by a desire to serve. They must not strut about airing their own importance, but rather must be humble examples to those they care for. In other words, they are to be good under-shepherds, faithfully caring for the community and following the example of Christ, the Chief Shepherd (1 Pet 5:1–4).

Paul also makes it clear that this type of leadership is expected of all Christian leaders, regardless of where they serve, when he tells all the Philippian Christians, regardless of their position, to follow Christ's example. Jesus Christ did not insist on his divine leadership prerogatives but instead made himself nothing by "taking the very nature of a servant" (Phil 2:6–7). The church needs leaders who are like Christ in that they are willing to take the lead in offering service to others.

In speaking of servant leadership, Peter and Paul are echoing the words of Christ himself. He told his disciples that whoever wants to be a leader of others must first of all be willing to be their servant:

> You know that the rulers of the Gentiles lord it over them, and their high officials exercise authority over them. Not so with you. Instead, whoever wants to become great among you must be your servant, and whoever wants to be first must be your slave – just as the Son of Man did not come to be served but to serve, and to give his life as a ransom for many. (Matt 20:25–28)

Here Christ is emphasizing that Christian leadership is not about being great. Rather, it is about being a servant to those one serves. This servant model of leadership is in harmony with the African philosophy of *ubuntu* which stresses the importance of interpersonal relations, even to the point of inconveniencing oneself for the sake of others. African Christians who obey their Lord should be more inclined than others to listen to others and to take a participative approach to leadership.

Our other New Testament model for leadership should be the apostle Paul who was a man of such integrity that he could say, "Follow my example, as I follow the example of Christ" (1 Cor 11:1). How many African Christian leaders in society and in the church could confidently make that claim? How many of us truly live like Christ, even when no one is watching?

Christian Leaders

Unfortunately, despite the Bible's clear guidance on leadership, it is not just secular leaders who set bad examples; so do many Christian leaders. Many of them are aware of corrupt practices and can give examples of exploitation of the weak and vulnerable, and some even participate in corruption and exploitation. They accept gifts knowing that they are meant as bribes, and they exploit the poor by demanding that they give sacrificially while making few sacrifices themselves. They model their lifestyle on wealthy chiefs and politicians, not on the humble life of Christ.

Why do Christian leaders fail to fulfil their responsibility to be the salt and the light of the world (Matt 5:13–16)? They should be in the forefront of those confronting evil and speaking out against it rather than remaining silent or succumbing to it. Yet few Christian leaders are willing to speak out. Some fear what might happen to them and their families if they were to oppose bad leaders and evil practices. Others are silent because they have lost their "saltiness" and do not see anything wrong with what is going on around them. When there is poor leadership in the church, the prophetic voice is often muffled or silenced.

If we want to be used by God to bring the change we need in Africa, then we should be willing to maintain our "saltiness" because we have been called to make a difference in our own way. Here are some biblical skills we should cultivate if we are to be servant leaders in Africa today.

- *Listening.* Leaders should always be listening and should listen carefully before making decisions. This is in line with James's reminder that all Christians should be "quick to listen, slow to speak and slow to become angry" (Jas 1:19). People who listen show that they care about the person who is speaking and about their ideas, even if those ideas differ from their own. A listening leader is one who has the interest of his people at heart.

- *Empathy.* Servant leaders embrace empathy. They live out Paul's instruction to "Rejoice with those who rejoice; mourn with those who mourn" (Rom 12:15). They understand what people are feeling and do not put their personal interests and the interests of their supporters before those of others.

- *Healing.* Our continent is riven with conflict, and there are many who are broken in some way. Nations and churches and communities are torn and bleeding. Leaders thus need to be people who have acknowledged their own wounds and have been healed of those wounds so that they can truly comfort others (2 Cor 1:3–4). Such people know how important it is to "make every effort to live in peace with everyone" (Heb 12:14). They bring healing and reconciliation rather than inflicting further wounds and perpetuating divisions.

- *Awareness.* Because servant leaders listen and care, they notice trends and recognize issues that are arising. But they are not only aware of the world around them; they are also self-aware. They know their own biases and shortcomings and so are willing to seek the help of others in carrying out their responsibilities.

- *Strategic thinking.* Servant leaders are able to look ahead. They recognize challenges that lie ahead and trends that will affect those they serve. They can formulate these insights in a way that shows their commitment to the growth of those they lead, and they can make plans to meet coming challenges rather than merely responding to the needs of the moment.

- *Community building.* Servant leaders are able to build communities. They seek to unite people rather than divide them and build up the confidence of the community by helping it to develop and use its own resources. Servant leaders do not assume that a community is helpless and can only prosper with the help of outside resources. Instead, they mobilize the resources within the community for the benefit of the whole community. President Magufuli of Tanzania modelled this leadership skill when he cancelled Independence Day celebrations in 2015 and urged all citizens to use the day to clean up the country, pointing out that "it is shameful that we are spending huge amounts of money to celebrate 54 years of self-rule while our people are dying of cholera."[10] He ordered "all regional leaders to oversee the clean-up exercise in their areas on that day," and he himself participated in the clean-up efforts.[11]

---

10. Henry Mwangonde, "Magufuli Strikes Again: Uhuru Day Scrapped," *The Citizen* (24 November 2016).

11. Wikipedia, "John Maguguli," Wikipedia, https://en.wikipedia.org/wiki/John_Magufuli#Presidency.

Contemporary Patterns of Effective Leadership

In contemporary Africa, we have plenty of exposure to bad models of leadership. But surely there are also some good models of leadership in Africa, people who can be held up as models for us to imitate? What do we actually know about contemporary patterns of good leadership in Africa today?

Our attempts to answer this question are thwarted by the fact that there has been very little research on what counts as good leadership in Africa. As can be seen from the names of the authors cited so far, "most of the academic leadership material currently available on political and other types of leadership comes from outside Africa, especially the West."[12] One of the few empirical studies that has been carried out is the Africa Leadership Study (ALS) which asked over 8,300 African Christians in Angola, the Central African Republic and Kenya to identify lay leaders, pastors and organizations that were offering powerful examples of good leadership. Those identified as good leaders were then interviewed at some length to determine what factors contributed to their success.[13]

One striking finding of this study was that almost 50 percent of the time, pastors were named as key influencers and models of leadership, which implies that lay leaders can also be very influential because their "professional positions and reputations positioned them to serve and influence more broadly than would be the norm for clergy."[14] These lay leaders included women and leaders in African-led parachurch Christian organizations. All of these leaders need to think carefully about how their style of leadership reflects their Christian convictions and how they can cultivate leadership skills in others.

The African Leadership Study also investigated the common factors shared by influential Christian leaders in Africa and came up with a list of five key characteristic of these leaders:

- *They are able to work with a people from an array of ethnicities and cultures.* Many "felt it was important that Christian leaders provide modelling and guidance for healthy interethnic relations." These leaders have thus moved beyond the precolonial model where leaders served only their own ethnic communities.

---

12. M. du Preez, "The Socrates of Africa and His Student: A Case of Pre-Colonial African Leadership," *Leadership* 8, no. 1 (2012): 7.

13. African Leadership Study, "17 Insights into Leadership in Africa."

14. "17 Insights into Leadership in Africa."

- *They are able to use the resources of the Internet to extend their ministries and train others.* In other words, they are immersed in the contemporary world and make good use of the resources it offers.

- *They have been mentored and are eager to mentor others.* This characteristic indicates that these leaders have the humility to be willing to learn from others and the generosity to want to share what they themselves have learned.

- *They are well educated.* The study notes that "most leaders have been shaped by some combination of high-quality formal education along with other forms of informal and mentoring relationships – with the combination being more important than any single one of these."

- *They make good use of relational networks.* In other words, they "build on extensive relationships of reciprocity and trust globally and within their own countries." These networks even extended to include Muslim leaders in countries where Islam plays a prominent role.[15]

Preparing the Next Generation of Leaders

It is striking that one of the key characteristics of the influential leaders in the Africa Leadership Study was that they are less concerned about maintaining their own position and more interested in mentoring young leaders. They do not feel threatened by promising younger leaders; instead they welcome them and offer them training. Their attitude can be summed up in the saying, "If when I die they say 'There is no one else like him,' I will have failed!"

It is also significant that the study showed that young leaders were willing to be mentored and trained. Too often a gifted young person will assume that they know more than anyone else and will confidently set off on their own, rejecting all guidance. This is a dangerous course for it deprives them of the ability to learn from the mistakes that others have made. Moreover, to be a good leader, one needs to have some experience of the joys and frustrations of being a follower. Only then will you have some idea of how to care for those who follow you.

Looking at the list of characteristics of Christian leaders, we can see that some people may be born with a natural aptitude for some characteristics of leadership; for example, some people are naturally more inclined to think strategically than others. But no one is born with all these characteristics fully

---

15. "17 Insights into Leadership in Africa."

developed. It takes time to acquire them, and it is our duty to work hard to develop them if we want to be Christ-like servant leaders. Moreover the "listening" mentioned above may also involve learning. As we listen to the needs of our communities, we will realize that we need more knowledge if we are to be able to formulate strategic plans that have some chance of success. We must therefore commit ourselves to acquiring the skills and tools we need to be effective leaders. The need for learning may explain why one of the characteristics of effective leaders is a high level of formal education. Nor did their learning stop when these leaders completed their academic degrees – the research showed that they continued to read extensively.

The Challenge

As Christians, we should not limit Christian leadership to those who serve from the pulpit; we should accept that God can call different people to serve in different capacities. What is important is that the people who are called to lead others are willing to be the salt and the light of the world. Leaders should know that their influence can help change the destiny of many people for the better. They should thus see their opportunity to lead as a calling from God and serve him and those they serve wholeheartedly and without concern for the personal benefits to be gained from being a leader.

As leaders we can affect all aspects of human community, from the family to the church to the village to the town to the state and to the nation. Are we as Christians willing to step up and take on the role of leaders? This question does not go out only to men but also to women. In the past, Africa has downplayed the role of women. As a result, we are not yet benefiting from the full potential of all the gifted men and women who may have been called by God to lead his people. To move forward and be successful, we need to change our view of leadership. We all know men who have failed as leaders and women who have done very well as leaders. So we should not let our cultural preconceptions blind us to the potential of those whom God has gifted with the ability to influence others.

In his grace, God also gives some of these leadership skills to people who are not Christians. We should not refuse to work with such people but should thank God for their gifts, listen to them and acknowledge our own failures to live up to the standards we profess to have as Christians. At the same time, we should encourage Christians to develop the leadership skills God has given them and to use them in a variety of vocations, and not just in the church. We need Christian leaders in homes, in businesses, in the education system, in the medical system, in government and in politics. Too often, we restrict our understanding of Christian leadership to church leadership and fail to support Christians who, for example, seek to participate in national or local politics. But it is the politicians who make the laws for our nations. If we leave this responsibility in the hands of non-believers, is it surprising if they make laws that force us to be involved in things not supported by the Scriptures? And if we leave government business to non-Christians, why are we surprised when government workers want bribes in order to carry out their duties? And if we leave business leadership to non-Christians, why are we surprised when business leaders act in ways that destroy the environment and exploit workers and consumers?

For the vision of *Agenda 2063* to materialize, Africa will need great leaders to empower the people to benefit others as a leader. Remember that your leadership role may be publicly acknowledged, or it may be a matter of exercising influence in quiet ways. Remember too that one day we will all be answerable to God when we are called to give an account of how we used the abilities he has given us and carried out the tasks he assigned us.

Questions

1. Who are the good leaders in your community, both the acknowledged leaders and the quiet influencers? Which of the qualities of servant leaders identified in this chapter do they show, and which do they still need to work on? Which of these qualities do you have, and which do you still need to work on?
2. Identify some men and women who are good leaders in your community and document their best practices. Can you use these to develop practical and workable guidelines for the leaders in any organization or community to which you belong?
3. How can you encourage leaders who work in areas outside the church so that they are reminded of their calling to serve God as leaders?
4. What steps can you take to promote the growth of future leaders?

Further Reading

Adeyemo, T. *Africa's Enigma and Leadership Solutions*. Nairobi: WordAlive, 2012.

Africa Leadership Study: A Seedbed Resource. https://www.africaleadershipstudy.org/.

Aseka, E. M. *Transformational Leadership in East Africa: Politics, Ideology and Community*. Kampala: Fountain, 2005.

Banks, R., and B. Ledbetter. *Reviewing Leadership: A Christian Evaluation of Current Approaches*. Grand Rapids: Baker Academic, 2004.

Bolden, R., and P. Kirk. "African Leadership: Surfacing New Understandings through Leadership Development." *International Journal of Cross Cultural Management* 9, no. 1 (2009): 69–86.

Boon, M. *The African Way: The Power of Interactive Leadership*. Cape Town: Zebra Press, 2007.

26

Intergenerational Issues

Nathan Hussaini Chiroma

Intergenerational relationships are key to a sense of identity and belonging. The baton of tradition and community values has been handed down from one generation to the next, with each generation recognizing what they can learn from their predecessors and that they are responsible to both their predecessors and their successors, that is, to both to their ancestors and parents and to their children.

But today things are changing. The currents of rapid political, social and technological change that are flowing through Africa are separating the generations so that they drift apart. Their separation is not just intellectual and emotional, it is also literal, for a generation growing up in cities is geographically remote from its parents and grandparents in rural areas.

As African societies, we have to deal with a range of issues that did not face us in the past. Young people are questioning the authority of the older generation, and the older generation is constantly in friction with the younger generation. Key values are being eroded and vices like corruption are taking root.

It is thus important that Christians and Christian churches think deeply about intergenerational relationships. Our goal should be to restore relationships and instil values that will help us gain the Africa we want, an Africa that is free of corruption and bad governance and where the church will flourish and accomplish its purposes. We do not want an Africa of which it can be said, as it was said of ancient Israel, "After that whole generation died, another generation grew up who did not acknowledge the Lord or remember the mighty things he had done for Israel" (Judg 2:10 NLT).

Traditional Intergenerational Relations

Understanding the major circles of influence in traditional African societies is pertinent to any discussion of intergenerational issues. While the details of how these circles operate may vary across Africa, the basic sources of influence are the same.

- *Family*. The family is the foundation of society and the pillar of intergenerational relationships. Family shapes conversations, values, culture and relationships. In Africa, the concept of family is far broader than the Western nuclear family of parents and children. It embraces the extended family and sometimes even neighbours. That is why in some regions, younger people are encouraged to address those older than themselves as aunts and uncles, even where there is no blood relationship. The extended family supported the parents in raising children and passing on values from one generation to the next.

- *Community*. The influence of community life in Africa is evident in proverbs like "it takes a village to raise a child" and "the child belongs to the community." A traditional African community was a place where people were committed to one another's welfare, to a common goal and to a common understanding of the way to reach that goal. As Agulanna says, Africans believe "that it is in the community of other human beings that the life of the individual can have meaning or significance."[1] That is why the concept of the will of the community carried such weight. Responsibilities were shared and each person was accepted based on their worth as a human being, not on what he or she could bring to the community. This context facilitated communication between generations and made for accountability in social life and matters of governance. Values were seen as shared, not private, and were passed on through intergenerational conversations.

- *Religion*. Religion has long contributed to shaping values, character and intergenerational relations. In most African communities, religion reinforced the apprentice culture in which both trades and the rituals associated with the worship of family or tribal gods were passed from one generation to the next. The accompanying values were also passed down through the generations. Elders and local priests were in charge of various rituals including the initiation rituals that marked the transition

---

1. Christopher Agulanna, "Community and African Well Being in Human Culture," *TRAMES* 14(64/59), no. 3 (2010): 282.

from childhood to adulthood. These initiation rituals often involved formal instruction in the community's beliefs and values. Those who violated these values were punished.

Contemporary Intergenerational Relations

Western sources classify generations as Baby Boomers, Gen X, Gen Y and Millennials, but these categories reflect the historical experiences of people in the West. In Africa, it makes more sense to categorize generations in terms of the eras and trends with which they identify. Using this approach, we can identify the following groups.

- *Traditionalists*, that is, people who have lived in rural contexts for most of their lives and live by traditional African values. Such people tend to be conservative and cautious. They assume that the elders are entitled to be the leaders and that younger generations should not challenge them in any way. Such views can become a major source of conflict in intergenerational relationships. Conflicts may flare up in churches served by a younger (and often better educated) pastor, as well as in cases where the youth want to see changes in the church and in the community. The older generation will regard the younger ones as rude and as turning their back on their cultural identity, and the young will see the old as intransigent.

- *Nationalists* are people who came of age during the struggle for independence from colonial powers and whose values were deeply shaped by that struggle. Those who took up arms experienced military-style discipline and have strong bonds to their former comrades. Those who did not fight in person honour those who did. This group were often raised by traditionalists and as young adults they were exposed to colonial and military styles of leadership. Thus they are comfortable with autocratic leadership styles and reluctant to allow women and younger people to assume leadership. They honour the leaders who brought them independence and will not criticize them. They feel that younger generations do not adequately respect them and appreciate their sacrifices, and younger generations see them as stubbornly ignoring leadership problems. This too can create tension in churches and society.

- *Migrants* are people who have moved to the cities as urbanization has taken hold but who still retain strong ties to their rural backgrounds. Their lives are often defined by the struggle and disorientation that transition imposes. Many of them may want to retire to traditional communities when they can no longer work, and they hold the values of traditional communities in high esteem. They may have the problem that their elders see them as losing their culture, while the younger generations regard them as too culture bound.

- *Urban Africans* have only known life in the cities and identify with city life more than with traditional Africa. They are better educated than earlier generations and may subscribe to Western economic values while looking down on those from traditional backgrounds. They are in general more open to women in leadership and have a more positive view of the young.

- *The digital generation* is the youngest generation. Their comfort with technology and access to mobile phones and the Internet means that they are exposed to a far greater range of cultures than any previous generation. They are more likely to question the culture of previous generations and to challenge authority.[2] They are now the largest generation in Africa and have established social networks far wider than anything their parents knew. They will be the future leaders of Africa, but they often find themselves in conflict with older generations, and their values are often still in flux.

Representatives of all of these generations can be found in African communities and churches, and it can be challenging for them to work together. Not only do they differ in age and experience but their world views and value systems are very different. Each generation values different aspects of African culture. But if Africa is to achieve the goals of *Agenda 2063*, these generations need to learn to work together, both in society and in the church, building on what is good from the past to construct the future.

Biblical and Theological Basis of Intergenerational Relationships

Our thinking about intergenerational relationships should be built not just on our cultural assumptions but on solid biblical and theological foundations. These foundations can then shape our practice. The place to begin is with our understanding of who God is. As we saw in chapter 4, God is and always has been a God of relationships. The relationship between the three persons of the Trinity serves as a model for our own human relationships, including our intergenerational relationships. Within the Trinity, the three different persons

---

2. Maggi Payment, "Millennials: The Emerging Work Force," *Career Planning and Adult Development Journal* 24, no. 3 (2008): 23.

are not in competition but work together in different ways to achieve the same goals. Their relationships are characterized by equality, unity and harmony.

When it comes to intergenerational relations within the family, the church and society, we would do well to adopt a Trinitarian perspective, which can be described like this:

> All the members of a family are equal in who they are as human beings. Each one is equal in value and dignity and worth; in this, they mirror the equality that we see among the three Persons of the Trinity. Because of this equality of dignity and worth, each member of the family ought to be accorded respect and be treated as someone created in the image of God.[3]

Adopting this perspective does not mean that the elders are not owed respect; they are. But what it does mean is that the young are also worthy of respect and cannot simply be dismissed as unworthy of a hearing. If both young and old can maintain a Trinitarian perspective on relationships, we will avoid much misunderstanding and many misjudgements.

God is a God of relationships not only within the Trinity but also with human beings. The Bible is the record of his relationship with those he chose as his people and commissioned to bring his blessings to the rest of humanity. It is striking how much generational imagery is used in the Bible to define God's ongoing relationship with us. He is our father and we are his children, and he speaks of himself as "the God of Abraham, Isaac and Jacob," referring to a relationship that spans generations. This generational focus underscores our understanding of the importance of a family's passing on the right values from one generation to the next so that successive generations trust in God. It may also be worth noting that although God names the three patriarchs in historical order, he does not distinguish them in terms of status before him. Despite our age differences, we are all equal in God's eyes.

God calls on those who know and love him to share their faith and the story of what he has done with the next generation. This call is deeply embedded in the Jewish tradition, as Moses's instruction to the parents and grandparents of his day makes this clear:

> These are the commands, decrees and laws the LORD your God directed me to teach you to observe in the land that you are crossing the Jordan to possess, so that you, your children and

---

3. Bruce A. Ware, "The Father, the Son, and the Holy Spirit: The Trinity as Theological Foundation for Family Ministry," *Journal of Discipleship and Family Ministry* 1, no. 2.

their children after them may fear the LORD your God as long as you live by keeping all his decrees and commands that I give you, and so that you may enjoy long life. Hear, Israel, and be careful to obey so that it may go well with you and that you may increase greatly in a land flowing with milk and honey, just as the LORD, the God of your ancestors, promised you.

Hear, O Israel: The LORD our God, the LORD is one. Love the LORD your God with all your heart and with all your soul and with all your strength. These commandments that I give you today are to be on your hearts. Impress them on your children. Talk about them when you sit at home and when you walk along the road, when you lie down and when you get up. Tie them as symbols on your hands and bind them on your foreheads. Write them on the doorframes of your houses and on your gates. (Deut 6:1–9; see also Ps 78:4)

The sharing of such stories and the passing on the faith can only be accomplished in the context of good intergenerational relationships. Such relationships provide the soil in which passing values from one generation to another is not only possible but also sustainable.

One other truth that is sometimes forgotten when it comes to intergenerational relationships is found in Paul's first letter to the Corinthians:

Just as a body, though one, has many parts, but all its many parts form one body, so it is with Christ. For we were all baptized by one Spirit so as to form one body – whether Jews or Gentiles, slave or free – and we were all given the one Spirit to drink. Even so the body is not made up of one part but of many. (1 Cor 12:12–14)

In these verses Paul groups people by ethnicity and status – but these are simply examples. They are not the only groups that can be identified within the body of Christ. There are also men and women, and young and old. Paul's argument is that people of all ethnicities and all social statuses, including young people, are valuable and important members of Christ's body (see also Matt 19:14). Moreover, we need to remember that each member of the body needs every other member of the body (1 Cor 12:21–26). "Children need the adult members of the Body of Christ to grow as fruitful, persevering members. Likewise, the elderly and adults need youth to grow as fruitful, courageous members."[4]

---

4. Ed Springer, "An Introduction to Intergenerational Ministry," Youthworks (2019), https://youthworks.net/articles/an-introduction-to-intergenerational-ministry.

We are reminded of the intergenerational nature of the early church when we read Paul's letter to Titus with its instructions to older men, older women, young women, young men and slaves. All had a role in the church, and all are to be a people of God, called to be "his very own, eager to do what is good" (Titus 2:14).

God has long valued intergenerational ministry in which it is not solely the elders who instruct the young, but also the young who instruct the old. We see this in God's words to Jeremiah as he commissioned him to be a prophet: "Do not say, 'I am too young.' You must go to everyone I send you to and say whatever I command you. Do not be afraid of them, for I am with you and will rescue you" (Jer 1:7–8). In the New Testament, we see the same situation with Timothy, to whom Paul writes, "Don't let anyone look down on you because you are young, but set an example for the believers in speech, in conduct, in love, in faith and in purity" (1 Tim 4:12).

In many respects, Timothy himself is an example of the fruits of intergenerational relationships. His grandmother and mother taught him the truths of the faith from his infancy on (2 Tim 1:5; 3:15), and as a young man he was mentored by the apostle Paul and travelled with him (Acts 16:1–5). Timothy then worked alongside other Christian leaders like Silas and Erastus (Acts 17:14; 19:22), and was eventually assigned responsibilities in major cities like Corinth and Ephesus (1 Cor 4:17; 1 Tim 1:2–4). His mentor, Paul could say that Timothy "is carrying on the work of the Lord, just as I am" (1 Cor 16:10).

Towards Intergenerational Relationships in Africa Today

In traditional Africa, people spent most of their time with those who were of their own generation, but there were also many opportunities for spontaneous interactions with older generations. The children and youth knew the elders, and the elders knew them. Each group could observe the other and know something of each person's character. The transition from childhood to adulthood was often marked by ceremonies and rituals in which the youth were given special instructions in their adult responsibilities by the community elders.

In today's urban environment, however, the only members of the older generation with whom youth have regular interaction may be their parents and teachers. There are fewer opportunities for interaction with other generations on a daily basis. While there is nothing wrong with associating with those of one's own generation – everyone needs to be part of a web of peer relationships – the lack of close intergenerational relationships presents a problem in that it makes it difficult to transfer values. It also creates a tendency for the different generations to view each other with mutual suspicion rather than with love and understanding. Older people mistrust the youth and complain that they do not follow the advice of their elders. Meanwhile, the youth are frustrated because they feel that older generations are attempting to make them conform to a world that no longer exists. For the African Union's *Agenda 2063* to be effective and sustainable, there is a need to consciously build intergenerational relationships. What follows are some suggestions for how this can be done.

Transferring values

Lectures and sermons are not enough to ensure that values are passed on from one generation to the next, for young people are exposed to even more powerful counter-influences in their world around them and in the media. By far the best way to teach young people morality and ethics is through modelling them in the context of relationships.[5] Morality and ethics cannot simply be taught; they must be caught, like viruses, through intergenerational relationships. Older generations must be prepared to spend time with younger people and to demonstrate what it means to live by the values they preach. Such modelling is not easy, for it requires living consistently at all times. It also requires humility. Older generations have tolerated conduct that will not help us to reach the goals of *Agenda 2063*. When the youth bring this to their attention, elders may need to listen and repent! They can do this secure in the knowledge that by deliberately modelling values, they can have a deep effect on the faith, social, academic and moral development of young people.

Creating opportunities

If one wants the older generation to be a model to the younger generation, it is important to provide opportunities for the generations to serve together or to deal with a moral issue together. It is as people work together on community projects that the generations are brought into contact and learn from each other. Often, however, we tend to think in terms of "youth projects" or "women's projects" and compartmentalize service so that there are few opportunities for generations to serve side by side. Intergenerational community needs to be established as a core value.

---

5. Albert Bandura, "Modeling Theory: Some Traditions, Trends, and Disputes," in *Recent Trends in Social Learning Theory* (Cambridge, MA: Academic Press, 1972), 35–61.

There is plenty of scope for intergenerational cooperation in opposition to corruption and bad governance. These evils affect everyone in the community and are thus intergenerational in their effects, so they need to be addressed in the context of intergenerational relationships. Addressing them should not be left to isolated individuals or to members of only one generation. An example of how generations can work together against corruption comes from Northern Nigeria, where a community group chaired by young people championed the removal of a sitting senator over verified allegations of corrupt practices and misappropriation of funds. It was initially the young people who pushed for this, but when they had explained their position to the elders in the community and provided proof of the senator's corruption, both young and old worked together without regard to their generational differences and achieved their common goal. If the power of intergenerational relationships can work in Northern Nigeria, it can also work in many other parts of Africa.

Encouraging participation

Young people must not be seen merely as agents who will carry out the plans of others. There are many who treat them in this way without concern for their long-term wellbeing. But treating people as tools falls far short of Christian love. Nor must young people be seen merely as participants in activities designed for them by others, no matter how well-intentioned those others are. As the example from Nigeria illustrates, youth must be active participants in initiating, planning and carrying out projects. In other words, they must have a voice in deciding what to do and how it should be done. If young people are merely consulted and all decisions and policies are made by others, the youth will not assume any responsibility for the outcome. But if they have been part of the decisions and the implementation, they will learn to take responsibility for the outcome.[6]

When our culture denies young people opportunities for involvement with adults and parents in working for the Africa we want, they go out into the adult world relationally, mentally and morally unprepared for the challenges of adulthood. Intergenerational relationships can provide realistic opportunities for mentorship and accountability while also empowering the young.

---

6. See Jones Adu-Gymafi, "Young People's Participation in Public Policy Formation: A Case Study of the National Youth Policy of Ghana," Doctoral thesis presented at the University of London, 2013.

Acknowledging gifts

Each generation has gifts that it can give to the other, but too often we misunderstand or make assumptions about each other's gifting. The older generation may assume that the gifts of the younger generation will take years to mature, and so may prevent youth from exercising those gifts in ways that will lead to mature use of them. On the other hand, the younger generation may think that the ideas of the older generation are no longer relevant today. Their eyes too must be opened to the gifts of their elders. In a village the generations would have been in close contact; in cities it is easier for the youth to exist as a completely separate cohort and to know little of the gifts of the older generation, and vice versa. But the only way the generations can discover and share their gifts with each other is if the youth and the elders spend time together.

Recognizing and working with youth-oriented organizations

A recent study on African Christian leadership in Kenya, CAR and Angola has shown the enormous influence of youth organizations.[7] Some are international organizations like the International Fellowship of Evangelical Students (IFES) which has been working in Africa for many years, but others are local organizations. It is well known that most African Christian leaders testify that their lives have been deeply influenced by such organizations, as well as by the church and choirs they belonged to in their youth. Youth organizations are the places where youth can learn basic leadership skills. The importance of choirs should also not be neglected.[8] Many young people belong to choirs where they socialize, learn biblical truth and discuss socio-political issues – often in the words of the songs. Music is a ministry that should not be neglected when establishing intergenerational relationships.

Obstacles to Intergenerational Relations

Listening to the voices of the youth will require a cultural change. African elders do not normally consult the young. The youth too will have to learn

---

7. Nupanga Weanzana, "Word and Deed: Patterns of Influential African Christian Organizations," in *African Christian Leadership: Realities, Opportunities, and Impact*, eds. Robert J. Priest and Kirimi Barine (Carlisle: Langham Global Library, 2019).

8. See the section on empowerment through choirs and music in H. Jurgens Hendriks' chapter "Empowering Leadership: A New Dawn in African Christian Leadership," in *African Christian Leadership*.

how to communicate their ideas clearly while still showing respect for the older generations. Such changes can be difficult, but the ideal place for them to start is in the church where the Trinitarian pattern of relationships lays a strong foundation for intentional intergenerational relationships, and the model of the body of Christ reminds us that every member is important and has something to contribute. The older generations have years of experience and practical knowledge to draw on; the youth can contribute their knowledge of contemporary culture and of technology as well as their energy.

But it is not merely traditional culture that can impose a barrier to communication between generations. There is also sometimes a language barrier! Young people may have a different vocabulary and reference concepts that are unfamiliar to their elders. They may use forms of address that their elders perceive as disrespectful without intending to be so. This is surely a case where both parties must take the words of James to heart: "Everyone should be quick to listen, slow to speak and slow to become angry" (Jas 1:19). Communication is possible if both sides are willing to make the attempt.

The best way to overcome these obstacles is for the leadership to demonstrate their own commitment to intergenerational relations. Others will follow the leaders' example. It is also advisable for the leaders to start the process slowly. Intergenerational relationships take time to develop. Trust has to be built up and cannot blossom overnight. We must also establish accountability and support structures that will sustain intergenerational relationships and a free flow of communication between the generations. These structures are especially important given that in most African cultures, young people cannot hold adults accountable. But intergenerational accountability demands that we hold each other accountable for how we got our wealth, our positions etc. We must be willing to answer tough questions from one another, especially when we suspect evil practices on the part of some members of the community.

Finally, it is important that congregations grasp the biblical and theological thinking underlying intergenerational relationships and understand that a commitment to such relationships is part of their Christian calling and an important element in the respect culture in many communities. A clear biblical understanding of intergenerational relationship will enhance the sustainability of our working together to fight corruption and bad governance in Africa by enabling communities to respond as biblical Christians and not just as cultural Christians.

Conclusion

The role of intentional intergenerational relationships in passing down values in the community is crucial for the African continent, especially as more than 50 percent of the population of Africa is under the age of twenty-five. Comprehensive discussion of intergenerational relationships with the goal of reaching a common understanding of our mutual responsibilities will strengthen us in our fight against corruption and contribute to our achieving the goals of *Agenda 2063*.

Questions

1. How can intergenerational relationships be enhanced in your community, church or sphere of influence?
2. Discuss how intergenerational relationships can be used to promote accountability in getting the Africa we want.
3. What are the opportunities and challenges in your church and community with regards to intergenerational relationships?

Further Reading

Alber, Erdmute, Sjaak van der Geest, and Susan Reynolds Whyte, eds. *Generations in Africa: Connections and Conflicts*. Berlin: LIT Verlag, 2008.

Hines, P. M., N. Garcia-Preto, M. McGoldrick, R. Almeida, and S. Weltman. "Intergenerational Relationships across Cultures." *Families in Society* 73, no. 6 (1992): 323–338.

Hoffman, Jaco. "What Motivates Intergenerational Practices in South Africa?" *Journal of Intergenerational Relationships* 1, no. 1 (2003): 173–176.

Larkin, Elizabeth, and Dov Friedlander. *Intergenerational Relationships: Conversations on Practice and Research across Cultures*. Binghampton, NY: Haworth, 2004.

Onyango, K.-M., and P. Onyango. *The Sociology of the African Family*. New York: Longmans, 1984.

Priest, Robert J., and Kirimi Barine. *African Christian Leadership: Realities, Opportunities, and Impact*. Carlisle: Langham Global Library, 2019.

Part 3

Public Theology and the Church

Much of what has been said so far involves action by individuals and churches, but now it is time to focus specifically on the role of the church in transforming Africa. So this section contains an overview of the state of the church in Africa and a chapter on how to set about mobilizing the African church.

Both this section and the book as a whole feed into the final chapter with its passionate call for the church to pray and act. This book will have failed to achieve its purpose if it is only read and not acted upon to further the kingdom of God and transform Africa and the church in Africa.

27

Christianity and the Church in Africa

Matthew Michael

Christianity occupies an important place in the cultural history, political development and religious landscape of the African continent. From Nairobi to Ndjamena, Cairo to Cape Town, there are visible marks of Christian presence in the architecture of emerging cities and the landmarks of the suburbs. Christian stickers appear on lorries and taxis, crusade posters on billboards and the unkempt walls of public buildings, and a million signboards announce churches in African megacities and African ghettos. These visual signs of Christian presence on the continent are supplemented by the sounds of Christian singing and preaching from the loudspeakers hoisted high on the walls of churches in almost every African town, the Makossa dance beats of gospel music on the airwaves of many African radio stations, and the Christian parades and celebrations in African villages and cities.

Christian motifs are also popular in Nollywood dramas, and in the testimonies to Christian miracles and healing that can be heard on many African television shows. There is also aggressive praying in monthly Pentecostal night vigils and emotional invocations of the imprecatory psalms in African Independent Churches. The Christian faith clearly has high social visibility in African communities.

In spite of pockets of violent resistance to Christianity, it has found a home in the warm hearts of African people, and the Bible has played a formidable role in shaping their religious consciousness. Christianity has not merely registered its presence in the length and breadth of the African continent; it has also led to social reengineering and cultural transformation of African communities through the education of elites, the empowerment of African people and the reconfiguration of the cultural identities of the African people along religious lines. In recent years, African Christianity has also been exported to Europe and North America and has growing significance among Africans in the diaspora.

In this chapter, we will consider the paradoxes and trends in the modern expression of African Christianity.

Some Definitions

Before dealing with the broader topic, it may be helpful to distinguish between Christianity in Africa and African Christianity, drawing on the distinction made by the South African scholar Tinyiko Maluleke:

> Although these two are often used interchangeably, perhaps they ought to be distinguished. The first seems to allude to the impact of Christianity on Africa and maybe of Africa on Christianity also. The second appears to go further and suggests that a peculiarly African form of Christianity has emerged and that such a form is both observable and describable as such. It is important that discussions of African Christianity keep both senses in view at all times.[1]

In this chapter I have endeavoured to keep Maluleke's words in mind and describe both African Christianity and Christianity in Africa.

The Paradoxes of Modern African Christianity

The warm reception of Christianity by African people has resulted in a geometric rise in the numbers of adherents to the faith across the African continent and has affected the social networks and the religious identities of African people. Yet there are at least six paradoxical elements in the expansion of African Christianity on the continent of Africa.

---

1. Tinyiko Sam Maluleke, "Of Africanised Bees and Africanised Churches: Ten Theses on African Christianity," *Missionalia* 38, no. 3 (2010): 373.

1) African Christianity has not been able to transform the economic destinies of the African continent.

In spite of Christianity's huge influence and the corporate goodwill towards it among the African people, Africa still endures numerous economic woes.

> The image of Africa with the widest currency in the rest of the world is that of a political and economic disaster area: the continent of dictatorships, corruption, oppression, civil wars, coups, refugees, ethnic strife, barbarity, and genocide. The statistics and the vignettes of poverty scandalise the informed observer who concludes that Africa is locked in a spiral of economic decline when much of the rest of the world is achieving remarkable growth.[2]

The church's presence in Africa has contributed little to the economic power of the ordinary people. Rates of poverty have skyrocketed in most African societies, and destitution has become the trademark of a continent with an overwhelming Christian presence. It is ironic that the church in many parts of Africa lives in apparent wealth, while the majority of its members endure poverty, destitution and lack. As Maluleke says,

> While the poor may not be the authoritative and formal voice in African Christianity, their sheer numbers makes them the living face of African Christianity. . . . This means that African Christianity is a Christianity of the poor, the women, the black and the underclasses. It is a Christianity of irony in the sense that though boasting numbers, it is the least powerful who swell its ranks.[3]

Admittedly, the church has empowered some of its members to engage in trade, develop vocational skills and acquire entrepreneurial knowledge. But the majority of church members are still poor, and poverty has become the albatross on the neck of the African church.

2) The influence of the church has grown at the expense of establishing industries and companies in Africa.

The church is present in almost every nook and cranny of the African continent, but companies and industries are more conspicuous by their absence in regions

---

2. Kenneth Ross, "Doing Theology with a New Historiography," *Journal of Theology for Southern Africa* 99 (1997): 94–98.

3. Maluleke, "Of Africanised Bees," 376.

and major towns across Africa. There are now more churches in Africa than companies and industries. The church itself has become the new industry of Africa, with various confessional and denominational varieties. It seems that this proliferation of churches in modern Africa comes on the heels of the decline of industries and companies, enabling people to psychologically redirect their focus and commitment to God in the face of harsh economic realities.

There are numerous stories of people abandoning their businesses and establishing ministries or churches. Thus the quest for more churches and ministries has taken centre stage rather than the need to establish new industries or seek new business ideas to combat the harsh economic tides.

The increase in the number of Christians entering full-time church work may seem like a victory because African ministries, churches and Christian organizations have the workers they need to maintain their structures. But this victory comes at a cost.

When the church treats the economic sector as a secular domain that is in eternal opposition to spiritual ministry, it contributes to the exodus of gifted workers and entrepreneurs from the public and economic sectors. Because so many committed Christians have opted out of thriving careers in business and the public sector and taken refuge behind the shielded walls of the church, there is an absence of Christ-centred professionals who can uphold the Christian presence in mainstream society. Thus the church has lost the ability to influence the larger society while the public sector has been deprived of those whose values and ethics could help in changing the larger society. The absence of committed Christians has had a long-term impact on the stability and flourishing of economic sectors.

3) African Christianity has failed to pursue a clear political manifesto that could contribute to defining societal transformation.

There are no doubt many cases of the romance of African Christianity with politics, but Christians have lacked the political will and power to transform the politics of African society. Recognizing this problem, Desmond Tutu rightly observed that in Africa there is often "no theology of power in the face of the epidemic of coups and military rule." Unfortunately in this hostile environment, the humanity of people is "constantly undermined by a pathological religiosity and by a political authority which has whittled away much personal freedom without too much opposition from the Church."[4]

---

4. Desmond Tutu, "Black Theology and African Theology: Soulmates or Antagonists?" *Journal of Religious Thought* 2 (1975): 42.

This situation is paradoxical for as the Ugandan scholar Emmanuel Katongole observed, "The reading of Scripture is not just some pious exercise, but a political exercise, and even a subversive form of politics."[5] In other words, the reading of the Bible itself should lead Christians to challenge "politics as usual," but unfortunately this point has eluded the African church.

In this context, it is important to reiterate the significant cultural synergy between religious institutions and the state in the traditional African world view. Ben Knighton says,

> The feature of African traditional religion has always been that it is inseparable from traditional politics, but Western intervention both to create desacralized states and churches that defied cultural norms meant that the separation of politics from religion was all the more vicious for not being natural. Mainstream churches often conscientized their members not to mix religion and politics, usually with the effect of stabilizing the colonial state. The theological dichotomy thus needs to be resolved without collapsing Christian faith into mere service of the state.[6]

In recent years, most of the churches in Africa have recognized the ineffectiveness of a passive strategy and have rhetorically drummed the need for individual and collective political participation of the church and its membership in mainstream politics. Nevertheless, they have been unable to concretely change the political processes of most African countries in any meaningful way. The church is largely seen as politically irrelevant because its communal influence has not translated into concrete transformation of the political direction of African society. The church has done little to deepen democratic culture, support equality and human rights, promote the rule of law or protect the rights of minorities, nor has it insisted on the need for accountability of political elites.

To give one example, the presence of the church in Africa has not affected the thriving corporate and individual corruption that characterizes most countries in Africa. In fact corruption is widespread even within the church. While the pathological commitment of African politicians to corrupt practices has become a disturbing reality, the African church has largely failed to root

---

5. Emmanuel Katongole, *A Future for Africa: Critical Essays in Christian Social Imagination* (Scranton, PA: University of Scranton Press, 2005): 88–89.

6. Ben Knighton, "Issues of African Theology at the Turn of the Millennium," *Transformation* 21, no. 3 (2004): 150.

out corruption among its members or to work towards the transformation of the values that lead to corruption and unethical practices.

4) The African church has largely held to conservative doctrinal positions, but its conservative values have not translated into the practice of ethical ideals that could transform African society.

The church has usually taken a firm, conservative stand on issues of modern society. Unfortunately, this stand is largely limited to doctrinal statements that are not mirrored in the practices of African Christians. For example, the African church has frowned on the use of condoms, the practice of polygamy, the use of herbal and traditional medicines and the patronage of traditional institutions of guidance. But in reality, all these practices are prevalent within the walls of the African church. Thus, while the leadership of the African church is conservative in its confessional stand, the members of the church often reject the official positions of the church.

5) The African church is highly superstitious.

African Christianity is generally a modern re-enactment of medieval spirituality with all its paraphernalia, assumptions, rituals and ideologies. Church members are largely uncritical of the clergy and will obey "the words of God" from the mouths of self-professed priests, pastors and prophets without seeking guidance from the Bible. The Bible itself is revered as the word of God, but the words of modern prophets are given almost the same weight.

Literal and superficial engagement with the Bible has not allowed deeper conversation about its theology. One seldom hears well-informed debate or conversation about the text of the Bible; rather, a quick reference to the words of a "man of God" or to the veracity of a miracle by a "man of God" is regarded as sufficient to settle any matter. People seldom engage in in-depth study of the Bible to support a theological position; rather, the words of a "man of God" are perceived to be sacred and sacrosanct.

The idolization of the clergy, especially of the Pentecostal brand, has contributed to the uncritical character of church members, many of whom have submitted their minds to the whims and caprices of so-called "men and women of God." In fact, most African Christians trust their pastors blindly and do not carry out the important duty of cross-checking the teachings and theologies of their churches and their denominational beliefs. This docility means that African Christians lack a critical disposition and do not challenge heretical and unbiblical teachings that have begun to find their way into the African church.

The uncriticalness of the African church presents a problem given that the African church and its form of Christianity are poised to be the next Christendom. There is a need for African Christians to be vigilant in protecting biblical Christianity.

6) The African church has a supernatural orientation and is more interested in spiritual and supernatural causation than in physical-social and concrete causation.

Churches in Africa like to "bind the spirit of poverty." In doing this, they divert the attention of the African masses from the socio-political causes of their perpetual poverty. Instead, churches host deliverance sessions and services to exorcise the spirit of poverty or to cast out the ancestral spirits that are believed to be responsible for the inability of most African people to enjoy abundant life. This orientation feeds into endless night vigils, fasts, and prayer meetings where evil spirits are cast out and people are delivered from the malevolent powers of these spirits.

Unfortunately, no attention is paid to the political roots of poverty such as voting for bad government and ineffective economic policies. Fatal road accidents are blamed on demons and evil spirits rather than on bad roads, speeding or individual negligence. The same attitudes attend the treatment of diseases, which are often seen as the work of evil spirits seeking to sabotage the health of the African people. There is not enough emphasis on the natural causes of ailments and sicknesses. Even though physical causation may be acknowledged in the diagnosis of physical ailments, priority is often given to their spiritual or supernatural origins. This attitude does not encourage scientific thinking and reasoning because the empirical world and its scientific laws are ignored or merely passively acknowledged, while the world of the ancestors and spirits is regarded as the real and concrete world.

This interpretation of natural phenomena also affects Africans' understanding of agricultural and farming activities. Instead of seeking the logical and natural causes of crop failures and epidemics, they blame bad harvests on the activities of witches who are said to have sent insect pests, viruses and bacteria to destroy the crop. Another popular narrative in times of plague, famine and harvest failure is that God is punishing the church or his people for their sins. Divine punishment is preached in sermons and discussed in public and private conversations.

The default thinking of the African church is to seek the spiritual causes of all misfortunes or ills. This mindset does not encourage empirical, scientific study in order to find appropriate solutions. Thus the African church in this modern age still advocates superstitious interpretations, diagnoses and analysis of natural phenomena.

Admittedly, scientific understandings of the natural causation of malaria, crop failure and epidemics are often acknowledged, yet the majority of African people still think within the mythical universe of a pre-modern world where evil spirits and forces are the sole cause of disaster and misfortune in the world. In this world of evil spirits, the activities of demons are hindered by prayers, and thus the dominant mindset is that aggressive prayer is the only key to the development and transformation of society. This perspective informs the noisy prayers, aggressive disposition, contentious character, "commanding God" theology and warfare mindset in the saying of prayers. In many places across Africa, silent prayers are regarded as an indication of lukewarm Christianity, whereas aggressive ones are thought to indicate a vibrant spirituality, given the mindset that aggressive forces of evil spirits must be confronted by aggressive prayer. According to such thinking, we need to confront evil spirits in aggressive prayer while we pray for people in governance.

Unfortunately, the mindset that promotes aggressive protest against evil spirits does not translate this aggression into confrontation of bad government, evil leadership, bad politicians and the dysfunctional character of most public offices in Africa. There is a disconnect between our aggressive prayers and our failure to protest against the bad governance that has reduced African people to paupers and left them destitute in their own countries. We deal with evil spirits, but we have no clear agenda in dealing with bad government.

Trends, Patterns and Trajectories

Besides the paradoxes discussed above, there are certain trends in Africa that come from the converging interactions of specific patterns. Four of these patterns need to be emphasized.[7]

First, an important pattern in the description of modern African Christianity is its association with missionary enterprise. The Western missionaries who came to the African continent in the eighteenth and nineteenth centuries contributed to the planting of African churches. Even though the missionary enterprise has come under serious scrutiny and criticism in recent times, it should be credited with the general thriving and successes of modern African Christianity. The Gambian scholar Lamin Sanneh argues that the missionary

---

7. For another approach to trends in Africa, see Josée Ngalula, "Some Current Trends of Christianity in Africa," *International Review of Mission* (2017): 228–240.

enterprise brought about the first theological discourse between Africans and missionaries, for Africans' involvement in translation aroused the need to debate word use and other considerations that are important for understanding the Christian faith.[8] This pattern has a rich presence in the founding of churches and the creation of theological institutions that have helped to nurture critical engagement with the biblical text. Unfortunately, the paternalistic control missionaries exercised over the churches they founded has not allowed rigorous engagement with the Bible and received ecclesiastical traditions.

The second pattern in the planting of the African church is the founding of African Independent Churches. This came about because of the general dissatisfaction of Africans with the liturgy, theology and hierarchical structures of the mainline churches founded by the missionaries. The perceived foreignness of missionary Christianity led African Independent Churches to seek to Africanize Christianity by merging it with certain aspects of African culture. Institutions such as polygamy, new rituals, prophetic practices, oracles, divination and other forms of traditional practices and norms were introduced into Christianity in these churches.

The third pattern in the story of African Christianity is the emergence of African Pentecostalism which has become an important force in global Christianity as it has been packaged and exported to all parts of the world. The Sierra Leonean scholar Jehu Hanciles has stressed the significance of African Pentecostalism and especially its exportation to Europe and America.[9] Similarly, Philip Jenkins has written about the exceptional importance of Pentecostalism in the configuration and description of Christianities in Asia, Latin America and Africa. As the seat of "the next Christendom," African Pentecostalism asserts its acceptability and popularity among African people with its promises of prosperity, wealth, healing and deliverance. This message has appealed to both the poor and the rich, thus penetrating different social classes and economic statuses.

The last pattern in African Christianity is the convergence of Pentecostal and conservative orientations so that both Pentecostalism and conservative Christianities seek to merge in a new movement that signals the harmony of conservative and Pentecostal elements.[10] The emerging synergy and

---

8. Lamin Sanneh, *Translating the Message: The Missionary Impact on Culture*, 2nd ed. (Maryknoll, NY: Orbis, 2015).

9. Jehu Hanciles, *Beyond Christendom: Globalization, African Migration and the Transformation of the West* (Maryknoll, NY: Orbis, 2008).

10. See Damaris S. Parsitau, "From the Periphery to the Centre: The Pentecostalisation of Mainline Christianity in Kenya," *Missionalia* 35, no. 3 (2007): 83–111.

collaboration between Pentecostalism and conservatism can be seen on several levels. The present trend suggests that Christians may now be tired of the emptiness and shallowness often associated with Pentecostalism – and the dryness and rigidity of mainline churches. The ecumenical impulses strive to merge, harmonize and harness the best of these theological traditions for the edification of the African church.

Denominational blunders are beginning to give way to a new development within the African church that can lead to celebration of Pentecostalism in mainline churches and conservative thinking in Pentecostal circles. There is a new consciousness on the horizon where reformed Pentecostalism is welcomed in conservative settings and the great doctrinal truths of conservative Christianity are cherished within Pentecostal thinking.

There are quiet agitations against the inadequacies of theological traditions in many parts of the African continent that are critical of both Pentecostals and mainline churches. On social media, for example, the abuse of tithes and offerings has occasioned a major critique of both Pentecostals and mainline churches. While it is unclear what the outcome will be, it seems that these critiques may lead to church practices that are more in harmony with the central teachings of the Bible. It is hoped that this criticalness on the fringe of the African church will lead to a healthier and more vibrant church where the gains of Pentecostalism and the doctrinal insights of conservative theology are beautifully merged for the edification of the African church.

Conclusion

African Christianity rejects monolithic simplification. The diversity of missionary activities, colonial encounters, cultural memories, political histories and polyvalent identities have conspired to produce a plethora of theological positions and a multi-faceted cultural entity. It is hard to describe it, let along map its character, drive and direction.

Yet in spite of its multidimensional character, African Christianity does present a certain homogeneity in its patterns and overall characteristics. While these patterns may not be present in every African country, there is an overwhelming recognition of their presence and significance in modern African Christianity.

Questions

1. Are the paradoxes discussed in this chapter present in the region of Africa with which you are familiar? Can you supply examples of how they do or do not apply?
2. Are the trends discussed in this chapter present in the region of Africa with which you are familiar? Can you supply examples of how they do or do not apply?
3. Are there trends or paradoxes you are aware of that are not mentioned in this chapter? If so, what are they?

Further Reading

Bediako, Kwame. *Theology and Identity: The Impact of Culture upon Christian Thought in the Second Century and in Modern Africa.* Oxford: Regnum, 2002.

Gifford, Paul. *Ghana's New Christianity: Pentecostalism in a Globalizing African Economy.* Bloomington: Indiana University Press, 2004.

Hanciles, Jehu. *Beyond Christendom: Globalization, African Migration and the Transformation of the West.* Maryknoll, NY: Orbis, 2008.

Katongole, Emmanuel. *A Future for Africa: Critical Essays in Christian Social Imagination.* Scranton, PA: University of Scranton Press, 2005.

Ngong, David Tonghou, ed. *A New History of African Christian Thought: From Cape to Cairo.* New York: Routledge, 2017.

28

Mobilizing the Church in Africa

Alfred uw'Imana Sebahene

A great opportunity lies before us as we in Africa face up to our greatest challenge since the days of the struggle for independence. The African Union has summoned us to take part in its *Agenda 2063* and work for the "Africa we want." As believers, we recognize that in many respects the "Africa we want" overlaps with the Africa God wants, one that will respond enthusiastically to the call, "Let everything that has breath praise the LORD" (Ps 150:6). We want an Africa that we can celebrate saying, "Let the heavens rejoice, let the earth be glad; . . . Let the fields be jubilant, and everything in them" (Ps 96:11–12), rather than an Africa that groans and suffers. But what is the role of the church in achieving this goal? How can it grow and stretch into the task God is calling us to?

The Purpose of the Church

Any reflection on the church's role in *Agenda 2063* must begin by exploring why the church exists. What is its purpose on earth? The answer to that question is clearly given in Scripture: it is that "through the church, the manifold wisdom of God should be made known to the rulers and authorities in the heavenly realms" (Eph 3:10). This verse should not be misinterpreted as meaning that the church only speaks to "rulers and authorities," for the way it speaks to them is through the lives of believers as they obey Jesus's command to "let your light shine before others, that they may see your good deeds and glorify your Father in heaven" (Matt 5:16). When the church does this, it can rightly be described as "a chosen people, a royal priesthood, a holy nation, God's special possession, that you may declare the praises of him who called you out of darkness into his wonderful light" (1 Pet 2:9). This is the role that was foretold for the church in the Old Testament (Isa 42:5–7).

In revealing God to the world, the church is expected to demonstrate how redeemed people live in community and partner with God in his mission. In the words of Buchanan, "The world cannot possibly begin to believe in the reality of an unseen God, extravagant in mercy, lavish in goodness, bent on redeeming and reconciling and restoring creation, until our churches are living object lessons of this very thing."[1] When African Christians truly grasp that God did not create the church merely as a place for believers to gather, they will begin to get a clearer understanding of their duty and responsibilities to Africa today and to future generations. They will start to live as a new community called to embody the principles of the kingdom and thus to have a saving effect on all the structures of life.

In Africa, we are blessed that such input may be welcomed, for here "religion is not relegated to the private spheres of life. In all public spheres there is a high level of hospitality to religion. Religion is welcomed in political life, economic life, ecological matters, civil society, as well as in the processes of public opinion formation and public policy formulation."[2] The research undertaken by the Africa Leadership Study has made it abundantly clear that the church exerts enormous influence in Africa.[3] We should neither take this privilege for granted nor neglect this opportunity God has given us to prepare church members for active engagement in the public sphere. The Africa we want cannot happen without careful and diligent teaching of the liberating truth of God.

Defining the Church

While we may readily agree on the nature of the church's mission, things may get a little more complicated when we ask, "But who or what is the church?" There are three possibilities. The first is summed up in the phrase "the church is not the building; it's the people." Here the focus falls on individual Christians who undoubtedly have a responsibility to live out their faith in their daily

---

1. Mark Buchanan, *Your Church Is Too Safe: Why Following Christ Turns the World Upside-Down* (Grand Rapids: Zondervan, 2015), 170.

2. Nico Koopman, "Public Theology as Prophetic Theology: More than Utopianism and Criticism," *Journal of Theology for Southern Africa* 133 (2009): 118.

3. African Leadership Study, https://africaleadershipstudy.org/.

lives at work, at home and in the community. Second, the church is the local church, the group of believers who gather together in one building for regular worship. In this book, many of the questions at the end of each chapter have been targeted to local churches to help their members discuss what they can do to address local problems. As discussed in chapter 10 on rural communities, a local church with a pastor and other leaders committed to action and service can have a positive impact on their local community. They are the ones best positioned to know the problems of the community, and as a group they can often accomplish more than can be done by an isolated individual. This point is so obvious in Africa that it scarcely needs to be made, although it is less self-evident in more individualistic contexts. However, this call for group action should not be used as an excuse to evade individual responsibility.

Third, the church may be a denomination, like the Anglican or Presbyterian Church. It may be possible for a larger group to mobilize resources that small local congregations cannot access. It may also be easier for a larger body to represent Christians when speaking to large organizations and even to the government – provided the denominational leaders are not co-opted by the government, a danger that is warned against in chapter 20 on theology and the state and in chapter 21 on theology and state power.

Denominations should not only work with larger groups. They should also support the ministry of local churches, providing advice and international connections of the kind that helped the college described in chapter 10 on rural communities. A denomination may also help by holding local churches and pastors accountable when funds are misappropriated or parishioners exploited.

In Africa there are, however, many churches that exist solely as local churches, without any larger oversight. In such situations, a heavy burden rests on the leaders and the church members. It is up to them to ensure that the corruption that is so common in Africa does not infiltrate their thinking and result in a church that does not reveal much about the goodness of God to those in the community.

The churches that are not part of any denomination, as well as all denominational churches, should never forget that they are also part of the full church of God that embraces all believers of all ethnic groups on all continents. This realization should prompt us not to see other churches as rivals but to work together to promote God's kingdom. It is not that we have to agree on every point of doctrine – our watchwords should be "in essentials unity, in non-essentials liberty, in all things charity." But it is time that we recognize that a divided and fragmented African church will hamper our attempts to bring about the Africa God wants: "Fragmentation [leads to] spiritual fatigue, and lack of zeal for prophetic social action."[4] It cripples the church and muddles its message. We should feel free to celebrate our God-given diversity (see chapter 4 on the Trinity), while also standing together in unity (see, again, the chapter on the Trinity) to prophetically denounce injustice and call on believers to live out their faith in their African context.

What best characterizes an African corporate church in action is its witness in the public square where it should speak out against the continent's darkest problems of bad governance, corruption, socio-economic injustice, religious competition, tribal and ethnic conflicts and political domination. When this is done well, the institutional church will be understood as one which is responding and faithfully following Jesus Christ and bearing public witness to the truth of the gospel.

Mobilizing the Church

In the Old Testament, God called his people to relationships rooted in responsibility, mercy, truthfulness and obedience to his law. In the New Testament, God revealed his nature of boundless love, and Jesus called on his followers to show love to their neighbours and to their enemies, a love that is revealed in deeds and in showing mercy. We are called to be a church in service to humanity because the Triune God entered into service with us and has shared with us the mission of the incarnate Word in the world.

God has given the church the resources it needs to carry out the task he has assigned it. His gifts to all Christian believers are the Bible and the presence of the Holy Spirit in their lives, but he has also given individual believers unique gifts that they can use in their vocations and in their communities. Thus one of the tasks of the church is to help believers identify and develop their gift, set them free for fruitful, faithful mission and ministry in all areas of African life, and support them in their work both within and outside church structures. The church should make followers of Christ the people that our God calls them to be, both for his glory and for the sake of our suffering continent.

Pastors and academics may understand the calling of the church, but how is this knowledge to be communicated to ordinary church members? The answer is that it can be done by breaking down the divide between the sacred and the secular, teaching, acting and empowering.

---

4. B. Goba, "The Role of the Church in Moral Renewal," unpublished paper presented at the annual meeting of the Diakonia Council of Churches, Durban, South Africa, 23 June 2007.

Breaking down the divide between the sacred and the secular

At the root of many of the failures of the church is what is called the sacred–secular divide, which allows Christians to think that their Christian faith involves only formal acts of devotion and piety and need not transform their everyday life and behaviour. In many churches, Christians hear the gospel and experience the love of God in Jesus Christ, but when it comes to other matters they are told to listen to what the secular or political authorities say and obey the law without questioning the local, state or national government. This problem is so deep-rooted that there are some Christian denominations and church leaders who argue that the pulpit must be used only for "sacred" matters and must not be contaminated by addressing "secular" issues. No wonder Christians have not been successful in bringing their faith to bear in their public spheres!

Pastors who hold to the division of the sacred and the secular cannot preach the whole word of God to the whole world, let alone to Africa. Their inability to do this undermines the power of their prophetic witness, and so their ability to minister to this suffering continent. They cannot equip believers to apply their faith in the contexts in which they live and will be unable to "incarnate the Christian message in African cultures."[5] In other words, they will not be able to establish any connection between the Bible and theology and the thinking of the local people, including their traditional views and insights, with the result that the Scriptures will be perceived as irrelevant to their lives.

In brief, pastors who cling to the division of the sacred and the secular will not be able to encourage Christians who are seeking to understand and present concrete interpretation of the Christian faith in accordance with the needs, aspirations and already existing thought-forms and mentality of people across the continent.

Teaching about the call to be salt and light for Africa

Pastors and teachers across Africa need to teach that the church in Africa does not exist merely to save souls but is also called to be salt and light in the public sphere in Africa in particular. Thus church members need to be constantly reminded of Christ's teaching in the Sermon on the Mount:

---

5. C. Nyamiti, "A Critical Assessment on Some Issues on Today's African Theology," *African Christian Studies* 5, no. 1 (1989): 10.

You are the salt of the earth. But if the salt loses its saltiness, how can it be made salty again? It is no longer good for anything, except to be thrown out and trampled underfoot.

You are the light of the world. A town built on a hill cannot be hidden. Neither do people light a lamp and put it under a bowl. Instead they put it on its stand, and it gives light to everyone in the house. In the same way, let your light shine before others, that they may see your good deeds and glorify your Father in heaven. (Matt 5:13–16)

People need to learn that our faith in Christ is manifested in and through personal spirituality, witness and actions. In other words, it is manifested as we follow Jesus, bear testimony and produce the "good works" that will lead to reconciliation, justice and peace in the church and society in Africa. Too often, this testimony is interpreted solely in terms of our personal or domestic lives, but as the previous chapters in this book have shown, we are also called to be salt and light in terms of democracy, citizenship and civil society, poverty, education, science, health, the environment, work, the economy, media and migration – or in every area in which we are called to serve. We are, as Mugambi says, to be the people who fulfil God's mission by adding "flavour and shine to the world."[6]

Acting to reveal the power of kingdom values

Agenda 2063 declares that the destiny of Africa is in the hands of Africans. In other words, Africa's development must be driven by its people, all its people, including men, women and youth. It is African people who must act to shape the future they want. Thus it is not enough just to talk about kingdom values in church. If Africa is to be transformed, these values must be understood and lived out in Christians' personal lives and should become moral values and ideals that are incorporated in the way they live in society.

The Christian faith is not supposed to be a matter of merely personal or private devotional life; it has to be part of all aspects of a believer's life, including those related to public life. So the church cannot focus only on spiritual matters but must also address Africa's challenges including its leadership styles, the inequitable distribution of wealth and resources, persistent poverty, gender-

---

6. Jesse N. K. Mugambi, *Democracy and Development in Africa: The Role of the Churches* (Nairobi: AACC, 1997).

based inequalities, social injustices and corruption, ecological abuse and misuse, war and terrorism, to mention only a few. The church in Africa needs to address these issues because it is meant to offer public hope amidst situations of despair and melancholy and public love in societies where public solidarity and compassion are absent.[7]

The biblical values Christians should be living out include compassion for the vulnerable, marginalized and oppressed (Exod 22:22); care for the poor (Lev 23:22); promotion of justice, for example, fairness in trade (Lev 19:36); fairness in not charging interest (Lev 25:36); and fair distribution of land (Lev 25:8–54) and paying fair wages to labourers (Mal 3:5). These values are of great importance for the social, economic and political development of Africa, and for the day-to-day administration of affairs. But many Christians may not understand their full implications, and thus it is up to the church to help people understand the implications of the norms and values that Christians bring to public discourse.

We hope that some of the topics discussed in this book will contribute to opening people's eyes to how they should live. But no book can offer all the answers in our changing political and economic landscape. Pastors who seek to adopt a holistic approach to the needs of their communities must spend time seeking God's direction for the appropriate responses to the challenges facing the continent.

Empowering the laity to stand up and walk

Even though we speak of the church as one body, comprising the clergy and laity, gathered and sent, who are together charged with continuing Christ's priestly work, these words are not translated into action. In fact, misunderstanding and confusion about who should do what and how has deeply affected the church's ability to carry out its responsibility of being a blessing to the whole of humanity. Rather than seeing ourselves as brothers and sisters in Christ, we have constructed a two-class society in the church with the "clergy" as the rulers and the "laity" as the ruled. The result has been a culture of arrogance and entitlement in which some church leaders feel free to make demands on their church members but exhibit a total lack of accountability to the members.

Many lay people have expressed their deep anger at this situation which undermines mutual growth in discipleship to Christ. It also denies people

---

7. Nico Koopman, "Some Contours for Public Theology," *International Journal of Practical Theology* 14, no. 1 (2010): 123–138.

the opportunity to work side by side with ordained ministers and ignores the unique role of the laity, who are well positioned to carry the gospel into their life-worlds and the world of work where ordained ministers can seldom go. That is why in this book we have stressed that public theology is not just about theologians and church leaders talking to the civil authorities and national leaders. Rather, at the heart of public theology is the local church and the understanding that all Christians in that church are to be involved in ministry in the world. In the past, it was baptized believers who contributed to the evangelization of Africa, and today they need to continue to do good and serve others in the society and the world in which they live. The church's job is to "strengthen the believers in their faith and prepare them for their service to each other and the world."[8]

Empowering the laity also means assigning them roles in leadership, for "lay leaders, regardless of gender, are key people because they sustain the daily life of congregations."[9] Thus the church needs to help members discover and use their spiritual gifts. It also needs to nurture and encourage lay persons with gifts of leadership, shepherding, faith and apostleship. The church will not raise up cadres of godly leaders unless it creates communities of whole-life disciples.

One way to empower lay leaders is to broaden our focus beyond the selection, training and ongoing ministerial development of clergy. Such training is an important task and one many churches have done well. But to be successful in transforming Africa, the church also needs to focus on inspiring and supporting faithful lay people in their discipleship and vocational journey. Lay formation and discipleship needs to become a matter of urgency. Books like this one are intended to be used as part of this training. But much more help is needed, and it needs to come from Africans who understand the culture, that is, the ordinary circumstances of family, work and social life in different communities across this continent. We need to work to build a network of Christians who will pursue integrity in their jobs, in their professions and in local and national governments.

---

8. D. J. Smit, *Essays on Being Reformed: Collected Essays 3*, ed. R. Vosloo (Stellenbosch: SUN, 2009), 449.

9. Jesse N. K. Mugambi, *From Liberation to Reconstruction: African Christian Theology after the Cold War* (Nairobi: East African Educational Publishers, 1995), 5.

Leading by Example: A Holy Church

We have been speaking of the church as a public institution whose vision is to meet the needs of human beings personally and publically. We have said that the church must engage with and prophetically challenge political and community leaders across the continent if it is to bring about change in society that will benefit all. But as we contemplate this task, we also have to recognize the problem that Jesus so neatly identified for us: "Why do you look at the speck of sawdust in your brother's eye and pay no attention to the plank in your own eye?" (Matt 7:3). Too often we focus only on the "speck" in the government's eye and totally ignore "the plank" in the church's eye. But while we ignore the church's problems, the rest of society does not. It is unfortunate that as the African Union seeks to transform Africa, the church's witness in most parts of the continent is undermined in the public arena by its own lack of integrity.

If the church is to call on the people to live out Christian values in their daily life, then the church must live by them too. People will not live out values that their leaders do not live out. Thus the church also needs to set an example as a place where Christian ethics affect the way the church is run, the way its finances are administered, how church leaders are appointed and what ministries are supported. If we call for competent, professional, rule- and merit-based public institutions to serve our communities, then the church must model what such an institution should look like. The church must be a community of character and model for other institutions its values-based mode of governance that prioritizes integrity, honesty, diligence, fairness and stewardship.[10] We cannot call for society to reflect God's rule if the church does not.

Becoming a holy church requires church leaders who are spiritually mature and who live out their faith at home, at church, in Africa and in the world. Such leaders will not confuse the sinful storing of earthly treasure with God-allowed use of earthly goods for the good of the African continent. Their lives will be characterized by humility, an assurance of God's calling and a focus on the potential of those they serve. Jesus must be their role model.

Conclusion: Where Does the Church Fit In?

To return to our original question: Where does the church fit in? We wish to emphasize that the church's involvement in identifying the "Africa we do not want" and working towards "the Africa God wants" is not a matter of choice

---

10. Smit, *Essays on Being Reformed*.

or a legal responsibility; it is an obligation that springs from our love for God and for the world which he has created and loves. James has warned us: "If anyone, then, knows the good they ought to do and doesn't do it, it is sin for them" (Jas 4:17).

God summons the church in Africa to share in Christ's own mission to Africa and the world. He calls the church to abundant life and to love as he loved us. God calls the church to service that includes applying gospel principles to social life and being engaged in dialogue with Africa the world around. The church should do these things because God is in dialogue with Africa and the world in human history.

The primary responsibility of the church in Africa is to witness to God in Jesus Christ through the power of the Holy Spirit in ways that can be heard and understood as the church builds up the common good. Our ultimate goal is to help Africa achieve the seven aspirations of *Agenda 2063*, but it is also to go beyond these goals and proclaim Christ, "admonishing and teaching everyone with all wisdom, so that we may present everyone [in Africa] fully mature in Christ" (Col 1:28).

Questions

1. What does the verse "You are the light of the world" (Matt 5:14) mean to you and your church? How does it relate to the sacred-secular divide?
2. How does your local church relate to other churches? What can be done to encourage cooperation rather than rivalry?
3. The chapter speaks about removing the plank from your own eye before removing the speck of sawdust from someone else's eye (Matt 7:4–5). What does this mean in terms of relations within your church, between churches, and with the surrounding community?
4. What training is available for the laity in your church or in your region? Can you think of any ways in which this training could be done better?
5. How can your local church prepare its members for life in the public sphere? For example, is it acceptable to pray for and commission members who are selling firewood, working as mechanics, mending tires or selling fruit and vegetables, or is such commissioning reserved only for those in professional careers like teaching and nursing?

Further Reading

Buchanan, M. *Your Church Is Too Safe: Why Following Christ Turns the World Upside-Down*. Grand Rapids: Zondervan, 2015.

Hendriks, H. J. *Studying Congregations in Africa*. Wellington, South Africa: Lux VerbiBM, 2004.

Khauoe, M. J. *The Awakening Giant: The African Church and Its Calling to Mission*. Wellington, South Africa: Christian Literature Fund, 2011.

Lausanne Movement. The Cape Town Commitment. https://www.lausanne.org/content/ctc/ctcommitment#capetown.

Sebahene, A. U. *Corruption Mocking at Justice: A Theological-Ethical Perspective on Public Life in Tanzania and Its Implications for the Anglican Church of Tanzania*. Carlisle: Langham Monographs, 2017.

29

Towards the Africa God Wants

H. Jurgens Hendriks

The African Union's *Agenda 2063* has the subtitle *The Africa We Want*. It was this subtitle that inspired Sunday Agang's opening words in chapter 1 of this book:

> Almost everyone in Africa acknowledges that we are currently living in an Africa we do not want. It is not that we do not love Africa – we do, passionately and deeply. There is much that is good and beautiful in Africa and much that we can be proud of in our past. But when we look around us, we see abundant evidence that all is not well in Africa.

This paragraph applies not only to Africa but also to the church in Africa. In many respects, the church in Africa is like Nigeria, which has vast oil reserves but chronic shortages of petrol and diesel. The church in Africa is in the same situation: there is a church on every corner and none of them has any fuel. Why not?

Sunday Agang identified one reason in chapter 1, "For too many people, there is a disconnect between their Christian life and the rest of their life, between the sacred and the secular world."[1] We tend to think of theology as part of the sacred world, as something academic and abstract dealing with topics like the Bible, the Trinity and identity. But if that is our only understanding of theology, it is far too limited. The Greek words that form the word "theology" imply that theology is words spoken after being in the presence of God. It is thinking born from an encounter with God that is not merely a private matter

---

1. See page 4.

but is shared and acted upon. Theology should lead to public action, which is why we speak of public theology.

God's word and guidance is something precious. It is the kind of truth that sets us free, the truth that can cut the cancer from our societies by addressing the ills of our continent. So we have striven to given expression to that word in this book. But books are merely collections of words on a page until they take root in readers' hearts and bear fruit in this world. For that to happen, we need to develop what Alan Boesak, a theologian who played a major role in the dismantling of apartheid in South Africa, calls "the tenderness of conscience."[2]

The Tenderness of Conscience

Theology sets a process in motion. It is born in the womb of prayer, gives birth to a spirituality received in the presence of God and then results in "good works," in just action and in bringing about the kingdom of God.[3]

Preaching, teaching and theology should be conceived "in the desert" or "on the mountain," that is, in the presence of God rather than just in the presence of other people. If these things do not come from an encounter with God, they are simply some form of selfish ideology that can never change the world. It is only when we surrender our own ideas that the ideas of the kingdom of God can take root and shape action. In allowing himself to be crucified, Jesus showed us the way.[4] That "way" is to never use the power we possess for our own benefit. We are to give to the point of sacrificing our own lives to show the world "the way."

The early Christians were called "the people of the Way." There is only one way to a new dawn for our continent, and for the world, and that is Jesus's way, the way of the cross, of example, of sacrifice. As we will see, this truth is deeply anchored in both the Old Testament and the New Testament.

---

2. Allan Boesak, *The Tenderness of Conscience: African Renaissance and the Spirituality of Politics* (Stellenbosch: SUN, 2005).

3. The same truth is well explained by Wes Granberg-Michaelson in "From Mysticism to Politics," *Oneing* 5, no. 2 (2017): 17. So, for the Christian, politics entails an inevitable spiritual journey. But this is not the privatized expression of belief which keeps faith in Jesus contained in an individualized bubble and protects us from the "world." The experience of true faith in the living God is always personal and never individual. Rather, it is a spiritual journey which connects us intrinsically to the presence of God, whose love yearns to save and transform the world. We are called to be "in Christ," which means we share – always imperfectly, and always in community with others – the call to be the embodiment of God's love in the world.

4. J. H. Hellerman, *Embracing Shared Ministry: Power and Status in the Early Church and Why It Matters Today* (Grand Rapids: Kregel, 2013); Richard Rohr, *The Universal Christ* (New York: Convergent, 2019), 139–158.

Micah 6

Micah prophesied at a time when the situation in Israel and Judah was bad with rampant idolatry and numerous false prophets. The people were yearning "for redemption, renewal, and a return to justice and blessing despite the corruption, poverty and violence."[5] They were asking.

> With what shall I come before the LORD
>   and bow down before the exalted God?
> Shall I come before him with burnt offerings,
>   with calves a year old?
> Will the LORD be pleased with thousands of rams,
>   with ten thousand rivers of olive oil?
> Shall I offer my firstborn for my transgression,
>   the fruit of my body for the sin of my soul? (Micah 6:6–7)

The Lord's response was simple:

> He has shown you, O mortal, what is good.
>   And what does the LORD require of you?
> To act justly and to love mercy
>   and to walk humbly with your God. (Micah 6:8)

It really is as simple as that: act justly, love mercy and walk humbly before God. Go public with what the Lord has told you, that is, with your theology. The Reformer John Calvin, the Dutch theologian and politician Abraham Kuyper and the South African Allan Boesak all affirm that acting justly, loving mercy and walking humbly *before God* lead to reformation. The image and likeness of the Trinity, the identity of Christ and the power of the Holy Spirit should convert our conscience, our spirituality and our lives.

Ora et labora is a Latin phrase that has long been used to summarize this process. It means "pray and work." We cannot work and get the Africa we want without prayer. It is in the presence of the Almighty that we are shown the way, that we are converted and saved from our selfish nature.

How to miss our goal is clear from Genesis. Adam and Eve tried to avoid the Lord by hiding. They did not want to take responsibility for creation. They preferred their own little garden. On a bigger scale, the same ethic is illustrated by the building of Babel-like empires with walls that keep out "the other," those in need of food, shelter and protection, so that the privileged few can enjoy the lush hanging gardens of their city.

---

5. *Africa Study Bible* (Carol Stream, IL: Oasis, 2016), 1309.

Peter Storey used four points to explain what Micah 6:8 implies in everyday life:

1. *Witness to the truth.* Do not be deceived by half-truths or blatant lies. Do not lie to yourself or others. Proclaim the truth without fear or prejudice and expose the lies that would destroy us.

2. *Bind up the broken.* In following the example of Jesus our Christ, whose name we bear, always side with the victims of injustice. No matter what your job or vocation, let your life be spent in the ministry of healing the wounded and restoring the downtrodden.

3. *Live the alternative.* Live in such a way that your life is a visible contradiction of the social, political and economic systems that destroy people and creation. There can be no greater calling than to offer your life as a "living picture" of God's loving and just alternative for society and creation.

4. *Replace evil with good.* Work tirelessly in non-violent, Christ-like ways to bring about the dispensation of God's justice, peace and love where God places you. Our lives are not measured by the nobility of our task, but rather by the measure of our cooperation with the God who is justice and love.[6]

Romans 12

In the New Testament and in another context, Paul's words in Romans 12 emphasize the same thing: transformation by the renewing of the mind and call for leaders who serve like Christ did.

Therefore, I urge you, brothers and sisters, in view of God's mercy, to offer your bodies as a living sacrifice, holy and pleasing to God – this is your true and proper worship. Do not conform to the pattern of this world, but be transformed by the renewing of your mind. Then you will be able to test and approve what God's will is – his good, pleasing and perfect will.

For by the grace given me I say to every one of you: Do not think of yourself more highly than you ought, but rather think of yourself with sober judgment, in accordance with the faith God has distributed to each of you. For just as each of us has one

---

6. Peter Storey, *I Beg to Differ: Ministry Amid the Teargas* (Cape Town: Tafelberg, 2018), 131.

body with many members, and these members do not all have the same function, so in Christ we, though many, form one body, and each member belongs to all the others. We have different gifts, according to the grace given to each of us. If your gift is prophesying, then prophesy in accordance with your faith; if it is serving, then serve; if it is teaching, then teach; if it is to encourage, then give encouragement; if it is giving, then give generously; if it is to lead, do it diligently; if it is to show mercy, do it cheerfully. (Rom 12:1–8)

If you want to listen to this passage in a more "applied" version, read these verses in *The Message.*

The Africa God wants will dawn if we are "people of the Way." But we cannot find the right way without the renewing of the mind and tenderness of conscience. *Ora et labora* holds the key to finding the way.

Starting a Movement

Since our 2015 Annual General Meeting, NetACT has been engaged in a discernment process on how to be obedient to the call to engage in public theology that addresses the woes of our continent. It became clear that we should produce a book on public theology that we can use as a handbook in our theological schools. We knew the book should also be written in such a way that it could guide Christians in all walks of life on how to be the salt of the earth and the light of the world *in Africa.*

We told ourselves again and again that this is not "our" thing. We should try to find our place in a much larger movement. We heard the cry from our continent, a cry like that of a woman in childbirth, a cry echoing from shore to shore, from east and west, north and south: stop corruption, give us servant leaders, create just societies, pity and help the poor. Africa is so beautiful; it has so much potential to be a new Eden . . . do something!

In this book we have tried to capture what we have heard in prayer and in the discernment processes taking place at our fifty-plus seminaries all over the continent. In 2019 we had four regional workshops in Angola, Kenya, Malawi and Nigeria where the editors of the book presented the concept and dream for this book to the NetACT network of Christian leaders and organizations. We listened and shared; we prayed and planned ahead. We linked our discussions to the 2019 publication *African Christian Leadership*, which is probably the best empirical study of Christian leadership on our continent.[7] This study confirmed without a shadow of doubt that Africa has outstanding servant leaders in all walks of life. The image and likeness of Jesus Christ is visible in their lives. It is clear that the power of the Holy Spirit working through them made a difference wherever they were. Such leaders are fountains of hope, biblical hope, in our continent. In 2020 and 2021, we would like to have further country-specific conferences where we invite you, the readers, and your organizations to keep the momentum of the Spirit alive.

The Africa God wants and that we dream of can only become a reality through a movement of its many peoples. Such a movement can only make a difference if it is empowered and led by God. When Jesus greeted his disciples, he assured them that all power/authority in heaven and earth has been given to him (Matt 28:18). Then he commanded them: "Therefore go and make disciples of all nations, baptizing them in the name of the Father and of the Son and of the Holy Spirit, and teaching them to obey everything I have commanded you. And surely I am with you always, to the very end of the age" (Matt 28:19–20).

Elsewhere, Jesus told his followers how the Holy Spirit would guide them (John 14:16–27; 17:26–16:15). In Acts 1:8, his precise words are, "But you will receive power when the Holy Spirit comes on you; and you will be my witnesses in Jerusalem, and in all Judea and Samaria, and to the ends of the earth."

We won't change a continent; this book can't change a continent. However, it may play a role and make a contribution to a Spirit-led movement. God can make it happen.

Three Guidelines to Test a Spirit-led Movement

History is one of the best tutors to guide all those who want to join the movement for the Africa God wants. This point is strongly made by the historian Andrew Walls who reminds us that the Christian story "is not a steady, triumphant progression. It is a story of advance and recession."[8] There is a way of introducing and expanding Christianity with a prosperity, health and wealth gospel that in the long run won't transform society but will instead lead to the decline of the church. Instead, Walls shows from historical data

---

7. R. J. Priest and K. Barine, eds. *African Christian Leadership: Realities, Opportunities, and Impact* (Carlisle: Langham Global Library, 2019).

8. Andrew Walls, *The Cross-Cultural Process in Christian History* (Maryknoll, NY: Orbis, 2002), 12. See also Andrew Walls, *The Missionary Movement in Christian History: Studies in the Transmission of Faith* (Maryknoll, NY: Orbis, 1996).

that what is key to transformation is an awareness that Christianity and the church are about Christ.[9] The source of Christian expansion and the driver of transformation is Christ.

Keep in mind that when we talk about Christian expansion, we are not talking about "church growth movements," which can become a numbers game. What we mean by "expansion" is the spread of the kingdom of God, of Christ's reign. Walls discusses three key tests for healthy Christian expansion, namely the church test, the kingdom test and the gospel test.[10] We need to look more at each of these.

The church test

The kingdom will come to Africa and the world if groups of saved people form groups, work in groups and live the values of the kingdom in groups. Such groups are usually called congregations, and they tend to develop their own styles of worship and their own liturgies and cultures. They will grow (expand) as long as their identity is Trinitarian and as long as they are communities of love and service that take responsibility for the world, for creation and for the "other" out there. History proves that the kingdom is not primarily about individual salvation and enlightened individuals. It is about the body of Christ. Only where Jesus reigns in *communities* and becomes visible *in communities* does the influence of those communities begin to change societies, countries and the world.[11]

The kingdom test

When John the Baptist sent messengers to asked Jesus if he was the one who would bring in the kingdom of God, Jesus replied with actions that demonstrated the presence of the kingdom:[12]

> At that very time Jesus cured many who had diseases, sicknesses and evil spirits, and gave sight to many who were blind. So he replied to the messengers, "Go back and report to John what you have seen and heard: The blind receive sight, the lame walk, those who have leprosy are cleansed, the deaf hear, the dead are raised,

---

9. Walls, *Cross-Cultural Process*, 9.
10. Walls, 1–26.
11. Walls, 1–13.
12. Walls, 13–18.

and the good news is proclaimed to the poor. Blessed is anyone who does not stumble on account of me." (Luke 7:21–23)

The sign of God's kingdom and reign is the demise of the principalities and powers, of evil and sin.[13] The work of the Holy Spirit is so powerful that nothing can withstand it. One of the most beautiful manifestations of this power is conversion, when a human being is saved or in other words turned around and restored to a right relationship with God.[14]

We know from history that when a church is not a sign of the kingdom, it actually becomes a countersign that in time leads to the decline of Christianity.[15] Mere rhetoric about the Africa we want will not lead to transformation and the Africa God wants. Without Christ-centred communities that live by the kingdom values in the same way that light expels darkness, transformation will not happen.

The gospel test

This third test is in a sense the hardest to apply. The gospel test refers to "the effect of Christianity upon mankind as a whole, or more specifically, the effect of Jesus on individual lives and civilizations. . . . The effect of Christ on people and on cultures."[16] The gospel is about the good news that Jesus died and rose again, that Jesus defeated the principalities and powers and freed us to love and care and reach out. This is the good news that changed the world. The gospel is not solely about something that is going to happen in a new dispensation on Resurrection Day. The gospel is about a reality that took place when the Holy Spirit was poured out at Pentecost and that continues to happen. Ask anyone who has experienced the miracle of conversion what happened. It is an indescribable joy that causes us to want to burst out in song and sharing.

---

13. Walter Wink, *Engaging the Powers: Discernment and Resistance in a World of Domination* (Minneapolis: Fortress, 1998); Walter Wink, *When the Powers Fall: Reconciliation in the Healing of Nations* (Minneapolis: Fortress, 1998); M. J. Dawn, *Powers, Weakness, and the Tabernacling of God* (Grand Rapids: Eerdmans, 2001).

14. Colin Brown, ed., *New International Dictionary of New Testament Theology* (Grand Rapids: Zondervan, 1975), 1.354.

15. Walls, *Cross-Cultural Process*, 15.

16. Walls, 18.

Conclusion

The patterns of growth and decline of Christianity over the last 2000 years give us some clues on the way forward as we seek to move out of the *humanly speaking* hopeless situation in our continent. We are reminded of the words spoken to the aged Sara when she doubted that she would conceive a son, "Is anything too hard for the LORD?" (Gen 18:14). Similarly, just before the nation of Judah went into exile, Jeremiah bought a piece of land near Jerusalem because God had promised that a remnant would return to the promised land. Speaking in faith, Jeremiah said, "Ah, Sovereign LORD, you have made the heavens and the earth by your great power and outstretched arm. Nothing is too hard for you" (Jer 32:17; see also Jer 32:27). When Mary, the mother of Jesus, was told by an angel that she would bear a son, she asked the angel how this would be possible because she was a virgin. The angel answered, "The Holy Spirit will come on you, and the power of the Most High will overshadow you. . . . For no word from God will ever fail" (Luke 1:35–37). Mary replied in faith, "I am the Lord's servant. . . . May your word to me be fulfilled" (Luke 1:38).

If we believe that nothing is impossible for God and that God can change the fate of a continent, we will have to answer like Mary: "I am the Lord's servant. . . . May your word to me be fulfilled."

God can change the continent, not us. Step one of *ora et labora*, pray and work, is a process of continuous conversion and learning to obediently follow Christ in all walks of life.[17]

The chapters in this book have focused on some of the most crucial areas in our societies. They offer guidance on what we believe the Bible teaches us about basic Christian principles that are applicable in those spheres. We have called on Christians to address corruption and to take arms against the principalities and powers that destroy, kill and maim our world.

In the previous chapter and in this one, we have thought about the role of the church. We are calling on the church to be a faith community, a house of prayer, where God the Holy Spirit can transform us into the image and likeness of the Trinity.

---

17. In 2 Corinthians 11:1–12:10, Paul bears testimony to how difficult it is to trust the Lord to do the impossible. He gives an overview of the dangers and challenges he had to face in his life. And then in retrospect, Paul shares the secret that the Lord told him: "'My grace is sufficient for you, for my power is made perfect in weakness.' Therefore I will boast all the more gladly about my weaknesses, so that Christ's power may rest on me. That is why, for Christ's sake, I delight in weaknesses, in insults, in hardships, in persecutions, in difficulties. For when I am weak, then I am strong" (2 Cor 12:9–10).

Ora et labora. If the church are people of the Way, following Jesus, our continent can change. Public theology is about being the hands and feet of Christ that serve a broken world. It does ask for sacrifice. The cross is the only way to resurrection and renewal. Christ triumphed over the principalities and powers. The Africa God wants is possible.

Questions

1. What are you going to do with what you have learned from this book?
2. *Ora et labora*: How will you make the time to pray and seek God's guidance as to what you should be doing?

Appendix

Agenda 2063:
The Africa We Want

AGENDA 2063 is Africa's blueprint and master plan for transforming Africa into the global powerhouse of the future. It is the continent's strategic framework that aims to deliver on its goal for inclusive and sustainable development and is a concrete manifestation of the pan-African drive for unity, self-determination, freedom, progress and collective prosperity pursued under Pan-Africanism and African Renaissance. The genesis of Agenda 2063 was the realisation by African leaders that there was a need to refocus and reprioritise Africa's agenda from the struggle against apartheid and the attainment of political independence for the continent which had been the focus of The Organisation of African Unity (OAU), the precursor of the African Union; and instead to prioritise inclusive social and economic development, continental and regional integration, democratic governance and peace and security amongst other issues aimed at repositioning Africa to becoming a dominant player in the global arena.[1]

This document played an important role in the planning of this book as we discussed "the Africa we don't want" and "the Africa God wants." All contributors were advised to read *Agenda 2063*, and we urge all those who use this book to read it and consider how they can contribute to fulfilling the vision.

The full popular version of *Agenda 2063: The Africa We Want* is available in several languages at https://au.int/en/Agenda2063/popular_version.

---

1. "Agenda 2063: The Africa We Want, Overview," African Union, https://au.int/agenda2063/overview.

Bibliography

Accra Confession, The. *World Communion of Reformed Churches*. http://wcrc.ch/accra/the-accra-confession.

Acemoglu, Daron, and James A. Robinson. *Why Nations Fail: The Origins of Power, Prosperity, and Poverty*. London: Profile Books, 2012.

Achebe, Chinua. *A Man of the People*. London: Heinemann, 1966.

———. *Things Fall Apart*. London: Heinemann, 1958.

Achiron, Marilyn. *Nationality and Statelessness: Handbook for Parliamentarians* (2014). UNHCR. https://www.unhcr.org/protection/statelessness/53d8ddab6/nationality-statelessness-handbook-parliamentarians-22.html.

Addai, William. *Reforming Leadership Across Africa*. Accra, Ghana: William Addai, 2009.

Adebisi, Y., and I. Ononye. "Untold Stories of Suffering in Government Boarding Schools." *Saturday Independent* (20 October 2018): 18–19.

Adegoke, Yemisi, and BBC Africa Eye. "Like. Share. Kill: Nigerian Police Say False Information on Facebook Is Killing People." BBC News, 13 November 2018.

Adeyemo, Tokunboh. *Africa Bible Commentary*. Nairobi: Word Alive; Grand Rapids: Zondervan, 2006.

———. *Is Africa Cursed*. Nairobi: WordAlive, 2017.

Adu-Gymafi, Jones. "Young People's Participation in Public Policy Formation: A Case Study of the National Youth Policy of Ghana." Doctoral thesis presented at the University of London, 2013.

African Commission on Human and Peoples Rights (ACHPR) and International Working Group for Indigenous Affairs (IWGIA). *Indigenous Peoples in Africa: The Forgotten Peoples? The African Commission's work on indigenous peoples in Africa*. Banjul: African Union, 2006. https://www.iwgia.org/en/resources/publications/305-books/2545-indigenous-peoples-in-africa-the-forgotten-peoples-the-african-commissions-work-on-indigenous-peoples-in-africa.

African Leadership Study (2016). "17 Insights into Leadership in Africa." http://www.africaleadershipstudy.org/wp-content/uploads/2016/07/AfricaLeadership_17Insights_v6.2.pdf.

African Union. *Agenda 2063: The African We Want*. Addis Ababa: African Union, 2015. https://au.int/en/Agenda2063/popular_version.

Africa Study Bible. Carol Stream, IL: Oasis, 2016.

Agoro, Saviour Nathan A. "A Study of Selected Themes in Christian Drama in Nigeria." 2002. http://www.globalacademicgroup.com/journals/the%20nigerian%20academic%20forum/Saviour14.pdf.

———. "The Notion of Christian Comedy." *Kiabara: Journal of Humanities* 17, no. 1 (2011). http://www.academix.ng/demo/search/paper.html?idd=3300014626.

Agulanna, Christopher. "Community and African Well Being in Human Culture." *TRAMES* 14 (64/59), no. 3 (2010): 282.

Akper, G. I. "The Role of the 'Ordinary Reader' in Gerald O. West's Hermeneutics." *Scriptura* 88 (2005): 1–13.

Al Jazeera English. *White Farmers Thrive in Zambia Years after Driven from Zimbabwe*, 23 November 2017. https://www.youtube.com/watch?v=5_Ym0M31MpE&vl=en.

Allen, John. *Rabble-Rouser for Peace: The Authorised Biography of Desmond Tutu*. New York: Random House, 2012.

Ango, Samuel P. "Educating for Justice and Righteousness in Nigerian Society: Applying Freire's Pedagogy of the Oppressed." *International Journal of Christianity and Education* 22, no. 2 (2018): 108.

Asamoah-Gyadu, J. Kwabena. "God Is Big in Africa: Pentecostal Megachurches and a Changing Religious Landscape." *Material Religion* (29 May 2019): 1–4, 6.

———. "Hearing, Viewing, and Touched by the Spirit: Televangelism in Contemporary African Christianity." In *Global and Local Televangelism*, edited by Pradip Ninan Thomas and Philip Lee. Basingstoke, UK: Palgrave Macmillan, 2012.

Asante, Emmanuel. "Ecology: Untapped Resource of Pan-vitalism in Africa." *AFER: African Ecclesial Review* 27 (1985): 289–293.

Atta-Asamoah, Andrews. "Youth of Africa: Unemployment, Social Cohesion and Political Instability." UNICEF, Office of Research-Innocenti. https://www.unicef-irc.org/article/1060-youth-of-africa-unemployment-social-cohesion-and-political-instability.html.

Babalola, A. "The Dwindling Standards of Education in Nigeria: The Way Forward." First distinguished lecture series, Lead City University, Ibadan, Nigeria, 2006.

Bagu, Kajit J. "Plurality, Peacebuilding and Islam: Gülen Optimism and the Cognitive Justice Prism." In *The Hizmet Movement and Peacebuilding: Global Cases*, edited by Mohammed Abu-Nimer and Timothy Seidel. Lanham, MD: Lexington, 2018.

———. *Peacebuilding, Constitutionalism and the Global South: The Case for Cognitive Justice Plurinationalism*. Abingdon, UK: Routledge, 2019.

Bandura, Albert. "Modeling Theory: Some Traditions, Trends, and Disputes." In *Recent Trends in Social Learning Theory*. Cambridge, MA: Academic Press, 1972.

Baranik, Lisa E., Carrie S. Hurst, and Lillian T. Eby. "The Stigma of Being a Refugee: A Mixed-Method Study of Refugees' Experiences of Vocational Stress." *Journal of Vocational Behavior* 105 (2018): 121.

Barbour, Ian. *Religion in an Age of Science*. New York: Harper Collins, 1990.

Barrow, J. "The Variables of Leadership: A Review and Conceptual Framework." *Academy of Management Review* 2 (1977): 231–251.

Bauer, Roxanne. "How to Use Social Media to Fight Corruption." World Economic Forum, 12 December 2014. https://www.weforum.org/agenda/2014/12/how-to-use-social-media-to-fight-corruption/.

Bedford-Strohm, Heinrich. "Prophetic Witness and Public Discourse in European Societies: A German Perspective." *HTS Teologiese Studies/Theological Studies* 66, no. 1 (2010): 1–6.

Beetham, David. "What Future for Economic and Social Rights?" *Political Studies* 43 (1995).

Belhar Confession, The (September 1986). https://www.pcusa.org/site_media/media/uploads/theologyandworship/pdfs/belhar.pdf.

Benhabib, S. "Towards a Deliberative Model of Democratic Legitimacy." In *Democracy and Difference: Contesting the Boundaries of the Political*, edited by S. Benhabib. Princeton: Princeton University Press, 1996. http://www.untag-smd.ac.id/files/Perpustakaan_Digital_1/DEMOCRACY%20Democracy%20and%20difference%20Contesting%20the%20boundaries%20of%20the%20political.pdf.

Bertot, John Carlo, Paul T. Jaeger, and Justin M. Grimes. "Promoting Transparency and Accountability through ICTs, Social Media, and Collaborative E-Government." *Transforming Government: People, Process and Policy* 6, no. 1 (2012): 78–91. https://www.emerald.com/insight/content/doi/10.1108/17506161211214831/full/html.

Bethell, G. *Mathematics Education in Sub-Saharan Africa: Status, Challenges and Opportunities*. Washington: World Bank, 2016.

Bloomberg, Business Tech. "Eskom's Massive Workforce Problem: Over-Staffed and Over-Paid." (3 April 2018). https://businesstech.co.za/news/business/235299/eskoms-massive-workforce-problem-over-staffed-and-over-paid/.

Boesak, Allan. *The Tenderness of Conscience: African Renaissance and the Spirituality of Politics*. Stellenbosch: SUN, 2005.

Bolden, R., and P. Kirk. "African Leadership: Surfacing New Understandings through Leadership Development." *International Journal of Cross Cultural Management* 9, no. 1 (2009): 69–86.

Bosch, David J. *Transforming Mission: Paradigm Shifts in Theology of Mission*. Maryknoll, NY: Orbis, 1991.

Brown, Colin, ed. *New International Dictionary of New Testament Theology*. Grand Rapids: Zondervan, 1975.

Browne, Evie. "Impact of Communication Campaigns to Deter Irregular Migration." Governance and Social Development Resource Centre Helpdesk Research Report 1248, University of Birmingham, 2015. https://gsdrc.org/wp-content/uploads/2015/09/HQ1248.pdf.

Brueggemann, Walter. *Journey to the Common Good*. Louisville, KY: Westminster John Knox, 2010.

Buchanan, Mark. *Your Church Is Too Safe: Why Following Christ Turns the World Upside-Down*. Grand Rapids: Zondervan, 2015.

Campbell, John. "South African Media Recognized for Exposing Zuma on Foreign Corruption." *Council on Foreign Relations*, 12 April 2018. https://www.cfr.org/blog/south-african-media-recognized-exposing-zuma-corruption.

Casberg, C. T. "The Surprising Theological Possibilities of Virtual Reality." *Christianity Today*, 11 November 2016. https://www.christianitytoday.com/ct/2016/november-web-only/surprising-theological-possibilities-of-virtual-reality.html.

Castells, Manuel. *End of Millennium: The Information Age – Economy, Society and Culture*, vol. 3, 2nd ed. Oxford: Blackwell, 2000.

———. *Networks of Outrage and Hope: Social Movements in the Internet Age*, 2nd ed. Cambridge: Polity, 2015.

———. *The Power of Identity: The Information Age: Economy, Society and Culture*, vol. 2, 2nd ed. Oxford: Blackwell, 2004.

———. *The Rise of the Network Society: The Information Age – Economy, Society and Culture*, vol. 1. Oxford: Blackwell, 1996.

———. *Rupture: The Crisis of Liberal Democracy*. Cambridge: Polity, 2019.

Charles, J. Daryl, and Timothy J. Demy. *War, Peace, and Christianity: Questions and Answers from a Just-War Perspective*. Wheaton, IL: Crossway, 2010.

Chitando, E. "Equipped and Ready to Serve? Transforming Theology and Religious Studies in Africa." *Missionalia* 38, no. 2 (2010): 198.

Chitiyo, Knox. "The Struggles for Zimbabwe, South Africa and SADC: Liberation War Theology and Post-Nationalism." *The RUSI Journal* 153, no. 3 (1 June 2008): 80–86. https://doi.org/10.1080/03071840802249638.

Christian Churches Together. *What Does the Bible Say about Refugees and Immigrants?* (2013). http://christianchurchestogether.org/wp-content/uploads/2013/01/What-Does-Bible-Say-Disciples-of-Christ.pdf.

Christian, Jon. "HTC Thinks Virtual Reality's Killer App Could Be Christianity: Christians Adapted Radio and Rock Music. Maybe VR Will Be Next." *Futurism* (16 December 2018): 6.

Claassens, Juliana M., and B. C. Birch. *Restorative Readings: The Old Testament, Ethics and Human Dignity*. Eugene, OR: Pickwick, 2015.

Cody, A. A. *History of Old Testament Priesthood*. Rome: Pontifical Biblical Institute, 1969.

Conradie, Ernst M. "Christianity and the Environment in (South) Africa: Four Dominant Approaches." In *Christian in Public: Aims, Methodologies and Issues in Public Theology*, edited by Len Hansen, 227–250. Stellenbosch: SUN Press, 2007.

———. "Notions and Forms of Ecumenicity: Some South African Perspectives." In *South African Perspectives on Notions and Forms of Ecumenicity*, edited by E. M. Conradie, 13–15. Stellenbosch: SUN, 2013.

Cornish, Sandie. "Welcoming Christ in Refugees & Displaced Persons: Discussion Guide to the Pastoral Guidelines." Social Spirituality (2013). https://social-spirituality.net/wp-content/uploads/2013/07/Discussion-Guide-Refugees-Displaced-Persons-Pastoral-Guidelines.pdf.

Crawley, Heaven, Franck Duvell, Katharine Jones, Simon McMahon, and Nando Sigona. *Unravelling Europe's "Migration Crisis."* Bristol: Policy Press, 2008.

Crisp, Jeff. *Beyond the Nexus: UNHCR's Evolving Perspective on Refugee Protection and International Migration.* New Issues in Refugee Research, Paper No. 155. UNHCR: Geneva, 2008. https://www.unhcr.org/4d9349ae9.html.

Curtis, Kimberly. "'Fake News' Is Shaping Hotly Contested Elections in Kenya: The Results Could Be Deadly." *UN Dispatch,* 2 August 2017. https://www.undispatch.com/fake-news-shaping-hotly-contested-elections-kenya-results-deadly/.

da Silva Almeida, L., and A. H. Rodrigues Franco. "Critical Thinking: Its Relevance for Education in a Shifting Society." *Revista de Psicologia* 29, no. 1 (2011): 178–195.

Dawn, M. J. *Powers, Weakness, and the Tabernacling of God.* Grand Rapids: Eerdmans, 2001.

Deb Roy, Rohan. "Science Must Fall? Why It Still Needs to Be Decolonised." *The Citizen,* 9 April 2018. https://citizen.co.za/talking.../1science-must-fall-why-it-still-needs-to-be-decolonised.

Dedji, Valentin. *Reconstruction and Renewal in Christian Theology.* Nairobi: Acton, 2003.

de Gruchy, J. W. *Cry Justice! Prayer, Meditations and Readings from South Africa.* London: Collins Liturgical Publications, 1986.

de Gruchy, Steve. *Keeping Body and Soul Together: Reflections by Steve de Gruchy on Theology and Development,* ed. Beverley Haddad. Pietermaritzburg: Cluster, 2015.

Dekker, H., and S. W. Wolff. "Re-Inventing Research-based Teaching and Learning." Paper presented at the European Forum for Enhanced Collaboration in Teaching, Brussels, 5 December 2016.

DeLong-Bas, Natana J. *Wahhabi Islam: From Revival to Reform to Global Jihad.* Oxford: Oxford University Press, 2004.

Dewey, J. *Democracy and Education.* New York: Macmillan, 1916. https://www.gutenberg.org/files/852/852-h/852-h.htm.

Diakonia Council of Churches. *The Oikos Journey: A Theological Reflection on the Economic Crisis in South Africa.* Durban: Diakonia Council of Churches, 2006. https://www.diakonia.org.za/wp-content/uploads/bsk-pdf-manager/39_The_Oikos_Journey_3.pdf.

Douglas, M. *Purity and Danger.* London: Routledge & Keegan Paul, 1966.

Dow, Philip E. *Virtuous Minds: Intellectual Character Development for Students, Educators and Parents.* Downers Grove, IL: InterVarsity Press, 2013.

Dube, Musa W. "Exegeting the Darkness: Reading the Botswana Colonial Bible." Presented in Atlanta at the SBL Annual Meeting, 2010.

———. *Other Ways of Reading: African Women and the Bible.* Atlanta: SBL, 2001.

Dube, Musa W., and G. West, eds. *The Bible in Africa: Transactions, Trajectories, and Trends.* Leiden: Brill, 2000.

du Preez, M. "The Socrates of Africa and His Student: A Case of Pre-Colonial African Leadership." *Leadership* 8, no. 1 (2012): 7.

Ecumenical Foundation of Southern Africa. *The Land Is Crying for Justice: A Discussion Document on Christianity and Environmental Justice in South Africa.* Stellenbosch: EFSA, 2002.

Egelhofer, Jana Laura, and Sophie Lecheler. "Fake News as a Two-Dimensional Phenomenon: A Framework and Research Agenda." *Annals of the International Communication Association* 43, no. 2 (2019): 97–116.

Estes, Steve. *I Am a Man!: Race, Manhood, and the Civil Rights Movement.* Chapel Hill: University of North Carolina Press, 2005.

Fam, Medhat. "Paulo Freire's Approach to Education." https://www.academia.edu/37432024/Paulo_Freires_approach_to_Education.

Faull, Andrew. "Corruption and the South African Police Service: A Review and Its Implications." *Institute for Security Studies Papers* 150 (1 September 2007): 20.

Fønnebø, L. "A Grounded-Theory Study of the Teaching Methods of Jesus: An Emergent Instructional Mode." PhD Dissertation 369, 2011. Digital Commons @ Andrews University Dissertations. https://digitalcommons.andrews.edu/dissertations/369.

Forster, Dion A. "Democracy and Social Justice in Glocal Contexts." *International Journal of Public Theology* 12, no. 1 (2018): 1–4.

———. "A Kairos Moment for the Methodist Church of Southern Africa? Engaging Nationalism and State Theology in the Democratic South Africa." *Methodist Review: A Journal of Wesleyan and Methodist Studies* 11 (2019): 1–23.

Forster, Dion A., and Johann W. Oostenbrink. "Where Is the Church on Monday?: Awakening the Church to the Theology and Practice of Ministry and Mission in the Marketplace." *In Die Skriflig* 49, no. 3 (2015): 1–8.

Francis (Pope). *Encyclical Letter Laudato si of the Holy Father Francis on Care for Our Common Home.* Vatican City: Vatican Press, 2015. http://w2.vatican.va/content/francesco/en/encyclicals/documents/papa-francesco_20150524_enciclica-laudato-si.html.

———. *Laudato si* (2015). http://w2.vatican.va/content/francesco/en/encyclicals/documents/papa-francesco_20150524_enciclica-laudato-si.html.

Freire, Paulo. *Education for Critical Consciousness.* New York: Bloomsbury Academic, 2013 (1967).

———. *Pedagogy of Hope.* New York: Bloomsbury, 1992.

———. *Pedagogy of the Oppressed.* New York: Seabury, 1973.

GAB. "The Global Anticorruption Blog." https://globalanticorruptionblog.com/about/.

Gabriel, E., C. Woolford-Hunt, and E. M. Hooley. "Creating a Christ-Centred Climate for Educational Excellence: Philosophical, Instructional, Relational, Assessment and Counselling Dimensions." *Catalyst* 23, no. 2 (2016).

Gambari, Ibrahim. "The Role of Religion in National Life: Reflections on Recent Experiences in Nigeria." In *Religion and National Integration in Africa: Islam, Christianity, and Politics in the Sudan and Nigeria*, edited by John O. Hunwick, 98. Evanston, IL: Northwestern University Press, 1992.

Geertz, Clifford. *The Interpretation of Cultures.* London: Hutchinson, 1975.

Gellner, Ernest. *Conditions of Liberty: Civil Society and Its Rivals.* Harmondsworth: Penguin, 1996.

Getui, Mary N., and E. A. Obeng, eds. *Theology of Reconstruction: Exploratory Essays.* Nairobi: Acton, 1999.

Gifford, Paul. *African Christianity: Its Public Role.* London: Hurst, 1998.

Giroux, H. A., and P. McLaren. "Teacher Education and the Politics of Engagement: The Case for Democratic Schooling." In *Breaking Free: The Transformative Power of Critical Pedagogy,* edited by P. Leistyna, A. Woodrum, and S. A. Sherbton, 301–331. Cambridge: Harvard Educational Review, 1996.

Gitari, David. "Church and Politics in Kenya." *Transformation* 8, no. 3 (1 July 1991): 7–17.

Gitau, Samson K. *The Environmental Crisis: A Challenge for African Christians.* Nairobi: Acton, 2000.

Global Policy Forum. "Failed States: Where Life Is Cheap and Talk Is Loose." Originally published in *The Economist* (17 March 2011). https://www.globalpolicy.org/nations-a-states/failed-states/49966-failed-states-where-life-is-cheap-and-talk-is-loose.html.

Global Witness. "About Us." https://www.globalwitness.org/en/about-us/.

Goba, B. "The Role of the Church in Moral Renewal." Unpublished paper presented at the annual meeting of the Diakonia Council of Churches, Durban, South Africa, 23 June 2007.

Goris, Indira, Julia Harrington, and Sebastian Köhn. *Statelessness: What It Is and Why It Matters* (2009), 5. http://hr.law.vnu.edu.vn/sites/default/files/resources/what_is_statelessness.pdf.

Granberg-Michaelson, Wes. "From Mysticism to Politics." *Oneing* 5, no. 2 (2017): 17.

Greenfeld, Liah, and Michael Martin. *Center: Ideas and Institutions.* Chicago: University of Chicago Press, 1988.

Habermas, Jürgen. *Knowledge and Human Interest,* translated by Jeremy J. Shapiro. Cambridge: Polity Press, 1987.

Haddad, B. "Theologising Development: A Gendered Analysis of Poverty, Survival and Faith." *Journal of Theology for Southern Africa* 10 (2001): 6.

Hanciles, Jehu. *Beyond Christendom: Globalization, African Migration and the Transformation of the West.* Maryknoll, NY: Orbis, 2008.

Harding, F. "Africa and the Moving Image: Television, Film and Video." *Journal of African Cultural Studies* 16, no. 1 (2003): 71. http://www.jstor.org/stable/3181386.

Hassan, Idayat. "Nigerian Political Parties Are Weaponising Fake News." *Mail and Guardian,* 21 February 2019. https://mg.co.za/article/2019-02-21-nigerian-political-parties-are-weaponising-fake-news.

Hathaway, Bridget, and Flavian Kishekwa. *Included and Valued: A Practical Theology of Disability.* Carlisle: Langham Global Library, 2019.

Hauerwas, Stanley. *In Good Company: The Church as Polis.* Notre Dame: University of Notre Dame Press, 1995.

Hauerwas, Stanley, and W. H. Willimon. *Resident Aliens.* Nashville: Abingdon Press, 1989.

Hellerman, J. H. *Embracing Shared Ministry: Power and Status in the Early Church and Why It Matters Today.* Grand Rapids: Kregel, 2013.

Hendriks, H. Jurgens. "A Change of Heart: Missional Theology and Social Development." In *Religion and Social Development in Post-Apartheid South Africa*, edited by Ignatius Swart, Hermann Rocher, Sulina Green and Johannes Erasmus, 278–279. Stellenbosch: Sun Media, 2010.

———. *Studying Congregations in Africa.* Wellington: Lux Verbi, 2004.

Hinsley, F. Harry. *Sovereignty*, 2nd ed. Cambridge: Cambridge University Press, 1986.

Hochschild, Adam. *King Leopold's Ghost: A Story of Greed, Terror, and Heroism in Colonial Africa.* Boston: Houghton Mifflin, 1999.

Holmes, Stephen. "A Theology of Social Media." Ethics Daily.com (3 December 2012). https://ethicsdaily.com/a-theology-of-social-media-cms-20248/.

Hunter, S. *Black Death: AIDS in Africa.* New York: St Martin's Press, 2015.

Inyang, Ofonime. *Introduction to Theatre and Media Arts Practice: A Beginner's Guide.* Lagos: Bezeliel, 2016.

Janvier, George. *A Vision for Teaching.* Bukuru: Africa Christian Textbooks, 2018.

Jenkins, P. *The Next Christendom: The Coming of Global Christianity.* Oxford: Oxford University Press, 2002.

John Paul II (Pope). "*Veritatis Splendor*, The Splendour of Truth." Rome: Vatican, 1993.

Johnson, Bridget. "A History of Hutu-Tutsi Conflict." Thoughts.Co (7 May 2019). https://www.thoughtco.com/history-of-hutu-tutsi-conflict-3554917.

Jordan Smith, Daniel. "Corruption, NGOs, and Development in Nigeria." *Third World Quarterly* 31, no. 2 (1 March 2010): 243–258.

Kaba Ahmadu, Jacky. "Africa's Migration Brain Drain: Factors Contributing to the Mass Emigration of Africa's Elite to the West." In *The New African Diaspora*, edited by Isidore Okpewho and Nkiru Nzegwu, 109. Bloomington: Indiana University Press, 2009.

Kalabamu, F. "Patriarchy and Women's Land Rights in Botswana." *Land Use Policy* 23, no. 3 (2004): 237.

Kamlongera, Christopher F. *Theatre for Development: The Case of Malawi.* Cambridge: Cambridge University Press, 2009.

Kanyoro, Musimbi. "Culture." In *Dictionary of Third World Theologies*, edited by V. Fabella and R. S. Sugirtharajah, 62–63. Maryknoll, NY: Orbis, 2000.

Kanyoro, Musimbi, and N. J. Njoroge, eds. *Groaning in Faith: African Women in the Household of God.* Nairobi: Acton, 1996.

Kaplan, A. M., and M. Haenlein. "Users of the World, Unite! The Challenges and Opportunities of Social Media." *Business Horizons* 53, no. 1 (2010): 59–68.

Karakoc, M. "The Significance of Critical Thinking Ability in Terms of Education." *International Journal of Humanities and Social Sciences* 6, no. 7 (July 2016): 81–84. https://pdfs.semanticscholar.org/8456/db20169266fb23758413dfcf5a11aa4b3c67.pdf?_ga=2.219698974.641678238.1571334140-1774160800.1571334140.

Kato, Byang H. *Theological Pitfalls in Africa.* Kumasi: Evangel, 1975.

Katongole, Emmanuel. *Born from Lament: The Theology and Politics of Hope in Africa.* Grand Rapids: Eerdmans, 2017.

———. *A Future for Africa: Critical Essays in Christian Social Imagination.* Scranton, PA: University of Scranton Press, 2005.

———. *The Sacrifice of Africa: A Political Theology for Africa.* Grand Rapids: Eerdmans, 2011.

Keener, Craig S. *The IVP Bible Background Commentary: New Testament.* Downers Grove, IL: IVP Academic, 2014.

Kenga, C. "The Role of Religion in Politics and Governance in Kenya." Thesis submitted to the University of Nairobi for an MA in International Studies, 2014. http://erepository.uonbi.ac.ke/bitstream/handle/11295/100199/Kenga-The%20Role%20Of%20Religion%20In%20Politics%20And%20Governance%20In%20Kenya.pdf?sequence=1&isAllowed=yIbid.

Kgatle, Mookgo S. "Social Media and Religion: Missiological Perspective on the Link between Facebook and the Emergence of Prophetic Churches in Southern Africa." *Verbum et Ecclesia* 39, no. 1 (2018): 1–6.

Kimotho, S. G., and R. N. Nyaga. "Digitized Ethnic Hate Speech: Understanding Effects of Hate Speech on Citizen Journalism in Kenya." *Advances in Language and Literary Studies (ALLS)* 7, no. 3 (2016): 189–200.

Knighton, Ben. "Issues of African Theology at the Turn of the Millennium." *Transformation* 21, no. 3 (2004): 150.

Koopman, Nico. "The Beyers Naudé Centre for Public Theology: Five Years On." In *Christian in Public: Aims, Methodologies and Issues in Public Theology,* edited by Len Hanson, 281. Stellenbosch: Beyers Naudé Series on Public Theology, 2007.

———. "In Search of a Transforming Public Theology: Drinking from the Wells of Black Theology." In *Contesting Post-Racialism: Conflicted Churches in the United States and South Africa,* edited by R. D. Smith et al., 211–255. Jackson: University of Mississippi Press, 2015.

———. "Public Theology as Prophetic Theology: More than Utopianism and Criticism." *Journal of Theology for Southern Africa* 133 (2009): 118.

———. "Public Theology in (South) Africa: A Trinitarian Approach." *International Journal of Public Theology* 1 (2007): 188–209.

———. "Racism in the Post-Apartheid South Africa." In *Questions About Life and Morality: Christian Ethics in South Africa Today,* edited by Louise Kretzschmar and Len Hulley, 165. Pretoria: Van Schaik, 1998. http://philpapers.org/rec/KOORIT.

———. "Some Contours for Public Theology in South Africa." *International Journal of Practical Theology* 14, no. 1 (2010): 123–138.

———. "Some Theological and Anthropological Perspectives on Human Dignity and Human Rights." *Scriptura* 95 (2007): 177–185.

Küng, Hans. "Declaration toward a Global Ethic." Parliament of the World's Religions (1993). https://www.global-ethic.org/declaration-toward-a-global-ethic/.

Kunhiyop, Samuel W. "Poverty: Good News for Africa." *Africa Journal of Evangelical Theology* 20, no. 1 (2001): 4. https://www.biblicalstudies.org.uk/pdf/ajet/20-1_003.pdf.

Lemarchand, Rene. *Burundi: Ethnic Conflict and Genocide.* Cambridge: Cambridge University Press, 1996.

Leo XII (Pope). "Rerum Novarum – Encyclical Letter of Pope Leo XIII on the Conditions of Labor" (1891). Providence College Digital Commons. https://digitalcommons.providence.edu/catholic_documents/13/.

Leonard, Gary S. D., ed. *The Kairos Documents.* Kwazulu Natal: University of KwaZulu Natal, 2010. For the full text of the Kairos Document, see https://kairossouthernafrica.wordpress.com/2011/05/08/the-south-africa-kairos-document-1985/.

Longman, Timothy. "Church Politics and the Genocide in Rwanda." *Journal of Religion in Africa* 31, no. 2 (1 January 2001): 163–186.

MacRobert, Jo. "Ungadinwa Nangomso – Don't Get Tired Tomorrow: A History of the Black Sash Advice Office in Cape Town 1968 to 1980." Unpublished PhD dissertation, University of Cape Town, 1993.

Mafeje, A. "Theory of Democracy and the African Discourse: Breaking Bread with Fellow Travellers." In *Democratisation Processes in Africa: Problems and Prospects*, edited by E. Chole and J. Ibrahim, 5–28. Dakar: CODESRIA, 1995.

Magezi, V. *HIV/AIDS, Poverty and Pastoral Care and Counselling.* Stellenbosch: African Sun Media, 2007.

Maluleke, Tinyiko Sam. "Of Africanised Bees and Africanised Churches: Ten Theses on African Christianity." *Missionalia* 38, no. 3 (2010): 373.

———. "Reflections and Resources: The Elusive Public of Public Theology: A Response to William Storrar." *International Journal of Public Theology* 5, no. 1 (2011): 79–89.

Mambo, Elias. "Embattled Chombo's Vast Property Empire under the Spotlight." *The Zimbabwe Independent*, 8 December 2017. https://www.theindependent.co.zw/2017/12/08/embattled-chombos-vast-property-empire-spotlight/.

Mambodiyani, Andrew. "Bank Loans beyond Reach for Zimbabwe Farmers without Land Titles." *Reuters*, 20 July 2016. https://www.reuters.com/article/us-zimbabwe-landrights-farming-idUSKCN1001R4.

Mamdani, Mahmood. "The Social Basis of Constitutionalism in Africa." *Journal of Modern African Studies* (1990): 360.

Manala, M. J. "'A Better Life for All': A Reality or a Pipe-Dream? A Black Theology Intervention in Conditions of Poor Service Delivery in the Democratic South Africa." *Scriptura: International Journal of Bible, Religion and Theology in Southern Africa* 105, no. 1 (1 January 2010): 519–531.

Mandela, Nelson. *Long Walk to Freedom.* Boston: Little, Brown, 1994.

Mangalwadi, Vishal. *The Book that Made Your World: How the Bible Created the Soul of Western Civilization.* Nashville: Thomas Nelson, 2011.

Masango, M. "Leadership in the African Context." *Verbum et Ecclesia* 23, no. 3 (2002): 707–718.

Mathebula, E. M. "A Critical Analysis of the Crime Prevention Role of the Military Police Division in the South African National Defence Force (SANDF)." Unpublished doctoral dissertation, University of South Africa (UNISA), 2018.

Mathope, Gosebo. "Zim's 'Most Corrupt Official' Reportedly Found with R140m Cash, 'Owned 100 Properties.'" *The Citizen*, 20 November 2017. https://citizen.co.za/news/news-africa/1733903/zims-most-corrupt-official-reportedly-found-with-r140m-cash-owned-100-properties/.

Maundeni, Z. "Why the African Renaissance Is Likely to Fail: The Case of Zimbabwe." *Journal of Contemporary African Studies* 22, no. 2 (2004): 199–202.

Mbiti, John. *African Religions and Philosophy.* New York: Doubleday, 1970.

McCombs, M., and D. Shaw. "The Agenda-Setting Function of Mass Media." *Public Opinion Quarterly* 36, no. 2 (1972): 176.

McIntosh, Esther. "Hearing the Other: Feminist Theology and Ethics." *International Journal of Public Theology* 4, no. 1 (2009): 1–4.

———. "Issues in Feminist Public Theology." In *Public Theology and the Challenge of Feminism*, edited by Stephen Burns and Anita Monro, 63–74. London: Routledge, Taylor & Francis Group, 2015.

———. "Public Theology, Populism and Sexism: The Hidden Crisis in Public Theology." In *Resisting Exclusion: Global Theological Responses to Populism*, 221–228. Geneva, Switzerland: Lutheran World Federation, 2019.

McKechnie, William Sharp. *Magna Carta: A Commentary on the Great Charter of King John.* Glasgow: James MacLehose & Sons, 1914.

Mda, Zakes. *When People Play People: Development Communication through Theatre.* Johannesburg: Witwatersrand University Press; London: Zed Books, 1993.

Mendieta, Eduardo, and Jonathan Vanantwerpen, eds. *The Power of Religion in the Public Sphere.* New York: Columbia University Press, 2011.

Migliore, Daniel L. *Faith Seeking Understanding: An Introduction to Christian Theology.* Grand Rapids: Eerdmans, 2004.

Miller, Sarah Deardorff. *Assessing the Impacts of Hosting Refugees.* World Refugee Council Research Paper No. 4 (2018): 1. https://www.cigionline.org/sites/default/files/documents/WRC%20Research%20Paper%20no.4.pdf.

Misra, Jagriti. "10 Facts about Africa's Education Crisis." The Borgen Project, 8 July 2017. https://borgenproject.org/10-facts-africas-education-crisis/s.

Moltmann, Jürgen. *Ethics of Hope.* Minneapolis: Fortress; Cambridge: Cambridge University Press, 2012.

———. *The Experiment of Hope.* London: SCM, 1975.

———. *Theology of Hope.* London: SCM, 1967.

Moltmann, Jürgen, Nicholas Wolterstorff, and Ellen T. Charry. *A Passion for God's Reign: Theology, Christian Learning and the Christian Self.* Grand Rapids: Eerdmans, 1998.

Moyo, A. "Material Things in African Society: Implication for Christian Ethics." In *Moral and Ethical Issues in African Christianity: A Challenge for African Christianity*, edited by J. N. K. Mugambi and A. Nasimiyu-Wasike, 50. Nairobi: Acton, 1999.

Mugambi, Jesse N. K. *Christian Theology & Social Reconstruction*. Nairobi: Acton, 2003.

———. "Christianity and the African Cultural Heritage." In *African Christianity: An African Story*, edited by Ogbu U. Kalu, 516–542. Pretoria: University of Pretoria, 2005.

———. *Democracy and Development in Africa: The Role of the Churches*. Nairobi: AACC, 1997.

———. *From Liberation to Reconstruction: African Christian Theology after the Cold War*. Nairobi: East African Educational Publishers, 1995.

Mume, J. O. "The African Traditional Doctor's Concept of Public Health." In *Principles and Practice of Public Health in Africa*, 6–10. Vol. 1, 2nd ed. Ibadan: University Press, 1996.

Mumuni, T. "Critical Pedagogy in the Eyes of Jesus Christ's Teachings: A Historical Study." *International Journal of Development and Sustainability* 7, no. 1 (2018): 340–354.

Mutonono, Dwight. *Stewards of Power: Restoring Africa's Dignity*. Carlisle, UK: HippoBooks, 2018.

Mutonono, Dwight S. M., and Makoto L. Mautsa. "Land." In *Africa Bible Commentary*, edited by Tokunboh Adeyemo, 290. Nairobi: WordAlive; Grand Rapids: Zondervan, 2006.

Mutua, Makau. "Why Redraw the Map of Africa: A Moral and Legal Inquiry." *Michigan Journal of International Law* 16 (1995): 1116. Available at: https://repository.law.umich.edu/mjil/vol16/iss4/3.

Mwangonde, Henry. "Magufuli Strikes Again: Uhuru Day Scrapped." *The Citizen*, 24 November 2016. https://www.thecitizen.co.tz/News/1840340-2969570-xr3dv6z/index.html.

Myers, Bryant L. *Walking with the Poor: Principles and Practices of Transformational Development*. Maryknoll, NY: Orbis, 1999 (rev. ed. 2011).

Nasiru El-Rufai, Ahmed et al. *Report of the APC Committee on True Federalism*. Nigeria: APC Adhoc Committee, 2018. https://pgfnigeria.files.wordpress.com/2018/01/volume-1-main-report-summary-of-findings-and-arecommendations.pdf.

Ndukwe, Olo. "Doing Theology in a Knowledge Society Today: A Nigerian Christian Public Theological Reflection." *Science Journal of Sociology and Anthropology* (14 April 2017). https://www.sjpub.org/sjsa/sjsa-164.pdf.

Ngalula, Jośee. "Some Current Trends of Christianity in Africa." *International Review of Mission* (2017): 228–240.

Nguru, F. W. "Development of Christian Higher Education in Kenya: An Overview." In *Christian Higher Education: A Global Reconnaissance*, edited by J. Carpenter, P. L. Glanzer, and N. S. Lantinga. Grand Rapids: Eerdmans, 2014.

Northouse, P. G. *Leadership: Theory and Practice*, 4th ed. Thousand Oaks, CA: Sage, 2007.

Nürnberger, Klaus. *Prosperity, Poverty and Pollution: Managing the Approaching Crisis*. Pietermaritzburg: Cluster, 1999.

———. *Regaining Sanity for the Earth*. Pietermaritzburg: Cluster, 2011.

———. "The Task of the Church Concerning the Economy in a Post-Apartheid South Africa." *Missionalia* 22, no. 2 (1994): 131.

Nussbaum, M. *Upheavals of Thoughts: The Intelligence of Emotions*. Cambridge: Cambridge University Press, 2001.

Nyaga, R., D. Njoroge, and C. Nyambuga. *An Introduction to Communication*. Nairobi: Oxford University Press, 2015.

Nyamiti, C. "A Critical Assessment on Some Issues on Today's African Theology." *African Christian Studies* 5, no. 1 (1989): 10.

Oberdorfer, Bernd. "Human Dignity and 'Image of God.'" *Scriptura* 104 (2010): 231–239.

Oden, Thomas C. *How Africa Shaped the Christian Mind: Rediscovering the African Seedbed of Western Christianity*. Downers Grove, IL: InterVarsity Press, 2007.

Oduyoye, Mercy Amba. *Introducing African Women's Theology*. Sheffield: Sheffield Academic Press, 2001.

Ogah Abah, Steve. "Vignettes of Communities in Action: An Exploration of Participatory Methodologies in Promoting Community Development in Nigeria." *Community Development Journal* 42, no. 4 (2007): 435–448.

Omollo, K. "Bishop Okullu: A Man of God with a Heart for Justice." *Standard Media Digital*, 13 Feb. 2014. https://www.standardmedia.co.ke/article/2000104598/bishop-okullu-a-man-of-god-with-a-heart-for-justice.

Orobator, A. E. *From Crisis to Kairos: The Mission of the Church in the Time of HIV/AIDS, Refugees, and Poverty*. Nairobi: Paulines Publications Africa, 2005.

Paeth, Scott R. et al. *Shaping Public Theology: Selections from the Writings of Max L. Stackhouse*. Grand Rapids: Eerdmans, 2014.

Palagashvili, Liya. "African Chiefs: Comparative Governance under Colonial Rule." *Public Choice* 174, no. 3–4 (11 January 2018): 277–300. https://doi.org/10.1007/s11127-018-0499-3.

Parsitau, Damaris S. "From the Periphery to the Centre: The Pentecostalisation of Mainline Christianity in Kenya." *Missionalia* 35, no. 3 (2007): 83–111.

Paul III (Pope). "*Sublimus Deus*: On the Enslavement and Evangelization of Indians." (1537). Papal Encyclicals Online. https://www.papalencyclicals.net/paul03/p3subli.htm.

Payment, Maggi. "Millennials: The Emerging Work Force." *Career Planning and Adult Development Journal* 24, no. 3 (2008): 23.

Phillips, Merran W. "The End Conscription Campaign 1983–1988: A Study of White Extra-Parliamentary Opposition to Apartheid." Unpublished Master's thesis, University of South Africa, 2002. https://core.ac.uk/download/pdf/43175117.pdf.

Phiri, Isaac. "Evolution of Anti-Corruption Journalism in Africa: Lessons from Zambia." *Global Media Journal – African Edition* 2, no. 1 (2008): 18. https://globalmedia.journals.ac.za/pub/article/view/32.

Pierson, Christopher. *The Modern State*. London: Routledge, 1996.

Pillay, J. "Faith and Reality: The Role and Contributions of the Ecumenical Church to the Realities and Development of South Africa since the Advent of Democracy in 1994." *HTS Teologiese Studies/Theological Studies* 73, no. 4 (2017): 2.

Plantinga, Cornelius, Jr. "Hodgson-Welch Debate and the Analogy of the Trinity." PhD dissertation, Princeton Theological Seminary, 1982.

Polkinghorne, John, and Michael Welker. *The End of the World and the Ends of God: Science and Theology on Eschatology*. Harrisburg, PA: Trinity Press International, 2000.

Pontifical Council for Justice and Peace. *Compendium of the Social Doctrine of the Church*. http://www.vatican.va/roman_curia/pontifical_councils/justpeace/documents/rc_pc_justpeace_doc_20060526_compendio-dott-soc_en.html.

Preamble to the ACHPR, Paragraph 7. http://www.humanrights.se/wp-content/uploads/2012/01/African-Charter-on-Human-and-Peoples-Rights.pdf.

Priest, Robert J., and Kirimi Barine, eds. *African Christian Leadership: Realities, Opportunities, and Impact*. Carlisle: Langham Global Library, 2019.

Publish What You Pay (PWYP). "Who We Are." https://www.pwyp.org/about/.

Reno, William. *Corruption and State Politics in Sierra Leone*. Cambridge: Cambridge University Press, 1995.

Ringson, John. "Zunde RaMambo as a Traditional Coping Mechanism for the Care of Orphans and Vulnerable Children: Evidence from Gutu District, Zimbabwe." *African Journal of Social Work* 7, no. 2 (2017): 54. https://www.ajol.info/index.php/ajsw/article/viewFile/165227/154687.

Robert, Dana L. *Christian Mission: How Christianity Became a World Religion*. Chichester: Wiley-Blackwell, 2009.

Rohr, Richard. *The Universal Christ*. New York: Convergent, 2019.

Ross, Kenneth. "Doing Theology with a New Historiography." *Journal of Theology for Southern Africa* 99 (1997): 94–98.

Sachikonye, L. *When the State Turns on Its Citizens: 60 Years of Institutionalised Violence in Zimbabwe*. Harare: Weaver Press, 2011.

Saliers, D. E. *Worship as Theology: Foretaste of Divine Glory*. Nashville: Abingdon, 1994.

Sam Maluleke, Tinyiko. "Reflections and Resources: The Elusive Public of Public Theology: A Response to William Storrar." *International Journal of Public Theology* 5 (2011): 79–89.

Sanneh, Lamin. *The Accra Charter of Religious Freedom and Citizenship*. Oxford: OMSC Publications, 2012.

———. *Translating the Message: The Missionary Impact on Culture*, 2nd ed. Maryknoll, NY: Orbis, 2015.

Schultz, John. *Commentary to the Book of Leviticus* (Bible-Commentaries.com, 2002). http://www.bible-commentaries.com/source/johnschultz/BC_Leviticus. pdf.

Schwab, Klaus. *United Nation's World Economic Forum's Global Competitiveness Report 2014-2015.* Switzerland: World Economic Forum, 2014. http://www3.weforum. org/docs/WEF_GlobalCompetitivenessReport_2014-15.pdf.

Schwenger, Björn. "'Heresy' or 'Phase of Nature'?: Approaching Technology Theologically." *European Journal of Theology* 25, no. 1 (2016): 44.

Setiloane, Gabriel. "Towards a Biocentric Theology and Ethic – via Africa." *Journal of Black Theology* 9, no. 1 (1995): 52–66.

Shaw, Flora L. *A Tropical Dependency: An Outline of the Ancient History of the Western Soudan, with an Account of the Modern Settlement of Northern Nigeria.* London: James Nisbet, 1905.

Shaw, Jeffrey. "Illusions of Freedom: Thomas Merton and Jacques Ellul on Technology and the Human Condition." *Religion and Theology* 25, no. 1 (2018): 152.

Sindima, Harvey. "Community of Life: Ecological Theology in African Perspective." In *Liberating Life: Contemporary Approaches in Ecological Theology*, edited by Charles Birch, William Eaken, and Jay B. McDaniel, 137–138. Maryknoll, NY: Orbis, 1990.

———. "Community of Life." *Ecumenical Review* 41, no. 4 (1989): 537–551.

Skinner, Matthew L. "Matthew 20:1–16: Justice Comes in the Evening." Blog posted on 2 November 2011. https://www.patheos.com/blogs/onscripture/2011/11/matthew-201-16-justice-comes-in-the-evening/.

Smit, Dirk J. "Does It Matter?: On Whether There Is Method in the Madness." In *A Companion to Public Theology*, edited by Sebastian C. H. Kim and Katie Day, 75. Leiden: Brill, 2017.

———. *Essays on Being Reformed: Collected Essays 3.* Edited by R. Vosloo. Stellenbosch: SUN, 2009.

———. "Liturgy and Life? On the Importance of Worship for Christian Ethics." *Scriptura* 62 (1997): 261–262. http://citeseerx.ist.psu.edu/viewdoc/download?d oi=10.1.1.1014.93&rep=rep1&type=pdf.

———. "Notions of the Public and Doing Theology." *International Journal of Public Theology* 1 (2007): 431–454.

———. "The Paradigm of Public Theology: Origins and Development." In *Contextuality and Intercontextuality in Public Theology*, edited by Heinrich Bedford-Strohm, Florian Höhne, and Tobias Reitmeier, 11–23. Münster: LIT Verlag, 2013.

Sookhdeo, Patrick. *Unmasking Islamic State: Revealing Their Motivation, Theology and End Time Predictions.* McLean, VA: Isaac, 2015.

South African Council of Churches, Climate Change Committee. *Climate Change: A Challenge to the Churches in South Africa.* Marshalltown: SACC, 2009. https:// acen.anglicancommunion.org/media/61434/climate_change_churches_in_sa.pdf.

Sow, Mariama. "Figures of the Week: Africa, Education, and the 2018 World Development Report." Brookings: Africa in Focus (6 October 2017). https://

www.brookings.edu/blog/africa-in-focus/2017/10/06/figures-of-the-week-africa-education-world-development-report-2018/.

Speckman, M. T. *A Biblical Vision for Africa's Development?* Pietermaritzburg, South Africa: Cluster, 2007.

Springer, Ed. "An Introduction to Intergenerational Ministry," Youthworks (2019). https://youthworks.net/articles/an-introduction-to-intergenerational-ministry.

Stackhouse, Max. *Public Theology and Political Economy: Christian Stewardship in Modern Society.* Lanham, MD: University Press of America, 1991.

———. "Reflections on How and Why We Go Public." *International Journal of Public Theology* 1 (2007): 426.

Stark, Rodney. *The Rise of Christianity.* New York: Harper Collins, 1997.

Stengel, Richard. "We're In the Middle of a Global Information War: Here's What We Need to Do to Win." *Time* (26 September 2019): 36–39. https://time.com/5686843/global-information-war/.

Steuernagel, Valdir R. "Doing Theology with an Eye on Mary." *Evangelical Review of Theology* 27 (2003): 100–112.

Storey, Peter. "Banning the Flag from Our Churches: Learning from the Church-State Struggle in South Africa." In *Between Capital and Cathedral: Essays on Church-State Relationships*, edited by Wessel Bentley and Dion A. Forster, 3. Pretoria: University of South Africa, 2012.

———. *I Beg to Differ: Ministry Amid the Teargas.* Cape Town: Tafelberg, 2018.

Stott, John. *Issues Facing Christians Today: New Perspective on Social and Moral Dilemmas.* London: Marshal Pickering, 1990.

Swanepoel, Hennie, and Frik de Beer. *Community Development: Breaking the Cycle of Poverty*, 5th ed. Cape Town, South Africa: Juta Academic, 2012.

Tangonyire, R. C., and L. K. Achal. *Economic Behaviour as If Others Too Had Interests.* Bamenda: Langaa RPCIG, 2012.

Taylor, John. *Christianity and Politics in Africa.* Westport, CT: Greenwood, 1979.

Tearfund. "Church and Community Mobilisation in Africa." https://learn.tearfund.org/~/media/files/tilz/churches/ccm/2017-tearfund-ccm-in-africa-en.pdf.

———. "Community Action Groups." Tearfund learn (n.d.). https://learn.tearfund.org/en/resources/publications/footsteps/footsteps_101-110/footsteps_106/community_action_groups/.

———. "Mobilizing Churches and Communities." Tearfund learn (n.d.). https://learn.tearfund.org/en/themes/church_and_community/mobilising_churches_and_communities/.

Theron, P. M., and G. A. Lotter. "Corruption: How Should Christians Respond?" *Acta Theologica* 32, no. 1 (2012): 96–117. https://www.ajol.info/index.php/actat/article/download/78840/69162.

Theuri, M. "Poverty in Africa." In *Theology of Reconstruction: Exploratory Essays*, edited by M. N. Getui and E. A. Obeng, 233. Nairobi: Acton/EATWOT, 1999.

Thomson, Jessie. *Durable Solutions for Burundian Refugees in Tanzania* (2008). https://www.fmreview.org/sites/fmr/files/FMRdownloads/en/protracted/thomson.pdf.

Tshaka, Rothney S. "African, You Are on Your Own!: The Need for African Reformed Christians to Seriously Engage Their Africanity in Their Reformed Theological Reflections." *Scriptura* 96 (2007): 533–548.

———. "On Being African and Reformed? Towards an African Reformed Theology Enthused by an Interlocution of Those on the Margins of Society." *HTS Theological Studies* 70, no. 1 (2014): 1–7.

Tshaka, R. S., and A. P. Phillips. "The Continued Relevance of African/Black Christologies in Reformed Theological Discourses in South Africa Today." *Dutch Reformed Theological Journal/Nederduitse Gereformeerde. Teologiese Tydskrif* 53, no. 3 & 4 (2012): 353–362.

Tutu, Desmond. "Black Theology and African Theology: Soulmates or Antagonists?" *Journal of Religious Thought* 2 (1975): 42.

———. *No Future without Forgiveness.* New York: Doubleday, 1999.

UNESCO Institute for Statistics. "Education in Africa." UNESCO (n.d.). http://uis.unesco.org/en/topic/education-africa.

UNICEF. "Trafficking in Human Beings, especially Women and Children." UNICEF Innocenti Resource Centre (2003), 3. https://www.unicef-irc.org/publications/pdf/trafficking-gb2ed-2005.pdf.

United Nations. "Transforming Our World: The 2030 Agenda for Sustainable Development." *Sustainable Development Goals Knowledge Platform* 21. https://sustainabledevelopment.un.org/post2015/transformingourworld/publication.

———. *Africa Sustainable Development Report: Towards a Transformed and Resilient Continent.* United Nations Economic Commission for Africa (2018). https://www.uneca.org/publications/2018-africa-sustainable-development-report.

United Nations Department of Economic and Social Affairs: Indigenous Peoples (2007). *Declaration on the Rights of Indigenous Peoples* (UNDRIP). https://www.un.org/development/desa/indigenouspeoples/wp-content/uploads/sites/19/2018/11/UNDRIP_E_web.pdf.

———. Population Division. *International Migration Report 2017* (ST/ESA/SER.A/403). https://www.un.org/en/development/desa/population/migration/publications/migrationreport/docs/MigrationReport2017.pdf.

United Nations Development Programme. *Human Development Report 1998.* (New York: Oxford University Press, 1998), 25. http://hdr.undp.org/sites/default/files/reports/259/hdr_1998_en_complete_nostats.pdf.

United Nations High Commissioner for Refugees (UNHCR). "Chapter 10: Information Strategy." In *Refugee Protection and Mixed Migration: The 10-Point Plan in Action* (Geneva 2011). http://www.unhcr.org/50a4c2289.pdf.

———. *Refugee Status Determination: Identifying Who Is a Refugee.* Self-study module 2 (Geneva, 2005). https://www.refworld.org/pdfid/43141f5d4.pdf.

———. *UNHCR Protection Training Manual for European Border and Entry Officials: 3 Who Is a Refugee?* Brussels: UNHCR Bureau for Europe, 2011. https://www. unhcr.org/4d944c319.pdf.

Vander Lugt, Wesley, and Trevor Hart, eds. *Theatrical Theology: Explorations in Performing the Faith.* Cambridge: Lutterworth, 2014.

Verster, P. *New Hope for the Poor: A Perspective on the Church in Informal Settlements in Africa.* Bloemfontein: Sun Media, 2012.

Villa-Vicencio, Charles. *A Theology of Reconstruction: Nation-Building and Human Rights.* New York: Cambridge University Press, 1992.

Waghid, Y. "On the Relevance of a Theory of Democratic Citizenship Education for Africa." In *African Democratic Citizenship Education Revisited*, edited by Y. Waghid and N. David, 1–12. London: Palgrave Macmillan, 2018).

Walls, Andrew. *The Cross-Cultural Process in Christian History.* Maryknoll, NY: Orbis, 2002.

———. *The Missionary Movement in Christian History: Studies in the Transmission of Faith.* Maryknoll, NY: Orbis, 1996.

Walton, John. "Deuteronomy: An Exposition of the Spirit of the Law." *Grace Theological Journal* 8, no. 2 (1987): 213–225.

Walzer, M. *Spheres of Justice: A Defense of Pluralism and Equality.* New York: Basic Books, 1983.

Wardle, Claire. "Fake News. It's Complicated." First Draft (16 February 2017). https:// medium.com/1st-draft/fake-news-its-complicated-d0f773766c79.

Ware, Bruce A. "The Father, the Son, and the Holy Spirit: The Trinity as Theological Foundation for Family Ministry." *Journal of Discipleship and Family Ministry* 1, no. 2. https://www.sbts.edu/family/2011/10/10/the-father-the-son-and-the-holy-spirit-the-trinity-as-theological-foundation-for-family-ministry/.

Weanzana, Nupanga. "Word and Deed: Patterns of Influential African Christian Organizations." In *African Christian Leadership: Realities, Opportunities, and Impact*, edited by Robert J. Priest and Kirimi Barine. Carlisle: Langham Global Library, 2019.

Weber, Max. *Economy and Society: Volume 1.* New York: Bedminster, 1978.

———. *Economy and Society, Volume 2.* New York: Bedminster, 1978.

Welch, Claude E. "The Organisation of African Unity and the Promotion of Human Rights." *Journal of Modern African Studies* 29 (1991): 535–555.

West, Gerald. *Biblical Hermeneutics of Liberation: Modes of Reading the Bible in the South African Context*, 2nd ed. Pietermaritzburg: Cluster, 1995.

West, M. O. *The Rise of an African Middle Class: Colonial Zimbabwe, 1898–1965.* Bloomington: Indiana University Press, 2002.

White, Lynn. "The Historical Roots of our Ecologic Crisis." *Science* 155 (1967): 1203–1207.